The Virgil Michel Series

Virgil Michel, O.S.B., a monk of Saint John's Abbey in Collegeville, Minnesota, was a founder of the Liturgical Movement in the United States in the 1920s and fostered its development until his death in 1938. Michel's writing, editing, teaching, and preaching centered on the relationship between liturgy and the life of the faithful—the Body of Christ.

The Pueblo Books imprint of the Liturgical Press honors Virgil Michel's life and work with a monograph series named for him. The Virgil Michel Series will offer studies that examine the connections between liturgy and life in particular communities, as well as works exploring the relationship of liturgy to theology, ethics, and social sciences. The Virgil Michel Series will be ecumenical in breadth and international in scope, recognizing that liturgy embodies yet transcends cultures and denominations.

Series Editor: Don E. Saliers

Don E. Saliers, who teaches regularly at Saint John's University in the summer program, is the William R. Cannon Distinguished Professor of Theology and Worship at Emory University, Atlanta, Georgia.

D1570561

Mary E. McGann, R.S.C.J.

A Precious Fountain

Music in the Worship of an African American Catholic Community

Virgil Michel Series

Don E. Saliers, Editor

A PUEBLO BOOK

Liturgical Press Collegeville, Minnesota

www.litpress.org

A Pueblo Book published by the Liturgical Press

Cover design by David Manahan, o.s.b. Illustration of African Kente fabric courtesy of Mary E. McGann, r.s.c.j.

Library of Congress Cataloging-in-Publication Data

McGann, Mary E.
    A precious fountain : music in the worship of an African American
Catholic community / Mary E. McGann.
        p. cm. —(Virgil Michel series)
    "A Pueblo book."
    Includes bibliographical references and index.
    ISBN 0-8146-6207-2 (pbk : alk. paper)
    1. African American Catholics. 2. Catholic Church—United States—
Liturgy. 3. Catholic Church—United States—Hymns. I. Title. II. Series.

BX1407.N4M34 2004
264'.0202'08996073—dc22

2004013677

Credits

Excerpts from *The Power of Black Music* by Samuel A. Floyd, © 1995 by Samuel A. Floyd. Used by permission of Oxford University Press, Inc.

Excerpt from the English translation of *The Roman Missal*, © 1973, International Commission on English in the Liturgy, Inc. (ICEL); excerpt from the English translation of the *Eucharistic Prayers for Masses of Reconciliation*, © 1975, ICEL. All rights reserved. Used with permission.

Excerpts from *The Spirit in Worship*, © 1978 by Clarence Jos. Rivers; *Soulfull Worship*, © 1974 by Clarence Jos. Rivers. All rights reserved. Used by permission of the author.

Permission has been granted by the copyright holders of the lyrics of the following songs for reproduction in this volume. Note: due to the exigencies of performance in a primarily oral tradition, lyrics as they appear in this text may vary slightly from the original.

"CHRIST IS ALL," by KENNETH MORRIS. Copyright © 1946 (Renewed) UNICHAPPELL MUSIC, Inc. All Rights Reserved. Used by Permission. Warner Bros. Publications U.S. Inc., Miami, Florida 330147

"FILL MY CUP," Chorus and Music by Isaiah Jones, Jr. Copyright © 1970 Davike Music Co. Assigned to Davike Music Company and Fricourt Music Company (ASCAP). USED BY PERMISSION. ALL RIGHTS RESERVED.

"GOD IS," by Dr. Robert Fryson. Copyright © 1976. Glori Gospel Music, Merrick, NY. (BMI). All Rights Reserved. Used by Permission.

"HOW GREAT THOU ART," Words and music by Stuart K. Hine. Copyright © 1953 by S. K. Hine. Assigned to Manna Music, Inc., 35255 Brooten Road, Pacific City, OR 97135. Renewed 1981 by Manna Music, Inc. All Rights Reserved. Used by Permission. (ASCAP)

"I FIND NO FAULT IN HIM," by Andraé Crouch. Copyright © 1966. Renewed 1994 by Manna Music, Inc., 35255 Brooten Road, Pacific City, OR 97135. All Rights Reserved. Used by Permission.

Every effort has been made to find and contact the copyright holders of other quoted lyrics not in the public domain. As this book goes to press, some remain unknown or contact impossible. Trusting that songwriters not only intend their creations to be sung but to be known by a wider audience, I have included this material with the intent of appropriate acknowledgment and remuneration if such information becomes available.

To my mother, Mary E. McGann,
who made her journey home to God as this book went to press;

to the
Community of Our Lady of Lourdes;

and to the memory of
Brother Jesse Lee Banks

Contents

Acknowledgments

My first debt of gratitude is to the Our Lady of Lourdes community without whose worship and music-making, as well as their love, support, and encouragement, this book would not exist. My special thanks to Father Kirk Ullery, Pat Goodall, Reed Fromer, and Sister Irma Dillard, R.S.C.J., who read and offered thoughtful feedback on each emerging chapter; to members of the Lourdes community and Gospel Choir whose insights and experience I record here; and to all who granted me permission to do so. I am likewise indebted to Father Don MacKinnon, C.S.S.R., and Sisters Martin de Porres Colemen, S.N.D.deN. and Helen Carroll, R.S.C.J., for oral histories of the renaissance of Lourdes in the late '60s and '70s. To the whole family of Our Lady of Lourdes, my enduring gratitude and love!

Mentors, colleagues, and friends have accompanied this work from its inception. My heartfelt thanks to John F. Baldovin, S.J., Michael B. Aune, Louis Weil, Bonnie C. Wade, and Olly Wilson, who supported and guided me through the initial research. My warm appreciation to Don E. Saliers and Toinette M. Eugene for urging me to undertake the writing of this book. Abundant gratitude as well to four colleagues—Eva Marie Lumas, S.S.S., Rawn Harbor, Lizette Larson-Miller, and Ann Jablonski, R.S.C.J.—whose encouraging response to the final manuscript brought the book to conclusion. I am indebted to Glen Hinson, author of *Fire in My Bones: Transcendence and the Holy Spirit in African American Gospel*, whose vibrant narrative style influenced the cadence and imagery of this volume. My thanks to members of the African American Worship Traditions Study Group of the North American Academy of Liturgy for ongoing conversations and shared interest in African American liturgy and music. My appreciation to Frances Flynn for research assistance, to Steven Schwartz and Charles Bultman for careful proofreading, to Irma Dillard, R.S.C.J., for assistance with illustrations and photos, and to Jerry Walker for creating several tables.

The research and writing of this book was funded in part by a Lilly Research Grant from The Association of Theological Schools, a Faculty Research Grant from the Graduate Theological Union, and the ongoing support of the Society of the Sacred Heart. I am grateful to the Franciscan School of Theology for granting me sabbatical time for the completion of this manuscript, and to the administration, faculty, and students of FST for their kind support. My appreciation as well to Peter Dwyer, director of the Liturgical Press, for his positive response to initial chapters of the book and for his encouragement to complete it.

Among the many who enabled and affected this book, a few stand out. My enduring thanks to friend and colleague Susan Marie Smith who believed in this work and urged me through multiple drafts of each chapter; to Dorothy Duff Brown, whose insight and wisdom guided many major decisions about the book's shape, content, and format; to Lois Landis for special help in completing the last chapter; to the leaders and members of my religious congregation, the Religious of the Sacred Heart, for their continued confidence and loving support; to dear friends and members of my family for their words of encouragement along the way; and most especially to my mother, Mary E. McGann, whose prayer, love, and interest accompanied the work from start to finish.

ON WRITING LITURGICAL ETHNOGRAPHY

*T*his book is a work of liturgical ethnography. As such, it probes the rich particularity of one worshiping community whose roots and practice are at once Black and Catholic, using music as a primary lens through which to explore the community's liturgy and embodied theology. Although small, the Our Lady of Lourdes community in San Francisco is part of a larger event in the American church: the emergence of a new paradigm of Catholic worship, one that is "authentically Black and truly Catholic." With other Black Catholic communities across the country, Our Lady of Lourdes has discovered what the Bishops' Committee on the Liturgy describes as "the joy and hope to be found when the African American religious spirit touches the heart of Catholic liturgy."[1]

But why this new genre of liturgical literature at the dawn of the twenty-first century? And why this community? And why music as interpretive lens?

Liturgical ethnography is first a necessary response to what Karl Rahner has identified as the most radical change in the life of the church since the first century—the change of the church into *a world Church* at Vatican Council II.[2] This revolutionary shift "from one historical and theological situation to an essentially new one," Rahner argues, has been paralleled only once in the church's long history—"the first century transition from Jewish to Gentile Christianity."[3] This "qualitative leap" from its century-old identity as a Western church to a new self-understanding as pluriform and multicultural—which Rahner contends has been brought about through the hidden and compelling grace of the Holy Spirit—confronts the church with a fundamental challenge: Either it recognizes the "essential differences [among] cultures . . . and with Pauline boldness draws the necessary consequences of this recognition, or she remains a Western Church and so in the final analysis betrays the meaning of Vatican II."[4]

Embracing the "radical difference of other cultures"—a task Rahner claims is most in danger of being missed or misunderstood[5]—has set a new agenda for the life of the whole church and specifically for the work of liturgical theologians. Not only must the church "be inculturated throughout the world," embracing a "pluralism of liturgies" and growing into a "pluralism of proclamations and theologies,"[6] as Rahner comments, but liturgical theologians must tap this rich reservoir of spirituality and theology that is erupting within the liturgical practice of its diverse cultural communities. Normative statements about the church's worship—important as they are for the church's sense of unity and the regulation of its practice—cannot carry the full burden of articulating the church's liturgical encounter with the living God. Nor can the comprehensive work of liturgical theology be shaped by the perspectives of a single culture. The time is ripe to deepen our probing of the "hidden treasures," the Spirit-gifted "genius" of multiple ethno-cultural communities: for forms of liturgical scholarship that search out the cultural intuitions—the structures of thought and feeling that shape their sense of divine mystery, of self-identity and relationship—that are foundational to their worship. Liturgical ethnography embarks on this challenge.

Liturgical ethnography, with its focus on the particularity of each community's worship experience, finds a second compelling *raison d'etre* in the insight of contemporary sacramental theologians into the nature of the church's liturgical/sacramental life. Exploring the "revolution" taking place in sacramental theology, Kenan Osborne asserts that *particularity* is of the very nature of sacramentality.[7] Just as local churches are not "simply cloned replications" of a universal church, so the particular sacramental action of one community is not a replication of some "objective 'essence' of sacrament."[8] Rather, Osborne posits, it is the unique encounter of a specific community with the living God in Christ, situated in the particularities of time, space, and the distinctive history and identity of that assembly. Sacramentality "is an event and a discourse that occurs only when there is a meeting of the primordial divine disclosing and the secondary human response."[9] The church's worship, its sacramental life, is thus always particular—lived out in the deep, experiential encounter of specific communities with the God of Christian faith.

Culture is essential to this encounter. Concluding his work on Christian sacraments in the third millennium, Osborne makes a striking statement: "If I were to write a book from the Asian standpoint, it . . . would require a total deconstruction and reconstruction, so that the reality of God revealing God's own self to human beings of another culture and their response to this revelation, in other words, the entire dynamic of a sacramental event, would be understandable, but only within a different *epistemé.*"[10]

Third, liturgical ethnography of an African American Catholic community is prompted by a strong summons—the call made by Pope Paul VI to the churches of Africa in 1969—that resounds to this day. Addressing the bishops of the African continent gathered in Uganda, West Africa, Paul VI claimed, "[Y]ou may, and you must, have an African Christianity."[11] He encouraged them "to remain sincerely African even in your own interpretation of the Christian life," and to "formulate Catholicism in terms congenial to your own culture." In sum, he issued this striking invitation: to bring "to the Catholic Church the precious and original contribution of 'Blackness' which she particularly needs in this historic hour."[12]

This call rang out throughout the African diaspora. It was heard and taken to heart by Black Catholics across the United States, especially the Black episcopacy. It fueled four decades of liturgical renewal and change. It was reiterated by Pope John Paul II in 1987 when addressing representatives of the African American Catholic community in New Orleans: "Your Black cultural heritage enriches the Church and makes her witness to universality more complete."[13]

Gifts given must be received. This book is a work of receiving that precious gift of Blackness from one of many Catholic communities that are offering the American church the originality and depth of their religious-cultural heritage. It is a work of receiving the fruit of their labor to unlock the potential of Catholic worship in ways that have previously been unimagined, or as Rahner has claimed, would have made no sense in another era.[14] The Black bishops of the United States proclaimed in 1987 that as Black Catholics "continue to probe the possibilities inherent in the Roman liturgy, they will recognize its limitations as well as its untapped potential. The entire church will be the richer for this journey and exploration made in spirit, in truth, and in love."[15]

Contextualizing scholarship. This book is contextualized in a great deal of scholarship. Since the early '70s, Black Catholic theologians, liturgists, historians, ethicists, and religious educators have probed the distinctive journey and legacy of African American Christians within the Catholic church. Cyprian Davis's *The History of Black Catholics in the United States;* Cyprian Rowe's "A Case for the Distinctiveness of Black Culture"; Diana Hayes and Cyprian Davis's *Taking Down Our Harps;* Joseph A. Brown's *To Stand on the Rock;* collections such as *Black and Catholic: The Challenge and Gift of Black Folk; This Far by Faith; Theology: A Portrait in Black;* as well as numerous articles and books by scholars like Thea Bowman, M. Shawn Copeland, Toinette Eugene, Jamie Phelps, Bishop Edward Braxton, Bishop James Lyke, D. Reginald Whitt, Glen Jean-Marie, J-Glen Murray, Eva Marie Lumas, Bryan N. Massingale, and Giles Conwell, to mention only a few, have laid out foundational understandings of Black Catholic life, history, and liturgy.[16]

At the heart of this ferment is the pivotal work of Clarence R. J. Rivers, whose music, lectures, and writings launched the Black Catholic Liturgical Renaissance of the '60s and '70s. It was Rivers who first articulated a Black Catholic liturgical aesthetic, rooted in the oral/aural, poetic, and holistic predilections of African cultures and spirituality.[17] This aesthetic is grounded in a sacramental view of the world that appreciates creation as inherently good; a biblical understanding of the Spirit of God at work in worship, accomplishing God's liberating intentions; a theological perception of emotion as a way of knowing the Other; and a Gospel realization that Spirit-induced *metanoia* is at the heart of Christian worship. Rivers's work became a catalyst for further scholarship and pastoral exploration. Summarizing his legacy in a recent article, I conclude that his insight continues to offer the church both timely wisdom and prophetic challenge.[18]

Tracing "The Emergence of African American Catholic Worship" over the past forty years, Eva Marie Lumas and I documented the unique liturgical journey of Black Catholics since the pivotal confluence of Vatican II and the Civil Rights Movement in the mid 1960s.[19] This journey makes clear that Black culture is not monolithic and that African American Catholic communities have shaped unique and differing expressions of Catholic worship that are rooted in a common religious-cultural heritage and a shared spirituality. The defining concept of "authentically Black and truly Catholic," articulated by the Black Catholic bishops, assumes a plurality of expressions around a common core of theological, liturgical, and cultural understandings.[20] The future of Black Catholic worship is yet to be discovered. Yet the fruit of the struggle of many communities to offer the church their "unique and precious gift of Blackness" is already being harvested, and offering its own seeds to future generations.

This present book is a companion to my earlier essay, *Exploring Music as Worship and Theology: Research in Liturgical Practice.*[21] In that volume I articulate the liturgical and theological necessity of attending to the lived experience of particular worshiping communities and underscore the centrality of music to their processes of meaning-making. *Exploring Music* creates a confluence of interdisciplinary perspectives on musical-liturgical practice, drawn from liturgical studies, ethnomusicology, and ritual studies, which in turn grounds the distinctive method of empirical research and ethnography on which this current book is based. In addition, *Exploring Music* identifies some of the theological themes that emerge from the worship-music of the Our Lady of Lourdes community, articulating those themes in a way that highlights their significance for the work of liturgical studies. That brief exploration would be incomplete without the richly contextualized, experiential narration of *A Precious Fountain.*

Liturgical ethnography as liturgiology. Liturgical ethnography has historic roots in liturgical scholarship. The fourth-century pilgrim Egeria stumbled on it as she created a travel-diary of her pilgrimage to the Holy Land for the community from which she came.[22] Motivated by the desire to describe a worship practice in which she found value and originality, she recorded the details of actual liturgical events—not only their structures and forms but also the sounds and sights of music and movement, of light and darkness, of space and time, and of what she experienced when caught up in the dynamism of the lived worship events of fourth-century Jerusalem. Despite its necessary limitations, Egeria's work has proved invaluable to liturgical scholars.

Ethnography is just emerging as a source of insight into contemporary worship and theology. It is uniquely suited to probing the cultural particularity of specific communities, the deep structures of thought and feeling that shape their practice and by which they interpret their defining encounter with the living God in Jesus Christ. Scholars have yet to formulate models for such liturgical ethnography—forms that remain faithful to the complex, ambiguous modes of a community's ritual action and true to the polyvocality of local interpretations.[23] Such texts must make evident the varied perceptions and interpretations of members of the worshiping community, allowing their voices and the events of their liturgical prayer to be at the heart of the account.

These challenges have given birth to the narrative, descriptive style of *A Precious Fountain*. Intended for scholars and pastoral leaders, this book is based on five years of focused research within the Our Lady of Lourdes community (1993–1997) and my continuing involvement in their liturgical and musical life. It draws extensively on the exigencies of actual worship events—the complex interplay of musical sound, movements, gestures, speech, objects, dress, time, space, light, and color. It contextualizes the community's liturgical practice within the larger rhythms of its life and faith; within the historical, cultural, social, and religious forces that have shaped its musical-liturgical practice; and within the emerging ritual patterns it shares with other Black Catholic communities. The voices of community members are heard throughout, offering commentary and interpretation of their musical-liturgical performance. I draw these accounts from interviews, from formal and informal conversations with musicians and other parish members, and from the worship events themselves. My purpose is to offer a "picture of the landscape of meanings" experienced by the community as these emerge within the "logic of lived musical and liturgical experience, a logic that is not primarily linear but interactive, dynamic, and holistic."[24]

This book is a work of contemplative scholarship. As stated in *Exploring Music,* attending to a community's worship and music requires a kind of "'spiritual discipline'—the ability to be with a community without judgement 'until you flow with the rhythm, the pace of its action; until your interior metronome is beating with theirs.'"[25] So, too, the work of writing liturgical ethnography is an act of "receiving," of attending to the lived logic and wisdom of the community's action and interpretive commentary. Receiving the other is a profoundly contemplative act, one of the most difficult of human activities, states Thomas Keating.[26] Yet the act of receiving constitutes the heart of contemplative prayer and, by inference, of contemplative scholarship. Reading this book requires the same kind of "spiritual discipline." It is neither meant to establish norms nor to claim a "model" of worship to be imitated but to invite the reader to experience one community's regular encounter with the living God, mediated sacramentally and liturgically through their being the "church" assembled.

The purpose of liturgical ethnography is to open to new insight, to receive new paradigms, to make new connections, to welcome fresh deposits of spirit. Its goal is appreciation rather than critique, understanding rather than evaluation. Within the work of liturgical studies, which necessarily seeks to establish normativity, contemplative ethnographic scholarship can bring to light and reflect on the salience of these new paradigms. For this reason it is integral to the work of critical liturgiology, inviting new paradigms to both confirm and critique our existing normative claims. It introduces new hermeneutics into the fabric of interpretive liturgiology, a process essential to a liturgical scholarship that can truly serve a world church.

A Black hermeneutic. Interpreting the music-worship of an African American Catholic community requires the incorporation of a multifaceted Black hermeneutic—one that resides first within the interpretive categories of the Our Lady of Lourdes community itself and then broadens to encompass the perspectives of Black theologians and scholars of Black music. This Black hermeneutic assumes that African musical traits, as well as ritual and cultural practices, "not only survived but played a major role in the development and elaboration of African American music" and worship.[27] It presupposes that enslaved Africans on American soil "took a twisted version of Christianity [by which they were evangelized] and retwisted it into a culture of liberation, transcendence, creativity, and wholeness."[28] This Black hermeneutic posits that African American music is the most comprehensive repository of Black theology in the United States; that within this tradition, music, narrative, and ritual are traditional forms of systematic theology, and that singing, dancing, and drumming in worship are not simply stylistic elements, incidental to a community's practice, but profoundly theological acts in and of themselves.[29]

The full impact of this Black hermeneutic has yet to be realized within liturgical scholarship. By incorporating it in this book, I underscore the importance of its interpretive strategies and outcomes, which have in large measure been missing from the fabric of our discourse, especially in Roman Catholic contexts. However, I write as a non-African American, whose perceptions were first shaped by another cultural history and its discourse and whose understandings of Black culture, worship, and music have been gained through adult experience and study. The "precious and original gift of Blackness" has been mediated richly to me by the Our Lady of Lourdes community and by numerous other Black scholars, musicians, and pastoral leaders. It has enriched my own understanding of worship and deepened my appreciation of the vital role of music in our voiced praise of the living God.

It is my assumption that in any work of interpretation there is no pure hermeneutic. Nor is there some objective truth waiting to be discovered in a community's worship practice. Rather, interpretation is richly interpersonal, rooted in conversation, interaction, and mutuality. *A Precious Fountain* is a work of collaborative scholarship. It could only have come into being with the full cooperation of the Our Lady of Lourdes community. They have worked in partnership with me from the beginning, offering their time and insight, their continued support and interest. As the writing progressed, a team of four members of the parish, including the pastor and key musicians, have engaged with me in a process of "dialogic editing"—reading drafts of each chapter, advising me about the accuracy of my interpretation, and offering suggestions for changes.

Music as critical lens. One last question remains. Why situate music as the critical lens through which to explore a community's worship practice and its embodied, ritualized theology? For all peoples, music expresses their deep intuitions about themselves and their world, the values they hold, and the particular ways they perceive and relate to the mysterious wisdom at the heart of life. More than "organized sound" with properties of rhythm, harmony, pitch, and timbre, music is "an encounter between human beings" through the medium of sound and movement[30]—a human negotiation involving intentionality, expectation, and outcome; a transaction of consequence. Music-making establishes "a set of relationships,"—person to person, individual to society, humanity to the natural and supernatural world—"and it is in those relationships that the meaning of the act lies."[31]

For Black Americans especially, music is critical to their cultural memory, their ritual assumptions, and their spirituality. Music has been a substructure of their history, life, ritualized faith—an integral part of their core culture.[32] Black sacred music is primarily an oral tradition—forged in the oppressive structures of slavery and the dynamic, ritualized call-response of the ring shout. Preserving rich African concepts of the world, music, and God, Black sacred music-making became a context for discovering the Christian God, present in the powerful, living Spirit of the risen Christ. To this day, it is cultivated as an oral performance practice that in no way precludes sophisticated musical literacy. Like the high art of jazz and blues, Black sacred music is a creative tradition—learned and transmitted orally, and creatively shaped by all its participants. Never conformed to a performance model that separates performers and listeners, Black sacred music-making strives for wholeness, considering all participants both musically gifted and part of the performance. Though it places high value on virtuosity in the service of powerful musical communication, Black sacred music is not an elitist knowledge nor an exclusive performance practice.

Black music, states Thea Bowman, "is a living repository of the thoughts, feelings and will of Black Spirituality."[33] It is a fountainhead of expectations and assumptions about ritual, Christian worship, social relationships, living faith, wholeness and integration in a society that tries to maintain a split between what it means to be Black and American—and a church that too often falls into the same divisive pattern. To enter the realm of an African American Catholic community's worship music, we must enter a web of expression that encompasses all aspects of its liturgical practice—prayer, preaching, and sacramental action—and that wells up not only in their Sunday gatherings but at the heart of the community's life.

Introduction

BORDERLANDS

*T*he streams from which music flows into the Our Lady of Lourdes community run very deep.[1] They well up as a great river of sound that reaches back to the earliest days of African presence on American soil. They flow through the hush-harbors of slavery—the sorrow songs and jubilees—and cascade through the revivals of the Great Awakenings—the uptempo shout songs and improvised gospel songs—gathering up a great reservoir of repertoire that has seeped into the hearts and voices of this community of Our Lady of Lourdes.

No one can be sure where this river began, where its first waters stirred, but it carries in its floodtide the rhythms of African drumming and the predilections of African song. It has run underground and over ground, through the adversity of African American migrations and resettlements—south to north, rural to urban—emerging reinvented and resilient.

It has shimmered and surged through the rituals of the Black churches, and carved out new courses in the song forms of African American prayer. It has been overheard on the voices of mothers and the humming of grandmothers, carried on the sounds of Sunday morning gospel singers on local radio stations.

It has now broken through the strong floodgates of Catholic worship, burst in like new wine filling old skins, releasing the energies of a long fermentation, the effervescence of a watercourse finding new tributaries and creating new forms, welling up within the voices of the Lourdes community as source of life and joy, washing across the hearts of all who share their worship like a cool spring, carrying in its wash deep assumptions about persons in community, about solidarity in the face of oppression, about not being defined by this world, and about an "unwavering faith" that will survive until we are "free at last, free at last!"

We meet this floodtide at a point of juncture—the matrix of its first seepage into the practice of the Lourdes community, ushered in by the faith-filled longings of a few parishioners and the prophetic vision of two Redemptorists. As these chapters unfold, we will experience its swelling tide, as it washes through their liturgy and life almost forty years later—flowing through their voices, running through their bodies, as they continue to claim their place in the church as both Black and Catholic, a church already changed by their genius.

This river of music, which erupts each Sunday in the voices, piano, drums, and rhythmic dance of this little community in Hunters Point, is, in their words, "a gift of God that enables us to worship Him better"; "a way of praising God from the heart," of "lifting Him up on our praises!" Singing, they say, is a way of "finding refuge and strength in the Lord"; a means of "making it through hard times"; a source of joy, of comfort, of healing; a precious nourishment that sustains our lives, giving us "something to feast on all week." Truly, music is for Lourdes *a precious fountain*—a wellspring of historical memory, a cultural model for preaching, praying, ritual, and relationship, and always the mediation of the "sweet sound" of "amazing grace."

❦ ❦ ❦

Our Lady of Lourdes parish, referred to affectionately as "Lourdes," is located in the southeastern corner of San Francisco. The area immediately surrounding the church, traditionally called Hunters Point, forms a peninsula jutting into San Francisco Bay. A major naval station, situated at the tip of this peninsula, has played a significant role in the history and development of the area and of the parish as well. During World War II, naval operations at the Hunters Point shipyard were greatly expanded, creating a surplus of jobs. Many who migrated to the area in the 1940s to fill these positions were African Americans from the southern part of the United States. A number of those who settled in this area were from Louisiana, among them individuals and families who remain part of Lourdes. To meet the needs of this rapidly expanding population, city officials hastily erected public housing on the "hill" above the current site of Lourdes, and a modicum of city services were extended to the newly developing area.[2]

Simultaneous with this first surge of employment, the Catholic Archdiocese of San Francisco, through the generous contribution of a single donor, founded the new church of Our Lady of Lourdes.[3] In 1942, a small Mission-style building was erected near the grounds of the Naval Station to provide for the religious needs of Catholics living in the area and especially for the catechetical needs of young people.[4] The church was designated a "mission" of neighboring All Hallows parish, and within a few years, became an independent parish.

As activity at the shipyard diminished after World War II, archdiocesan authorities moved the church building a few miles inland to its current site at the corner of Hawes St. and Innes Ave. Once again, Lourdes became a mission of neighboring All Hallows parish. For a time, regular Sunday liturgy at Lourdes was provided by clergy from All Hallows. But as clerical resources dwindled, liturgies at Lourdes became less frequent. Most members reaffiliated elsewhere, leaving only a small number who considered themselves parishioners. The church building fell into disrepair, despite attempts by a few members to care for it.

"We came here right after they pulled the tanks out," recounts Father Donald MacKinnon, former pastor of Our Lady of Lourdes, remembering his arrival in Hunters Point.[5] It was May of 1968—a turbulent time in this and other predominantly African American districts of San Francisco. The city "never came to grips with racial discrimination," writes one historical commentator.[6] By the mid-1960s,

> the Black community had grown increasingly frustrated . . . with the lack of progress . . . [a frustration that] culminated in a race riot in 1966. The riot erupted after a white policeman killed a black teenager who had allegedly stolen an automobile. When news of the slaying was reported by black Hunter's Point residents and the local media, the entire city exploded for five days. The riot seemed to take many white San Franciscans by surprise, for they had grown complacent and ignored the disparity between themselves and the black community[7]

Two years later, the National Guard was finally withdrawn from Hunters Point. The stage was set for Lourdes' renaissance.

"The little church was pretty much abandoned," comments Father MacKinnon about his arrival with Brother Gary Pometta on that warm day in 1968. "The archdiocese like everyone else had abandoned the place." But, these two Redemptorists would soon learn, there were embers in the ashes left to cool as parish life diminished. Mrs. Margaret Fisher, joined by two companions, Mrs. Coleman and Mrs. Joseph, gathered regularly near the church to pray the rosary. "I *believed* this church was going to reopen," Mrs. Fisher commented to me years later. "The other women and I would come and stand by the statue of Our Lady of Lourdes out in front of the church and pray. Then," she added with a twinkle in her eye, "we'd go and have lunch or something."[8]

Their hopes would be satisfied in 1968. Alarmed by the social turbulence that erupted in Hunters Point two years earlier, archdiocesan authorities determined to reestablish a presence among the African American community there. Thus, they welcomed the request of Father MacKinnon and Brother Pometta to reopen the parish. Father MacKinnon notes that his desire to do this was sparked in large measure by an experience of living in Harlem for several years. There, a small group of women religious, working among the Black community, had shaped his vision of how the church might be involved in the social fabric of people's lives. With the blessings of the archdiocese, Father MacKinnon and Brother Pometta moved to Hunters Point and took up residence in the housing project on "the hill" behind the church.

Slowly, the embers were reignited. The period from 1968 to the late 1980s was a time of progressive growth for the parish.[9] The new pastor's strategy was to involve as many persons as possible in the rebuilding process, calling on the specific gifts of each. He himself began door-to-door contact with persons in the surrounding neighborhoods, while reestablishing regular times for worship and religious education classes for the children. Gradually, members rejoining the parish were enlisted as teachers, assisted by seminarians and women religious from around the Bay Area who served on a volunteer basis.

"We were a kind of magnet," recalls Father MacKinnon, attracting persons who wanted to minister in the Black community. In time, a few women religious became regular members of the parish staff, among them Sister Martin de Porres Coleman, S.N.D.deN., and Sister Helen Carroll, R.S.C.J. Without major financial resources to call on, much of what was accomplished was due to the hard work and untiring efforts of numerous persons. Close human interaction between families and the clergy and religious who served them created strong bonds within the developing parish community. "You read about 'comunidades de base,'" comments Father MacKinnon. "We had it at Lourdes!"

From the outset, persons in parish leadership were concerned to recognize and develop gifts for leadership within the community. Women were prepared to be catechists and encouraged to use their gifts to train children in the faith, first in neighborhood settings and later at the church itself. Teenagers became involved in tutoring younger students in the parish. Brother Gary Pometta, having assisted Father MacKinnon through the first years of rebuilding the parish, decided to prepare for priesthood. Ordained in 1980, Father Pometta succeeded Father MacKinnon as pastor shortly afterwards.

Social outreach was an extremely important focus of the rebuilding process.[10] The African American community of Hunters Point was often denied social and educational services available in other parts of the city. "Kids would [come knocking on] our windows," recalls Father MacKinnon, "knowing that they had to have my [white] voice on the phone to get an ambulance." Informal GED classes were started. Spearheaded by the parish and its growing network of friends, including the Religious of the Sacred Heart of San Francisco College for Women (later renamed Lone Mountain College) who became an indispensable educational link, this initiative grew into the founding of the Bayview-Hunters Point Community College, which today is part of the City College of San Francisco. Two law offices were brought to the area and parish assistance given them. Through the help of a Jesuit priest, also a lawyer, a Criminal Defense Office was established to assist criminal offenders. Personal support of every kind was offered to persons in need. Soon the word got around, "If you need help or anything, just go down to that church at the bottom of the hill, they'll help you."[11] In Father MacKinnon's words, "Every time we went to the jails or took someone to the hospital, our membership grew."

Ecumenical contacts were crucial to this process. "To do the things I wanted to do in the civil arena, I needed allies," recalls Father MacKinnon. Through contacts with Baptist ministers and service on the San Francisco Council of

Churches, he and other staff members helped build a concerted effort among religious leaders to address the needs of the area. "Mission Possible," a halfway house for ex-offenders, was initiated by the newly formed Ecumenical Ministerial Association. In this collaborative process, a specific friendship grew between members of Lourdes parish and Reverend John Lane, pastor of Grace Baptist Church. Some years later, when the community of Grace Baptist needed a new place for worship, they were invited to hold their services in the Lourdes church house on Sunday afternoons.

"It's in the music, the poetry," suggests Father MacKinnon, describing the "soul" of a liturgical renaissance that took place at Lourdes during these years of rebuilding. In 1970, Sister Martin de Porres Coleman, S.N.D.deN., a classically trained musician, vocalist, choral director, and teacher, was invited to join the parish staff.[12] Prior to her affiliation with Lourdes, Sister Martin was already engaged in recovering the riches of Black musical traditions for Catholic worship. Beginning in the mid-1960s, she worked with Father Clarence Rivers, a priest of the Archdiocese of Cincinnati who is recognized today as the major catalyst in bringing the artistic genius of African Americans to Catholic worship.[13] During the late 1960s and 1970s, Father Rivers, Sister Martin, and various other musicians, liturgists, and composers led national workshops under the auspices of the National Office for Black Catholics.

Within the parish, the process of shaping worship and music patterns began from the ground up. First, the church building had to become a home for the community again. Windows were replaced[14] and the room repainted and refurbished. Furnishings were adapted to meet the new liturgical directions taken by Vatican II, and new vestments were made. Concerned to allow all aspects of the church to reflect the African American culture of its members, the pastor called a parish meeting to discuss the European-style plaster statues present in the church. After initial resistance on the part of some because of life-long association of this kind of art with Catholic life and worship, the decision was made to replace them with carved wooden statues of the Black Madonna of Montserrat and of St. Martin de Porres.

Music was pivotal for the gradual evolution of the worship patterns of the Lourdes community. Shortly after her arrival, Sister Martin founded a youth Gospel Choir, the first of its kind within the Archdiocese of San Francisco. Four musically talented members of a single family, well-versed in contemporary soul and gospel music, became the core members of what grew into a forty-voice youth choir. Attracted by the involvement of their children, older members of the parish began to appreciate this new integration of "gospel sound" and Catholic liturgy. The youth choir's ministry included singing at other churches as well, in some cases introducing Catholic communities to the use of

African American musical styles in worship. Within a few years, a small adult choir was also formed, giving birth to what is today the Lourdes Gospel Choir.

Both choirs served as a context for developing the musical and liturgical leadership of choir members. Sister Martin introduced these parish musicians to an understanding of worship that flowed from the reforms of Vatican II, and to a sensitivity regarding the appropriate use of music in worship. She engaged members of both choirs in weekly liturgy preparation and in the selection of repertoire for Sunday worship. She worked to develop their gifts for solo and choral singing, and in the case of some, for instrumental accompaniment on organ, piano, or drums. Under her tutelage, several young members became proficient percussionists. Given this formation, choir members were prepared to take leadership and self-direction in the future.

One of Sister Martin's concerns was to develop a liturgical repertoire that responded to the needs of this parish community—one that integrated music of their African American heritage while remaining truly "catholic." African American gospel music, gospel hymns, spirituals, and newly composed settings of liturgical texts, such as Grayson Brown's *Mass for a Soulful People,* were introduced to the parish. Traditional Catholic hymns and some Gregorian chants were also used, since these were part of the repertoire familiar to older members of the community.

Sister Martin's departure from the parish in the mid-1970s was a sadness for the parish, especially for the women. In addition to her musical leadership, Sister Martin had been part of their lives, visiting their homes, helping with the care of their children. In her absence, Mr. Hilliard Patterson, a pianist from the Baptist tradition, was employed to accompany the Gospel Choir, and for a brief time, George Quigley, S.J., a young Jesuit theology student in Berkeley, took over its direction. A few years later, when George Quigley was ordained to the priesthood and Mr. Patterson responded to an inner call to "street preaching," Charlene Edwards, a choir member trained for leadership by Sister Martin, became director. Soon after, Reed Fromer was employed as the community's pianist.

Preaching and the preparation of lay liturgical ministers became a final focus of the liturgical renaissance that took place at Lourdes between 1968 and the late '80s. Father MacKinnon was especially concerned to develop Black leaders who could represent the community. For this reason, Lourdes joined some five other parishes, each with predominantly African American membership, in preparing lay Eucharistic Ministers.[15] After a year of formation, communities gathered to confirm and bless their ministry. Among these new ministers was Mr. Jesse Banks—better known at Lourdes as "Brother Banks"—who would serve the parish for many years to come as a treasured "elder" and assist at liturgical services in the role of deacon.

*T*he warm October sun drenched my face as I parked in front of Our Lady of Lourdes church for the first time.[16] It was 1991. I had recently begun doctoral studies in Worship and the Arts at the Graduate Theological Union in Berkeley, and was eager to explore the liturgical life of communities in this culturally diverse area surrounding San Francisco Bay. My motivation was more than curiosity. The goal of my incipient doctoral studies was to probe deeper into the practice and theology of Christian liturgy, and specifically into the multifaceted role of music in worship. I was convinced that to do this, I needed to learn from the wisdom and experience of particular communities. I realized that, given the great cultural diversity of our churches, there were stories to tell that were missing from our academic conversations about Christian liturgy, and more specifically about Catholic worship. I knew there were musical traditions that were nourishing the faith life of praying assemblies that were not yet fully recognized as Catholic liturgical music. It was my intent to tap something of this richness.

My first acquaintances with the Lourdes community were occasional visits for Sunday liturgy. At the time, Lourdes was a growing community of perhaps one hundred families—a buoyant, resilient, "church community," proud to be who they are, taking ownership of their lives, their social situation, their worship, their families. I would soon learn that Lourdes is a community because of geography, attraction, commitment, choice, and history. Many of its members grew up in Hunters Point, although some now live in other parts of San Francisco and the greater Bay Area. Others have been drawn to Lourdes in recent years, often by the vitality of its Sunday worship. Most adult members, including many of retirement age, are employed; their occupations include early childhood education, sales, secretarial services, youth counseling, nursing, and various transportation services. Most have modest incomes, yet financial support of the parish is a priority. Many retired members remain remarkably active, caring for grandchildren or other family members, and offering varying kinds of service on a volunteer basis. Several young adults are enrolled in college or have recently graduated.

The cultural complexity of the community has evolved over the years, although most members are African American. In 1990, the Redemptorist priests, who had served the parish since 1968,[17] withdrew because of new ministerial demands. Father MacKinnon, who had returned for a second brief tenure as pastor, encouraged members of the community to petition the archdiocese to staff the parish so it would not close. Father John Isaacs, a priest of the archdiocese, was named pastor and served until early 1991, when Father Kirk Ullery replaced him as the current pastor of Lourdes.

I would learn, as well, that the religious background of Lourdes' parishioners is diverse and ecumenical. Perhaps the majority have been Catholic all their lives. Yet the traditional worship style of their childhood Catholicism was significantly different from what they experience here. This is especially true for those who grew up in Louisiana and certain other areas of the South where Catholic practice was conservative and quite restrained. One young member describes the liturgies of his childhood as quiet, usually without song, and most often limited to forty-five minutes. Some who had been raised Catholic attended the worship services of other denominations with friends or family members. In fact for some, church attendance on Sunday included Catholic Mass in the mornings and a Baptist service in the afternoon, or throughout both afternoon and evening. Others were raised Protestant, several in the Baptist tradition. Some, both Catholic and Protestant, had stopped attending church in their adult years because there seemed little connection with their daily lives. Worship at Lourdes was pivotal, in most cases, for their decision to become active again. Yet no matter what the pattern, members of Lourdes report that faith in God was always central to their lives. Faith was cultivated in their family life, and music was often a deep expression of that faith. Songs still sung by this community carry memories of their childhood and of the faith witness of parents. But all this learning would come in the future.

*F*rom my first visits to Lourdes, I was stirred by the dynamism, conviction, at times communal passion of Sunday worship. I was moved by the candor with which people expressed their faith. I was warmed by the hospitality and acceptance I felt. Each Sunday, visitors were welcomed, even thanked for being present, and always encouraged to return. Lourdes has much the feel of an extended family—a network of children, young adults, adults, grandparents, and great-grandparents. Family ties are strong. Children are especially cherished—hugged, caressed, cared for by parents and grandparents, as well as other members of the community. But people are bonded beyond blood ties— joined by experience, by a common history, and by deep affection.

What attracted me most, though, was the vibrancy of the community's music. I was intrigued by the timbral intensity of the women's voices, the energy with which people engaged in making music, and the sense of communal ownership that seemed to suffuse the music. Hymn books were markedly absent, yet everyone knew the songs. Moreover, I was engaged in the study of Black gospel music, exploring the impact of various worships contexts on its historical evolution and performance practice. Here, the tradition was incarnate— alive and recreated each week.

Despite the hospitality I felt from members of the community, I knew that I stood at an intersection, a complex border-crossing. I was attracted by the art of their communal modes of song and worship, and realized how much I could learn from them. Yet it was clear that I would be changed in the process. Although I shared their Catholic tradition, I would need to discover new rhythms of prayer and praise, new patterns of thought and feeling, and a new freedom to participate in a worship practice that was significantly different than what had shaped my understandings of liturgy. It would take time to develop mutual trust and understanding, for me to know members of the community, and for them to know me. I knew that my experience as a white American woman of Irish heritage would be stretched, even challenged. And I sensed that articulating my learning in a scholarly context, or bringing it to bear in pastoral conversations about liturgy, would likewise be challenging.

In the fall of 1993, I explained my interest to Lourdes' pastor, Father Kirk Ullery, and three leaders of the choir, Pat Goodall, Jean Alexander, and Judy Brown. With their blessing, I began an intentional affiliation with the community, participating regularly in Sunday worship and parish celebrations. With their permission, I tape recorded, and at times videotaped, each liturgy. I initiated conversations, at times longer interviews, with the pastor and various members of the community, seeking out different points of view on how they experience music and worship at Lourdes. I sought out those who had guided the parish through the years of rebuilding—Father Don MacKinnon, Sister Martin de Porres Coleman, and Sister Helen Carroll. With the consent of the choir leaders, I attended weekly rehearsals, getting to know members of the choir, observing the musical processes at work, engaging, on occasion, in conversation with the whole choir about their musical ministry, and after a year, becoming a choir member. On numerous occasions, I met at length with individual musicians to explore aspects of repertoire and performance. Accompanist Reed Fromer, Director Pat Goodall, and many of the choir members were generous with their time and insight.[18] In all this, I was hardly a detached observer. Gradually, my attitudes, insights, assumptions, and research agenda were changed and reshaped by my interaction and prayer with this community, and by the deep friendships that have grown over the years.

In both my conversations and my experience of worship at Lourdes, I was struck by the community's well-formulated, interpretive discourse about their worship and musical practice. Although there is no single perspective, people articulate their experience, comment on it, describe it, ascribe meanings to it through recurring images and metaphors that signal a shared and cultivated discourse about the significance of what takes place from Sunday to Sunday. These images have significantly shaped my own interpretive categories and have been part of the dialogic process by which this book has come into being.

One of the striking things I came to know about this community is their comfort with both suffering and joy. Struggle is considered a normal part of life and is meant to be shared. Something of the drama of each Sunday gathering is the communal entrance into the struggles of its members, into the dynamic juxtaposition of liturgy and life. For me to understand what was at the heart of their music and prayer, I needed to enter these rhythms and allow them to touch my own—to partake of both the suffering and joy, to embrace not the "drama of worship" but the drama of our lives lived together before

God. As a scholar, this deep personal involvement allowed me a depth of understanding that might otherwise have eluded me.

Within a year of my affiliation, Lourdes faced one of the most significant turning points in the life of the community. In November 1993, the Archdiocese of San Francisco announced the closure of nine of its parishes, among them All Hallows, the "parent church" of Lourdes at its founding and again before its reopening in 1968. Given bonds of family and friendship among members of both parishes, many from All Hallows gravitated to Lourdes. This included the large Samoan community affiliated with All Hallows who, through their spokesperson, approached Father Ullery seeking membership. By the following July, Lourdes had doubled in size. A second Sunday liturgy (8:30 a.m.) was inaugurated, with the Samoan Choir offering musical leadership, while the original Lourdes community, under the musical leadership of the Gospel Choir, rescheduled its worship for 10:00 a.m.[19] Three years later, Archbishop William Levada, then the new prelate of San Francisco, decided to reopen All Hallows Church as a "chapel" of Lourdes parish.[20]

My engagement with the Lourdes community has continued through the present, although my most intensive research spanned the years 1993–1997. In the Spring of 1996, I completed a first interpretive presentation of my learning in the form of a doctoral dissertation.[21] This systematic portrait of the role of music in the Lourdes worship left me wanting to write more—to capture in a more narrative mode the dynamic and vibrant musical practice that is so integral to this community's Catholic liturgy. It is this desire that has prompted *A Precious Fountain*.

I write this book from a busy intersection: first, from within the experience of worshiping with the Lourdes community for several years, from conversations I have had with many community members, and from all the wealth of new insights regarding music and worship that these experiences have opened for me. I write as a musician and member of the Lourdes Gospel Choir, engaged in an ongoing process of learning, singing, and treasuring new music. I write, as well, from the practice of systematic reflection what I have experienced and learned—through regular field notes, listening to audiotapes of each Sunday's worship, tracking of new questions, and infiltrating this process with readings/conversations with others who study the African American religious and liturgical experience. I write as a scholar in the complex field of liturgical studies, seeking to discover new treasures, to tap new theological-liturgical wellsprings within the culturally diverse practice of our Catholic tradition. And lastly, I write as a person of faith who has been deeply enriched by the flow of spirituality and commingling of spirits that are integral to my engagement at Lourdes.

Even as I write, I continue to stand at a border-crossing. I have been deeply integrated into the life of this community. But I can only speak from the juncture where my experience with and of them meets my own life, personal and scholarly. Writing from this intersection, I invite others to taste and learn what I have experienced. I suspect that many of the readers of this book will come from backgrounds similar to my own. I invite them to learn with me. But I do not speak alone. The voices of the community, that great exuberant chorus of voices, *are* the story. I speak and sing with them. I hope to present a "portrait" of their dynamic music and worship practice—to invite the reader, through stories, events, descriptions, and analysis, into the micro and macro rhythms of the community's prayer and song.

*T*he distinctive format of this book enables the reader to access the musical-liturgical practice of the Lourdes community from several vantage points. The numbered chapters are narrative and descriptive in character. Each is organized around a significant song title, aphorism, or image from the community's "orature" that captures a key interpretive perspective. Here I speak *with* the community, weaving vignettes, stories, commentary, and descriptions of specific worship events that invite the reader to experience the complexities of the community's music, worship, and life. The first six chapters introduce the reader to the community—the ethos and patterns of their worship; the role of musicians, elders, and children; and the significance of "home" to their identity as Black Catholics. Chapters seven through twelve focus on key dimensions the worship itself—the proclamation of the Word in song and preaching, as well as the words, prayers, gestures, and attitudes through which the community enacts Eucharist. The final three chapters bring the narrative full circle by highlighting three pervasive aspects of the community's liturgical practice—singing and dancing as revelatory of divine presence; the distinctive role of women musicians; and the incorporating action of the Holy Spirit. Throughout, music unfolds as a multifaceted jewel—embraced as a potent performance medium and a vital communication of faith; remembered as an intricate part of the community's historical journeys; treasured as a repository of wisdom and source of shared spirituality. The entire narrative is necessary to capture the full spectrum of this jewel's radiance.

Punctuating these chapters are a series of *Intermezzi*—pauses in the narrative flow that allow me to assume a different interpretive stance, one more reflective and analytical, in order to probe what can be learned from this community's practice about musical-liturgical action. Each intermezzo is organized around an important dimension of both music-making and ritualizing: Time, Space, Words, Flow, and Embodiment. Taken together, these intermezzi create a path of interpretive analysis that flows from the opening images of this Introduction—describing the wellsprings of music at Lourdes—to the theological reflections of the last chapter.

"Speaking Theologically," the concluding chapter, mines the rich theology embedded in the narrative chapters and signaled in the intermezzi, identifying the specific intersection of this community's lived practice with the theological formulations of liturgical scholars. Moreover, it probes how Lourdes' unique fusion of African American and Roman Catholic sacramental life, and especially its musical practice, introduces distinctive liturgical and theological understandings that enrich Catholic practice.

The primary time frame of this book is the period between 1993 and 1997—all the events described fall within this period, with the exception of a few more recent occurrences that appear in the latter chapters—and it is from within this time frame that the account has been written. Hence, an *Epilogue* 2003 has been added to bring the reader "up to date" on significant events and dynamic changes that have taken place in the life of the Lourdes community in recent years.

Several appendices complete the work—diagrams of the Lourdes worship space, an overview of the patterns of Sunday worship, a glossary of musical terms, and a detailed sampling of the Lourdes repertoire. Information regarding songs mentioned in the narrative, including published sources, can be found in this latter table.

Throughout the book, excerpts from liturgies, conversations, and interviews will be quoted, either briefly or at length. In so far as possible, all personal references, names, and quotations are used with permission. When citing spoken interaction—in the form of preaching, prayers, conversations—I have attempted to represent the sound of the speakers' voices. For this reason, I have engaged a pattern of "coded speech" by which to capture something of their vocal inflection and emphasis. I encourage readers to consult the table of "coded speech," which can be found in Appendix 1, before embarking on the narrative chapters.

Throughout the text, I have capitalized "Black" to indicate a critical consciousness—a life-affirming embrace of Blackness as gift and graced heritage. I have also attempted to capture something of the patterns of Black English [22] that are cultivated within the community's discourse: for example, the regular use of "soft endings," such as "singin', prayin', workin'," that are part of what Henry Mitchell describes as the "'down home' drawl" of Black speech—a cultivated practice of "soft velvet sounds" that have a "capacity to communicate warmth and avoid harsh overtones," and that "signal value in the Black speech community."[23]

In all of this, I invite the reader to enter imaginatively into the sights, sounds, feelings, and faith expression that comprise the worship-music of this dynamic community.

Chapter One

"HAVING A GOOD TIME IN THE LORD!"

—ENJOYING WORSHIP—

*F*ebruary 14, 1994—Opening night of the annual Lourdes Revival. A soaking rain envelops the car as I cross the Bay Bridge and make my way through the dimly lit streets of east San Francisco to Lourdes. Finding a parking space among the cars that already line the corner of Hawes Street and Innes Avenue, I take refuge from the miserable weather in the warmth and light of the church. The entranceway at the rear of the church bustles with activity—people arriving, greeting each other, embracing. Members of several guest choirs are vesting in brightly colored choir robes, each bearing the insignia of the church to which they belong. St. Paul of the Shipwreck Inspirational Choir in tan with a touch of Kente cloth. Rose Olivet Emmanuel Baptist Choir in deep maroon. Sacred Heart Gospel Choir in brilliant gold and deep blue. The Stockton Travelers in black and white. Blue-robed singers from the Lourdes Gospel Choir are welcoming guests and members of the parish who press through the crowd exchanging hugs and greetings. Meanwhile, people are slowly moving to the seats on the left side of the church, reserving most of the thirteen pews on the right for the guest choirs and musicians. Any lingering notions I might have had of "revival" as a serious, pleasureless, "shaping oneself up" are shattered by the mood of expectation, enthusiasm, and festivity that abounds.

The pews are filling quickly. I notice Mrs. Amanda Winslow, one of the great-grandmothers of the community who is known and loved by all as "Mama Winslow," seated some eight pews from the front, beneath the window image of Sojourner Truth—the spot where she can be found each Sunday morning. Walking a bit further, I slip into the third row next to Shirley Valmore, whose two grandnephews, Tyree and "little" Darsky, are already settled on her lap. A small group of clergymen are gathering near the front-right of the church, just this side of the "sanctuary" area. Reverend John Lane, the short, stately

1

Black minister of Grace Baptist Church, whose congregation shares the worship space with Lourdes. Reverend Kenneth Westray of Sacred Heart, one of the few Black priests of the Catholic archdiocese. Reverend Kirk Ullery, Lourdes' pastor. Reverend Jim Goode, the African American Franciscan pastor of neighboring parish St. Paul of the Shipwreck. Over his black suit, Father Jim Goode is wearing a tunic of African cloth, brilliantly designed in red, orange, and purple, and a matching Kufi hat. I smile, remembering that tonight's preacher is a woman, curious to see how she will meet the high expectations of this community and its guests.

Already there is music in the air. To the left of the front, just across from the clergy, Reed Fromer is seated at a well-worn baby grand piano. As he begins to play, eleven-year-old drummer, Isaiah Brown, moves to a large trap set nearby. Reed begins to trace song lines beneath the animated greetings, improvising a medley of familiar melodies, punctuated by Isaiah's occasional drum or cymbal flourish. Between the musicians on the left and clergy on right, you can see the well-lit sanctuary area, altar recessed for the evening to make space for the performing choirs. At the rear, a colorful tapestry made by members of the parish for this year's revival.

*R*evival. The word is markedly absent from the vocabulary of most Catholics.[1] Yet for the Lourdes community, this pre-Lenten triduum is an indispensable part of the spring rainy season. Webster's Unabridged offers a glimpse. "Revival: a restoration to life, consciousness, vigor strength; . . . an evangelistic service or series of services for the purpose of effecting a religious awakening." But Catholic? you might ask. Black theologian Diana Hayes describes "Black Catholic Revivalism" as a distinctive form of worship, a "rich synthesis" of "the unique contributions of the African past, the ongoing Black life experience, and Catholic ritual and sacramentality . . . which celebrates being Black and Catholic in a way which is . . . self affirming . . . community-building and nurturing. It is a celebration of the Spirit and of thanksgiving. . . ."[2]

Lourdes held its first Revival in 1985, just eleven years after Reverend Jim Goode, present this evening, launched the Black Catholic Revival Movement in Chicago. "It's not just about feeling good for three days," comments Father Goode about revivals. "It is about renewing our spirit. It is directing us as a people in what our ancestors handed down to us—that God is still in charge. When we begin to pull on our faith experience, it renews our spirit. And this renewed strength that comes from above should move us to take up the cause of justice and liberation for our people."[3] At Lourdes, evenings of revival are meant to move people toward greater surrender to God, toward receiving God's blessing and anointing through a laying on of hands and prayer over each one who desires this ministry. Song, prayer, the Word of God, and preaching seem to coalesce to create a pathway, a watercourse, if you will, along which people can make a personal journey, buoyed up by the faith and enthusiasm of others.

*T*he hours begin to dissolve. The stirring rhythms of an opening song seem to galvanize this church house full of people into a single, pulsing body. I can feel people around me swaying and clapping to the infectious beat, joining their voices to proclaim for the first time this evening that "Jesus is all right with me!" One by one, the guest choirs walk rhythmically "in step" down the center aisle to their designated pews. The singing continues, "I've tried Him / and I've found out / that He's all right with me!" The Lourdes choir is last, moving to the front to fill in the seating area in the sanctuary. Sister Renee de Porres Fenner, guest preacher this evening, takes up the rear of the procession. Dressed in white alb, a bright Kente cloth stole over her shoulder, she "dances" her way through the assembly to join the other ministers seated in the front.

"Are you looking for joy?" queries Barbara McKinney, mistress of ceremonies for the evening, from the ambo, after welcoming everyone to the first night of revival. *"Yes!"* returns the resounding volley. "Then you've come to the right place! Are you looking to have your spirits revived?" *"Yes!"* is once again the reply. "Then you've come to the house of the Lord. You are certainly in the right place! Sit back and relax and have a good time in the Lord. . . ." "Lourdes is like a family," adds Alexis Alexander, another woman from the parish who is now standing at the ambo. "If you come as a visitor, you come back, because you feel so welcome. That's why I come back, and keep coming back. So, tonight," she adds, "there'll be some spirit-lifting, *(Oh, yes!)* some foot-stomping, *(Yes!)* some hand-clapping, *(Yes!)* and some souls touched!" *(Amen! Yes!)*

Applause subsides as Brother Jesse Banks, Lourdes' elderly deacon, moves to the front of the church. The cadence of his voice penetrates the now-hushed room. The rhythmic rise and fall of his heartfelt prayer evokes responses from people around the church. Reed Fromer continues to improvise, catching the flow of Brother Banks's words with his musical phrases.

> We're here on the first night of our revival. *(Oh, yes!)* In times like this, it's necessary that we get close to Jesus. *(Amen!)* *Everything else* seems to be failin'. *(Al'right! Amen!)* We're so glad to see so many here. *(Amen!)* You could have been some other place, but you say, *"I want to be a guest of Jesus!"* *(Yes!)* We pray to the Almighty God tonight, that he will bless everybody that is here. Bless all these choirs who have come to sing. *(Yes!)* We pray, Father, that it will *not be in vain!* Things are goin' so bad. *Unless you be* **with us Father,** we cannot make it. *(Amen!)* We need your help. *(Yes!)* We ask you to bless all the minsters, especially our speaker tonight—*one who has come a long way.* When someone asked her where she was goin', she said "I'm goin' to be a *guest of Jesus.*" *(Amen!!)*
>
> We pray Father, bless our musicians, everybody here. *(Yes!)* *We hope that this will bring us closer together,* *(Oh, yes!)* that we will **love one another** the way *God loves us,* *(Yes! Amen!)* that we will become *true brothers and*

sisters, and say, *"**He's not heavy,** he's my brother; **She's not heavy,** she's my sister!"* Help us, Father, to do the will of God. *We cannot make it, Father, unless you hold our hand.* **Lead us and guide us** *in the way you would have us go. (Yes!)* Give us that *ol' time religion, Father, (Oh, yes!)* that we may *love* one another, not only here, but tomorrow and every day Father, *like they did in the old days,* Father, *(Yes!) workin' in the cotton fields, when they didn't have anything!* Mules pulling the wagons. They would always say, *"I love the Lord, (Yes!) for he heard my cry!"* Sometimes they'd break out with that song, **"He's sweet I know!"** *(Yes!)* We ask you to bring us together, Father. Sometimes we have disturbance in our churches. Sometimes we have disturbance in homes. *(Yes!) But we know Father that you can make it all right. Jesus said he would be with us, and he **never comes short of his word!** (Amen! Yes!)* Oh, Lord have mercy! Father we know we can make it if you help us. But, Father, we need to do the will of God, no matter what it may be, no matter what we need to go through, we must say, *"Here I am Father, take and use me! I will say yes to you!"* Lord have mercy!

We pray for everybody here, that you will be blessed, that we will become true brothers and sisters in Christ, so that when it is over, *Father, when it is over—*we don't know *when it is goin' to come,* we don't know *where we're going to be at,* we don't know *how it is goin' to be—*but if you *lead us, Father,* **that "old ship of Zion" will come over!** *(Amen!)* We *know it will be all right,* because *Jesus can speak to the wind and the waves! (Yes!)* He can speak to the water! *(Yes!)* We *need you Father to speak to our leaders, 'cause they're takin' the poor people, who are down and out.* They seem to think that more jails will help. *Father, something is wrong!* Jesus said, "I am a peacemaker," and *unless he comes to be with us,* we cannot find you. We pray, Father, that this revival will help to bring us all together, will bring peace, like a cool wind on a hot day, in all the places that it is needed. That we will *love one another, walk together, pray together, so that when we reach that place we call heaven, we will be able to walk around the throne and cry,* **"Holy, Holy God almighty!"** *and say* **"Free at last, Free at last!"** No more **sorrow,** *no more* **pain,** *no more* **suffering,** *only peace and happiness! (Al'right! Amen!)* We ask this in the name of Jesus. *(Amen! Amen! Amen!!!)*

It is clear to the community that Brother Banks has been touched by the Holy Spirit's power. His voice and body have become so animated as he prayed these last phrases that Jean Alexander and Pat Goodall are now standing beside him and gently lead him back to his seat among the clergy.

*T*he first part of the evening is given over to singing and readings from Scripture. Music, it is understood, "prepares a way for the Spirit," awakens the soul, and allows tired bodies to relax and "lay down the burdens" of the day.

One by one, guest choirs are invited forward to engage us in song—to offer an "A and B selection" chosen in light the prayerful energy they experience in the church house tonight. Each is welcomed with applause. People spontaneously join the singing, catching the often repetitive flow of words, of praises sung like mantras: "I Will Sing, Hallelujah! I Will Sing to the Lord!" sung by St. Paul of the Shipwreck's Inspirational Choir; "I Love to Praise His Name!" chorused by Rose Olivet Emmanuel Baptist Choir; and "I Will Bless You, Precious Lord!" led by the Sacred Heart Gospel Choir. Each choir has its own tone, style, and repertoire. For those who have come without accompanists, Reed Fromer's presence at the piano, and Isaiah Brown's at the drums, are indispensable. Listening only briefly to catch the key, melody, and rhythms, they slip in to add their support. There's an electricity in the air, an enthusiasm, a sense of rapport. People respond like tiny sparks colliding in a conflagration of delight—some rocking gently to the rhythms, some with hands raised, others on their feet, toes tapping and hands clapping to the alternating beats of their swaying bodies. "Tarrying with the Lord," they sometimes call this. Tuning in. Remembering, in the lyrics of the songs that "Trouble don't last always!" and that "I shall overcome!" because "God is faithful," and "God will make a way where there is no way!" The room warms with the exchange of energy, prompting Jean Alexander to move down the center aisle passing out small paper fans.

In the midst of this musical exchange, Sister Irma Dillard comes forward to read from 1 Corinthians 12: 4–11. "Now there are a variety of gifts, but always the same Spirit; *(Amen!)* and there are varieties of services, but the same Lord; *(Well . . .)* and there are varieties of activities, but it is the same God who activates all of them in everyone. *(Yes!)* To each is given the manifestation of the Spirit for the common good. . . ." *(Oh, yes!)*

It's not difficult to see these manifestations in what is taking place tonight. In the early days of rebuilding Lourdes, "ecumenism was a strategy for survival."[4] Tonight, ecumenism is a cause for celebration, a strategy for reclaiming a shared religious heritage that crosses denominational lines. On subsequent nights of the Revival, other Black choirs from around the Bay Area will weave their own threads in this musical tapestry. Old spirituals, gospel praises, new arrangements of favorite hymns—all an expression of a shared faith, a common Black aesthetic and performance practice that is deeply ritual and spiritual in its roots.

*A*fter an hour or more of singing, Rose Isles comes forward to introduce tonight's "revivalist." Sister Renee de Porres Fenner, she tell us, is a Daughter of Charity who serves on the pastoral staff and preaching ministry of St. Alphonsus "Rock" church[5] in St. Louis, Missouri. Spontaneous applause makes it evident that people are ready and eager for what is about to happen. The evening has been building to this moment.

5

Sister Renee moves to the center of the room—her tall, youthful presence accented by the movements of the white alb she wears. An expectant hush envelops the church house. She calls out for the elders of the Lourdes community to bless her and then kneels down on the floor in the open space between the congregation and sanctuary. Liz Bell and Brother Banks hesitate but a minute before coming from either end of the church to lay hands on her. You can feel people praying with them in the silence.

Standing once again, Sister Renee begins to speak. Her contralto voice is full of enthusiasm. Despite her youth, she is skilled in the strenuous art of revival preaching. For well over a half hour, she weaves biblical stories, phrases from well-known songs, bits of folk wisdom, and the testimony of her own conversion experience into an evocative invitation to "step out on faith" and hear God's call to change—all the while engaging those present in an animated dialogue of voices and spirits, a repartee much like the flowing exchange of a good conversation.

"It's a blessing and a delight to be with you this week," she begins, "as we come to be revived // renewed // and ready! (Amen! Al'right!) I come here to share what is in my heart (Amen!) because my faith tells me // that everything // is going to be alright! (Amen!! Yes!!! Clapping . . .)

Picking up the enthusiastic responses of people around the church, she leads us into a well-known spiritual: "When I woke this morning, I didn't have no doubt!" Immediately, piano and drums join in what soon becomes a delightful, communal dance. People are on their feet, singing, clapping, moving freely, even playfully to the rhythms of the song:

> When I woke this morning, I didn't have no doubt [*repeated twice*],
> I didn't have no doubt in my heart.

As if to keep the energy flowing, Sister Renee "lines out" the next verses:

> When I saw that bright sunshine, I didn't have no doubt . . .
> When the Spirit spoke to me, I didn't have no doubt . . .
> When I got down on my knees, I didn't have no doubt . . .

After several minutes, she brings the song to a final cadence. Energies continue to spill over as she begins to speak once again. There's a pregnant passion in each of her words, a persuasive presence in each phase.

> I want to talk a little bit, Church // about stepping out on faith, (Al'right!)
> because it is by *faith* // that we will move mountains (Amen!)
> and remove the shackles // that hold us down. Amen, Church? (Amen!!!)
> Jesus tells us // that if only we had faith (Amen!) // the size of a mustard
>   seed, (Tell it, Sister!)
> *everything*, Church, // is going to be all right! (Amen!)

6

God our creator and covenant-maker // has told us through the ages
that everything // would be all right. *(Amen!!)*

"Didn't God deliver Daniel?" she asks, setting up a litanic call and response.
"Didn't God assure Jeremiah // that he was not too young? *(Oh, yes!)* . . . Didn't
God give Abraham and Sarah a son in their old age? *(Yes!)* . . . Didn't our God
lead Moses and the children of Israel // into the land of milk and honey, *(Yes!)*
even if it took them *forty years to do it? (Amen!* Applause and laughter . . .) Why?" she
asks, goading people's response: "Because they // stepped out on faith!"

Sister Renee's tone shifts a bit, signaling a segue into a story, this time from
the New Testament.

Now I'm gonna ask you to walk with me, . . . *(Well. . . OK!)*
to take a walk with the Man of Galilee, . . . *(Yes!)*
to walk with the Master along Jordan's banks. *(That's right!)*

Evoking images of Jesus' baptism, his call to leave his family and work behind,
to take up his mission, to heal, to touch, to forgive, she invites us to "gather at
the river," to recognize our call to the Jordan, our call to ministry, our call to
prophecy, our call to be equipped with that "same sweet Holy Spirit" that made
Jesus "ready for active duty." She invites us to "make that move, . . . make that
decision," to "come forward and be identified, . . . to be sealed with the Spirit
in 1994," to be "fueled by the same Sprit that empowered Jesus to make his new
beginning . . . to discover that new Renee // that new Corey // . . . that new
person who is a little more tolerant, a little more compassionate. . . ."

That Spirit // will give us comfort // in the midst of our tears. *(Al'right!)*
Those who mourn, // your tears will dry! *(Al'right!)*
Those who fear, // you will be strengthened! *(Oh, yes!)*
Those who feel alone, // you will be filled! *(Yes!)*
Those who lack courage, // you will be fortified! *(Yes!)*
Anxious, // you will be given peace; *(Yes!)*
knocked down, dragged down, *(Yes!)* put down, *(Yes!)* set down, //
you will be righted! *(Oh, yes!)*
You who are silenced, // remember: // the truth // will set you free!
(Amen!!! Applause . . .)
When we've forgotten how to pray, // when we've forgotten how to
forgive, *(Oh, yes!)*
when we've forgotten how to love, *(Yes!)* // the Spirit will be there. *(Yes!)*
But we must allow the Spirit to work in us! *(Yes!)* // We must let the
Spirit fill us! *(Amen!!!)*

Opening her Bible now, Sister Renee turns to Mark's Gospel, chapter 1, verse
14 through 20—Jesus' call to the disciples by the lakeside. She reminds us that
at Jesus' invitation, fishermen Peter, James, and John "walked off the job, left

their father Zebedee, just walked off the job!" . . . "Come after me, and I will make you fishers of people!"

> And when Jesus calls [her gaze is fixed on us now, her words intent]
> we better hush, *(Yes!)* // 'cause somebody is calling my name! *(Oh, yes!)* . . .
> This call will make us // walk off the job.
> Now you all know what I mean // when I say walk off the job?
>   *(Laughter . . .)*
> It means we'll walk off the corner //
> where we've been hanging on *(Al'right!* Intermittent clapping . . .)
> to make a *change* in our lives *(Yes!)* . . .
> O yes, we too, by our baptism, // have been chosen. *(Yes!)*
> We too, are God's beloved sons and daughters. *(Oh, yes!)*
> We too, are called to preach the good news // of truth, *(Yes!)* hope, *(Yes!)*
>   peace. *(Yes!)*
> We too are called as witnesses, *(Amen! Yes!)* // as prophets and prophetesses
> to God's *mercy,* God's justice and hope! *(Yes!)*

This call to "come follow me," she continues, "doesn't require that you be any more // than a child of God! So, Church, if anybody asks you // who you are? What you gonna tell them?" The response is spontaneous: "A child of God!!!" Reed Fromer anticipates the ensuing song and intones the opening chords. "Go ahead!" she prods. In a flash, people are on their feet again, singing the old Spiritual,

> If anybody asks you who I am? who I am? who I am?
> If anybody asks you who I am? Tell them, "I'm a child of God!"

After two verses, Reed leads into a final cadence, but Sister Renee calls out,

> Don't sit down! Who are you? *(A child of God!!!)* Who are you? *(A child of God!!!)*
> If you know you are a child of God, stand up!

The song erupts again, goaded to new repetitions by her calls, "Who are you?" "Tell me one more time!" Clapping merges into enthusiastic applause, which only gradually dies down again.

At this point, Sister Renee walks from her position behind the ambo and comes into the "open space" in front of the pews. She begins to tell the story of a young woman, the tale of a "child of God," who had her sights on religious life from her earliest years. "But because of circumstance, because of the way the church *appeared* to be . . . [this] Black child of God didn't think there was any 'room in the inn' for her. *(Well . . .)* Y'all know what I mean, don't you?"

Laughter and shouts of *Amen!!! Oh—yes!!* from around the church make it clear that they do!

Well, she continues, this young women grew up, went on to pursue a college degree, a career in theater, then in broadcasting, all the time trying to have a good time. But "the Hound of Heaven // was nipping at her heels!" She moved away from home and tried, at first, "to do the right thing." She went to church one Sunday morning in Springfield, Illinois. The usher standing near the door looked at her as if to say, "What's she doin' here?" *(Al'right!)* Oh, she tried to sing, she tried to pray. "But the church was so *cold*" that "*Sistah-girl had to come out of there!*" *(I hear you!* Laughter . . .) So she went on, having a good time—acting, teaching, dancing. "But the Hound of heaven // was nipping at her heels!" One morning, she doubled over with pain. "Oh, somebody take this chil' to the hospital!" She needed emergency surgery. But "Oh, she knew . . . she wasn't ready to see Jesus!" A first surgery, then a second. Then one day "something just came upon her. She asked the Lord to change her life. . . . She felt in her heart // that a change had to come." She "let the Lord into her life." Things were no longer the same. "She saw things // with a new light, // new vision, // new maturity." A few years later, she was selected as a delegate to the National Black Catholic Congress in Washington, D.C. "Here I am, send me!" read the banner that greeted her arrival. For the first time, she met Black sisters, Black priests, Black deacons. She'd never seen many of them before. *(I heard that! Al'right!)* Something changed. "Here I am, send me!" Oh, yes, she'd been having a good time—she'd started as a production assistant at the public TV station, then director, then assistant producer, and, before she left, was training to direct the weekend news.

> But somehow // the Hound of Heaven kept calling her. *(Yes!)*
> And praise God! Praise God! *(Amen!)*
> The call of the Lord // will make you do some crazy things! *(Oh, yes!)* . . .
> Her Mama, they tell me, didn't believe her *(Laughter . . .)*
> until one Christmas, // she put in her mother's Christmas stocking,
> the new diamond ring she had bought for herself. *(Oh . . .)*
> Sistah was serious. *(Yes! Al'right!)*
> So I'm here to tell you, // that if the Lord can change *my* life, *(Yes!* Bits of
>   clapping . . .)
> he can change *yours too*! *(Amen!!!* Clapping increases . . .)
> So if anybody asks you, // who you are?
> If anybody asks me, // who I am? *(Yes!)*
> I *know* the answer I've got for them. *(Yes!)*
> I'm a child of God!!! *(Yes!!!* Applause . . .)

The piano slips in under the excited exchange, joined by drum flourishes that punctuate the flow of Sister Renee's final, cadenced appeal. "We, Church //

have heard the voice say, // *'You* are my beloved!' *(Al'right!) Come follow me just as you are!"* Piling image upon image, she reminds us that if we answer that call, it will be with new eyes that we look on God's creation, "new ears . . . new actions . . . new enthusiasm . . . and new hearts // that we can love our brothers and sisters // be they red, // brown, // yellow, // green, // pokkadot . . . // no matter what religion, // because no one church has a corner on the Holy Spirit!" *(Yes!* Clapping breaks out again . . .*)* All are given "the gift of wisdom // or the gift of knowledge, // the gift of healing // or the gift to work miracles."

> If everybody could proclaim // that *"Jesus // is the center of our joy," (Yes!)*
> then the world will be a different place! *(Yes! Amen!)*
> Church, *oh* Church!
> I boldly ask you to *declare war* // on the things that might hold you
>   back! *(Yes!)* . . .
> Don't hesitate to *step out on faith! (Al'right! Amen!)* . . .
> Be *witnesses* // of your faith! *(Yes! Oh, yes!)*
> Be *bearers* // of the good news! *(Yes!)*
> Be *bearers* // of justice and equality. *(Al'right!)*
> Allow each other // to share your roots, *(Yes!)*
> your gifts, your talents, // your songs, your music, your art, *(Yes!)*
> your story, // your dance, your history, // your joys and your sorrows.
>   *(Yes!)*
> Share your laughter, step out on faith! *(Al'right!)* . . .
> So, if anybody calls you, // what will you say?
> If he *calls* you, // will you answer? *(Yes!!!)*
> If he calls *you,* // will you answer? *(Yes!!!)*
> If he calls *you,* // or *you,* // or *you,* // even you, baby, [looking at Isaiah
>   Brown] *(Laughter . . .)*
> What you gonna' do? (Applause . . .)
> Our Lady of Lourdes and all our guests,
> *step out* // on faith! *(Yes!! Amen!!!)*
> *because the Lord will give you // what you need! (Yes!)*
> And let the church say, *(Amen!!! Amen!!! Amen!!!)*

Amens give way to a burst of applause. People are on their feet, some calling out *Hallelujah! Thank you, Jesus! Amen! Yes!* Sister Renee's voice can be heard repeating "When he calls // *answer!"* as she returns to her seat with the other clergy. *Thank you, Jesus! Oh, hallelujah!*

Amidst the excitement, Barbara McKinney returns to the ambo. The applause subsides just enough for her to be heard: "Sister Renee de Porres Fenner, you are really a blessing to us! We love you very much!" Reed continues to weave his music beneath the lingering commotion, creating a gentle segue to what will follow, all the while negotiating a "cool down" time to allow the intensity of people's response to subside a bit. As people begin to take their seats again, Barbara calls on the Lourdes Gospel Choir for a song. At her request, choir members seated in the sanctuary fan out across the front of the church. You can feel the mood shift as Ernestine Harris comes forward to take the microphone.

Reed and Isaiah set up an easy beat—the gentle rhythms of a favorite gospel piece, "What Shall I Do?"[6] The song, chosen on the spot by director Pat Goodall, is well selected to rekindle the challenge of Sister Renee's preaching while orchestrating a communal response bathed in deep feeling and a meditative fervor. Ernestine begins reflectively, her soprano voice clear and confident:

> What shall I do? What steps shall I take?
> What move shall I make, O Lord, what shall I do? *(Oh, yes!)*
> I'm going to wait *(Oh, yes!)* for an answer from you, *(Well . . .)*
> I have nothing to lose, O Lord, I'm going to wait.
> I know you'll come through *(Yes!!)* with a blessing for me, *(Yes!)*
> Please, Lord, set my soul free, O Lord,
> I know you'll come through. *(Oh, yes!)*

"Sing it daugh'eh!" calls someone from the front, anticipating Ernestine's lead into a first verse. You can feel the energy begin to build, the flow of the music carrying us along channels of response.

> I can't live *(can't live!)* without your hand! *(Oh, yes!!)*
> I am weak all by myself! *(Multiple responses . . .)*
> Lord, please give me the strength I need //
> so I can possess eternal peace!

The choir takes up the refrain, joined by voices around the church, freeing Ernestine to soar above the choral queries of "What shall I do?" answering each with her own responses: "I know you'll come through!" "I'm going to wait on you, Lord!"

Ernestine presses into a second verse, her voice rising once again to the melodic apex of the song. Shouted responses from around the church become more insistent.

> No one else *(No one!!)* can count my fears! *(That's right!)*
> God a-lone *(Yes!)* can wipe away my tears! *(Amen!)*
> And glo—ry to the mighty King!
> In Je–sus Christ I have everything!

Borne aloft on Ernestine's lucid voice to this profession of faith—that "in Jesus Christ I have everything!"—we are carried now by the choir's compelling response, matching the stately strength of her voice with the intensity of their sound:

Oh, oh, there's no one else! *(No one!)* no one like Jesus!
Who can heal a broken heart
and put it back together again!!

"*Woo! Thank you Jesus!*" shouts a choir member as *Amens!* are heard from around the church. "*Woo! Thank you Lord! Woo! Thank you Jesus! Woo! Nobody but Jesus, Lord!*" A last, "*Woo__!*" and her voice gradually subsides. A woman in front of me is standing now, her waving hand etching an arc in the air. *Amen! Amen, Lord!*

Gradually, the floodtide of response ebbs a bit as Reed modulates to a tone higher. Once again, we are drawn into the gentle questions of the song's refrain, "What shall I do?" only to be carried afresh through a spiral of energy into its core message: "In Jesus Christ I have everything!" Ernestine's voice sails again above the chorused words:

Oh, oh, there's no one else! *(No one!)* No one like Jesus!
Who can heal a broken heart
and put it back together again!!

For a final time, the intensity subsides, as we are led back into the gentle rise and fall of the refrain's queries, "What shall I do?" and its faith-filled acknowledgment, "I know you'll come through with a blessing for me."

Please Lord set my soul free, O Lord,
I know you'll come through!
I know you'll come through!
I know you'll come through!

As Ernestine's voice rises a last time above the chorused sound, a surge of applause all but drowns out Reed's last chords.

Barbara McKinney has returned to the ambo. The hours have passed unnoticed, but there's no lagging in people's spirits. "Church," Barbara announces, "it's now time for the altar call!" At her prompting, clergy members who have been seated to the right spread out and take places along the single step into the sanctuary area. "Sisters and brothers," she entreats, "please come forward if you would like a special blessing. Some of you may be burdened with the cares of the world, have personal problems, health problems. Or perhaps you would just like a prayer. Please come forth for the laying on of hands by our ministers. Do not be shy," she adds. "You are in our Father's house, and he accepts all of us just as we are!"

Immediately, people seated in various parts of the church begin to move into the center aisle. You can sense a readiness, an almost palpable desire, as they make their way to the ministers at the front of the room. Something has stirred among us. I hesitate momentarily but feel compelled to approach Sister Renee, to ask the prayer of this Black woman of God. People around me are moving freely toward the lines forming in the front. The room is humming. The gentle sound of the ministers praying over person after person, the din of quiet conversation, all sustained by Reed Fromer's gentle improvisation. No one is in a rush in this free flow of people. Alexis Alexander takes my hand as we wait in line, she clearly moved by what has happened. "Some souls," as she predicted, have indeed been "touched."

Arriving finally before Sister Renee, I ask her prayer for courage and freedom from fear. I feel the press of her hands on my shoulders, the warmth of her flushed face next to mine. I close my eyes. The voices of ministers praying on either side of me recede. The last bits of tension in my body seem to melt away. "The Lord is my light and my salvation," she begins gently, "whom need I fear?" I'm touched at hearing the words of a favorite psalm. She asks God to enable me to "step out on faith," to live freely, to love freely. I feel a flow of spirit between us, an exchange of womanly strength, the healing touch of a God come very close. We embrace.

As I turn to make my way back to my seat, Zettie LeBlanc reaches out to hug me. I feel her moist face against mine. Our tears mingle. Others returning seem equally moved, comforted by friends or family members who sit near them offering an embrace, or a hand resting on the other's shoulder. Reed is singing now. His voice seems to capture the feel of the moment. "There'll come a time," he begins, others joining in, "when you will find // that you are free of the troubles of today. // There will be light, // things will be right, // There is a Power that will set you free some day." Something has opened in us. We've come through something together. There's a sense of promise.

The lines begin to dwindle now. I notice that one by one, the ministers turn to each other for a moment of prayer, hands resting one on the other, before returning to their places. The song reiterates one last time, "There is a Power that will set you free some day."

"Amen, Church! Amen!" adds Barbara McKinney from the ambo, as if to punctuate this holy exchange. "God is so good! . . . He keeps blessing us, blessing us, blessing us!"

"*T*he evening is coming to a close," says Judy Brown who is now at the ambo. "We want to acknowledge all our visitors. . . . You're in the Lord's house, so you're at home." (*Amen!!*) She thanks each of the clergy by name and offers words of appreciation to each of the choirs who have "shared in the spreading of the Good News." Thanking parishioners and all who have come, she encourages them to "come back tomorrow night. It will only get better! We're just laying the foundation tonight! The next two nights we'll be building the house of the Lord." (*Amen!!*) Judy announces that Father Ken Westray will have copies of Father Cyprian Davis' new book, *The History of Black*

Catholics in the United States,[7] for sale after the service. "As Black Catholics, we have all been part of this book," she claims. "In some ways, we've helped to write this book. *(Yes!)* Now," she concludes, "please join us in the hall for fellowship, and come back tomorrow night." (Applause . . .) I'm aware that, despite the late hour on a week night and the miserable weather outside, many people will make their way to the church hall for refreshments and conversation.

Before anyone can stir, Barbara McKinney has returned to the ambo. "Religious leaders, guests, our own people—thank you for being with us. Take the blessing of this evening to someone at home who could not be here." Reminding us that tomorrow is youth night, she urges, "Let's do what our mothers and fathers did in the good old days. *(Well . . .)* Don't *send* your children. *(That's right!)* Please *bring* them! *(Amen!)* And now, it gives me great pleasure to present this next person, who will lead us in benediction. He is the pillar of the foundation of Lourdes, a person who sees the importance of including the congregation in all church affairs *(Amen!!! Yes!!)*—our pastor and friend, Father Kirk Ullery." *(Al'right!* Applause . . . Piano flourish . . .)

"Church, do you feel blessed?" asks Father Kirk, who has come to the center of the room. *"Amen! Yes!!"* is the resounding response. "The Lord has already blessed us tonight—in our songs, the people who have come, but mostly in our speaker. *(Amen!!)* We thank the Lord because of you, Sister Renee!" *(Amen!)*

"So now, Church, please stand. If you believe that you have the Lord in your heart, share in this blessing, and let this blessing flow out of you." As is the custom here, people stretch out their hands in blessing of each other and repeat each phrase of the blessing after him:

> "Lord // come upon us // with your strength tonight. // Let us go forth now // to be the faithful people // you have called us tonight to be. // Bless us *again,* and *again.* // Bless our *families,* // bless our *community,* // bless our *city.* // **Lord,** *bless our world,* // and make us always // true lovers of you. // Amen!" *Amen!* echoes from around the church.

Barbara McKinney signals that she has one last word. "Tonight, Reverend and Mrs. John Lane celebrate their thirty-fifth wedding anniversary." Applause breaks out as she continues to address these two friends of the Lourdes community, "I hope joy was brought to your hearts tonight, as you have witnessed the many beautiful voices of praise." And finally, she says to all assembled, the "fantastic, dynamic Lourdes choir" will "leave you with a powerful message of their true devotion." Taking her cue, Reed and Isaiah strike up a lively praise song. People, singing and clapping, join the choir in adding this last punctuation point to this very full evening.

> This joy that I have, the world didn't give it to me! *[repeated three times]*
> The world didn't give it, the world can't take it away!

*I*ntentional joy. Cultivated joy. A joy that "the world didn't give" and "the world can't take away." "Upright but not uptight," is Sister Renee's playful rendition. Claiming a freedom to be "at home" in God's house. "If you're looking for joy, you've come to the right place!"

In my years at Lourdes, I've come to realize that joy is cultivated here as both an attitude of heart and a purposeful strategy of community prayer. Joy, like the breath of God's Spirit, creates a sense of elan, a security in one's self, a readiness to encounter the other. Joy liberates. Joy releases. Joy is a gateway, not an impediment. A climate of joy, a mood of celebration generated by a pervasive hospitality and a proclivity for song, gathers up tears, frustrations, and troubles, opening a path by which people can "keep on keepin' on." I've learned again that joy is a godly emotion.

Chapter Two

"I NEEDED THAT SONG!"

—RHYTHMS OF LIFE AND LITURGY—

*S*unday at Lourdes is pivotal. A day for "having a good time in the Lord!" For being "church." A day not to be missed! A point of convergence. A confluence of many streams of life. A unique juncture in a set of interlocking cycles, at once social, liturgical, familial, personal, and cultural.

It took me some time to recognize the patterns, and even longer to realize their complexity. What was clear from the start was that each Sunday is an "occasion." No time is ordinary. Sunday worship bears the imprint of people's lives, makes room for an influx of their struggles and rejoicing. Sunday is a time for naming, claiming the community's seasons of grace. For acknowledging the events that mark the lives of individuals and families. For enfolding these events into the community's prayer. Worship and life are not simply juxtaposed. They blend. They flow into each other. They fuse. And people leave, some two to two-and-a-half hours later, feeling nourished.

*T*ake, for example, the Second Sunday of Easter, 1995. The sun was shining brilliantly after a night of heavy rain. I detoured into the Haight-Ashbury district to pick up choir director Pat Goodall. It was a rare Sunday when Reed Fromer, Lourdes' pianist and Pat's usual driver, would not be present—he was touring with a blues singer in Alaska. As we set out across the city to Lourdes, Pat and I talked of many things. So much had happened in the past few weeks. Brother Banks's recent illness—concern for his continued health— the sense of loss when he is not present on Sunday. The Easter liturgies—the first attempts to bring together the community from All Hallows with the original Lourdes community—grace-filled yet a bit awkward—differing styles of worship, touching everything from decorations to dress to music—the challenges that lie ahead in growing together as one parish. Making our way along Army Street, we spoke of Martha Hurt, a member of Lourdes who died recently without next of kin—of state officials' reluctance to release her body so that Lourdes could give her a proper funeral—after all, Lourdes was her family—Father Kirk's Palm Sunday appeal for signatures on a petition—political negotiation—an appeal to Willie Brown—finally, last Wednesday, a chance to celebrate her life and to commend her into God's hands. Nearing Lourdes, our conversation shifted to David and Lea Schermerhorn's anniversary celebration that afternoon at the Slavonic Cultural Center—most of the choir would be there. Then, that morning's musical challenge—singing without Reed's accompaniment—acknowledging his importance to the community's music—how difficult it would be, I muse, to find a substitute pianist since the repertoire is oral—scheming how to get the choir started on the right pitches—knowing that in the end, the spiritual energy generated by the choir and drums would carry the day.

Arriving at the church, we noticed a few children playing in the grassy lot between the church and the small building that serves as parish hall—searching, we imagined, for stray chocolate eggs left behind from last Sunday's Easter-egg hunt. The 8:30 liturgy had just finished, and many of those exiting the church were clad in Samoan national dress. Small groups of families and friends lingered in conversation near the church as cars exchanged places along Hawes Street, some leaving, others arriving. Folks emerging from just parked cars called greetings to each other, exchanging hugs, laughter, conversation. Inside the church doors, Brother Banks stood handing out colored programs, a kind word for each one arriving. Despite the bustle of comings and goings in the small entryway, there's a sense of peace here. I noticed a faint scent of lilies in the air. A beautiful tapestry hung on the far wall of the sanctuary, depicting in its pastel shades the poignant meeting of Jesus with Mary Magdalen near the tomb that first Easter morning. I'd been told it was the work of an African artist who visited Lourdes several years ago.

"*G*ood morning, Church!" exclaimed Father Kirk some quarter of an hour later, gathering up the energy of extended greetings, a vibrant opening song, and Brother Banks's animated welcome to parishioners and visitors. "Good morning, Father Kirk!" came the returning volley.

"This morning, Church, we are remembering one event that is very happy and one that is not so happy." The juxtaposition is not unusual, and Father Kirk never shies away from naming both. "David and Lea Schermerhorn are celebrating thirty years of marriage together!" Applause and loud *Amens!* break out around the church, people turning around to see David and Lea seated with their extended family towards the back of the church. "Lea and David," he continues, "we hold you in our hearts, and we lift you up to the Lord in this worship. We thank God for the blessings you have received, and we ask that they will continue for many, many more years! *(Amen!! Amen!!)*

"We're also remembering Danny Williams, Betty Cooper's son, who was gunned down a year ago on Third Street *(Oh Lord have mercy!)* in one of those *insane* acts of violence! *(Amen!)* Young people against young people!" *(Yes!)* The story is well known to the community, the tragic killing of young people an all-too-familiar event. Danny was twenty-one years old. "We're lifting up Danny to the Lord this morning, *(Yes!!!)* as well as his mother."

"We're also remembering, as a nation, *(Oh, Lord! Yes!)* the shame *(Yes!)* that has come upon us *(Amen!!! Oh, yes!)* because of Oklahoma!" *(Yes!)* There's a poignancy in his voice as he reflects on the recent bombing of the U.S. Federal Building in Oklahoma City. "We'd begun all the wheels of hate to point the finger at the Middle East, *(Yes!!!)* and all of a sudden we have to *point the finger at ourselves!*" *(Yes! Amen!)* Responses heard from all over the church persist as Father Kirk continues. "What happened there is the result of our hatred for one another! *(Amen!)* We lift that up, and we ask the Lord to cleanse us!" *(Oh, yes!)*

"And so we begin, in the name of the Father, (a few voices join in . . .) and of the Son, and of the Holy Spirit." *Amen!*

"The grace and peace of the *Risen Lord* be with each of you!" *And also with you! . . .*

Death and life. Heartaches and joys. How these rhythms of life flow into Sunday worship is less the work of a single person, or the result of elaborate planning or scripting, and more the fruit of people's willingness to be present to each other and to give witness to how God is working in their everyday lives. Their concerns, struggles, joys, and challenges well up like fugal entries throughout each week's liturgy. On that warm April Sunday in Eastertide, you could hear the influx in the prayers of intercession that were voiced at length from around the church. You could sense the inrush in the *Amens!* that punctuated the prayers, songs, and Scripture readings. You could recognize it in the images of Father Kirk's preaching, as he called the community to commit itself "totally to the way of Jesus," to the "way of resurrection," which is "life over death, love over fear, peace over violence," lest there be "many more Oklahomas!" *(Amen!)* You could touch it in the embraces and bits of news exchanged during an extended offering of Peace. You could suspect it when a song was changed near the end of the service, making room for the community to plead with God in song,

> We need to hear from You! *(Yes!)* we need a word from You!
> If we don't hear from You, what shall we do? *(That's right!)*

Wanting You more each day to show us your perfect way,
there is no other way that we can live![1]

There's time and space for people to enter the flow of the worship, to allow their lives to be present here. In fact, it's expected. "We're in God's house," they tell me, assuming I'll understand the implications. Whatever the concern, whatever the occasion—be it a death, baptism, anniversary, graduation, or achievement of any kind—there's room for it to be gathered into the patterns of Catholic liturgy that Lourdes shares with the larger church. Worship, at Lourdes, breathes. And it does so with the lungs of this community.

*O*f course, there's a tension in all of this. A concern some might have for the integrity of "the liturgy"—the age-old flow of symbols, readings, gestures, and prayers that constitute the Catholic rite. Are they not overwhelmed by this floodtide of a community's daily experience? The universal patterns upstaged by the inrush of local concerns?

It's a question of rhythm, I've discovered. Of Black rhythm, that is. Here, Sunday—the gathering, the prayers, the patterns of worship—is as regular as the recurring "beat" of African American music. And as engaging. Beat is perhaps the most obvious and infectious aspect of Black music. It's difficult not to move, or at least tap one's foot, to the persistent, driving pulse of an upbeat Gospel song.

Yet rhythm in Black music is generated by more than beat—it requires the tension of two divergent impulses. One is stable and recurring, as regular as the human heartbeat, as persistent as Isaiah Brown's drumbeat from the left side of this little church house. The other impulse is improvised, syncopated, unpredictable, ever unfolding, and constantly reconfigured by those making the music—as inventive as the the flow of Reed Fromer's keyboard improvisation.[2] Only when these two rhythmic impulses are held in creative tension does the music "swing." At times, the accents disagree, even clash, generating cross-rhythms, polyrhythms, and metrical ambiguity.[3] But in the crossrhythms, there's movement, there's life, there's energy. Herein lies the genius of Black rhythm.

And herein, I've come to see, is a touchstone of liturgy at Lourdes. In this familial setting, the improvised, unpredictable, unfolding experience of everyday living creates an ever changing counterpoint with the regular patterns of Catholic worship. Liturgy doesn't filter out the everyday. Rather, life filters through the mesh of these words and actions. It penetrates the recurring feasts and seasons of the liturgical year. The tension generated in these polyrhythms is creative and full of life.

*I*t's also nourishing. "I have something to live on all week!" I've heard the comment over and again as people leave the church on Sunday. "I *needed* that song!" is another recurring refrain. In fact, music seems key in how people feel they've been fed. Particular songs become a point of convergence between their everyday lives and the thrust of a particular Sunday's liturgy, as imaged in its readings and prayers. Songs seem to hold the tension. It's striking that the lyrics of the community's gospel repertoire fuse the predicaments of daily living with the hope-filled images of the Scriptures. They make personal the challenges of faith and discipleship.

On that Second Sunday of Easter, the Gospel reading was from John 20:19-31 —Thomas's coming to faith in the Risen Christ, and Jesus' blessing of those who "have not seen and yet believe." As Ernestine Harris intoned the first un-metered phrases of Darryl Gates's "Unwavering Faith," I could feel in the responses of those around me that her words were touching home.

"Lord," she began slowly, "give me *(Oh, yes!)* an un-wav-er-ing faith!" *(Yes! Take your time!)* "to help me stand the storm," she continued, delivering each word on the richness of her resonant voice, "when I would do wrong! *(Oh, yes!)* Un-wav-er-ing faith! *(Yes!)* An un-wav-er-ing faith!" *(Oh, yes! Al'right!)*

As she moved into the more rhythmic second verse minutes later, you could feel the responses swell:

I need faith *(Yes!)* to climb that mountain *(Yes!!! Oh, yes we do!)*
I need faith *(Oh, yes!)* to climb that old, old rugged hill! *(Yes, Lord!)*
Faith! *(Yes!)* to insure God will answer, *(Well . . . Oh, yes!)*
if I only do his will! *(Yes!!! Oh, yes! C'mon, sing it!)*
Faith! *(Yes! C'mon, daugh'er!)* to say no *(That's right!)*
when others say yes! *(Al'right! Yes!)*
Faith! to know that God is there, when I stand my test *(Yes!!!)*
Unwav-er-ing faith! *(Yes!!)*
An unwav-er-ing faith!" *(Yes! Oh, yes! Al'right! Amen!!!)*

The applause that welled up as she reached her last, deliberately placed words did not drown out the exclamations being voiced around me: *Thank you, Jesus! Glory! Hallelujah! Thank you, Jesus! Oh, hallelujah!"*

"*I* needed that song!" I'm beginning to understand what they mean. The songs get inside you, especially the slow ones. They meet you where you least expect to be touched or challenged. They inscribe wisdom. They formulate a response that had been, until that moment, only tentative. They remind you that you can make it. That "trouble don't last always!" That "God will make a way where there is no way."

It's evident, here, that music ministers. I'd introduced that concept to students many times before coming to Lourdes. But it's taken on new significance here. Music ministers to *people,* and in a very personal way. Father Kirk noted this in one of our first conversations as we sat for coffee in the rectory kitchen. Songs are chosen each week to reflect the themes and images of that Sunday or feast, he remarked. But there is a more important purpose at work—to encourage the faith and life of the people. In other settings, he added, where the first of these goals dominates, people often feel uninvolved. The music seems to be more about "the liturgy" than about the faith of the people. Not so at Lourdes.

"All that beauty I've [experienced] today," commented Joan Dill after one Sunday gathering, "that will take me all through next week! Until next Sunday!"

*T*he weekly flow of life and liturgy finds a larger pattern—an intentional weaving of the "feasts and seasons" this community considers holy into the pattern of the church's "year of grace." The annual spring Revival is but one of several customs that have become a regular part of the community's liturgical calendar.

The commemoration of "Lourdes' Saints" is another. November, with its opening feast of All Saints, provides an occasion to keep alive the memory of those who have "gone home to God." Each year, on the Sunday closest to the feast, individuals and families enter new pages in the "Book of Lourdes' Saints"—a beautifully crafted binder, covered by one of the women of the parish in bright African cloth. Already it holds the memories of many dear ones. Each page is richly decorated with photos, poems, words of remembrance, even drawings done by young relatives, prepared to honor a deceased loved one.

*M*y first experience of this remembrance took place on a chilly November Sunday in 1993. As we arrived that morning, the Book of Lourdes' Saints rested on a stand just in front of the altar and remained there throughout the liturgy.

"Sign me up for the Christian jubilee!" Who could resist the spirited beat of this opening song, as the choir moved through the assembly "in step," Judy Brown "lining out" each phrase:

> (Sign me up) Sign me up for the Christian jubilee!
> (Sign my name) Sign my name on the roll!
> (I've been changed) I've been changed since the Lord has lifted me,
> (I wanna be) wanna be ready when Jesus comes![4]

"Ready when Jesus comes!" exclaimed Brother Banks, as *Amens!* concluded the song. The image recurred mantra-like throughout the service.

"The Lord himself will come down from heaven at the word of command, *(Yes!)* at the sound of the archangel's voice and God's trumpet," proclaimed John Brown from 1 Thessalonians minutes later. "And those who have died in Christ will rise first. *(Oh, yes! Amen!)* We, the living . . . will be caught up with them in the clouds to meet the Lord in the air. *(Amen!)* Henceforth, we shall be with the Lord. *(Amen!)* Therefore, console one another with these words!"

As if to anticipate the great "meeting in the clouds" just described, the community welcomed the Gospel with a well-loved spiritual:

> Will the circle be unbroken
> by and by, Lord, by and by?
> There's a better home awaiting
> in the sky, Lord, in the sky?[5]

"What are the qualities we need as we wait for the Lord to return?" queried Father Kirk, preaching on Matthew's parable of the wise and foolish virgins who await the bridegroom's return. What wisdom will make us ready? The answer lies in how we live with one another, he claimed; in five Spirit-given qualities that prepare us to meet the Lord as he comes "in the least of these brothers and sisters"—a compassion that looks beyond another's faults; a peace-making that works for a just world; a faith that is willing to let go of our seeming control of life; a hope that is sure of God even in the darkest night; and a love that does not manipulate or try to change others but gives freely of what we have and what we are. His words flowed easily into the ceremony which followed.

Returning to his chair, Father Kirk invited people to "lift to the Lord" their loved ones. Reed Fromer wove a gentle improvisation as, one by one, members of the congregation came forward. There was a hush in the church as Liz Bell and Bessie Brooks—Bessie a choir member since the days of Sister Martin—acknowledged their beloved parents. Later in the service Bessie would sing "Precious Lord, Take My Hand," dedicating it to their memory. Sister Irma Dillard placed photos of two members of her religious community in the album, then paid tribute to her father and a cousin. Pat Goodall remembered a dear sister, Odessa Costello. Everette Edwards, Sr., recently deceased in Louisiana and patriarch of a great network of siblings, cousins, grandchildren, and great-grandchildren here at Lourdes, was honored by a grandson. Who suspected that just a year later, Tiffany Isles would pay tribute to Everett's wife, Elsie—Tiffany's grandmother—and place her photo, adorned with messages from family members, beside his.

These gestures evoked a whole litany of remembrance. At Judy Brown's invitation, voices of young and old around the church began to call out names—parents, spouses, friends, sisters, brothers. Some had died tragically, too young to have left us. Others had lived among this community for many years. Family held dear. It was a tender moment. Each name surrounded with love. "Will the circle be unbroken . . .?"

The following Thursday, as I browsed through the pages of the Book of Lourdes' Saints before choir rehearsal, Isaiah Brown, Lourdes' youthful drummer, came and stood at my side. Minutes later, two of his aunts, Jean Alexander and Rose Isles, had joined us. We talked of Everett Edwards, their father and Isaiah's great-grandfather. At my invitation, Isaiah guided me through the many tributes to members of his extended family, telling me stories he had been told of his ancestors in the faith. "Will the circle be unbroken, in the sky, Lord, in the sky? . . ."

*P*erhaps the most striking integration of cultural and liturgical seasons begins each year on the Sunday after Christmas. Since 1992 the community has set aside seven weeks for the African American festival of Kwanzaa, incorporating the celebration into Sunday worship. Spanning January and half of February, this keeping of Kwanzaa creates a counterpoint with feasts of the Christmas season—Holy Family, Epiphany, and the Baptism of the Lord—and with the African American celebration of Dr. Martin Luther King's birthday and Black History Month. The seventh and final Sunday of Kwanzaa coincides with "Lourdes Day," the patronal feast of the parish, celebrated on the second Sunday of February. Spring Revival follows directly.

The particular density of this "season" yields a unique expression of the community's identity— and worship, we say, is about identity, a community's Christian identity. "Who we are and Whose we are," as Sister Thea Bowman phrased it.

Kwanzaa is already a cultural synthesis—a family celebration of "first fruits" that links African harvest customs to the traditions of Black Americans.[6] Usually celebrated in the home, families gather between Christmas and New Year's Day to draw strength from the remembrance of seven principals, each named in Swahili: *umoja* (unity), *kujichagulia* (self-determination), *ujima* (collective work and responsibility), *ujamaa* (cooperative economics), *nia* (purpose), *kuumba* (creativity), and *imani* (faith).[7] The festival was created by Dr. Maulana Karenga, a professor at California State University, Long Beach, in 1966. In fact, Omar Butler, a young married parishioner, studied with Karenga some years later.

Rose Isles and Sister Irma Dillard proposed the Lourdes Kwanzaa celebration and crafted its integration into Sunday worship. On each of the seven weeks, a chosen parishioner, often a young adult, addresses the assembly about one Kwanzaa principle, claiming it as spiritual-social value for this community. These testimonies are played out against the backdrop of that Sunday's prayers and biblical readings. The counterpoint is striking. The principle of *umoja*, unity, for example, coincides with images of the Holy Family. The value of *kujichagulia*, self-determination, mingles with themes of Christ's Epiphany.

The dedicatory thrust of the Baptism of the Lord intertwines with images of *ujima*, collective work and responsibility, made even more potent by the witness of Dr. Martin Luther King, whose memorial coincides with that feast.

"*L*et us rise in the name of Jesus!" Brother Banks calls out from the front of the church, signaling that the Gospel is about to be read. It has already been an exhilarating morning—the first all-parish liturgy since Lourdes has swelled with new members from All Hallows. Everything in the church is ablaze with color. People dressed in their finery fill every inch of the church, including its tiny rear gallery. Gospel choir members flank the altar, adorning the sanctuary with vivid African attire. Samoan choir members dressed in multi-toned blue robes embellished with bright red ribbons fill the front pews on the left side. Magnolia blossoms fragrantly bedeck the mahogany statue of the Black Madonna of Montserrat, situated in a little niche just above Isaiah Brown's trap set.

It is Sunday, February 12, 1995. Lourdes Day and the close of Kwanzaa. A small table, covered in African cloth, stands just in front of the altar. Seven weeks ago seven children from the parish were called forward by Rose Isles to place the symbols of Kwanzaa on the table, as she reminded the community of the significance of each symbol. First, the *mkeka*, a straw mat. Then *mazao*, bright orange and yellow squashes that image an abundant harvest. *Muhindi*, small ears of corn. *Zawadi*, several tiny gifts wrapped in colorful paper. *Kihombe cha Umoja*, a wooden Unity Cup, from which families drink on the last day of Kwanzaa. And seven candles, the *mishumaa saba*, placed in a decorated seven-branch candelabra or *kinara*. The candles are colored red, green, and black, the traditional colors of Black liberation—black representing the ebony skin of the African peoples; red, the blood shed by some so that others might be free; green, the color of hope for the future. Only one candle remains to be lit. Walter Turner will ignite it today before addressing the community on the last principle, *imani*.

Images of faith, *imani*, are already awash in the gathering. Readings from 1 Corinthians and Hebrews have invited us to a faith that rests "not on human wisdom but on *God's* power." Now, as Brother Banks heralds the Gospel, Reed Fromer's fingers capture the gusto with which the community will take up its acclamation:

> We've come this far by faith, leaning on the Lord!
> Trusting in his holy word, He's never failed me yet!
> Oh——— can't turn around,
> we've come this far by faith![8]

There's a poignancy in the singing. Only a year ago, "we've come this far by faith" gave voice to Lourdes' trust in God at a time of uncertainty about the fate of the parish.

"Go tell John what you have seen and heard," declares Father Kirk, standing with open lectionary in the clearing between the sanctuary and first pews. "The blind receive their sight, *(Yes!)* the lame walk, the lepers are cleansed, the deaf hear, the dead are raised, *(Thank you, Jesus!)* the poor have the good news brought to them! And blessed are they who take no offense in me. . . ."

Father Kirk offers brief reflections on this Lukan Gospel passage, then invites Rose Isles to come forward. It is Rose's task to reweave the story that has emerged over the past Sundays. She recalls images from each of the six Kwanzaa speakers, noting the themes that have emerged and intertwining them like a woven tapestry. Today is the climax, she claims. "Faith is the root" on which all depends! "Faith, *Imani*, is the root!"

At her invitation, a tall, well-built man strides from the choir, and places his feet firmly in front of the Kwanzaa table—his brilliant dashiki a patterned ochre, gold and red, with touches of green. As he reaches to light the last taper, Naja, his little daughter, bedecked in black velvet, emerges from the front pew and wraps her arms around his right leg. Leaning over, he speaks softly to her, places a kiss on her head, and sends her off to join her mother seated among the sopranos.

"*Imani*, faith," begins Walter Turner assuredly, standing at the ambo. "I didn't prepare this talk," he notes characteristically. "I ask the Lord to speak through me. *(Al'right! Yes!)* I have to show you my faith! *(Amen!)* In order for *you* to have faith, we need to see each other's, and *I'm stepping out here this morning on faith!* *(Amen, Walter!)*

"There are a lot of things we need to know," he continues. You can sense that people are with him as he begins to weave a story of faith in the midst of the cruelest hardship. "We're gonna start way back a long time ago, *(Well . . .)* when those ships rolled over to Africa and took those slaves. See, people think that Black people can't get along. . . . But there was a lot taken out of us. *(Yes! Amen!)* Those ships didn't just roll over there to a port and say, 'Come on, get on board!' *(Amen!)* We were *tricked* onto those ships . . . by our own people! *(That's right!)* There was division. Who could we trust? Who could we believe? *(Amen! Well . . .)*

"When those ships started rolling to America, that was a living hell. *(Yes!)* We have to imagine those slaves in the bottom of the ship, being whipped all day and all night. . . . You rowed till you died! And then they put someone else in your place. *(That's right! Amen!)* But there was *faith* on that ship, *(Yes! Amen!)* 'cause we *brought* it here! *(Yes!)* We brought our faith with us! *(Yes!)*

"Then after that ship landed in America, those slave masters. . . . Understand one thing!" he exclaims, interrupting his train of thought. "We should all teach our kids to understand our heritage! *(Yes!)* The men [had to] work in the fields. . . . The slave master came to those huts and took whatever women he wanted. *(Amen!)* And if the man said anything, he sold him or killed him! *(Yes!)* But *she* was the one who was bringing food back *(That's right!)* to that man and her family *(Yes!)* . . . Still, there were a lot of Black slaves on their knees praying! *(Yes!)* See, we are the only race on earth that doesn't speak its native tongue! *(Yes! That's right!!)* . . . They took that out of us! *(Yes!)* But with the Lo—rd," Walter stretches the word as if to emphasize its importance, "*we still made it! (Amen!) We're here today (Yes!) through His grace! (Preach it! Yes!)*

"See, our faith starts with the Lord, . . . but it's also through us. *(Yes!)* We have to start having faith in each other. *(Al'right! Yes!)* Some people say, 'I can't trust them. . . .' We have to *start* trusting each other. *(Amen! Yes!)*. . . Let's pray and ask the Lord to change that. *(Yes!)* All things are possible with God!" *(Amen!)*

Lifting this Sunday's bright green program, Walter reads the text of the principle of *Imani:*

> "To believe with all our hearts in our Creator, in our people, *(Yes!)*
> in our parents, *(Oh, yes!)* our teachers, *(Yes!)* our leaders, *(Yes!)*
> and the righteousness and victory of our struggle."[9] *(Amen!)*

You know, we have to believe with all our hearts! For some people that's hard to do. But how can you say you have faith in God [when] you do not have faith in me? *(Yes! Amen! That's the truth!)*

"You know, the Lord left us down here to do some things. . . . Right now, a lot of our Black kids out there on the streets are killing each other. *(Yes!)* Owning a gun can only result in one thing, *(Yes!)* the harm of someone else. *(Yes, Lord!)* The Bible hasn't changed! The Bible says, 'Thou shalt not kill.' *(Yes!!!)* It doesn't say, under conditions! *(Laughter . . .)* . . . *All* of you that have guns, what for? *(Yes!)* The Lord said, 'Thou shall not kill.' *(Amen!!!)* If you tell me you believe his Word . . . Mothers and fathers, pass it along to the kids. *(Yes!)* [We must] do Jesus' works! *(Amen!)* . . .

"Everything we own [belongs to Him.] *(Amen!)* . . . Jesus makes it possible for us to go to work! *(Amen! Yes!)* We don't own anything! *(Yes!)* It's all his, [including] this church. . . . If you didn't pay for your house, that bank is gonna take your house, or that landlord is gonna put you out. *(Yes!)* But a lot of us come to church and don't pay our tithes. *(Al'right!)* How do we expect this church to run? Jesus could take care of it, but he left it for us to do. *(Amen!)* That's his money in our pocket. *(Amen!! Amen!! Yes, Lord!)* It's all His! 'The Lord giveth and the Lord will taketh away.' *(Yes!!* Applause *. . .) It's time for us to wake up! This church shouldn't be in need. (Amen!!!)* . . . We're all prosperous. I'm blessed every day that I wake up! *(Yes!! Amen!!* Multiple responses *. . .)*

"In the church I used to go to, I used to sing a song, and it was called 'I Get a Blessing.'" Walter's clear tenor voice rings out:

> One day I might not have but one thin dime,
> but oh, the next day the Lord will step in on time! *(Yes!!* Clapping *. . .)*
> I get, O Lord, I get a blessing every day! *(Yes!!!)*

"I haven't worked in four months!" he adds, as if to give testimony. "I've been back and forth to the doctor. But I have been truly, *truly* blessed. *(Amen! Al'right!)* And I have been passing that blessing on! *(Yes!)* You don't keep it to yourself! *(Applause and animated responses . . .)* Last week Father was saying that we have to meet $3,000," he recalls, referring to an assessment placed on the parish by the archdiocese. "Some of us don't have it, *(Yes!)* but for those that do, go in your pockets. *(Yes!)* What you give to the Lord, believe me, he is going to give back. *(Amen! Yes!)* I'm standing here before you this morning! I'm going to pay for my family this morning, but I'm also gonna pay for another family who don't have it. *(Al'right!! Yes!! Shouts from around the church . . .)* We all have to do that, *(Clapping . . . Yes!)* because the Lord has truly been blessing us. *(Yes!!)* Step out on faith. *(Yes!)* Trust in his word! *(Al'right!)* You're *never* going to be alone. *(Yes!)* . . . If you hang out with Jesus every day, what better friend can you have? *(Amen!!!)*

"Now I know everybody believes. 'Oh, I believe.' But we have to stop believing and start knowing!" *(Yes!)* As if to illustrate, Walter retells a little story. [They asked a man once,] " 'Is this your son?' 'Oh yes, this is my son.' 'Do you *believe* it' [asks the first]? 'I don't *believe* it' [the second answers], 'I **know** this is my son!' *Then why you don't know that this is your Jesus?"* Walter retorts. *(Yes!* Applause . . .*)* That he *died* for you! *(Yes!)* We have to start *knowing!* . . . Believing turns into *knowing. (Al'right!)* And I **know** *what he's done for me! (Yes!)* And you know what? He's going to keep on doing it! Your landlord and your bank, they'll take your house. Jesus won't ever turn you away! *(Amen!)* But if you want him to represent you to his Father, you better get on board! *(Al'right!)* *Imani.* Faith. That's our foundation. *(Yes!)* That's what we build on. *(Yes!)*

"So let's start teaching these kids. *(Yes!)* . . . [You know] they walk around with earrings in one ear, earrings in the other ear," he notes, returning to his first theme. "I wear an earring in this left ear because of those slaves *(Yes!)* who died before me! *(That's right!)* And I want those kids to know *why* they wear earrings. They think it's just a fad. *(Yes!)* But back there a long time ago, it was the only way we could identify the ones that wasn't telling on you, and getting you killed. . . . They pierced their ears and wore burnt straws in their ears *(That's right!!!)* so they could identify those who were going to the Underground Railroad! We have to pass that along. *(Al'right!)* . . . They died trying to be free! In 1861, forty thousand slaves had made it to Canada to freedom. We need to let our kids know that! I want to leave you with that faith!" *(Amen!)*

"Oh, before I go," adds Walter, "let me show you something." Laughter erupts. "What ya' got, Walter?" someone calls out as he reaches down to pick up a large white package that has been resting just to the side of the ambo. There's much curiosity and laughter. Slowly, Walter unwraps a large, Louisiana red fish which his mother sent for the occasion. "Go ahead, Walter!" shouts someone from the front.

"I imported this," he claims proudly, "because I wanted you to see it. . . . I heard somebody say the other day, 'If you're going to church, you better get there early because you might not get a seat!' (Laughter . . .) Think about when Jesus fed those five thousand people. *(Amen!)* If the ones in the back had said, 'If we don't get there early, we won't get no fish!'" *(Al'right, Walter! Laughter . . .)* Then recounting the legend of the "red fish" and its peculiar tail marking, Walter continues, "What I want to show you . . . is the fish that Jesus fed those people with! It's called the red fish. Do you see that fingerprint on the tail?" he asks, holding the fish high so that all can see. "That's were Jesus held it up to bless it. Those fish have been marked since then. They say that if you eat some of this fish, it will give you that "full" feeling. This is a red fish that a lot of these kids would never get to see. That's the print where Jesus held it up to bless it. I want to leave you with that little bit of faith. *(Amen!)* . . . Those five thousand who were in the back—*they got full!"* *(Amen! Amen!!)*

People are on their feet instantly, applauding, cheering, shouting, *Amen! Amen, Walter!* Moved by his own story, Walter is in tears, as is his wife Rita. Naja, obviously proud of her dad, runs up to him again, embracing both legs with her tiny arms.

I, too, am touched by Walter's words, moved by his reweaving of "blood lines" lost in the slave trade. Claiming that his people's history is not an accident of fate but the arena of God's grace. Believing that even the worst situations, the most severe sufferings, have been avenues of God's redemption. Passing on the good news! Breaking open the "work of God." I sense the rightness of this moment, feel the power of personal faith communicated from person to person, see the rejuvenation of a community caught up in the images of its own story, the hope and communion it generates.

Kwanzaa closes with a brief ceremony and a song. I stand with those around me as a mighty sound swells from the whole congregation. Locking arms, we begin to sway to the stately, eloquent phrases of James Weldon Johnson's "Black National Anthem,"[10] summing up seven weeks. Or, perhaps, a lifetime.

> Lift every voice and sing, till earth and heaven ring,
> Ring with the harmonies of liberty.
> Let our rejoicing rise high as the list'ning skies.
> Let it resound loud as the rolling sea.
> Sing a song full of the faith that the dark past has taught us.
> Sing a song full of the hope that the present has brought us.
> Facing the rising sun of our new day begun,
> Let us march on till victory is won!
>
> Stony the road we trod, bitter the chast'ning rod,
> Felt in the days when hope unborn had died:
> Yet with a steady beat, have not our weary feet
> Come to the place for which our fathers sighed?
> We have come over a way that with tears has been watered;

We have come, treading our path through the blood of the slaughtered;
Out of the gloomy past, till now we stand at last
Where the white gleam of our bright star is cast.

God of our weary years, God of our silent tears,
Thou who hast brought us thus far on the way;
Thou who hast by thy might, led us into the light,
Keep us forever in the path, we pray.
Lest our feet stray from the places, our God, where we met thee;
Lest our hearts, drunk with the wine of the world, we forget thee.
Shadowed beneath thy hand, may we forever stand,
True to our God, true to our native land!

Chapter Three

"TAKE YOUR TIME!"

—MUSICIANS AND THEIR CRAFT—

Music is a very human process, as social as it is sonic—a truth we some-times miss with the availability of CD recordings, radio programming, and handy "walkmen." Music readily available, in just the right quantity, at just the right time. Sound at our command, without all the human trappings. No preparation. No waiting.

At Lourdes, music takes time. Time is integral to how individuals come to know their musical skills, discover the spiritual power of their song, and learn the gifts and limits of their own voices. Time is essential to how new music comes into the repertoire—to how songs are chosen, prepared, arranged, learned, and eventually brought to the community's prayer. Taking time is necessary so that this preparatory process can be communal, egalitarian, open to the input of all, negotiated. Engaging together over time, through thick and thin, is the crucial groundwork for the desired action of the Spirit—enabling musicians to be of "one accord"—an experience which cannot be produced purely by effort, but must be prepared for through the very stuff of human en-gagement, struggle as well as joy.

"Take your time" someone often calls out to a new singer who feels nervous or unsure, or to an experienced singer who is full of emotion. "Take your time!" Words of reassurance, support. We want you to do your best! We'll be there for you! We won't leave you alone! Your ability to do well is important to who we are! Music takes time.

*T*he fragrance of Louisiana gumbo wafted through the doorway of Jean and Wilfert Alexander's home on Innes Avenue that cold January morning. Several weeks before, I had asked Jean to recount for me the history of the Gospel Choir. She responded with an invitation to lunch in her home after Sunday liturgy. Entering Jean's living room that morning, I was surrounded by a gallery of family and friends whose photos covered the walls. Lingering, I recognized several faces who were now familiar to me from Lourdes. Atop the open sewing machine in the corner I noticed one of the royal blue and white dresses Jean was hurrying to complete for Lourdes Day, each dress tailor-made for one of the women choir members. Jean's voice summoned me to the kitchen. A quick grace over two steaming bowls of gumbo, and our conversation began.

Jean, educator and mother of two, grew up in a small Catholic town in Louisiana, the fifth of Elsie and Everette Edward's ten children. She was cared for by godparents as a child while her mother worked in the fields, and eventually came to live with them. Although staunchly Catholic, Jean accompanied her godparents to their Baptist services on many occasions, exposing her to both traditions and their distinctive approaches to Black membership. To my surprise, Jean, now an experienced "lead" in the Lourdes choir, did not grow up singing. Public school children were not welcome in the Catholic parish choir, and their own schooling provided little opportunity. At twenty Jean moved to the Bay Area, living for a time in the projects on the hill above Lourdes, and making All Hallows her parish. In 1963, she and Wilfert were married.

It was by chance that Jean first came to Lourdes. One cold morning, when Denise, the first of her two children, was a few years old, engine trouble sent Jean off on foot, child in arms, to the nearest church. Reaching Lourdes, Father McKinnon greeting them warmly at the gate—a welcome reiterated inside the church by Sister Martin de Porres Coleman, the first Black nun Jean had ever met. Unlike the Irish and Scottish religious she had known in Louisiana, clad head to foot in black habits, Sister Martin wore ordinary dress. A new world of church, of music, and of liturgical leadership was opening up for Jean that day.

Sister Martin soon convinced her and a few other women—Bessie Brooks and Charlene Edwards, Jean's sister-in-law, among them—that they could sing well enough to form the first Gospel Choir. Still, believing that she could sing "lead" took Jean more time, experience, and the encouragement of Sister Martin's successor, Deacon George Quigley, s.j. Jean still sings some of the "old songs" she learned then—a gospelized version of Charles Gabriel's "His Eye Is on the Sparrow," and James Cleveland's "God Has Smiled on Me." Having emerged as a musical leader, Jean soon took on other roles in the parish, eventually training in the archdiocesan program for lay leadership. To this day, she serves as choir president.

*T*he stories of other musicians at Lourdes bear similarities to Jean's. As we conversed over breakfast at Mel's Diner on Geary Street one Sunday, Pat Goodall spoke of her childhood in St. Louis. Growing up in a Catholic setting, devoid of Black music or any reference to Black culture, and with the Latin Mass her primary liturgical nourishment, Pat wandered away from the church in her adult years. She searched for a tradition that could better feed her religious longings. Short experiences with Lutheran and Baptist churches failed to satisfy her, and for twelve years Pat eschewed regular churchgoing. Moving to San Francisco in the mid-'70s, Pat worked first as a drug counselor at one of the hospitals, then for the Pacific Gas and Electric Co. Her friend Louise Wood, knowing that she had yet to find a church, invited her to Lourdes. Pat hesitated. After several months of coaxing, Pat arrived one Sunday, but chose to sit in the back of the church so as to have a ready escape. To her great surprise, "the priest could preach, the music was good, and the people were so friendly!" In her words, "The Catholic church had made a 360 degree turn since Vatican II!" She spoke with Louise and other choir members after liturgy, and to her own surprise, agreed to join the choir. Ten years later, when Charlene Edwards handed over the direction of the choir, Pat stepped in, almost by default.

Witnessing Pat's leadership today, it's difficult to believe that she never aspired to being a choral director. "This is God's work, this is God's plan, not mine," she comments. Her gifts for music are natural and intuitive, and her knowledge of the gospel tradition has been shaped over the years through listening to gospel performances and singing. "I have a good ear, I can learn [the music] quickly. . . . [Still,] I'm not in this position because of my own choosing . . . but because I have the energy, that support from the Spirit, so that I can help the choir feel a song, can draw the best out of them." In the beginning, Pat claims, she tried to be very subdued. But "the music set off fireworks in me. . . . I guess that was God's way of letting me know, 'You can't shut me down!' I stopped trying after that. When I feel the music, you all know it!"

In fact, Pat's role is pivotal. She coordinates the complex interaction among singers, instrumentalists, and other participants in the liturgy, all of whom have a role in the music-making. Every ounce of her petite body becomes engaged by the music. Her expressive hand gestures and body movements communicate a song's dynamic rhythms. Her fingers, eyes, and head deliver signals the musicians need in a performance style that is always somewhat improvisatory. I asked her how she makes decisions on the spot about how to shape or sustain certain portions of a song. It's a matter of "feel," she responded—a complex, intuitive sense of when a song has accomplished its desired spiritual-musical purpose, based on her own inner experience and on how she perceives participants and musicians are being moved by the song's message.

Catching a light supper with me at the Amerasian Café on Union Street one evening, Reed Fromer recounted his arrival at Lourdes. "The last place I expected to find myself was in a Catholic church!" Reed grew up in a Jewish family across the bay in Marin County. Religious services were not part of his upbringing. His father and uncle were semi-professional musicians, and Reed learned to play piano by ear at an early age. In 1987 when Lourdes was searching for an accompanist—note, they had been left stranded when the Baptist pianist serving them felt a sudden call to street preaching and left town for Atlanta overnight—Reed was a part-time student at Marin Community College. Urged by a musical associate to consider Lourdes' position, Reed agreed to pay a visit. He loved to make music, and he needed the money. Reason enough. It took only part of his first liturgy there to realize that he was ready to slip onto the piano bench. Which is exactly what he did.[1] "It was a marriage right from the beginning," noted Pat Goodall to me once. Reed quickly learned the choir's repertoire, "catching" the style and guessing the chordal structures. Tutelage by jazz and rock musicians over the years had made this second nature, giving him the enormous versatility necessary to perform in an oral tradition, where scores are not used, and songs often need transposition to match the range of particular singers. Little did he dream, then, how life-changing his affiliation with the parish would become.

"I felt welcome at Lourdes from the beginning," Reed commented, "and connected with the community's commitment to issues of social concern and social justice. I love the fact that the preaching has a human content and a social context. I come from a family of activists and can easily identify with Lourdes' concerns for the city, the neighborhood, the homeless." And, he added, with their familial ways of relating to each other. The children are his special love. When not needed at the piano, Reed is often found sitting in the front pew, interacting with a varying cast of three to five year olds.

Reed's easy manner and unassuming way of being might belie his accomplishments as a professional musician. Composer and occasional recording artist, Reed leads a rhythm and blues band, and performs as pianist/vocalist with other ensembles in the Bay Area. Over the years, he has composed several songs for the Lourdes choir. I asked what most prepared him for making music at Lourdes. "From a strictly musical point of view, the fact that I'm a singer and accompany myself has created an acute awareness of what it takes to accompany singers. [And, I can sense] what is appropriate. . . . I've always felt that the best musician is not necessarily the one who has the most ability but one who can apply that ability to a particular song or context.

"In terms of my having an appreciation of the music, the *feeling* of it, that comes from my involvement in the Freedom Song Network.[2] I've been in situations where I was one of a bunch of people, united, singing about a cause. It's just that here there's a different content to the message. In addition, a lot of the songs that fueled the Civil Rights marches and union rallies were directly adopted from the Black churches. By tweaking a lyric here or there, you could apply songs like "This Little Light of Mine" to whatever struggle you happened to be involved in. So in a sense, I grew up amidst gospel music. I just knew it with its adapted lyrics, rather than its original church-oriented content. And from that experience, I have an appreciation for what gospel music means to people here."

"That in the singing, the music takes on a significance greater than itself?" I asked.

"Yeah. There's a solidarity [among people] that's very real, not just a show, which is something I really appreciate. That's the feeling I have when I'm singing with [others in the Freedom Song movement]. I'm not old enough to have been in Selma, but there's a definite, firm belief in the validity of what we are singing. A certainty that gives the music a kind of religious quality. Something different from just singing 'Baby, I love you. . . .'"

*A*t six, Isaiah Brown, who had been drumming with an intuitive expertise since age three, took his seat at the trap set and became the Lourdes full-time drummer. He recounts shyly that his mentor and cousin, Darsky Alexander, left to get a drink of water one day, and Isaiah took his place. It was 1990. Son of two choir members, Judy and John Brown, Isaiah grew up with a passion for playing the drums. At age eleven, he claimed to have played for eleven years. His innate musical sensitivities were first guided by Darsky, a cousin and young member of the community, and have been honed through the experience of making music at worship, listening to other drummers, and occasional coaching from Reed Fromer. The entire set of drums are at his command—bass/kick drum, toms, snare, hi-hat, and cymbals. But his ability to sense appropriate and engaging patterns, to maintain an interplay between strong primary beats and a range of syncopated secondary beats, flourishes, drum and cymbal rolls, enables him to add the intensity and color essential to the musical style. In gospel singing, rhythm is crucial to how musical sound engages people in bodily modes of participation. At Lourdes, Isaiah's drumming is a catalyst.

*U*nlike many of the other choir members, Judy Brown, Isaiah's mother, came with experience. "Our family has a Baptist background, a Holiness background," she comments as we talk after liturgy one Sunday morning. As a child in Louisiana, Judy went with her aunt to the Holiness church where she had her first experience of singing at worship, performing solos such as "Oh, how I love Jesus" at an early age. When her own Catholic church initiated a choir, Judy joined. The repertoire was different—"Catholic" music instead of gospel—but participation prepared her to join the Lourdes choir when she moved to the Bay Area in 1975. Offering her musical gifts at Lourdes "was like second nature to me," she comments. "I love singing. I love praising God, and that's why I sing—for the grace of God and all the blessings he's given me. Singing is just giving back. It's a ministry . . . giving back to him what he's given me in my life."

When Charlene Edwards left her position as director of the choir, Judy assumed responsibility for selecting music for each Sunday's liturgy. Knowing the Scriptures well from Bible study, and after "meditating" on the appointed passages each week, Judy listens for how the choir's song might nourish the prayer and lives of those who gather. Moreover, Judy's ministry as lead singer is powerful. "Sometimes when Judy sings, she gets 'taken away,'" comments Sister Irma Dillard. "The Spirit takes over," and others are deeply affected. "The song she's singing uplifts you, it takes you somewhere. . . . Your whole being is swept up into God. Your body and soul. . . . The words of her song cause you to remember the times when God has gotten you through. It brings tears of joy. Tears of thanksgiving."[3]

*F*or Rose Isles, it was a long journey from Louisiana to lead singer at Lourdes. Sharing lunch one Saturday in the small CCD room adjacent to the church, where Rose had just completed a morning of teaching youngsters in the parish "School of Religion," she recounted the tale. A woman of gentle spirit, sister of Jean Alexander, Rose is both mother and grandmother. In 1979, she moved to San Francisco, affiliating with All Hallows for a time. Her first visit to Lourdes made her resolve, "I *have* to come back here . . . a church where I felt I was welcome, like home." Her musical gifts were still unknown to her, but were soon recognized by the pianist, Mr. Patterson, who overheard her singing from the front pew. "You should be in this choir," he urged on several occasions. She finally succumbed to his prompting. "I think it was just the will of God, the Spirit working through me," she comments. "I've grown so much in faith since I've been here."

Once in the choir, Rose was encouraged by many to become a lead singer. Director Charlene Edwards took up her cause. "Give her time!" Four years later, she agreed to lead a verse on the relatively calm "Blessed Assurance." "The first song I sang on my own, though, was 'Hold Out,'" she recalls, referring to one of the most beloved songs in the Lourdes repertoire, "Lord, Help Me to Hold Out!" "It's a song Reverend Cleveland sings. . . . I was listening to [the album] one night and the words really caught me. I said, I think I can sing this!" Gradually, the process began of arranging and learning the piece. "The song has to become part of you. You have to sing the song the way you feel it or it never gets across to others. . . . The first time I sang the song, I was afraid! I prayed, 'Please Lord, help me do this right!' Even now, before I sing, I'm sometimes nervous. . . . [But] the first word you sing, all the nervousness goes. . . . It took me about three times and then I knew, 'This is my song!'"

*E*ven before Rose joined the choir, she was recruiting others. "Rita [Johnson] used to sit in back of me every Sunday. One Sunday, I heard her sing. She had a beautiful voice. . . . I turned around and said, 'Why are you not up there? God gave you this [voice], you better use it.' Her grandmother, Mrs. Fisher, [agreed]. 'I've been trying to get that girl to join the choir and I just can't get her.'"

Rita, a slender, attractive woman, mother of three and recently grandmothered, was not baptized a Catholic as a child. Conversing in the small CCD room before choir rehearsal one evening, Rita recounted that her mother was Baptist. But because her grandmother, Margaret Fisher, was Catholic, Rita participated in religion classes at Lourdes. Discovering as an adult that she could be baptized, she was thrilled. Rita learned to sing and harmonize from her mother. "We sounded so good together," Rita comments, telling how she loved the sound of her mother's voice blending with hers. Of the many songs she learned as a child, Mallot's "Lord's Prayer" remains her favorite. Yet despite this early experience, Rita had to be coaxed into the choir, and was only gradually convinced that she could sing lead. There's a shyness that persists today, but there's also a power in her gentle, clear voice. Andraé Crouch's "I Find No Fault In Him"[4] was one of the first she learned, she recalled, singing a few bars. I've heard her sing this song only once, but I remember how her voice soars in a heartfelt act of believing as she reaches the end of each verse:

> They pierced him in his side,
> and his blood came streaming down!
> And that's how he purchased my salvation!
> I find no fault in him!

"You have to make the song your own," she commented, echoing Rose's sentiment. "It has to connect with your life before you can give it to others."

Her husband, Walter Turner, seated beside her, agreed. Walter grew up on "the hill" overlooking Lourdes. I remember him commenting once that the projects were a difficult place to live. But "at nighttime, we had a beautiful, beautiful view of the city. My body would be in those projects, but my mind was always somewhere else!" It was the expansive "view from the hill" that gave him a sense of purpose, a reason for leaving the projects, and a reason for returning now to Lourdes, to give back.

Walter's mother was pianist in a Baptist church. At two, standing on the piano bench next to her, Walter sang in public for the first time. A path was set. Professional singing—on stage, on recordings, with a Baptist "Mass Choir"—became an important part of his adult life. Yet his musical involvement at Lourdes came gradually. Meeting Rita Johnson, whom he would later marry, Walter was drawn to Lourdes. Sitting in on a rehearsal one evening, Pat Goodall invited him to learn the lead on a new arrangement of "Near the Cross," a hymn he remembered well from his childhood. David Curry's adaptation of the song was made for Walter's voice—tapping his full range, from clear, high tenor falsetto tones, honed in gospel quartet singing, to those deep chest tones that seem to resonate within his entire 6′ 3″ stature. When he performed the song for the first time in March, 1994, Pat Goodall commented to the community at the end of the liturgy, "I don't know why he hasn't joined the choir. Perhaps he's afraid of the women. But he's more than welcome any time he wants to come." Walter has been a member ever since.

*I*t was my own musical journey that had brought me to Lourdes. Rehearsals afforded me time to get to know the musicians, their ways of interacting, and to learn the music. It was all new to me—the repertoire, the styles, and the musical processes of learning and performing. But unlike the children who were always present at rehearsals, having accompanied parents or grandparents, I was not learning *tabula rasa*. Rather, assumptions about music long embedded in my consciousness were being stretched, reappraised, and reformulated. Likewise my assumptions about choir rehearsals. I had attended many in my life. The primary objective was usually to get down to business—that is, to the musical business—and to finish as close to "on time" as possible. Lourdes was different. Both in rhythm and intent. Arriving from a day's work, from family obligations and numerous other responsibilities, choir members spent the first part of the evening catching up, embracing, talking, sharing news, listening to each other, connecting, "tuning in." Clearly, the bonds among people came first—the necessary rapport, I would learn, on which the music is built.

Slowly I recognized, within the informality and fluidity of Thursday night gatherings, that rituals of rehearsal had much in common with those of Sunday morning. Once a quorum of musicians had arrived—quorum here is a relative term—and had engaged long enough in conversation, Jean Alexander would lead a time of prayer, inviting those present to add their petitions. The concerns voiced were often very personal, prayed at times through tears. Jean would draw the prayer to a close, asking, with deep feeling in her voice, "for the serenity to accept what we can't change, the courage to change what we can, and the wisdom to know the difference." Announcements were next. Places where the choir would sing. A meal for the homeless on the steps of City Hall or at a neighboring Baptist church. A choir festival in a nearby city. Dates needed to be cleared. Calendars. Commitments made. My amazement grew. With all the demands made on the lives of these musicians, their ministry overflowed into so many places, into so many lives.

Once the singing got underway, the choir would work in earnest, sparing nothing in their investment of energy. Learning notes, pitches, harmonies was never enough. What needed to be discovered was the full impact of the music—sound, energy, *and* communication. Despite the almost empty church, the choir stood in precisely the same place from which they would sing on Sunday morning—arced across the sanctuary. Lead singers rehearsed with microphone in hand, balancing their vocal leadership against interlocking sounds of the choir, the piano, and drums.

During my first year with them, I was an observer to this process. From where I usually sat, some four or five pews from the front, I could watch the musicians at work, tape-record, and jot down melodies in my shorthand *solfège*—one aspect of my training which, in the absence of musical scores, aided my learning process. I was hardly an invisible presence. From time to time, Pat Goodall or someone else would call out, "What do you think, Sister?"—always happy to have a listener.

A chilly Thursday evening in February of 1994. Billows of fog are gliding in from the bay as I pull up in front of Lourdes. Two cars have preceded me, their passengers already inside the church. One is a grey Buick belonging to Reed Fromer, whom I left a half hour ago at the Amerasian Café. I turn off the engine. Stillness envelops the car. A distant siren sends a muted flare through the hushed moment. In the dim ochre glow of the corner street light, I can see that the gate of the chain-link fence surrounding the church has been opened, unlocked no doubt by Pat Goodall. I pause, expecting that another car might pull up beside me. At night, I prefer to enter the church in the company of others. The rumbling sound of a souped-up Fiesta, bass booming, barrels down the Innes Avenue hill and heads off along Evans Street toward the shipyard. Quiet returns. I walk quickly from the car to the red door on the left side of the church. Inside, a gentle peace and the sound of Reed's fingers on the keyboard. A few lights are on near the front. I see Pat busy changing the altar linens, and Bessie Brooks seated a few pews back on the left side. Even from a distance, I sense the tiredness in her body. Reed calls me to come listen to some new compositions he recorded this afternoon at a local studio. Other choir members gradually congregate.

Like a sudden gust of fresh air, Louise Wood arrives exuberant. Cassette tape in hand, she walks to the front of the church exclaiming, "We *must* learn this song for Easter!" At her urging, a quick shift of tapes in the small black "boom-box" tape-recorder resting on the piano. A few of us huddle nearby to listen. In no time, the strains of Brenda Moore's majestic piece "Perfect Praise" are pressing the acoustic limits of the tape-recorder: "Oh, Lord, how excellent!

How excellent! How excellent is thy name!" Louise sings along, her body catching every wave of the song's energy. The soprano voices of the performing choir are soaring: "Every knee shall bow, and every tongue proclaim that he is Lord! Jesus excellent!" We listen. Someone mentions having heard the piece performed by another choir, commenting that the arrangement was a bit different. I notice that unlike most of Lourdes' songs, this one is choral throughout and has no lead singer.

As always, I'm full of questions. Who composed the song? Who recorded it? Where can I find a copy of the music? Most often, these are my questions only, part of my quest to get some handle on the expansive, sometimes elusive Lourdes repertoire. To fit the pieces together like a jigsaw puzzle. Not that others aren't interested in my questions. But they seem more concerned with the song's message, its power, and how it might sound in this choir's voices. My search begins to find a recorded version of "Perfect Praise," and if possible, a musical score.

Louise offers to make a copy of her tape for Reed and Pat. I'm learning that this is how it all begins, and fascinated by the way the repertoire develops. Songs are not simply chosen by a director, as in most of the choirs I've known. Rather, each song has a story. Like Louise, people bring the choir new pieces that have touched them, and that they believe will become fitting vehicles for the community's worship. Often, it's the bearer of the new song who feels ready to sing lead, who has imagined him- or herself into the song's message. Suddenly, a new image emerges in my mind. Lourdes' repertoire is a map of the social and spiritual journeys of the community. Up until this time, I've thought of it as a vast reservoir, a seemingly endless storehouse of hymns, gospels, spirituals, and praise songs that everyone here knows. Except for me. Now, I image this evolving repertoire as the "songlines" that the Aboriginal peoples of Australia retrace in the desert as a way of reliving the spiritual journeys of their ancestors. To sing a song at Lourdes is often to retrace a songline, a spiritual journey.

Reed and Pat take up Louise's challenge, agreeing to learn the song apart from rehearsal and devise a first arrangement, one that suits the voices and scale of this choir. But much negotiation will remain—the hard work of shaping and reshaping the vocal parts, adjusting key and tempo, feeling the song's dynamics, and reaching a mutual sense of how Lourdes will perform it. These require the whole choir. Everyone's input is valued.

Aural learning, I'm beginning to see, is a strenuous process. I feel adrift without the "shorthand" of a musical score, but realize the value of what I witness here. Music is transmitted "person to person," performance to performance —albeit from recording to live event—without the intervention of a written version, a codified reduction, which I've come to realize filters out all the human elements, suggesting, perhaps, that "music" exists apart from those who make it. In this setting, memory—a holistic, bodily consciousness—becomes the slate on which the music is written. Once learned, it is rarely forgotten. Moreover, in the gospel tradition, each choir has its own version of a song, its own arrangement. Scores and hymnal versions, when they exist, are seen as blueprints, but never a substitute for "making the song your own." Originality is what is prized, even expected. The repertoire I'm learning at Lourdes, indeed, bears its own imprint.

"*I* Have a Father," Pat Goodall calls out, signaling a shift to one of the choir's newest pieces. Louise's "Perfect Praise" has been set aside, and Sunday's music rehearsed. Some forty-five minutes remain—time for a bit of hard work. Tonight, there's an urgency. A new song, "I Have a Father,"[5] is slated for Lourdes Day, two weeks hence.

I've watched the choir rehearse this song for many months now, listened to its journey into their voices, observed the processes of arranging choral parts and negotiating the timing. Jean Alexander, who brought the song to the choir, sings lead. I learned the story from her as we talked over gumbo in her kitchen a few weeks before. On first hearing, "I Have a Father" reminded Jean of the godfather who cared for her as a child, and who was ill at the time. A few years passed, and Jean made intermittent attempts to learn the song. But only when her own father "went home to God"—he, the beloved patriarch of their large family—did Jean begin in earnest. Returning from his funeral in Louisiana with her sisters Rose Isles and Shirley Valmore, Jean resolved to ask the choir's help. Singing it now evokes memories of her godfather and father, images of their faith and constancy.

This "contemporary gospel" piece has been particularly challenging to the Lourdes choir. Their preference is for the "traditional gospel" sound. "We sing old-style gospel," they say, referring to the hard driving rhythm of more traditional pieces. Gospel "done from experience and with gut feeling!" as Rose Isles phrased it. The gentle, ballad style of a piece like this makes timing and musical cues more difficult to catch. Clearly, the softer, orchestral sounds of contemporary gospel are aimed to evoke a listener's quiet reflection and not the exuberant *Amens* of a spirited congregation. Jean's lead is more gutsy and her voice more raspy than the smooth, sleek tones of the recorded vocalist. Mahalia Jackson would be proud.

Mastery of the song has come through repetition—much repetition: relying for a time on printed lyrics distributed to choir members; rehearsing the piece in sections; returning, from time to time, to the taped original version for inspiration and clarification, but never imitation; hammering out the details; "fighting a lot," as Pat would sum it up. Over the months, I've watched how differing types of musical expertise, varying ways of "knowing" the music, play themselves out: Reed's technical knowledge, often translated into straight-forward images, such as "jumps" to describe interval changes, as he teaches the choir their various parts; Jean's "feel"—shorthand for her inner sense of timing and intuitive grasp of how her lead should go. Singing "from the heart" is her bottom line. Don't get too technical. But always the goal is the same—to communicate a song in such a way that people are touched and fed.

"It's dry," shouts Pat Goodall, a good half hour into the work. "It has nothing! Let's take it again from the top!" Reed circles back to the introduction. As if by some magic, things seem to fall into place this time. Jean is right on cue, her entrances as secure as they've ever been. Head back, right hand aloft, she's in command. The choir's vocal parts gel as never before. I watch Jean "working" as she sings, her body, seen in profile, totally engaged; her movements downward as her voice becomes more animated. Each phrase seems to come from some place deep within. Each line invested with intensity. As they reach the vamp section near the end of the piece, I notice that members of the choir have moved closer together, circling in as if to close ranks, moving as a single body to the undulating rhythms, arms motioning downward as they feel each animated word of their back-up:

I // have // a Fa-ther! I // have // a Fa-ther! I // have // a Fa-ther!

Energy builds with progressive repetition, aided by Reed's piano and Isaiah's drum, then subsiding a bit as they near the end, allowing Jean to take a final lead,

I have a Father . . .

only to be joined again by the choir for an exhilarating crescendo and octave leap to the last word:

who can_____!!

"We did it!" someone shouts as applause breaks out. Pat and Jean embrace. "We did it!"

"What I love about this choir is that it's not stiff and starchy," commented Pat Goodall to me over lunch at a Berkeley café one Saturday.[6] Lourdes is different from other choirs, she continued. "We don't aim for perfection. We have fun with the music!" We're concerned less with performance than with getting across the spiritual feeling of the music. Best of all, she adds, this choir "is not a dictatorship!" It's not focused on one or two personalities. Everyone is involved in the decision-making!

As I listened, I recalled the many times I've heard Pat ask for "comments, criticisms, suggestions" when the choir was learning a new piece. It's got to be this way, she reiterates. Each one's sense of the music counts! It strikes me that efficiency is not the goal here, but valuing the individual. It takes more time to include everyone, to experiment with diverse, sometimes conflicting, suggestions about how a song should be arranged, before setting a course. Everyone's voice counts musically as well. Even fledgling members of the choir are invited to "sing a verse" on a familiar Communion song. It's a kind of apprenticeship, if you will. A chance to allow a less experienced singer to grow strong.

The uniqueness of each voice matters to the ensemble, too. There's no attempt to "blend," as I've experienced elsewhere. The distinctive resonance of each is valued in the heterogeneous contours of vocal fabric.[7] The convergence they seem to seek is more a spiritual one—a being of "one accord." Being in tune with the Spirit. "Spiritually, when we're all at the same place, we can't be beat!" claimed Louise Wood at rehearsal one night. "When we're really, *really* good is when, as a group, we've gone through a difficult time together and it becomes rejoicing—we're all of one accord. . . . Sometimes it happens [on a Sunday, and sometimes] at rehearsal. All of a sudden, everything falls into place. When it's like that [when the Spirit takes over], we cannot be beat!"[8]

*D*avid Alexander, a handsome young man, joined the choir shortly before I came to Lourdes. Although an enthusiastic member of the ensemble, David had yet little experience singing lead. One warm April Sunday, he was slated to sing a verse on an old, well-loved hymn, "Is Your All on the Altar." It was Communion time. David moved into place behind the ambo as his verse neared. A few notes into his first line and difficulty set in. Losing his sense of timing, David began to speed up the words. Pat motioned him to wait, but David was off course. In a flash, she was at his side. Support rather than judgement is her approach to a faltering singer! *"It's al'right!"* someone called out. Soon Jean had moved in to flank him on the other side, resting her arm on his shoulder. *"Take your time!"* someone else shouted. Gently, Pat began to mark the beat with her hand, mouthing the words, enabling David to catch the rhythm again. Instinctively, the choir began to hum beneath his voice, and soon he was singing with a modicum of composure. Pat signaled a repeat of the verse. Choir members, standing now, began to sing full voice, but David was heard above them all, as he stood surrounded—vocally, physically, psychologically—by those who cared that he offer his gift well. Singing here is not about glory. *David needed to sing, so that the community could receive his gift.*

*T*ake your time! . . .

Intermezzo

TIME

K*airos* is a rich biblical word replete with images of "God's time" intersecting human history. *Kairos* moments erupt within human time, revealing God's hidden purpose, God's intentionality. They are full of promise and unforseen opportunity. Yet they are decisive moments that demand decision, and call a community of faith to choices and commitments.[1]

Black theologian M. Shawn Copeland claims that the 1960s were a *kairos* time for Black Catholics. The intersection of the African American Civil Rights movement with Vatican Council II created a unique juncture, a singular challenge. "Change in the social mood," she writes, "without change in the ecclesiastical mood might have forced Black Catholics in the United States to abandon their centuries-old religious tradition." On the other hand, "change in the ecclesial mood without change in the social mood might have compelled them to barter their racial-cultural heritage for silver. There was a propitiousness to these times," Copeland contends. "This was God's time: this was *kairos*."[2]

K*airos* is likewise an apt word for the historical frame and the generative forces we see at work in the music and worship of the Lourdes community. Bear in mind that *kairos* moments, while pregnant with possibility, are fraught with paradox and uncertainty. Like all moments of conversion, they offer life through death, rebirth through struggle and suffering. They lead us more deeply into our own history.

In the late 1960s, when Father Don MacKinnon, Brother Gary Pometta, Jesse Banks, Margaret Fisher, and a few other parishioners established the fragile beginnings of the new Our Lady of Lourdes, the word "inculturation" had not yet been coined.[3] Only their bold, courageous choices, guided by the Spirit, could have paved the way for the fusion of horizons that marks the community today—a new weaving of Catholic identity and Black religious experience. Here we witness a reclaiming of the church's age-old tradition of discerned interplay between Christian faith and a community's lived cultural experience. This process was denied generations of Black Catholics, choked off by the dynamics of racism and misunderstanding. The people of Lourdes know that history well—a history captured in an image from Sr. Renee de Porres' preaching, as she described her longing to enter a religious community: "This Black child of God didn't think there was any 'room in the inn' for her. Y'all know what I mean, don't you?"

The creativity that has been released at Lourdes is akin to the genius at work in the earliest centuries of Christian faith that gave birth to a Christian calendar forged in the experiential matrix of cultural life. The counterpoint of the Christmas season and Kwanzaa, or the juxtaposition of Revival and Lent, are but symptoms of the creative ferment that marks this local community's search for authentic faith.

Music has been key to this search. Father MacKinnon's intuition was prophetic —"It's in the music, it's in the art." To sing, to make music, is to awaken a "cultural memory."[4] For the Lourdes community to incorporate Black sacred music in their worship has been to release that memory—to unlock a whole compendium of understandings, ritual assumptions, and ways of being in the world. This cultural memory is described by one scholar as an embodiment of

> [those] nonfactual and nonreferential motivations, actions, and beliefs that members of a culture seem, without direct knowledge or deliberate training, to "know"—that feel unequivocally "true" and "right" when encountered, experienced, and executed. [Cultural memory is] . . . a repository of meanings that comprise the subjective knowledge of a people, its immanent thoughts, its structures, and its practices . . . [that] are transferred and understood unconsciously but become conscious and culturally objective in practice and perception. Cultural memory, obviously a subjective concept, seems to be connected with cultural *forms*—in this case, music, where the "memory drives the music and the music drives the memory."[5]

It is striking that in years following Vatican II, when Catholic communities around the United States searched for new vernacular music, Lourdes and other Black Catholic communities could reach back into a centuries-old tradition of vernacular song—could reclaim a tradition of sacred music forged in the face of oppression and celebrating the fearless faith that had brought African Americans "safe thus far" and would doubtless lead them home. Deep within this tradition of sacred music—of sorrow songs and jubilees, of metered and improvised hymns, of traditional and contemporary gospel music—are culturally rooted perceptions of time and ways of being in time that flourish today at Lourdes.

Circles in motion / ritual matrix / generative center: Where did this musical tradition come from?

*C*ircles are places of participation, of inclusion, of wholeness. Listening to the Lourdes community sing about "unbroken circles" as part of their November commemoration of "Lourdes's Saints" invites one to ponder what perception of time might be captured in these unpretentious lyrics: *"Will the circle be unbroken / by and by, Lord, by and by? There's a better home awaiting / in the sky, Lord, in the sky?"*

Singing about unbroken circles, about circles that reconnect loved ones, about circles that ring 'round the tides of change—loss and gain, suffering and joy—seem to reveal a cosmic connection between past and future as God's own time of fullness, to be realized in that "better home awaiting," where loved ones will once again be joined in the great circle dance of life in all its fullness. This perception of life as unbroken circle shapes a community's way of being together in time, here and now.

Circles-in-motion, rings-in-motion, like the "wheel in a wheel" that Ezekiel saw[6]—these images open for us a path of insight into the genesis of Black sacred music and its impact on worship at Lourdes. Black music scholar Samuel Floyd traces the origins of African American music to the experience of the "ring shout"—a ritual practice that emerged during slavery, in which participants move in a circle, shuffling, swaying, and dancing with increasing velocity, accompanied by call-and-response singing, hand clapping and foot stamping, all of which create cross-rhythms and multi-metric patterns, and culminating in a collectively improvised, even ecstatic experience of worship and communion with God.[7]

Clearly African in origin, the ring shout was a primary context in which transplanted Africans could recognize values they held in common.[8] In this distinctive cultural ritual, Africans on American soil "fused the sacred and the secular, music and dance," and perpetuated the African-derived tendency to "eschew distinctions between religion and everyday life."[9] The ring preserved African musical practices that are now recognized as the foundational and characteristic elements of African American music. Many of these can be heard in the music-making of the Lourdes community:

> . . . call-and-response devices; additive rhythms and polyrhythms; heterophony, pendular thirds, blue notes, bent notes, and elisions; hums, moans, grunts, vocables, and other rhythmic-oral declamations, interjections,

and punctuations; off-beat melodic phrasings and parallel intervals and chords; constant repetition of rhythmic and melodic figures and phrases (from which riffs and vamps would be derived); timbral distortions of various kinds; musical individuality within collectivity . . . hand clapping, foot patting . . . and the metronomic pulse that underlies all African American music.[10]

It was within the "ring" that the spirituals were born, as images of Christian faith were fused with the predilections of African song and dance. It was from the ring that other genres of Black music would flow: "the shuffling, angular, off-beat, additive, repetitive, intensive, unflagging rhythms of shout and jubilee spirituals, ragtime, and R&B; the less vigorous but equally insistent and characteristic rhythms of the 'sorrow songs' and the blues; and all the musical genres derived from these and other early forms. All were shaped and defined by black dance, within and without the ring."[11]

Gospel music was born of this same spiritual floodtide. The early decades of the 20th century were the "right time" for a new, urban expression of Christian faith—a musical formulation of "good news in hard times" that could keep hope alive in the often hostile environments in which Black Christians found themselves. Melding elements of the blues with those of religious hymnody, Thomas A. Dorsey, the "father" of gospel music, created a genre of Black music that transformed the emotional and inspirational force of Black preaching into song. Like other offspring of the ring shout, gospel music synthesized African and African American elements of music, dance, poetry, and drama—distilling "the aesthetic essence of the Black arts into a unified whole," and becoming, in the image of one scholar, "a crystallization of the Black aesthetic."[12] Gospel flourished in the worship practice of the Black folk church[13]—drawing its genius from the "free-style collective improvisations of the Black church congregation and the rhetorical solo style of the black gospel preacher," and fueled by the same potent spirituality known best as "soul."[14] Today, the performance of gospel music at Lourdes roots this community in its dynamic and generative past, while creating a contemporary "ring"—a place of participation, inclusion, and wholeness.

Remembering song / dynamic memory / *anamnesis:*
What distinctive perspective on time is integral to this musical tradition?

"*I*'m so glad trouble don't last always!" Sung mantra-like over and again, creating an almost ecstatic moment of delight within a night of revival at Lourdes, this phrase captures the distinctive perspective on time that is shot through the performance tradition of Black sacred music. Those making music are situated in a dynamic present, while both actively remembering the past and looking to a future which they, in some measure, actively create.

Caught in the image of an African proverb, "in order to know where you are going you must know where you've been."[15]

Experiencing music at Lourdes, it's not surprising that Black music has been described as "remembering song"—a "translation of memory into sound and sound into memory."[16] Past experience is named—"God of our wearing years, God of our silent tears . . ."—but always as a point from which to claim the future: "Facing the rising sun of our new day begun / Let us march on till victory is won."

The dynamism is not only textual. It resides in the liturgical action of a performing community such as Lourdes who, hands joined on a day of remembrance of Martin Luther King, Jr., recall that "*We* have come over a way that with tears has been watered. / *We* have come, treading our path through the blood of the slaughtered." But, once again, "trouble don't last always!" The God who has "led us into the light" will "keep us ever on the path . . . lest we stray from the places . . . where we met thee." This is dynamic memory, situated in the lived experience of this community's history—this is *anamnesis*.[17] Gathered up in the singing, swaying rhythmically to its steady meter, the Lourdes community juxtaposes old and new—God's action in the past claimed within the particular circumstances of their contemporary lives, so as to release new meaning,[18] new hope, new determination to stay on the journey. This is "bringing the circle 'round." This is holding dear the memory of a people, just as Lourdes holds dear the memory of those "saints" who have gone ahead to that "better place awaiting . . ."

Sacred time—sacred space / / church time—church space: How does the realm of worship relate to other realms of time and space?

Worship is often described as "sacred time" and "sacred space." Implicit in this designation are two assumptions: (1) that liturgy exists in a sacred realm somehow distinct from a more secular one, and (2) that this distinction will be present in the temporal/spatial strategies of a community's liturgical action: that is, in how persons enter the worship event, and in what modes of interaction take place.

My experience at Lourdes and conversations with community members indicate that this sacred/secular dichotomy is not assumed. Rather, all life and all time are presumed to be sacred, the realm of God's grace. God can and must be worshiped at all times and in all places. This lived belief in an overlapping realm of the sacred—encompassing worship and everyday living—is evident in Sunday gatherings, as people's concerns, struggles, joys, and challenges flow into the prayer and liturgical action. It is likewise heard in the expressions of praise and testimony—which other communities might reserve for worship— that slip into the everyday speech of community members.

Moreover, Lourdes' use of gospel music within their worship further corroborates this lack of sacred/secular distinction. While powerfully religious in its message and intent, gospel music has never been restricted to liturgical contexts. Its religious vitality does not spring from the distinction of its rhythms and stylistic elements from what might be considered secular or popular music, but in its power to speak timely words of faith in the most concrete of human circumstances.

It seems more accurate to describe liturgy/music at Lourdes as "church" time and "church" space. This does not undermine the centrality or profundity of God's action or self-disclosure in their liturgy. Nor does it deny that what takes place is sacred. Rather it underscores that what is most characteristic of Lourdes's liturgical prayer is that the action of God, revealed in worship, is inexorably bound up with the action of the community. Liturgy here is fundamentally about being "*ecclesia*"[19]—the "convocation" of God that transforms the community's identity and empowers it to be the healing action of God, one to another. What distinguishes liturgical action here from other realms of action, and liturgical time and space from other times and places, is that the "church," as convoked by God, is gathered, acting, and acted upon.

Temporal frame / tempo and pacing:
How does music affect and participate in the temporal logic of the worship?

"At Lourdes, we're not on clock time! We're not at the office!" "Who watches the time at our worship? . . . Once we get started, I don't know where the time goes." "The liturgy generally takes two hours, but it never seems like it's taking too long. . . . However long it takes, it seems appropriate."

These striking comments by members of the community signal a particular temporal logic at work in the worship as a whole and in each of its musical moments. It's not on clock time. Unlike the time preoccupations that mark much of American life—efficiency, punctuality, control, and getting the job done in an expedient manner—here, time seems at the service of a deeper spiritual goal. Time spent together is fluid, expandible, protracted, and responsive to spiritual and social processes that cannot be rushed. Persons need to be strengthened, nourished, refreshed by God's word and table. Burdens need to fall, a new perspective on life needs to be gained. Images of being "on time" are replaced with attitudes of "take your time"—of taking and making the necessary time, musically and liturgically, to foster a quality of life and prayer that is attentive and responsive to the needs of each one.

This temporal logic is especially evident in music-making. The "temporal frame" of a musical piece—where a song begins and ends, how long it lasts, how its parts are performed—is not fixed or rigidly bounded, but fluid. A musical score, were one used, would only be a starting point. The musical and lyrical elements of a song are often stretched, repeated, prolonged so as to allow the music to fulfill its spiritual purpose. The introduction to a song may be extended, for example, as a lead singer addresses the community offering words of comfort or encouragement. Verses of songs may be repeated "just one more time" so that the power of its message can touch the hearts of those participating. Within songs that everyone knows, there's a level of indeterminancy, of choice, of improvisation, which makes room for the liberative power of the Spirit to work within the community.

The fluidity of time evident in each musical piece is mirrored in other aspects of the liturgy. The temporal frameworks of prayers, preaching, and other actions are flexible. They "stretch" according to the engagement of the community. The tempo and pacing of the whole worship—clearly more protracted than what might be found in many Catholic communities—is geared to make room for an ongoing dialogue within the community. The deliberate pace and cadence of Father Kirk's prayer creates a temporal space within which others can participate in the prayer through responses of *Amen! Lord have mercy!* or *Oh yes, Lord!* The community's intercessory prayer extends long enough so that all who wish to voice their needs or thanksgivings may do so. The altar call on a night of revival is prolonged until all those seeking the laying on of hands have received that prayer.

In moments of music-making, as in the worship as a whole, no single person controls the timing. As Pat Goodall intuits the appropriate moment to bring a song to a close, she is attentive not only to her own inner experience but to how she perceives others—singers, musicians, community members—are being moved by the song's message. Within a whole Sunday liturgy, sensing the appropriate length of any portion of the rite is an interactive and interdependent process that involves all those in leadership, as well as other community members. As a result, there's an open-ended quality about the community's prayer, be it Sunday worship or a night of revival—an expectation that something will happen, will change; that time is not our enemy ("there's never enough time") but our ally; that time will satisfy rather than rob us of what we most desire.

Qualities and density of time / tension and counterpoint: What is it like to be "in time" together?

*M*usic "makes time audible," makes it available to human perception, claims Suzanne Langer. Making music together mediates time in such a way that those participating can hear its tone, sense its timbre, feel its textures, and experience something of their temporal identity as individuals and as a community.

At Lourdes, musical time is densely textured with rhythmic complexity. The persistent, almost metronomic "beat" of an uptempo song galvanizes the community into patterns of swaying and clapping that are regular, predicable, and unified. Yet against this rhythmic anchor, people create intricate layers of movement and sound—hands, heads, and feet in motion; voices and instruments creating complexities of sound that are unpredictable, syncopated, and individually contributed. These complexities of counterpoint build a creative tension in which individuality—each one's unique contribution—and corporate action are not dichotomous, but all are integral both to the musical experience and to the identity of the community.

These complexities of rhythm[20] experienced at Lourdes are not simply musical characteristics but are ways of being together "in time." They require a mutual "tuning in," a social rapport, an attentiveness to the other, and a recognition that each one's musical contribution is important to the whole. They are mirrored, as we have seen, in the contrapuntal complexities of each Sunday and each "season" at Lourdes—in the cultural, liturgical, social, and personal rhythms that intersect temporally on any given occasion, and the community's willingness to shape and adapt the time spent together to include all these aspects of its lived experience.

Being "in time" together at Lourdes, musically and liturgically, is a lived art that is quite distinct from being "on time"—that is, the imposition of an external norm by which the community makes judgments about the temporal unfolding of its worship as well as its overall time frame—for example, the worship will last one hour. Notions of being "on time" are more spatially conceived, the product of cultural frameworks preoccupied with clocks and calendars—devices that segment time visually into predictable and equal parts, and mark the temporal points at which events are meant to begin and end. Being "on time" ensures a measure of control—a norm, a social contract to which one is accountable. Being "in time" is a more organic measure, a more internal norm that springs from interdependence and mutuality. At Lourdes, one enters a dynamic, relational experience of time in which the outcome is unpredictable—much like the drama of narrative and everyday life.

The fruits of this "lived art" of being "in time" are certain qualities of temporal experience— "enjoying oneself in the Lord," "having a good time"— drawn into an engagement from which one emerges revived, refreshed, and ready for what lies ahead.

Inbreaking of God's time / awakening to God's presence / *kairos*: How is music-making revelatory of God's action-in-time?

*T*here seems a shared assumption at Lourdes that God acts in God's own time—that although God is faithful and "will never come short of his word," God's action in time is unpredictable. As Brother Banks reminds the community often, "We don't *know* when Jesus will come!" "We don't know *when it is* *goin' to [happen]*, we don't know *where we're going to be at*, we don't know *how it's goin' to be. . . .*" Music-making becomes a place, a means of waiting on God's time, of "tarrying," of awakening to God's action in time, of remembering that although "one day I may not have but one thin dime," "the next day the Lord will step in *on time!*" Over and again, song lyrics focus this expectation: "What shall I do? I'm going to wait for an answer from you," because "I know you'll come through . . ." "I want to be ready, ready when Jesus comes!" But "Lord, help me to hold out until my change comes." A communally shared expectation that the Spirit of God—who "does not descend without song"—*will* act creates a spiritual context within which the musical process unfolds.

We see this expectation in both the macro- and micro-rhythms of the community's practice. Listening to the stories of how musicians came to be part of the Lourdes choir, we hear over and again of how they discovered God's action in their lives, inviting them, at times through the voices of others, to offer their musical gifts for the good of the community, to build up the community's worship. Their membership in the choir, as well as their readiness to become lead singers, is based more on their inner sense of God's timing, God's *kairos*, than on external credentials that "qualify" them for musical leadership. Likewise, Pat Goodall's direction of the choir was assumed at a moment when several factors converged—a need, an opening, a sense that "this is what God wants me to do," and the affirmation of others that she is gifted for this ministry —rather than because of any "formal" music training. What is revealed in this evolution of musical leadership is that the Spirit has prepared ministers for this community, providing gifts that have unfolded in God's good time.

God's action-in-time, apparent in these larger musical journeys, finds a parallel in the particular musical process that unfold within worship. Being together "in time," within the improvisatory temporal framework of a song, holds the attention of those who participate, engaging their bodies, allowing lyrics to attune their spirits and the power of a singer's message to stir their hearts and minds. *Amens* voiced by community members, erupting spontaneously and in syncopated rhythms, are testimonies that God is indeed acting now, in my life, in this present moment. As the music unfolds, unexpected moments of being "of one accord," which musicians contend can only come about when God's "Spirit takes over," are likewise reminders of the inbreaking of God's time within our own temporal, musical processes.

Ultimately, it is God who is "on time." A treasured aphorism, framed in the lyrics of a gospel song, make this truth clear: "God may not come when you want him, but he's *right on time!*"

Chapter Four

"I'VE BEEN A GUEST OF THE ALMIGHTY!"

—BROTHER BANKS—

*I*t's Sunday morning. A slight, wiry man, clad in white alb, brightly colored stole, and an embroidered African style Kufi hat, makes his way down the center aisle. Undaunted by the din around him—the church is buzzing with people still finding places, hugging each other, greeting visitors—"Brother Banks" walks to the ambo. "In the name of the Father, and of the Son, and of the Holy Spirit!" His voice rings out through the church. "May we give honor to God! Let us *rise in the name of Jesus,* our service is about to begin!" "Oh yes!" he sighs, as Reed Fromer strikes up the sturdy tones of Albert Goodson's classic gospel piece "We've Come This Far by Faith."[1] Isaiah Brown is right with him, etching the song's catchy rhythms on the resonant air. The procession, no doubt, is forming in the back—one of the men of the parish as crossbearer, the choir, the children carrying the Lectionary and the Sacramentary, and Father Kirk. But it's Brother Banks at the ambo that I can see best—his body leaning slightly forward, his hands moving to the insistent beat. "Oh, yes!" I hear him say. "Can't turn around!" *"Let us praise him! Praise him!"*

Reaching the front of the church house, the choir propels us into the song's first chorus:

> We've come this far by faith, leaning on the Lord,
> Trusting in his holy word! He's never failed me yet!
> Oh—— can't turn around!
> We've come this far by faith!

Judy Brown has left the line of altos, taken a mike in hand, and stands now in the "open space" just in front of Brother Banks, adding her vocal embellishments to the rhythmic lyrics: "every day I'm just a' leanin'!" Brother Banks, in the background now, is clearly engaged. I can almost catch his exclamations as we reiterate a full-voiced, "We've come this far by faith, leaning on the Lord! . . ."

Judy takes up the first verse, her voice straining a bit as she chides us,

> Don't be discouraged when trouble's in your life! *(Oh, yes!)*
> He'll bear your burdens, remove all misery and strife!
> Thank God we've . . .

". . . come this far by faith, leaning on the Lord!" Another chorus surges. Brother Banks's arms are aloft, his moving hands inscribing the rhythms in the air. Judy takes the lead again, a note of testimony in her voice as she sings,

> Just the other day *(Yes!)* I heard a man say, he didn't believe in God's word.
> *(Oh, yeah!)*
> All that I can say, God has made a way, and he's never failed me yet!
> Thank God we've . . .

". . . come this far by faith," we chant exuberantly, "leaning on the Lord! Trusting in his holy word! He's never failed me yet. . . ." Reed's quick modulation upward triggers a new chorus. Something has caught fire. It's not just the recurring choruses, or the intensity of the singing. The community seems to own this song.

As our last phrases slow into a spreading *ritard,* Brother Banks leans toward the microphone before him, ready to fan this fire into flame. Above the applause that breaks out, a great *Amen!* wells up as if from his very soul—gliding up a good half octave, and moving like a wave of sound out into the exuberant church house. Without missing a beat, he catches the spillage of our singing, repeating its wisdom like pearls worth savoring.

"Oh, yes! We've come this far by *faith!*' he shouts, "**Leanin' on the Lord!** *(Well . . .) Trustin'* in his holy name! *(Yes! Amen!)* He's *never failed* us yet!" *(Thank you, Jesus!)* Reed hasn't missed a beat either. Like the fingerings of a blues singer embellishing his sung lines, Reed echoes each of Brother Banks's exclamations with a flourish of piano improvisation.

Looking out at the gathering now, Brother Banks continues: "We're so glad to see that our sistah Joan, who's been sick, is back here with us! *(Amen!)* We *know* that God is a merciful God! *(Amen!)* We're glad to see that they've brought this little baby to be baptized this morning!" Unaware of his attention, little Kaelin, dressed in white, fusses in her mother's arms in the front pew. "Another friend of Jesus! " he adds. "We want to welcome all of you! Our pastor, choir leaders, choir, musicians, the *whole church body* want to *welcome you* to Our Lady of Lourdes **Holy Catholic Church!** *(Yes!)* We hope that when it is over you'll say, *I'm* **glad** *that I came!* I have somethin' to feast on all week! Somethin' that will help you when things don't seem to be goin' right *(Amen!)*—at home, on the job. We hope that no matter *what you have to go through,* you'll say,

I'm *glad* that I came! *(Yes!)* In Jesus' name!" As Reed completes his last several-octave flourish, Brother Banks haltingly climbs the three steps at the rear of the sanctuary to take his place beside Father Kirk.

"*Good morning, Church!*" exclaims Father Kirk. "*Good morning, Father!*" echoes throughout the church house.

*I*t all seems so natural. The easy flow of leadership from Brother Banks, to the choir, to Brother Banks, to Father Kirk. The effortless outpouring of Brother Banks's welcome, the cadence of his voice creating a music of its own against Reed's facile repartee. The shared sense among those who have gathered of how to enter the flow with their voiced acclamations.

How did it come to be this way, I wondered? And who is this man, "Brother Banks"? I've heard others comment about him. "He's the soul of the community. . . ." "He's an unusual blessing to this parish. . . ." "He never prays for himself. . . ." "He's a tower of strength. He's really the pillar of the church. . . ." "He's a man of God. If anybody's ever known or seen a child of God, he is one!" "It's just not right when he's not standing beside me. . . ." "As long as he's here, the soul of Our Lady of Lourdes is alive!"[2]

*A*s Father Kirk continues his greeting—welcoming little Kaelin, our new sister in baptism, her family, and all the church—Jesse Lee Banks stands ready beside him, hands folded against his chest, palms together, fingers slightly bent. Bits of grey hair and a tight curly beard surround his strong, black face. Above the collar of his white alb, the tips of a black bow-tie emerge. His body, it seems, is always ready—ready to move, ready to affirm, ready to embrace. Now, as Father Kirk invites the community to ask for "God's best gift of mercy," Brother Banks's hands open and begin to move with the music. "Oh, yes!" escapes from his lips, as the choir intones a soulful "Lord, have mercy!"

"*I* came to Lourdes in April, 1965." As we share a bite to eat after Sunday liturgy one warm April afternoon, sunlight streaming through the open door of the small CCD room, Brother Banks recalls his discovery of this little church.[3]

"At that time," he begins, "there was nothin' going on here. There wasn't no singin'. . . . All the windows of the church were broke! I was a member of All Hallows. I had children in All Hallows School and had to buy all those uniforms. There was no help, you had to do it yourself. By helpin' around the parish, I got some help with the tuition. I wanted my children to go to Catholic school. Myself, I'm from the country. I'm from Louisiana and I just didn't have the opportunity. . . . But I wanted them there, no matter what it costs," he continued, mentioning that he was working two jobs at the time. "I wanted them to learn about Jesus Christ. . . ."

"Up until that time, I'd never heard about Our Lady of Lourdes. It was just a mission." Father Oringo, pastor of All Hallows, "asked me to go down . . . and see if I could get a little of the glass out." The church had fallen into disrepair, and broken window glass covered the floor. "I came here to clean out, and the first thing I saw was the statue of the Holy Mother and Bernadette outside." There's a note of wonder in his voice as he describes his encounter with the image of Our Lady of Lourdes that still stands in front of the church. *"Somethin' struck me,"* he said emphatically. "Father told me that nothin' was going on down here. But I looked at that [statue] . . . and somethin' struck me. . . . There was some beautiful roses behind it. Nobody was waterin' them, but they were some of the most beautiful roses you've ever seen in your life. . . . I say to myself, this is where I want to come! . . . There was something here. . . . I felt like I was fulfilled. . . ."

Brother Banks goes on to tell of Father MacKinnon and Brother Gary's arrival from New York in 1968. The bishop had agreed that they could reopen Lourdes parish, and directed them to the church at the corner of Innes and Hawes. But Father MacKinnon "passed by and said, 'I don't see no church down there,' because it was all grown up with bushes in the yard. All kind a' wrecked cars" filled the lot beside the church. "All that stuff—it looked like a junkyard! I thought to myself: Father MacKinnon—he's from New York. He's gonna see the church and say 'Drag it into the ocean.' . . . But he saw it, and decided he's goin' to try it."

"At first, I hid from Father MacKinnon, thinkin', 'Well, I'm not going to meet him because I'm not an educated man. I don't have no money. I have a houseful of kids. . . . I don't want to get involved with those big time New Yorkers!'" Although secretly fearing that Father MacKinnon would change his mind and abandon Lourdes, Brother Banks would come to church, "sit in the back . . . and get out quickly so they couldn't meet me. I'd still come down early in the mornin' and work. Clean up what I could. Get on my knees and try to get out the glass and things."

One day, "Father MacKinnon came to my house and brought a chocolate pie and said 'I've been tryin' to meet Brother Banks, but he's too fast for me!'" "Finally I met him," recalls Brother Banks. "He talked like a Christian man, and he seemed to understand [our situation] here in Hunters Point." That was enough. "'You can depend on me!'" Brother Banks promised, although he quickly apprised the new pastor of the limits of his education. Think about Jesus' disciples, was Father MacKinnon response. They were fishermen, and Christ didn't tell them to go to school. "From that day, we became very good friends."

"You can depend on me!" That simple commitment marked the beginning of years of dedicated service to the parish and the surrounding community.

"Hunters Point was a jungle at that time," recalls Brother Banks. "The little children," always his special concern and a constant part of his prayer, were especially at risk. Brother Banks became instrumental in founding the Hunters Point Youth Park "on the hill" above the church. Using an old building that the city deemed unfit for a school, he and Aunt Bea Julia Middleton, the Youth Park's director, worked tirelessly to provide a place where children could come during lunch hour or after school to find help with their schoolwork and a bite to eat. Each Christmas, there are gifts for all the children, no matter how many. Until his recent decline in health, Brother Banks was present every day, caring for the children, supporting other staff members. "These children are our future," he said to me once. "They make mistakes, but they're human beings."

Whatever the need, Brother Banks is there—be it joining Liz Bell on Fridays to make sandwiches to distribute to homeless persons downtown, in the South of Market district, or setting up tables and chairs in the church hall, a task which he now must forego because of his weakened heart. "Brother Banks shows up!" commented one longtime member of Lourdes. "He just shows up! No matter what's happening, no matter how difficult it is to get there, he's there. He's present. Everybody counts on him. He doesn't need to do anything. It just means the world that he shows up!"

"Early in my time as pastor," recalls Father MacKinnon, "I realized the importance of Black liturgical leadership"—a concern shared by other predominantly African American parishes served by white clergy.[4] In the early 1970s, he and his small "staff" selected four men who were strong and faithful members of the Lourdes community. Jesse Banks was among them. The archdiocese had recently invited parishes to train lay ministers of the Eucharist. This became the context for raising up these Black men for liturgical leadership. Five other parishes joined the Lourdes initiative.

"For a year we worked with them, prayed with them, read Scripture with them . . . gave them a sense of liturgy and of what they were to do," recalled Sr. Martin de Porres in one conversation. They were to be more than altar servers, she stressed. "They were there to represent the people at the altar." These men would be "the forerunners of the permanent deaconate," she added, referring to a development that would emerge in the American church later in that same decade.

After a year of training—including prayer, Scripture study, liturgical preparation, and training for ministry—community members from the six parishes gathered at St. Paul of the Shipwreck for a ceremony of blessing and accepting these men for ministry. Brother Banks remembers the scene—his standing with the others, dressed in white albs, the church filled with people, some eleven priests, and the bishop present. Not only clergy but "everyone who was there came up and laid hands on them," noted Sr. Martin—a sign of the people's affirmation and acceptance of their important ministry.

Brother Banks's role in the Lourdes liturgy evolved gradually. But the importance of the community's "raising him up" for ministry remains. He's an elder of the community who functions liturgically as deacon—"but with the approval of the church!" emphasized Father Kirk as we spoke over coffee one December morning. "It's a whole concept of ecclesiology," he added. "The church *elevated* him . . . to that role and *accepts* him in that role, although he has more difficulty now because of his age and declining health. . . . But the church brought him forth. Today is the feast of St. Ambrose, and Ambrose was proclaimed a bishop by the people of Milan. *That's* the concept, *that's* the ecclesiology!"

"*I*t's now time for the prayer of the faithful," proclaims Brother Banks, standing beside Father Kirk on the platform at the rear of the sanctuary. The rain beat down insistently on the roof of the church house that first Sunday in Advent, 1993—just three short weeks after the archdiocese announced that Lourdes would remain open, despite the closure of nine other parishes. The church had been "reclothed" for the season in blues and purples. A large blue banner hung to the right of the sanctuary area, announcing a single word: "Watch!"

Minutes ago, Father Kirk challenged us to Wake up! this Advent, as he preached on how the season calls us to pay attention to what God is doing in our personal lives, in our relationships, and in how we are living as a community of faith. Returning to the chair, he invites a threefold profession of faith. "I do!" rings out three times, as people affirm their belief in a God who has come to dwell among us in Jesus.

Brother Banks now takes up the leadership, creating a framework of heartfelt prayer within which persons around the church can voice their needs, their concerns, and their thanks to God. Brother Banks begins slowly, his tone solemn and full of reverence. As he prays, the emotion of his heart seems to shape the rise and fall of his speech.

"We want to thank and give honor to God, for *waking us up this morning! (Oh yes!)* Another day in the land of the living. For giving us this day our daily bread." You can feel, in the hushed church, that people are with him, drawn into the prayer. He continues with a litany of thanks,

> for our pastor, who tells us the good news . . .
> for those who worked so hard on this church *(Yes, Lord!)* . . .
>   how beautiful it is, how clean . . .
> for our choir leaders and choir who carried the good news of God to a
>   great church last Sunday, where *people were **standin'*** because they felt
>   the Spirit o' God *(Amen!)* . . .

for our musicians, little Isaiah, for the blessin's he gives us in playin'
   that music *(Oh yes!)* . . .
for *our little children*, those round the altar, helpin' to serve God . . .
for our sister Amanda, whose recently passed her husband on to glory,
   (Oh yes, Lord!)
      who's come here to serve God . . .
for all those who are doing something in this parish . . .
      even though *times are rough* . . .
      they will **not give up**, but have *faith in God* . . .

Brother Banks's litany changes to intercession, as he asks the Almighty God

to help all those in need . . . the old people . . .
those who are out in the rain today . . .
those sleeping under the bridges, waiting to get a piece o' bread.

With great emotion he asks that "God will *forgive us* **all our sins** and guilty
stains," *(Yes!)*

make us *ready to* **accept** *him* and be awake . . .
that he will **keep us near** *to the sacred heart of God,* *(Oh yes, Lord!)*
no matter *what* we have to go through, *how* it may be,
we will *still wait* and be **ready to answer** when he comes. *(Amen!)* . . .
We pray, Father, for this parish, that it may stand *(Yes!)* . . .
that we may reach out to those who come, no matter *how* they come,
and say *"You are my sisters and brothers! We love you!"* *(Amen!)*
[For all this,] we pray to the Lord! *(Lord, hear our prayer!)*
Now, we invite your prayer. . . .

   For several minutes, persons from all parts of the church hold before God
and the community their needs and concerns, at times giving testimony to
God's faithfulness, thanking Him for "all the blessings of my life." Sensing
that these many prayers are complete, Brother Banks continues:

We ask God to take all these petitions . . . to his *throne of grace,*
and let his will be done, *(Yes!)*
but most of all help us to accept it . . . *no matter what it may be,*
as long as it's *his* will, we will say *thank you*, thank you. *(Amen!)*

   "We go now to the Holy Mother," he concludes, "asking her to go to her
Son . . . to help us in times like these." "Hail Mary . . ." begins the community, invoking their patroness, the "Holy Mother" whose "presence" first
touched and drew Brother Banks to Lourdes, to "pray for us, now and at the
hour of our death. Amen."

*A*s I listen this morning, I realize that Brother Banks's praying is part of the musicality of the whole liturgy. Simple prose becomes poetry on his lips. The cadence of his voice, the rise and fall, the pacing, the buildup of tension and resolution, and most of all his sense of timing, make music of his speech. His prayers seem to flow directly from the songs, or perhaps are at the heart of them. The fervor of his voice makes audible the community's shared spirituality. His doctors have warned him not to get excited—a sheer impossibility when he prays aloud, because it is on the wings of emotion and the movements of his body that his prayer rises to the throne of God. "When I pray I just gets happy!" I heard him say once.

"*B*rother Banks keeps the oral history alive, through his prayers and his storytelling," remarked Sister Irma Dillard one evening, nuancing my musical reflections and opening them in a new direction. "For Black Americans, oral history is *so* important! He never lets us forget! He makes us remember—where we came from and who we are. We are here today due to the struggles and sacrifices made by our parents and grandparents. Although I'm California born, educated, and citified, I am always reminded of my roots through Brother Banks's prayer and his storytelling. For many of us, our roots are in the rich soil of the South. Our roots are in the oral history—I cannot forget; we cannot forget. Brother Banks's simple and precious gift to us is that he never lets us forget!"[5]

*T*wo decades before he "discovered" Lourdes, Jesse Banks moved from Louisiana to San Francisco. The Second World War was underway. Like so many other African Americans, including some of the current members of Lourdes, he was lured from the South by the promise of employment. The Navy Shipyard in Hunters Point was in full swing with the war effort. Black Americans were being recruited as a workforce. Brother Banks tells of becoming a cook in the Navy, and of struggling to send part of his salary to his parents in Louisiana so they could buy a home. Raised in the Baptist tradition, it was while he was in the Navy that Jesse Banks became a Catholic. Following the war he married and, with his wife Deona, raised seven children, supporting them with two jobs—driving a Muni streetcar and working for the Caltrans Highway Maintenance Division.

*O*ne Sunday after liturgy, as Joan Dill, Brother Banks, and I sit in a small room adjacent to the church, we talk about the significance of music in his early religious experience.[6]

"Brother Banks," begins Joan, "you were raised on a Louisiana plantation. From what I know about plantation life, spirituals were always sung. Music was . . . a form of support, a form of protest. . . . They sang about their life, they sang about the time, they sang about what kept them going, the faith that kept them going."

"Oh, yes," replies Brother Banks, eyes twinkling behind his hornframed glasses as he spoke. "They would sing until the tears ran out of their eyes, because it was from the heart. . . . In those days, you'd meet someone, and if you talked with 'em about the president, they didn't know nothin' about that! But if you said somethin' about Jesus . . . 'Oh yes, I know somethin' about Him!' They firmly believed in God and firmly believed in what they were singin': 'Oh, how I love Jesus!' 'He's sweet I know!' 'Leaning on the Lord!'" he continues, inviting us into a litany of images from the songs of his youth. "'He brought us this far!' He takes care of us. . . . The songs were based on the way they lived, what they went through. And they sang them from their heart. . . . My mother used to sing all the time—'Oh, how I love Jesus!' . . . 'At the Cross'. . . 'Christ loved me first,' songs like that. . . . Songs was the only consolation they had . . . when they were worried. Maybe they didn't sing it just the way it's in the book, but they would sing from their heart. . . . The songs seemed to help them to carry through on the journey . . . seemed to give them faith, belief, strength to carry on.

"When we used to come together on Sunday," he continues, remembering their weekly worship gatherings, "they would sing the songs, and it was upliftin' to them. And they believed in God in those songs. . . . They gave testimony. . . . One would tell what he went through, 'What God did for me!' and 'God will do the same thing for you.' No matter what the situation may be, it would bring them joy. . . . They would get strength through that. . . . That's why they would want to meet together. . . . They looked at the strength of God, what *God* was doin' for them, what he would do for them. Through these songs, through their bein' together, they would strengthen one another.

"That's the way the old gospel hymns came, back in those days," he says, as if to conclude. "God, he didn't care about no color or race, he just cared for people. No matter how poor I am, or how ignorant I am, I have a friend in Jesus who will care for me . . . if I only believe and do his will. That's where they got their faith from in those days, because they knew that they may not have no doctors, no lawyers, but they could always go to him, to God, anytime of day or night. They didn't have to worry about the language they used— they didn't need this verb, this noun. They could go to God in their own way, in their heart, and he'd hear them."

"My mother, she could talk about Jesus, because she knew what he'd done for her!" The image became a recurring refrain in our conversations. Perhaps

Brother Banks's most touching story—a tale of faith lived, of strength in the face of injustice, and of song that wells up in a heart that trusts God—was recounted in a rare but treasured Sunday afternoon conversation.

"I love God," Brother Banks began. "I *believe* in God, because I *know* what he brought me from! The old cotton fields. My people back in the country were poor people. My father went to school three days in his life. My mother went to the fourth grade. In the country we had no school buses, no regular school. We went to school from October to March in Louisiana. In winter time it would rain. In December and January it would freeze up, so we'd be just stayin' in the house. Like in the Bible, sometimes it don't rain in the summertime, so we didn't raise anything. We had two rooms and a kitchen; the kitchen had a dirt floor. We were living poor.

"My mother, the faith she had in God! She *believed* in God. One summer it didn't rain, so we didn't raise nothin'. The boss man came one day when it was cold. He had to have more food for his cows and horses, he said. My father told him we didn't have anything, and showed him a few potatoes. 'I got to have what you have,' he said. He took everything we had in the house in the middle of the winter! No stores around, nothin'. No jobs. My father—it was the only time I saw him get on his knees and cry. He wanted to talk about the white people, but my mother said 'No, those are my sisters and brothers. We have to love them. They think they're doin' what's right.' I never forgot that. She didn't see no race! She said, 'That's our brothers and sisters, we've got to love them.'

"They'd taken everything!" I sense the pain in Brother Banks's voice as he remembers the scene. "Mother said, 'We have an old gum tree out in front. I can boil the bark with rock salt in the cooker. We can live off that. . . . God will take care.' My father, he'd go to work on the cane farm. They wouldn't let him come home until all the cane was cut. After Christmas, the house was leakin'. He had to leave to work on the cane farm. The children didn't have shoes. My mother, she was smilin'." This last comment catches me of guard. Noticing my surprise, Brother Banks interprets the wisdom of her smile. "I seen that God would take care of you if you had that faith! No matter *what*, he would make a way!

"The children came down with whoopin' cough," he continues. "No doctors. Mother would make her own tea, but that wasn't doin' any good. 'I'm going to town,' she said. 'I'm going to beg for them to give me a bone so the children will get better." None of the medicine we made was doing any good. We had rags we used to wrap our feet in. Called 'em our Sunday shoes.

"We were happy to go into town with mother. She knocked on the boss man's door. 'Just give us a bone. The kids are sick.' 'I would,' his wife answered, 'but my husband has these coon dogs, and I have to boil the bones and give them to the dogs.' My mother said, 'I understand.' But before she got out of the house, the woman said, 'Wait! I just thought of something. I'll take these bones and throw them out into the yard. And if you can get to the bones before the dogs do, you can have them. But if you get bit, you can't holler! You can't tell nobody, because you'll get *me* in trouble. And you know what they'll do to you!'

"I seen my mother, then." His eyes flash and his voice full of emotion as he recounts the scene as if for the first time. "The dogs were prancin'. The woman took that big bone and threw it out in the yard. The gates were open. My mother went in there, and those dogs ran as if someone was shootin' at them. I'll never forget it! My mother went in that mud, and picked up those bones. And the dogs didn't bother her! I tell you," he comments again, "faith in God! What he can do for you! God can take care of you! He can do these things!"

Tears run down Brother Banks's cheeks as he continues the story. "She brought the bones, and she said, 'We'll go home through the valley 'cause there's no snakes. We'll boil these bones!' We had pots to boil the clothes in. . . . We were walkin' behind her, holdin' each other's hands. She stopped and said, 'Lord have mercy!' I thought it was a turtle. They have turtles in Louisiana. 'Look children, under the vine!' There was somethin' we call "poke salad"—something green that grows like mustard, but it's bitter. They don't grow in the wintertime; but it was green under that vine! For as far back as you could see was these greens, and they were about that tall." He motions to indicate the height. "She said, 'Look what God give us! We have meat and greens to eat!' *That's* why I have faith in God. I *know* what he can do!

"Mother said, 'Go tell the children to come and we can get the greens.' We hadn't had anythin' to eat but bark. The children went out and they blowed the horn!" he exclaimed, adding as if to explain to me: "We didn't have no telephone. But they had a tune they'd blow [on the horn] if it was good news, and a tune they blew if someone died. This was a good tune! People came and said, 'What's wrong?' 'Sister Sue's in the valley, and she has greens!' 'What kind of greens in the wintertime?' I went back there and my mother was singing, 'Oh, how I love Jesus because he first loved me. . . .' She boiled them greens, and the children got better.

"That's what give me so much faith in God. I *know* he helped us. I seen what he did when you didn't have nothin'. Nowhere to turn. No welfare. Nobody give us nothin'. But *God* provided. He didn't just feed the Hebrew children! . . . I *know* what God can do!"

*T*his touching story of Brother Banks's childhood speaks eloquently of a triumphant faith in the face of prejudice, racism, and injustice—a faith spontaneously expressed in song. The simple lyrics his mother sang in the field of greens—"Oh, how I love Jesus, because he first loved me"— belie the depth of spirituality, a belief that God's justice will triumph no matter what forces work to oppress. It's no wonder that "the old songs" are a treasured part of this community's repertoire.

Brother Banks's stories have alerted me to the layers of family, social, and religious history that are deeply intertwined in the music of the Lourdes community. He exemplifies a legacy of songs learned as children and handed on from one generation to another—songs that embody a belief that we "can't turn around [because] we've come this far by faith"; songs that continue to shape and express the community's spirituality and worship. In his experience, singing was never reserved for a few, but something everyone did. Spontaneously. It was a mode of testimony, a way of resisting the forces that worked to cripple, oppress, overtake, or to rob them of their God-given dignity and rights.

I've learned that the songs Brother Banks remembers from his youth and young adulthood and which he identifies by title or significant line—"He's sweet I know," "Leaning on the Lord," "In the cross," "Christ loved me first," "Oh, how I Love Jesus," "He brought us this far," "He takes care of us"— represent a significant strand in the tapestry of gospel music.[7] His childhood coincided with a period of development in Black religious culture, around the turn and early decades of the last century, when European American hymns were incorporated into the tradition of Black sacred song. During this time Black Christians were developing their religious institutions and borrowing from others what might be useful for their religious purposes—in this case hymns with lyrics that spoke to the religiosity of Black communities. However, while retaining their lyrics and in some measure the basic melodic/harmonic shape, Black congregations transformed them according to their own aesthetic and improvised performance practice. These "gospelized hymns" became part of the living tradition of Black sacred music that continues to be handed on from generation to generation at Lourdes.

*F*rom my earliest days at Lourdes, I was aware of the fragility of Brother Banks's health. On August 15, 1993, my first Sunday at Lourdes, he told the community of a recent hospitalization. The doctors warned him that he needs serious surgery but fear he would not survive it. Months later, Brother Banks recalled the experience:

"I know that God has been with me through this. . . . I have such terrible pain in the heart area, now. . . . The veins are leakin'. . . . Once I was in the hospital, and they said, 'If you don't have this operation, you're not gonna make it!' I said, 'I'm gonna believe in God.' . . . When I got out, that song Brother Walter sings, "Near the Cross," that song came to me. I told Sistah Pat," referring to Pat Goodall, "'cause I figured it would probably be my last time here. . . . [That Sunday] I came to church. I wasn't able, but I came to church anyway 'cause I figured that was going to be it. And I told her I wanted to sing that song. She got me a chair and put me down in the front. She let me sing it."

As he recounted the story, I remembered the scene well. Just after Communion time, Brother Banks, escorted by John Brown, walked to the front of the choir. Pat Goodall brought a chair and placed it near the altar. Moving slowly, he sat down, and in halting phrases, began to sing, "Jesus, keep me near the cross . . ." Reed slipped a gentle piano accompaniment under his singing, and the choir joined softly so as not to drown out his voice: "there's a precious fountain . . ." he continued. Completing one verse, he realized the effort was enough. Leaning on John Brown's arm once again, he returned to his seat. As I left the Bay area four months later for my Christmas travels, I wondered to myself if Brother Banks would still be alive when I returned. But alive he was! This was only the first of several experiences of serious illness and hospitalization. Each time he returned to the community more grateful for "another day in the land of the living."

On the eve of his seventy-seventh birthday in September, 1994, Brother Banks came to a Thursday night rehearsal. One by one, he thanked members of the choir by name for all the help and encouragement they have given him. Like an African *griot*, he honored each of them, speaking eloquently of the importance of their love in these his later years. At seventy-seven he now works to complete his G.E.D., since his childhood education extended through the tenth grade only. Yet it's clear that the wisdom he carries in his heart and mind are not measured in degrees or diplomas. Father Kirk, who was present that September evening, expressed it well: "Brother Banks, as long as you are here, the soul of Our Lady of Lourdes is alive."

*F*ather's Day, 1995. "Let us rise in the name of Jesus!" Arms aloft, Brother Banks invites us to welcome the Gospel. "I am the Bread of Life . . ." we sing. The slow, stately rhythms fill the church house, as Father Kirk readies to proclaim the Lukan text—Jesus' feeding of the crowd at sunset. . . . "Taking the five loaves and two fishes, Jesus raised his eyes to heaven, pronounced a blessing over them, broke them, and gave them to his disciples to distribute to the crowd. They all ate until they had enough. *(Amen!)* What was left over filled twelve baskets." "The Gospel of the Lord!" he concludes. *"Praise to you, Lord Jesus Christ!"*

Reed Fromer plays gently as Brother Banks makes his way slowly down the three steps to join Father Kirk at the front of the gathering. "A few weeks ago," comments Father Kirk, "we had an eminent preacher speak to us on the values of motherhood." There's a ripple of affirmation as people turn to acknowledge Jean Alexander. "Today is the feast of Corpus Christi, the Body and Blood of Christ, which is a feast of sharing. And one of the great examples of sharing and of fatherhood has been Brother Jesse Banks. *(Amen!!!)* And so I've asked Brother Banks to speak to us on fatherhood." *(Amen! Amen! Applause . . .)*

Brother Banks has clearly orchestrated what will follow. Reed's improvisation shifts, and Pat Goodall, now standing beside Brother Banks, begins to sing slowly, "Lord, give me an un-wav-er-ing faith!" Before her first line is set down,

Brother Banks's voice can be heard: *Oh, yes!* ". . . to help me stand the storm," she continues, "when I would do wrong, *(Oh, have mercy!)* Unwavering faith! *(Oh yes!)* An unwavering faith!" *(Have mercy!)* Brother Banks's exclamations punctuate Pat's phrases as the song swells to a climax . . . "Faith when this life *(Yes!)* has knocked me to my knees, *(Yes, Lord!)* faith in the midnight hours when my mind needs relief, Un-wav-er-ing faith. *(Yes, Lord!)* Un-wa-ver-ing faith."

When the *Amens* and applause have died down, Brother Banks begins. "My brothers and sisters, this is a day that is set aside to honor fathers. . . . We're thankful to God that we're here, *(Amen!)* not only because it's Father's Day, but because we've come to serve God! *(Amen!)* Here in Hunters Point, if you look at conditions, it's not a happy Father's Day. *(Hum . . .)* . . . As Sistah Goodall was singin', we need that *unwaverin'* faith. That's what's brought us this far, and that's the only thing gonna save us! *(Amen!)* You know back in slavery, Abraham Lincoln freed the slaves, but he didn't do it alone. It was those old people, people with their children, prayin' and goin' to God, having that faith in God, *(Yes!)* that freed them. *(Yes! Amen!)* And if we are to make it in Hunters Point, that's what we're gonna need. *(Al'right!)* That unwaverin' faith. *(Oh yes, Lord!)*

"I'm Brother Jesse Banks, for those who don't know me. I'm a member of this parish. I've been here since April, 1965. An old man now. And when I first came here, they didn't have these beautiful windows and things around—only a few members. *But I stayed here* because *somebody had that unwavering faith.* I didn't come to worship this building, I came to serve God. *(Al'right! Amen!)* . . . And I'm telling you, God has heard their prayer *(Yes!)* and has brought me safe this far. *(Oh, yes!)* Friday night I was in my home. . . . I couldn't breathe and I couldn't get up. They had to *call the emergency* to come get me and take me to the hospital. But I'm here today! *(Thank you, Jesus!)* If it had not been for you and our pastor, I would a' been packed under the ground many years ago. But if we have that *unwaverin' faith*, as Sistah Pat was singin' . . . we can make it! I don't care *how steep* those mountains is, or *deep the valleys* is, we can make it! *(That's right!)* That's what we're gonna need. *(Amen!)*

"I came out here to Hunters Point in the early part of 1950. I moved out here because they sent those pamphlets around sayin', Come out to Hunters Point, where there's room where you can raise your children. The rent gonna be cheap. Gonna fix the houses up. They didn't do that. Rent never got cheap. *(Laughter . . . Amen, Brother Banks!)* They've been fooling us ever since we've been out here. Then, next thing, they were gonna build a school out here, all the way up to the 12th grade, so our children won't have to be bussed. *(That's right!)* . . . Gonna build a swimming pool . . . gonna put a tennis court out here, and our children would be able to come home at night and sleep in their own beds. But the answer was, 'We don't have the money.' . . . The next thing came up, they was gonna build homes out here. . . . Our Lady of Lourdes was involved. . . . There was men and women ready to work. . . . When the contractors come out the next day, they went back home. We went out to see what happened.

They said, 'They're not trained. They can't even drive the nails through.' When we asked why didn't they train 'em like they promised, they said there was no money. So the young men and women didn't get no jobs. They didn't get no homes. It's been that way ever since we've been here in Hunters Point. *(Amen!)* . . . We need that *unwaverin'* faith! We need to go back to God! . . .

"Now, I'm from Louisiana. Yes, I picked cotton, pulled them sacks, two hundred pounds. *(That's right!)* . . . Sometimes had nothin' to eat, nothin' to drink. *But my mother would come out,* '*Oh, how I love Jesus!*' She didn't let nothin' come between her and God! *(That's right!)* And that's what we're gonna have to do. We're gonna have to go to God and ask him to take over . . . ask him to help us out here. . . . They want this hill now," referring to the hill behind Lourdes, "[to build] beautiful homes. *(Yes!).* . . . They want to rezone it so they can do just like they did in the Fillmore," referring to another predominantly African American part of San Francisco. "When you come back and try to get a home they say, you ain't got no money! *(Yes! Al'right!)* You're gonna have to move on, after all these years you've been livin' here. *(Yes!)* We need to go back to God *(Yes!)* with that unwavering faith. . . .

"What I'm tryin' to tell the fathers of today, grandfathers, and all other fathers —you're gonna have to have faith in God. *(Yes!)* . . . You know Job, who lived a long time ago. He had faith in God. *(Yes!)* Sometimes when people get doin' good, they forget about God. *(Amen!!!!)* We need God in our lives. *(Yes!)* . . . All this stuff they tell us out here, that it's gonna be a little better. Now, after all these years, they're gonna come out here and start training. . . . But remember, this is election year. *(That's right! That's right!)* *They* **always** *do that!* *(Every time!)* . . . They're gonna come out here and say, *look what we've been doin'.* *(Yes!)* But what have they been doin'? *(Nothin'!)* Poor people out here starvin', can't get no jobs. *(Yes!)* . . . Some nights you can't sleep with those sirens! Runnin' after our boys and girls like we used to run rabbits back in the country. . . . They catch 'em, and take 'em to jail. *(Yes!)* . . .

"In 1945, I was in the United States Navy. Just came from Hawaii. . . . I got a job with Muni, driving streetcars. . . . The news was all over: *There ain't gonna be no more war! We're not gonna fight war no more!* They had people comin' here from every country," Brother Banks recalls, referring to the founding of the United Nations. "Gonna make history here in San Francisco. . . . [But when] they were gettin' ready to sign [the agreement], the speaker of the house said, 'One minute! I have a priest back here, I have ministers. Let 'em come and ask God's blessin' on this.' 'No, we don't need God!' [came the response]. 'We don't need God! This is somethin' for man, now.' They had to go and tell the priests and [ministers], 'You can go home. We don't need you.' That's like tellin' God, 'You can go out the door now.' *(Amen!)* Before they left the city, *wars had started breaking out! Places we never heard of! And there's been wars ever since! People starving to death!* You see, *without God,* we can't do it. *(Amen!)* We don't know *how* to do it. We *need* God. *(That's right!)*

66

"That's what I'm sayin' to these fathers, we must keep that unwaverin' faith in God. *(Amen!)* We must trust him. We need him in Hunters Point. *(Yes!)* We need him in our church, *(Yes!)* in our jobs, *(Yes!)* in the homes, *(Yes!)* and everywhere. . . . We need God everyday! . . . Now they don't allow 'em to bring up the name of our Lord in schools. . . . The reason they're doin' that is because they see where God brought us. And *God* is not gonna tell us that he run out of money. *He's* not gonna tell us that he don't have time. He's gonna bless us. *(Amen!)* And that's what fathers have to do. . . . *Our only hope* is Jesus! *Ask him* to lead and guide us! Every morning! I can't get on my knees now, but I can get on the side of my bed and thank him for givin' me this day our daily bread. *(Amen!)* Let's do that from our heart, everyday of the week." *(Amen!!)*

Now, as if to gather up his whole message in an act of praise, Brother Banks invites "Sistah Louise" to come forward to sing. To Reed's accompaniment, Louise Wood takes the mike in hand, puts her arms gently around Brother Banks, and begins slowly:

When Christ shall come *(Take your time!)* // with shout of acclamation, *(Oh, yes!)* and take me home, *(Sing it, Louise!)* // what joy will fill my heart! *(Oh yes, Lord!)* Then I shall bow *(Oh, have mercy!)* // in humble adoration, *(Yes!)* and there proclaim, *(Oh, yes!)* // my God how great thou art! *(Yes!)*

Voices around the church join in, swelling the sound in a chorus of reverent faith:

Then sings my soul my Savior God to thee, *(Yes, Lord!)* How great thou art, *(Oh, yes!)* // how great thou art! *(Oh, yes!)* Then sings my soul, my Savior God to thee, *(Oh yes, Lord!)* How great thou art, // how great thou art![8]

"*H*ere I am an old man," Brother Banks remarked to me one day, "but here I am. And comin' here to Lourdes, I can be with you all and hold up my head and say, '*Praise God!* **Praise God!** *Praise him! Love him!*' And I can still pray, 'Help those who have gone on, that they may rest with you, in peace with you, where there won't be *no more sorrow*, no pain, no misery, for *you have prepared a place!*' O Father, when you see 'em you will say, '*Well done! Come on in!*' Oh, have mercy!" His voice trails off a bit, and then as if musing to himself, Brother Banks adds, "Must be a wonderful place over there! . . . Hear those angels come before the throne of God, singin', singin'. . . like we've never heard before! . . ."

*S*ingin', singin'. . . like we've never heard before!

Chapter Five

LOURDES' MIRACLES

—GROWING UP IN THE CHURCH—

*T*o grow up at Lourdes is to grow up in the music. Rarely is there enough room on Reed's piano bench for all the children who like to slip in beside him. Seldom does Isaiah Brown leave his trap set that another child doesn't sit down, eager to experiment with sticks against drum heads or brushes against cymbals. To grow up at Lourdes is to "catch" the sounds and rhythms of a vast repertoire, to learn the emotions generated, the ritual behavior expected, and the collective assumptions about faith that are carried on the lyrics, melodies, and rhythms of those who sing. To grow up in the music is to receive a legacy of song and faith. It is to find one's voice. To know that one's voice is appreciated and welcomed. Your voice counts! "You are our future!"

A tussle broke out in the fifth pew one Thursday evening during rehearsal. Three-year-old Tyree McDuff was intent on grabbing the microphone of my tape-recorder despite my resistance. Being the stronger and the more determined, Tyree secured the mike, lifted it to his mouth, and began to imitate the lead singers he'd watched so often. A bit embarrassed by the confusion—I was still new to Lourdes and to my role of "sitting in" on choir rehearsals—I tried to stop his "performance," but to no avail. To my amazement, this three-year-old had mastered one of the community's best loved songs: "Lord, Help Me to Hold Out!" Curly black head aloft, microphone raised to his mouth, his body moving rhythmically as he sang, Tyree was now inscribing its lyrics on my tape.

Like several other children, Tyree was a regular at Thursday rehearsals. His mother, Denise Alexander, "grew up in the choir" herself, learning some of the repertoire she now sings as she "played on the floor of the church" during rehearsals in the early days of the Gospel Choir. My tussle with Tyree over the microphone was one of many—he intent on taking his role, and already familiar with lyrics and rhythms of many songs. One evening, I watched him climb onto a chair which he had carefully placed behind his grandmother, Jean Alexander, as she rehearsed one of her leads. Just outside her range of vision, Tyree drew himself up to his full stature, and with right hand to his mouth as if to hold a microphone, imitated her every move.

Ebony Baxter, a slender child, tall for her eight years, was another regular during my first years at Lourdes. One evening I noticed her dancing and singing unselfconsciously in the center aisle as the choir rehearsed. Minutes later, she slipped into the pew beside me, and at my prompting, recounted the events of her day at school—scenes from the life of a fourth grader. Of all her activities, she informed me, singing and dancing were by far her favorites. Our conversation lulled momentarily as the choir began to rehearse Grayson Brown's "My Shepherd is the Lord." To my surprise, Ebony began to sing the alto line, clearly able to hold her own against the other vocal parts and accompaniment. "I'm an alto," she informed me minutes later. The soprano line was much too high for her voice. Like her grandmother, Aline Bobbitt, who sang with the choir, Ebony has her sights set on doing the same. Next I knew, Ebony was on her feet again. After a brief exchange with Naja Turner, she walked to the front of the church, stopping just behind Pat Goodall. Like a well-trained mime artist, Ebony began to mirror Pat's every move, catching each rhythmic gesture, echoing each energetic sway, as Pat directed the choir through the spirited verses of "He Keeps Doing Great Things for Me!" So this is how it happens, I mused to myself.

Intrigued by the growing musical astuteness of Tyree and Ebony, I began to pay more attention to the children on Sunday morning, inquiring in my own mind about how they learned the music. It was late in the liturgy one Sunday. The choir was singing the final chorus of a Communion meditation, "What Shall I Do." Ernestine Harris's voice soared above the ensemble, adding her last, "You'll come through!" above the choir's final chord. As the ensuing *Amens* subsided, I heard a small child repeating the choir's closing line. Glancing down, I noticed a young boy, no more than three or four years old, his grey trousered legs swinging to the rhythm as he finished *his* song, unaware of those around him. It took me a week to discover that this was Cameron Isles, Rose's grandson. "He's such a musical child," commented Tina Edwards, a cousin of his, some months later. And he loves the music at Lourdes. When the family is getting ready for church on Sunday, Cameron often urges, "Hurry up! We're gonna miss it!"

Children naturally congregate in the front pew on Sunday morning, and Cameron is often among them. I sat behind a row of youngsters one week, each one dressed with care, each "lookin' as good" as anyone in the church house. Naja Turner's well-braided hair sparkled with pink hair clips. Coy Lacy looked smart in a freshly ironed white shirt. Tyree McDuff sported a new vest of bright orange African fabric, his grandmother's handiwork no doubt.

It struck me, as the liturgy progressed, that this front pew location puts the children at the center of the action. No wonder it holds such attraction. From here they can see choir members emerge from the center aisle at the beginning of the liturgy, watch them move "in step" to their places in the sanctuary. They can hear the feeling carried on the voice of a lead singer, and observe every movement of her body. They can feel the vigor of Father Kirk's preaching and watch his energetic movements around the front of the church as he speaks. They can see Brother Banks's hands in motion and hear the nuances of his emotion-filled prayer. Inches away from the baby grand piano, they can feel its vibrations, or at times slip over behind Reed or Isaiah to watch them play. They are drawn into the joining of hands, the reaching out across the center aisle, as the community prays the Lord's Prayer just before Communion time. Most importantly, they are free to enter the music on their own terms—to move their bodies freely, uninhibited by pews or kneelers—to clap, to sing, or just to watch the music happening around them.

I was marveling to myself at how well-behaved this string of youngsters were, how engaged in the music, when suddenly a skirmish broke out between two of them. In no time, the woman next to me had swooped up the smaller of the two and set him down on her abundant lap. The gesture made it clear that prayer was the most important thing going on here. And in a community where kinship is not limited to bloodlines—where it takes a village to raise a child—the correction of a neighbor is how children learn. I mused to myself that love is perhaps the best discipline, and in this church house, love is abundant. The dispute was put to rest instantly. Moments later, the tot was resting content in the woman's arms, soothed by her voice and the undulating movements of her body as she rocked gently to the ebb and flow of an old spiritual, "Thank you, Lord! Thank you, Lord! Thank you, Lord, I just want to thank you, Lord."

Watching the children that morning, I realized that for most youngsters at Lourdes, an ability to participate in the music is just a question of time, of lived experience. They are socialized into the music in a very organic way— learning through imitation, observation, and participation. At the same time, they are absorbing the cultural sensitivities that allow them to appreciate, to value, and to participate knowledgeably in the community's musical prayer in ways that are bodily, spiritual, and emotional.

Moreover, they learn the music "ensemble" in the midst of a music-making community. This insight dawned on me one Sunday as I watched two small girls next to me in the pew—the younger, held aloft in her mother's arms, hands waving and feet swinging; the older, dancing in place beside her. Suddenly, I had a new way of perceiving what I was witnessing. In the early twentieth century, Carl Orff and Zoltán Kodály built their alternative systems of music education around the concept of ensemble music making.[1] In contrast to the model of a child learning music alone—struggling to make little fingers perform piano scales or tiny windpipes to execute a steady trumpet pitch, only to join a performing group much later—Orff and Kodály place children within a performing ensemble from the start. Each child is given a musical role they can achieve "without mistakes." They are free not only to play or sing assigned parts, but to make up their own.[2] As I mused on this, the younger of the two girls began to "sing" rather loudly—a child's approximation of what she was hearing, while her sister continued her dancing—both lost in the mosaic of sound the swirled around them.

My train of thought went further. I remembered the great *Tshikona*, the national dance of the Venda of southern Africa. In *Tshikona*, points out ethnomusicologist John Blacking, the number of unique parts expands to match the number of persons participating.[3] Each has a distinctive role in the singing and dancing. This flies in the face of a common wisdom: reduce the musical complexity so that many can partake. Create a simple line, an uncouplex rhythm. The result, as often experienced in contemporary worship, is usually boring and unmemorable. *Tshikona* performance creates an alternative, one not unlike what I was finding at Lourdes. Everyone contributes to the polyphonic whole—adding a rhythmic bodily movement, a shout, a bit of harmony. For the Venda, the goal is to develop individuality-in-community.

The liturgical and spiritual implications are astounding.

*T*here's an assumption at Lourdes that everyone has something to contribute. Roles have been created so that children can take their part. On a cold, November Sunday, I watch eleven-year-old Niesha Smith seated next to Father Kirk on the sanctuary platform, just opposite Brother Banks. A brightly colored stole draped over her lovely high-bodiced dress marks her ministry. She sits poised, the Sacramentary resting comfortably on her lap, awaiting the moment when she will lift it high so that Father Kirk can pray with arms outstretched. Earlier in the service, she and Maurice Moran processed behind the choir, each carrying one of the ritual books—Lectionary and Sacramentary—to their resting places in the sanctuary. A bit later in the liturgy, Pat Goodall will announce, "It's now time for the children to bring up the gifts!" A small trio, chosen this morning, will wander down the center aisle, carrying "gifts of bread and wine" to the altar, as two parishioners prepare it for Eucharist.

During Communion, little ones carried in arms or led by hand will come forward to receive a blessing from Father Kirk, and most often a word of love and encouragement.

One of the most cherished and engaging roles taken by young members of the community is to lead the sung "Amen" at the conclusion of the Eucharistic Prayer. Mike in hand, one or two children intone their acclamations—"Sing it over!" "Praise the Father!" "Alleluia!"—in rapid call and response with the familiar strains of the "'Lilies of the Field' Amen." Niesha Smith and Ebony Baxter are already initiates. Others wait in the wings for their turn.

I was in the choir loft one Sunday taking photos—an adventure I chose not to repeat because I felt so distant from the action!—but a vantage point from which to watch Ebony as she assumed her lead. There she stood in the open space between the sanctuary and pews, surrounded by the community, her head just taller than the altar top behind her. Bright ribbons adorned her braided hair. A printed stole, reaching almost to the tips of her black strapped shoes, bedecked her salmon-colored frock. Her grandmother looking on from the choir, who were now positioned on the steps behind the altar. As Ebony began, "Sing it over!" against the clapping, rhythmic swaying, and jubilant "Amens" of those around her, I could see young Juwan Graves slip out of the second pew into the center aisle—a better place from which to see the action.

At four and five years old, Naja Turner and Tyree McDuff seemed ready to take their turn at this ministry. Melodies were well-practiced at choir rehearsal the previous Thursday. Sunday dawned, and the two youngsters arrived dressed for the occasion. Long before Father Kirk reached the closing Doxology of the Eucharistic Prayer, Tyree was standing just behind Pat Goodall, gently tugging on her choir robe, lest she forget to hand him the microphone! Naja, a bit more shy, hesitated a moment then took her place beside him in front of the altar. Applause and *Amens* erupted as they sang their last "Alleluia!" Delight! Appreciation! *Amen!!*

*I*t was the feast of Corpus Christi, 1994. I arrived early with a friend from Brazil. Already, the church and parish center were abuzz with activity. As we parked the car, Ebony Perryman—a petite, slightly reserved child, who is the apple of her grandmother's eye—walked quickly past us along the sidewalk ahead. Her long, silk white dress floated just above her patent leather shoes. A white veil framed her black ringlets. Other children scurried around, several dressed beautifully in white dresses, some quite elaborate, boys in white suits. One white-clad youngster, a crown of pearls circling her dark hair, paused with her family near the doors of the church for a photo.

First Communion Sunday is always a bit chaotic, as visitors and extended family members swell the usually crowded church house, anxious to catch sight of the children as they walk in procession and take various roles of leadership. That June morning was no exception. The front rows were crowded with First Communicants, each with two "sponsors," who would sit with them throughout the liturgy—one of Louise Wood's many preparations to make this a very special event. Families squeezed into the pews around them, some with video cameras in hand.

It was almost midpoint in the liturgy—a certain calm having settled over the church house—when Father Kirk, completing his proclamation of the Gospel, looked out at the children in white before him, and invited each to come forward to give a brief "testimony." The custom was no doubt Louise Wood's initiative, a way to allow the children to tell the community what First Communion means to them. One by one, the children came forward to offer a "word of faith"—some more timidly than others—a poem or prayer they've composed, a story, or a little statement they'd prepared. You could feel people leaning forward in their seats, trying to catch a glimpse and hear the voices of these little witnesses.

As Ebony Perryman's turn arrived, she walked confidently across the front of the room to the piano—displacing Reed who, as her sponsor, was about to assume a new role as her "godparent." Despite her young age, Ebony already sang with a youth gospel choir in the Bayview district, and was learning to play piano under Reed's guidance. Ebony seated herself and began to play, "Yes, Jesus loves me!" —a song generations of African American children have known and loved. Immediately, a humming began to arise from people around the church, then unabashedly they joined the song to Ebony's accompaniment: "Yes, Jesus loves me! Yes, Jesus loves me! Yes, Jesus loves me, the Bible tells me so!" Terse words, simple truth. As Ebony and the other children completed their testimonies, Father Kirk commented, "The children have just preached the homily!"

It's not only the children who shine that are noticed. Awards are one way Lourdes expresses appreciation, love, and support for its members, and children are part of the family.

"We the people of Our Lady of Lourdes, thank God for the gift of our children," read Father Kirk from the colorful certificate he held in his hand. It was the second ceremony of its kind during the spring of '94. Then calling several of the youngest members of the community to come forward—Maurice Moran, Anna Marie Molina, Cameron Isles, Niesha Smith, Coy Lacy, David Wood, Telisha Molina, Juwan Graves, Jessica Howard, and Ebony Perryman—Father Kirk offered each of them a small gift and read the citation inscribed on the accompanying certificate:

May the Lord bless_____, a child of God upon whom His favor rests.

Several young adults were offered similar words of affirmation:

We the people of Our Lady of Lourdes,
recognizing that the future of our church rests in the hands of our young adults,
do herewith honor_____ for the good he/she has already accomplished
and voice our hope for what is yet to be.

Inviting young adults Denise Alexander, Michael Edwards, Chantal Vez, and Tina Edwards to come forward, Father Kirk recognized them as holding "the future of our church in their hands."

*T*here's no safe place for children in Hunters Point!" commented a health-care professional to one of the mothers of the parish. In a single week of May 1995, four young people had been shot to death in Hunters Point. One of these killings took place in front of her home and was witnessed by her seven-year-old son. The experience affected him deeply.

The support and "incorporation" young people experience within this church house is in marked contrast to the dangers they face on the streets and in their neighborhoods. The shootings of that unseasonably warm week in May of '95 are but the tip of an iceberg. Senseless killings. Children gone before they reach their adult years. Parents and grandparents among the Lourdes community have lost their "babies" to an epidemic of violence.

Drugs are another omnipresent challenge. "I remember strong mothers and fathers helping us around the community," commented Corey Monroe, a young adult, in his Kwanzaa address one year. "For some reason, a lot of them got strung out on drugs. Drugs are bigger than us!" he added. "And we didn't bring them into our community!"

"I messed up!" confided a teenage girl to me as I hugged her one Sunday. "I'm pregnant."

Drugs, shootings, violence, teenage pregnancies. These are but a few of the challenges that face the younger members of the Lourdes community. The son of a choir member was jailed for a year and a half for being present with a group of young men who robbed a store—he, while not involved in the theft, was unwilling to tell on his friends. A week after he was released, I watched him walk with his young son down the center aisle of Lourdes to receive Communion, and I imagined the immense joy of his mother.

"Parents Who Care," an initiative taken by a small group of Lourdes' parents to guide their young people through these challenges, might well be titled "Kids Who Matter." "We wanted to provide a safe place where they could get off the street and get help with their homework after school," commented Jeannette Howard, one of its founders. "Many come just to get something to eat," she added. "We provide weekly movie nights with pizza at the parish hall, tutoring, basketball competitions, and field trips to places they'd never been before—sports events, museums, concerts, Great America, Santa Cruz. Many have never been out of their neighborhoods. They enjoy just being on the bus, watching the scenery!"

> *W*anna *sing* for some-*bod*-y, sing for *Je*-sus!
> Wanna *sing* for some-*bod*-y, sing for *Je-sus!*
> Wanna *sing*, (la, la, la, la) wanna *sing*, (la, la, la, la)
> Wanna *sing* for some-*bod*-y, sing for *Je*-sus!

A chorus of little voices, a lively tune, an upbeat tempo, and a meandering line of fifteen youngsters, dressed in black and white, make their way down the center aisle. The Gospel Choir follows. From my place at the back of the line, I can just catch sight of the tops of their heads as they file into the front pew on the right side. It's Sunday, March 16, 1997. A dream has been realized. The "Miracles" have been born.

For months, Judy Brown has talked with other parents about re-forming a youth choir, the third in Lourdes's history,[4] as a way to incorporate children more fully into the community's prayer, to provide them with faith formation, fun, musical development, and an alternative to the negative lures of their neighborhoods. Judy will train and direct them. Reed Fromer will accompany and create musical arrangements. Rose Isles, Jeannette Howard, and Rita Johnson, parents or grandparents of children in the choir, will serve as assistant directors.

Tots to pre-teens, these Miracles grew quickly into their musical ministry. Wiggly at first, more than one feeling shy, missing a cue, losing their places, or at least their tongues, they needed Judy's constant tending. At times, she'd stop a piece altogether so they could begin again, in sync. But never a ripple of discontent from the community. Rather *Amens,* applause, appreciation—a willingness to enter the faith process on their terms, singing and swaying to their songs.

> Wanna *sing* for some-*bod*-y, sing for *Je*-sus! . . .
> Wanna *shout* for some-*bod*-y, shout for *Je*-sus! . . .
> Wanna *clap* for some-*bod*-y, clap for *Je*-sus! . . .

Within three months, the Miracles took a regular place in the music leadership of the parish, replacing the Gospel Choir on the third Sunday of every month. Yes, the wiggles continued. But there was room for them to grow into their ministry. On that premier Sunday in March, the Miracles knew two songs—"Sing for Jesus," composed by Reed and Judy, and the old spiritual "This Little Light of Mine." By June, their repertoire had swelled to eight songs and several liturgical acclamations. A year and a half later, thirty-five. Who could have imagined then the CD that would follow in another three years.

At first they sat in the front pews, moving to the open space in front of the altar to sing. Individual Miracles would take turns as lead singers—Judy Brown passing the mike from one to another so we could hear their sometimes hesitant voices. They were a sight to behold—Tyree McDuff, now six, looking confident. Dante Dow, almost a head shorter, a bit more bashful. Simone Mackey, already eight but not having reached her growth spurt, looking out shyly from the second row. From month to month, you could watch them grow—in their presence to the community, their musical assurance, and their ability to remember musical lines. Soon, their blue and beige choir robes arrived—monogrammed *OLOL,* the initials of the parish—and they had taken their new places in the sanctuary, seated now where the Gospel Choir sits.

*T*he Black gospel tradition assumes that songs are meant to be reinterpreted—that new, creative ways of performing treasured pieces keeps the musical tradition alive, keeps the faith memory living. Children at Lourdes are drawn into this artful process. Take, for example, the Spirituals that are part of the Miracles' repertoire—"Every Time I Feel the Spirit," "Get on Board, Little Children, the Gospel Train's a Comin'," "This Little Light of Mine," "Somebody's Knocking at Your Door." These reach back into the early memory of Black Africans on American soil. At that time, spirituals were performed without instruments—drums were forbidden—but accompanied by rhythmic movements and percussive bodily sounds, clapping, and foot-stomping. Nineteenth-century "concertized" versions, performed *a cappella,* without rhythmic expression of any kind, were themselves a reinterpretation. Once again, the Civil Rights Movement transformed these spirituals into the freedom songs of the '60s, performing them at protests and bus boycotts.

The process continues at Lourdes, as cherished songs are reinvented, rearranged, to match their bodies, their spirits, their life experience.

Over my *head,* I hear *music* in the air!

The beat is strong. Swaying side to side, the Miracles perform an up-tempo arrangement of a traditional favorite, full of vitality, energy, and movement, spurred on by Isaiah Brown's infectious drum beat and Reed Fromer's inventive piano improvisation.

Over my *head,* I hear *music* in the air!
Over my *head,* I hear *music* in the air!
there *must* be a *God* (Oh, yes!) // some-where!

A living memory, made fresh and vibrant. A profound intuition handed on—that music announces the presence of the living God.

Brother Banks's mother would smile to hear a new generation of believers sing "Oh, How I Love Jesus!" with youthful "lead singers" chanting the verses. "Yes, Jesus Loves Me" has likewise been reimagined, with young leads now rapping the verses.

> Jesus loves me, this I know! For the Bible tells me so!
> Little ones to him belong, / / they are weak but he is strong!

The regeneration process gives birth to new compositions as well, as the idioms of contemporary gospel are woven together with treasured images of faith.

*I*t's a rainy Sunday in March, the Second Sunday of Lent, 2000. The Miracles, now numbering over twenty, ages seven to twelve, spread themselves three lines deep across the open space at the front of the church house. Communion ministers have just returned to their places. There's a sense of expectation in the air. Reed sets the easy beat of a song he's composed for the children, "I Love You, Lord!" It's amazing to see how their confidence has grown over these three years—finding their voices, singing their faith, finding resonance in the community's support, bonded in a sense of common purpose, emerging as leaders of prayer. Catching Judy Brown's signals, they begin to sway in sync with the song's flowing energy. The sound is smoother, less driven than many of the uptempo gospel pieces that characterize much of the community's repertoire, yet the message is as direct. You can hear people singing along as the Miracles begin crisply,

> I love you Lord! You are my strength when life has me down,
> There's so many mountains you've led me around,
> And I love you, Lord. *(That's right!)*

It's the kind of song that sets your body rocking gently, the lyrics running through you on their way into your soul. Words to live by. "I love you, Lord!" they continue,

> You are the source of light in my day,
> And I'll keep the faith every step of the way,
> 'Cause I love you, Lord. *(Amen!)*

The first chorus in place, Amber Bryant, ten years old but standing head and shoulders above most of the others, takes the lead, a youthful soulfulness in her voice:

> I may be lost and far from my home,
> but I know inside that I'm never alone: *(Yes!)*
> you are there, (you are there) guiding me. (guiding me) *(Amen!)*

> I cannot think of a greater victory!
> I love you, Lord! . . .

Another chorus, and Sonia Cosey takes the mike, singing with all the flair of a seasoned gospel singer:

> Give me the courage to change what I can, and what I can't,
> help me understand,
> It's your will (it's your will), and not mine (no not mine)
> and I know in the end that I won't be left behind!

"I love you, Lord!" we chorus again, enjoying the play of lyrics against the subtle syncopations of the accompaniment, "You are my strength when life has me down. . . ."

Then the beat becomes more insistent, the tonality shifts to minor, the harmonies stall, and like a parting of the waters, blue-robed Miracles reconfigure themselves into two parallel lines—girls to the left and boys to the right—moving to the beat. "C'mon now!" calls one of the young women, as girls on the left side take up their rhythmic mantras:

> I love you Lord! *(Yes!)*
> You know that I love you!

After several repetitions, the choir of boys to the right adds its own chanted phrases, creating call-and-response patterns with those of their youthful counterparts:

> Take my hand! Help me stand!
> Fill my cup! Lift me up!

It's hard to resist the building energy. I join the others around me who are on their feet, echoing the children's rhythmic interplay in the movements of our bodies. It's a moment of shared delight, as the undulating patterns of interchange wash over us.

| I love you, Lord! | Take my hand! Help me stand! |
| You know that I love you! | Fill my cup! Lift me up! |

Then, without the least *ritard,* the Miracles' voices merge again into a last, almost shouted:

> I love you, Lord! You know that I love you!

The song is over! Delivered! The rebound of applause is just as sudden. *Amen! I love you, Lord! Yes, Amen! Amen!*

*F*or those who have grown up at Lourdes, songs continue to have an impact on their lives. "There's a song the choir sings," stated Omar Butler near the close of a Sunday liturgy in June of '94. "'Lord, Don't Move that Mountain.'⁵ That song gave me strength to complete my years at college." Corey Monroe introduced Omar that morning and congratulated him for his accomplishment. The struggle to finish had been real, Corey noted, since there are few role models for Black college students. Omar responded, recalling the lyrics of the song he'd mentioned and the power with which Jean Alexander sings it.

> Lord, don't move that mountain, but give me the strength to climb it!
> Lord, don't take away my stumbling block, but lead me all around it!

Yes, the Lord had led him around many stumbling blocks and enabled him to earn a bachelor's degree from California State University, Long Beach.

Corey Monroe, a young adult himself, counsels teenagers at the Potrero Hill Community Center. I spoke with Corey and a friend, Mike Edwards, some months later. "That song [referring to Omar's touchstone] says a lot," he commented. "You go through so much in a lifetime, and sometimes we run into problems. . . . That song lets you know not to give up. 'Lord, don't move that mountain!' Don't make it easier for me, but give me enough strength to make it over. That says a lot about life. . . . You go *through* the challenges! That song says so much—just gives me strength to keep going!"

"Are there times when these lines come back to you when you're not at Lourdes?" I inquired.

"Yeah, always," Corey responded, and Mike agreed. "I tell kids about that song; I use it when I talk to the teenagers."

"I drive a lot," remarked Mike, a deputy sheriff for San Francisco county. "My job has me going where I'll be driving by myself sometimes. . . . Up to Tahoe, Susanville, northern California. I'll be coming back home at night, eight or nine o'clock, by myself, and I start singing some of the songs. Or I think about why God put me here—what's my purpose? . . . Or I just start talking to him . . . in my own way. . . . I talk to him every day, and I think about all the songs. I'd be singing songs like 'Excellent!'" referring to Brenda Moore's "Perfect Praise." "It gives me energy. . . . When I really get into a song like that, I can feel it . . . and I know something is coming into me. . . ."

Tiffany Isles, a pre-med student at the University of California, Santa Cruz, with her sights set on Howard University Medical School, and Tina Edwards, a mechanical engineering student at San Francisco City College, joined me for coffee one warm April Sunday in 1995. They reminisced about singing in an earlier Lourdes' youth choir which Judy Brown had also directed. "We practiced after religion classes," recalled Tiffany. "I was about ten, maybe even younger.

. . . I used to sing [the old spiritual], 'I want Jesus to walk with me.' . . . That's when I got courage to sing in front of the church!"

In their young adult years, music continues to be a place of solace. "When I'm having a really bad couple of weeks," remarked Tiffany, "I can come to church. . . . And all of a sudden, someone will sing . . . and if they're really singing the song, I can feel it up and down my spine. . . . [It opens me.] The wall I put up comes crumbling down. . . . It fills me with emotion. . . . It helps me think. It makes me realize that we're all human, we all struggle."

"You can put the following week into perspective," added Tina. "It opens your mind to new questions and new ideas. . . . If you're going through hard times . . . you can [let go] and surrender yourself to God."

"Are you saying that music has a power to touch?" I inquired.

"Exactly! . . ."

*T*ina, Tiffany, Corey, Mike, and Omar are among the young adults who have found their voices at Lourdes. Speaking at one of the yearly celebrations of Kwanzaa, Corey Monroe put it this way:

"This community has played a big role in my life. At fourteen I lost my mother to cancer. It's very hard for a young man to keep going—there's no one like your mother! [But people here shared] the problems they'd been through, and helped me surpass my own. I was blessed to have my father with me. . . . 'We're gonna make it, Corey!' [he said]. I want you to make something out of yourself.'

"In tenth grade I went with my friend Omar to the Omega Boys Club. [I saw] brothers and sisters doing homework, studying after school, learning our history . . . talking about problems they had gone through. . . . Mr. Marshall [founder of Omega] talked about respect. . . . Respect comes from within, [he said]. I don't have to prove myself! I remember Mr. Marshall telling us about drugs, alcohol, negative views of women—[stressing that] we had to tell our brothers and sisters. . . . I was shy. I never wanted to go out and speak to nobody. I had a lot to share, but I felt I might say something wrong. I might not use the proper way of English. [But I learned], it's not the way I use my English, it's the message! I remember going out for the first time—talking to a group of teenagers. . . . This young brother came up to me afterwards. 'You know, I like what you said. . . . My mother died when I was young.' I had shared something that might help that young brother keep going. . . . It's amazing how God can take my problems and make them work for someone else.

"Three months [after I graduated from high school], my father passed away. Again the community came. . . . They didn't want me to fall to the wayside. . . . Omega Boys Club sent me on a college tour to Atlanta, Georgia. Something I'd never seen—brothers and sisters learning!. . . I had never heard about this on the evening news. All I'd seen was brothers killing and shooting each other. I never knew that we went to school and were smart in chemistry! . . . It motivated me. . . . I went to Morris Brown for two years, then came home. . . .

"One thing I've learned—I will never give up! As long as I have my church with me! Some days, I come down here and I'm tired and fed up. . . . Seem like everything I'm telling [the kids] is not working. Then, I realize, it takes time. . . . I come here, I meet someone . . . and when I leave I feel good. . . . Whenever you get a chance to help somebody, do it! If someone calls you in the middle of the night and says, I need help, I need to talk—please talk to them, because you might be saving their life!. . . . We need our elders. . . . If someone would have turned their back on me and said, 'That's not my kid,' I don't know where I would be. . . . I could call Mrs. Alexander and say, 'Mrs. Alexander I'm hungry!' I know that people . . . are there to help me. . . .

I see a lot of children. I have to talk to them. . . . One day they are gonna get older . . . and have to make decisions on their own. The least I can do is guide them on their way. . . . Some kids don't know where to get help. I need to reach out and say 'I'm here for you!'" [Remember]:

I am // because we are,
and because we are, therefore I am.

In appreciation, the entire community rose in applause. Beneath the *Amens* and shouts of affirmation, I could hear Reed weaving the theme of his composition "Heroes"—a song about the little people who make a big difference. As the applause tapered off, Father Kirk came to the ambo.

"A few minutes ago, we heard proclaimed in the Gospel that *we* are the salt of the earth. *We* are the light of the world. We've just had an example of that! Corey, *you* are a light for us. Thank you! *Thank you!*"

*L*ourdes is full of Miracles. . . .

Chapter Six

"WHEN I HEAR MY SAVIOR SAY, 'WELCOME HOME!'"

—BEING HOME—

"*L*et us rise in the name of *Jesus!*" rang out Brother Banks's voice from the front. "Our service is about to begin! Our choir will be singing, 'What a Mighty God We Serve!' Oh, yes! *It is a mighty God we serve!*" His words were all but drowned out by Reed Fromer and Isaiah Brown's vibrant introduction to the song he'd just announced. In no time, everyone was standing, moving to the compelling beat. Rhythmic clapping rang out like shots penetrating the room. No cues needed. I didn't know the song, but the tune Reed was playing seemed familiar, like others we'd sung for the opening of a liturgy. "Walking music," I thought to myself, feeling its syncopated, shuffle like beat. Despite the paucity of space around me, my feet began to "walk," moving from side to side, alternating my steps with hand claps as others around me were doing. The choir was not in sight yet, but I could feel their approach and imagine their moving down the aisle in festive "step"—the hallmark of Black choirs. As the tenors neared the front of the church, Pat Goodall shouted, "What a mighty God!" and the song erupted:

> What a mighty God we serve! What a mighty God we serve!
> Angels bow down before him! Heaven and earth adore him!
> What a mighty God we serve!

One hearing, and I could join the singing. The tune was catchy, the lyrics easy to remember, and the song surged forward as syllables anticipated the beat. But what took me by surprise were the choir's gestures. As we chorused the third line of the song, they paused momentarily. "Angels bow down before him!" Blue-robed arms reached to the floor, bodies bent forward. Then, arms outstretched, bodies thrust upright again, "Heaven and earth adore him!"— only to resume their "stepping" toward the front of the church.

By the next repeat, I had the choreography down as well. Despite the pew inches ahead of me—the choir had the luxury of an open aisle!—my body was now caught up in this exuberant act of praise. *Sing out, Church! It's a mighty God we serve!* shouted Jean Alexander from the rear of the sopranos as another repeat ensued. I liked the repetition. I could feel my body and voice more engaged with each reiteration of the mightiness of God, my arms reaching up each time as if to touch the heavens. Waves of sound and praise surrounded me!

*T*he church had been humming that morning long before the song began. I'd come a good half hour early, hoping to learn the names of a few more parishioners. I envied the long-term members who knew everyone's first and last name and was still sensing the nuanced ways people greeted one another, especially elder members of the community—"Mama Winslow," "Mama Levy." But I was not the first to arrive. I could see that Brother Banks had placed a light-green songsheet and a parish bulletin on each of the choir seats in the sanctuary. He was now greeting and making conversation with folks as they came through the doors. Pat Goodall had already prepared the Communion vessels and ritual books and was spreading a linen cloth on the altar table. Rose Isles was in the front watering a few thirsty plants. I lingered in the entryway, talking for a time with Liz Bell. She'd been asking the community for clothing donations for the St. Vincent de Paul Society these past weeks and had her large bags ready today. As more people arrived, I was caught up in the hugs and greetings that seemed to overflow like a river—people catching up on the "trials and tribulations" of the past week. "Oh, I'm gonna make it!" I heard one say. A few choir members had joined us in the now crowded entryway. I could spot the blue robes of a few others making their way down the center aisle, greeting people already seated in the pews. "OK, choir, let us pray!" called Father Kirk, signaling that it was time to join hands for prayer. I realized I had better find a seat and headed off toward the front. As I walked, I caught sight of the stained-glass image of St. Augustine among the gallery of saints that line the left side of the church. His mitered head and dark complexion reminded me that he was an *African* bishop. Was it not Augustine, I mused to myself, who described the church as the "one Christ loving his own Body"? The image seemed so apt in this setting.

"*W*hat a *peaceful* God!"shouted Pat Goodall, "lining out" the one-word change that would launch us into the next stanza. With his split-second timing, Reed modulated to the next highest key. You could feel a new burst of energy as we sang:

What a peaceful God we serve! What a peaceful God we serve!
Angels bow down before him! Heaven and earth adore him!
What a peaceful God we serve!

The choir had reached the sanctuary by then. Their voices met ours directly as we faced each other; their rhythmic movements echoed back the swaying and clapping I could feel and see around me. Father Kirk was no exception, his green chasuble rocking from side to side as we praised this "peaceful God" that we serve. Beside him, Maurice Moran stood a bit more stationary, as if not to disturb the large, red Sacramentary, draped with its Kente-cloth sash marker, which was resting against his chest. It seemed that this whole assembly was moving as one body, caught up in a compelling inrush of musical energy. "What a *mighty* God!" shouted Pat, sensing that we needed one last repeat for the song to have knit us together as a praying body. Applause broke out as we neared the end, as did shouts of *"Amen!"* "It's a *mighty* God we serve!" Reed's improvisation continued to spill over.

"We welcome you to Our Lady of Lourdes *Holy Catholic* Church!" resumed Brother Banks, as if to complete his words of welcome. "We're so glad to see so many of you here this morning. With all the things goin' on, you could have been somewhere else. But you *chose to serve God!* To put God first! . . . What we do here today they're doin' in heaven. . . ."

*P*eople talk about Lourdes as a "home," a "haven," a "home away from home," a "family." A comment by Tiffany Isles sums it up best: "You can feel the love radiating."[1]

"You've heard people say that they are at home [at Lourdes]," remarked Sister Irma Dillard to me over dinner one evening, "that church is their second home. . . . It's all about relationships," she explained. "It's about the church supporting [them]." You notice that after the liturgy "people 'hang out' and still talk," she added, referring to the lingering conversations and laughter that continue for some time. You can see them there each Sunday clustered around the benches near the church hall, their spirited interaction silhouetted against the purple bougainvillaea that graces the entranceway. "If you came to someone's house for a dinner party, and it was gracious," she concluded, "the party [may be] over, but you've had such a great time together that you still are talking to each other."[2]

"This is home," stated Pat Goodall emphatically one Saturday as we drove across the Bay Bridge. "The very first day I walked through the door, it was like God was there saying, 'Open the window, you're home!' I haven't left since then. . . . I think that my time away from church was so that Lourdes could be [ready], when I got there, to give me what I need, . . . to hold me, and let me know that I had come home. . . . I knew I was home! The love, the real genuine love . . . it was like I knew these people all my life! . . . I would never leave this church. . . . This is what God meant church to be. It's not about color. It's not about money. It's not about power. . . . It's the people's church."[3]

"It's good to be home," whispered a woman to me as we exchanged the Peace one Sunday. "It's good to be home." She hardly needed to explain that she'd been alienated from the church for several years. Her tears said it all. Leaving a funeral on another occasion, I overheard two visitors debriefing the ceremony. "See why I always love to come here," commented one of them. "It's like a home!!"

From my first months at Lourdes, the threat of parish closure was evident. In September 1993 the Archdiocese of San Francisco announced a process of "reorganization"—a neutral term for parish closures. At the encouragement of community members, Father Kirk immediately called a town-hall meeting to talk about how Lourdes would participate in the process. A small group of parishioners were sent to "cluster" meetings, in which diocesan administrators conferred with parish representatives. Unlike parishes that viewed the possibility of closure as remote, the Lourdes community knew it was vulnerable. It was both small and poor and, at that time, dependent in some measure on the financial assistance of the archdiocese.

Knowing that they had much to lose, Lourdes' delegates were outspoken about how they valued the life, worship, and outreach they shared at Lourdes. To support their efforts, forty-nine parishioners turned out for an archdiocesan prayer service at St. Mary's Cathedral on October 24 to pray for God's guidance in the reorganization process. Lourdes' attendees outnumbered those from any other parish. "It was a fight for survival," remarked Pat Goodall several months later—the survival of a way of life and a style of worship that responds to their religious longings.[4]

This wasn't the first time the parish faced closure. In the late 1980s personnel shortage forced the Redemptorist community to withdraw from Lourdes. Father Don MacKinnon, then in his second term as pastor, encouraged the parishioners to speak directly to the archbishop. Make your desires heard! Speak about what Lourdes means to you! Ask the diocese to staff it! "We had a session, I'll tell you!" recalled Pat Goodall, a delegate to that negotiation as well. The exchange had been frank, at times impassioned. "When the deal was [made], the archbishop came and we didn't close. They sent us Father Jack instead," referring to Father Jack Isaacs, who was then appointed pastor by the archdiocese.[5]

It's an old struggle. Sister Martin de Porres Coleman tells of growing up in the Bay Area in the era of "national parishes," where persons from various ethno-cultural communities could find a home. "[Everyone] knew that St. Paul of the Shipwreck was the Maltese national parish. They built it, they came back and supported it. St. Dominick's was the German national parish. Out in North Beach, Sts. Peter and Paul was the Italian national parish." But the story was different for the African American community. "The older [Black] folk know that St. Benedict's Center for the Deaf, off Divisadero . . . was really theirs," stated Sister Martin. "When I was a child, [the S.V.D. Fathers had a small chapel] called St. Benedict the Moor. That was the church where most of the Blacks in the city would come. For many years they sold sweet-potato pies to get money to build a church. They built it, and it was likewise named St. Benedict the Moor. [Within a few short years], the diocese took it for a center for the deaf."[6]

"What does it mean to be Black in the church and in society?" The question was posed by Black scholar, musician, and poet Sister Thea Bowman, addressing the Catholic bishops of the United States assembled in June of 1989.[7] Seated before them in a wheelchair, the result of a debilitating and progressive cancer, Sister Thea spoke boldly, "I want to tell you about the church," she continued. Then invoking the poignant lines of a beloved Spiritual, she began to sing, her resonant voice filling the hushed assembly hall:

Sometimes I feel like a motherless child!
Sometimes I feel like a motherless child! Sometimes I feel like a motherless child,
A long way from home!

"Can you hear me, Church?" she inquired of the room full of black-suited men before her. "I am a long way from home. . . . I'm a pilgrim in the journey looking for home, and Jesus told me the church is my home. . . . Cardinals, archbishops, bishops! . . . Please help me to get home!"

Throughout her presentation, Sister Thea recounted the struggles of Black Catholics to find a welcome in the church, an effort that continues to the present. "Surviving our history, physically, mentally, emotionally, morally, spiritually, faithfully, and joyfully," she pointed out, "our people developed a culture that was African American, that was formed and enriched by all that we experienced. And despite all this, despite the civil rights movement of the '60s and the socio-educational gains of the '70s, Blacks in the '80s are still struggling . . . still trying to find a home in the homeland, and a home in the church."[8]

I was looking forward to this moment—a warm September Sunday in 1994. Ever since Louise Wood burst into a choir rehearsal in late February, announcing that the choir *must* learn "Perfect Praise," they had rehearsed it intermittently. These past weeks, they'd worked in earnest. Today the choir would offer it as a Communion meditation.

A sense of expectation settled over the room as the choir fanned out. Reed modulated into a gentle, stately introduction. I could almost feel the choir members getting into the piece as they began their rhythmic sway from side to side. Just then, Ernestine Harris peered out at me from the sopranos and motioned for me to come into the sanctuary. Stunned, I watched her gestures become more emphatic. "Come up here, Sister!" she said in a stage whisper. My body felt immobile, glued to the third pew. She turned to Pat and said, "Get Sister to come up here. She sang it with us on Thursday, she can sing it with us now!" Pat turned around and motioned to me. Embarrassed by the confusion, I realized I had no choice. I was exposed! Yes, I had asked to "try out the song" with them at rehearsal, but to sing with them this morning? Sheepishly, I walked forward and slipped in between Ernestine and Rita Johnson, feeling conspicuous as I stood among the blue-robed singers without a "wedding garment." But no matter. The song was underway, and a sense of reverence had returned. My heart pounded as we began softly,

Oh, Lord, how excellent! How Excellent!

Then, like a geyser shooting its burst of water toward the sky,

How Excellent is your name!!

Questions raced through my mind. Had I paid enough attention on Thursday? Did I remember the soprano entrances? I fixed my gaze on Pat, relieved to notice that her gaze was intent on me, ready to prompt me should I falter. My body relaxed a bit, and the song began to take over. At one point I glanced out into the church, startled by the scene before me—pew after pew of faces seemingly entranced by the song. But quickly I looked back at Pat, afraid I'd miss the subtle timing of another "Excellent!"

By now, the tenors were leaning into their penetrating line:

In all the earth, in all the earth, in all the earth, in all the earth!!!

The altos took it up with a new melody. Now it was our turn. My eyes watched Pat to catch the split-second, off-beat soprano entry,

Every knee shall bow, and every tongue proclaim that He is Lord!!!

"Jesus, excellent!!" we concluded together. I hardly remember how many times we layered those three lines into a great contrapuntal dance. But by the time we swelled to our last "Jesus, excellent is your name!" a roar of applause burst out. People were shouting, "Excellent!!! He's excellent!!" When I finally looked out, I could see that the whole church had risen to its feet, exhilarated by the volcano of praise into which they had just been drawn. The air was tingling. The intensity of those high-pitched "Excellent!"s were still bouncing off the wooden rafters of the vaulted ceiling, reverberating from the tiny "rose window" I could now see at the rear of the high gallery. Someone came up and hugged Pat, I don't remember who. Choir members were in tears, exhilarated by this burst of praise and relieved that they had navigated their way through a new piece. In the midst of the commotion, someone walked up to me and said emphatically, "Chil', you need a robe!"

The robe was the easy part. Jean supplied it the next Thursday—freshly washed and ready for a new owner. We tried it for size, and it fit. What took longer was the dawning realization of what had happened that September Sunday. I had been catapulted across a border, welcomed into the choir before even asking to join. They had made a home for me in the music and at the heart of their ministry. My learning curve had just taken a sharp turn. I was now in the sanctuary on Thursday evenings, intent on mastering the lyrics and melodies, learning to read Pat's signals, and feeling how to stay in sync with the choir. But other patterns changed as well. On Sundays I entered the church through the small "choir room" to the right of the building—once a parish office, before that, the tiny "rectory" into which Father MacKinnon and Brother Gary Pometta moved on their arrival. How could they have managed in this one room and small bath, I wondered! Now it was filled with choir robes, a Xerox machine, and lots of storage—only enough room for singers to robe. Then I would take the backdoor into a small sacristy, tuck my purse into a cupboard, greet Father Kirk, usually vesting, and others making preparations, and enter the church through a door at the rear of the sanctuary. Bowing to the tabernacle on the right side of the room—a custom that is in people's bodies here, part of the choreography of the whole event, yes, a sideways bow, but taken for granted—I would walk through the church, stopping to greet Joan Dill, Alexis Alexander, Mercedes Salguero, Margaret Fisher, and other early-comers who were already in their pews. I'd seen other choir members do it before me and realized intuitively that it was part of the ministry. Oh, yes, a slide into the pew beneath Sojourner Truth to greet "Mama" Amanda Winslow, seated with a coverlet over her lap, always a lovely hat in place on her loose black curls, and a pause to hug dear Gloria Stith in the second-to-last pew on the left side, then each of the grandchildren seated beside her. Yes, Lourdes had made a home for me here, but I'd thrown my lot in with them as well. My second oar was in the water.

"*M*y mother was a very devout Christian," remarked Joan Dill to me one Sunday. "She always had gospel music on, every Sunday. . . . Now you can hear gospel music [on the radio] at six every morning. We only had it on Sunday. . . . We had gospel records in the house, and a lot of music I hear brings back memories of my childhood and my mother. . . . The last [song we sang] today, 'God be with you,' " she said, referring to a piece by Thomas A. Dorsey, "my mother would sing that all the time. That's a very old song. And 'Near the Cross,' " she continued with a sigh. "That is *such* an old spiritual. . . . I remember that my mother would sing it all the time. It just brings back emotional feelings about my life."[9]

Remarks like Joan Dill's have taught me how integral music has been to creating a home at Lourdes—a place that feels, sounds, and looks like home—a cultural climate, a psychological space, an aural context, a faith environment within which members of the community and visitors can say, "I'm home. I belong here!" Performing gospel music is a way of saying, This is *our* music! This is the music we created as a testament of faith to our survival as a people—overcoming hardship, putting things in God's perspective, creating feelings of hope in the midst of struggle. Moreover, this is the way we *make* music. "When we sing, we move our feet to the music, we keep the beat, we feel the spirit," commented Sister Irma Dillard. "It's our prayer—our movements are as personal as anyone's prayer."[10]

Music is only one way the whole "liturgical aesthetic" has been transformed since the late '60s. In 1984 the community commissioned and installed a procession of stained-glass images that line the two sides of the church—early Christian African saints on the left, African American spiritual leaders on the right. "Every time we enter this church," claimed Sister Irma, addressing the community during Kwanzaa one year, "we are surrounded by our strong history, our kinfolk in the faith and in the struggle."[11]

"Liturgy [here] is the work of the community," mused Father Kirk as we sat in his office one January afternoon. "I am presider, preacher, leader of the Eucharist. [But] this is an African American church, and I am a white man. I'm not trying to be Black. I bring my culture, experience, faith, to serve. But there *has* to be a strong Black spirit in this church. I can't do that. Mr. Banks does that, the choir does that, the people speak up from the church—that's valid. If that's turned off, there would be something [wrong]. I don't diminish my voice, but recognize the value, the importance of exactly how things are done. I stand up there, front and center, and if Mr. Banks is not with me, I feel something important is missing. When he was sick, something was wrong. He is a long-time member of this African American community—he's spent fifty years of struggling to be a child of God."[12]

"*C*an you imagine what it would be like to be homeless?" The question was not rhetorical. Nor was it the first time Father Kirk's preaching of the Word of God had addressed the plight of homeless persons in San Francisco, especially now that Mayor Frank Jordan had taken hold of the reins. That last week of August 1995 the newspapers had been full of the story. Homeless people camping in Golden Gate Park. The mayor embarrassed by this blight on the city. A new disturbance. A new crackdown.

"Now there may be some of you who are saying to yourselves, 'Well, you know they shouldn't be in our parks—our parks are meant for the recreation of everybody,'" continued Father Kirk. "That's true. But what happens when you have no home, Church? *(Amen!)*

"Everyone of us here has some place to go back to. Right? *(Yes, Lord!)* It may not be a mansion in the northern part of the city, but it's a home. *(Yes!)* It's a place where, when I get there, I can just be myself, I can let my hair down, I can kick off my shoes, I can do what I want. That's my space, *(Yes!)* and nobody can take it from me! *(Yes! Well . . .)* Can you imagine what it's like to be homeless? *(No!)* It's almost *unthinkable*—to have no space that is yours! Well, these [homeless] folks have decided that Golden Gate Park has a few square inches that are worthwhile looking at, saying, 'Well, at least I can sleep here.' Just a few days ago a transient man who was deranged, out of his mind, starting shooting at the homeless—*(Uh huh! . . .)* *at the homeless, Church!* They called 911 to get assistance from the police, and guess what? *They became the victims.* *(Amen!)* It was used as an *excuse* by our mayor to vacate the park. *(Yes!)* Tomorrow morning at 5:00 a.m.—now there's a sacrifice—some of us are going to stand in front of the police station at Stanyan and Waller, because from that station will come the corps of police to evict the homeless from the park.

"What has this got to do with the readings today? What has this got to do with the Word of God? It's got *everything* to do with the Word of God that we're hearing this morning. *(Amen!)* We are all called not only to worship the Lord—and we do worship the Lord here *beautifully!* As I've said before, I've been to other places where God does not get the praise that the Lord receives here, and I hope that He is pleased and that His ears are opened to us, to all of us. *(Amen!)* But the Lord is also asking of us what He asked of the people in Isaiah's time, what He asked of the people in Jesus' time. He's asking of us—be mindful of those who are hurting. *(Amen!)* Be mindful of those who are being thrown away as outcasts that nobody wants!" *(Amen!)*

*T*hursday, October 5, 1995. There was a chill in the air as I arrived for rehearsal that night. I'd brought along an extra sweatshirt, knowing that we would go directly to the rally at Golden Gate Park sponsored by the "Religious Witness with the Homeless." After rehearsing Walter Turner's new song, "We Worship Christ the Lord," making a few changes in the choral parts, we set out in small groups for the nine o'clock vigil. I followed the other cars closely, not sure of the route across town, then walked with Bessie Brooks and Gaye Hyde into the darkened southeast corner of San Francisco's most splendid park. Father Kirk was already there, preparing to join some twenty other persons who would sleep in the park that evening in solidarity with the homeless and in protest of Mayor Jordan's Matrix program. Arrests were possible, but they hoped to make a peaceful statement without spending time in jail.

The Lourdes choir was first on the program. We huddled to find a common pitch, then launched into "What a Mighty God We Serve"—setting a tone that seemed to match the ecumenical nature of the gathering. Few vigilers knew the Black repertoire, so the choir was on its own for this one. But we had another song ready, with freshly devised words worked out while waiting for the event to begin.

We *shall* not, we shall not be moved!

rang out the words of an old freedom song.

We *shall* not, we shall not be moved!
Like a tree planted by the water,
We shall not be moved!

Vigilers old enough to remember the Civil Rights Movement joined the singing, then smiled as Lourdes gave the song a new twist:

Go and tell Frank Jordan, we shall not be moved! . . .
We may go to jail, but we shall not be moved! . . .

As we delighted in the repartee, I noticed little Naja Turner leaning against her mother, captivated by the candlelight that glistened in the darkness around her.

Prayers and songs were offered by Father Louis Vitale of St. Boniface Catholic Church; Reverend Charles Lerrigo, Calvary United Methodist; and Dorothy Merson, Congregation Emmanu-El. Reflections followed by Rabbi Alan Lew, Temple Beth-Shalom and Rev. Jeff R. Johnson, First United Lutheran Church. Then Syed Saifullah, imam of the Muslim Community, and Mary Jane Brinton of the Religious Witness led us in prayers of intercession. As the service neared completion, Father Kirk Ullery commissioned Brother Lou Bordisso and his Salvatorian associates to distribute blankets to homeless persons around the city— a sign of compassion and support. Then he invoked God's blessing on the little band of witnesses who had gathered here and prayed for all who would sleep that night in this verdant piece of God's bounteous creation. We concluded with a heartfelt song: "The Lord hears the cry of the poor, blessed be the Lord!"

As the crowd of some sixty people began to dissipate, Gaye, Bessie, and I lingered in conversation with Father Kirk. Yes, he had a sleeping bag, but nothing to keep the dampness from penetrating its thin casing during the night. A quick trip to our respective cars and we produced a canvas mat and a few thin blankets—more than his homeless "companions" would have, he reminded us. The four of us joined hands, prayed for a safe night under the brilliant stars that had appeared overhead, and left Father Kirk to continue his vigil.

☙ ☙ ☙

"*C*hurch, do you realize that it's been two years since God took our brother Al Winslow home?" began Father Kirk that warm November Sunday in 1995. "I know that Amanda has never gotten over that loss, *(Amen!)* because he was *so* important, and they had such a *wonderful* relationship!" *(Oh, yes!)*

"Mama" Winslow was seated in the second pew that morning, surrounded by four generations of family members. "Amanda," Father Kirk continued, "we're *lifting up Al* today, on this his anniversary, *(Yes!)* and we're *lifting up you, too,* Amanda! *(Oh, yes!)* I can't see you, but I know your head is nodding!" From the choir, I could only catch a glimpse of Amanda's black felt hat among her standing relatives—no doubt her lap-robe in place over her arthritic knees—but I suspected how appreciative she was for this moment.

It was a Sunday like many I had experienced at Lourdes before, when death was stared down by life, when the trials of this life—named, owned, and embraced—were caught up in God's victory. Here and now. The prayers that morning spoke eloquently of this mystery. Father Kirk, voicing the great Thanksgiving, addressed the "all powerful and ever living God," giving thanks for Christ who "has made us children of the light, *(Yes!)* rising to new and everlasting life. He has opened the gates of heaven to *receive* his faithful people. *(Yes!)* His death is *our* ransom from death; *(Amen!)* his resurrection is *our* rising to life. *(Amen! Well . . .)* The joy of the resurrection renews the whole world. . . ."

Mama Winslow's prayer during the lengthy intercessions translated those rich theological images into the vernacular. She thanked God for "my church. If it hadn't been for you, I wouldn't have made it!" She prayed for Father Kirk, "who's been so good to me"; and for her family. "They were hurting right along with me. *(Amen!)* But sometimes it seems that you're all alone. *(Amen!!!)* The nights get so long *(Have mercy!)* until you can't hardly *stand* it. *(Oh, yes!)* The fears are so close. *(Have mercy!)* . . . But I want to thank God that I've come this far! *(Yes!)* I have a long ways to go, *(Amen!)* but with the Lord and all of you, I will make it!" *(Yes, Lord! Amen!)*

The Scripture readings and preaching were full of the same wisdom. The treacherous tale of seven courageous Maccabee brothers and their faith-filled mother was carried on Lea Shermerhorn's gentle voice. A hymn of God's goodness from 2 Thessalonians proclaimed by Zettie LeBlanc—a poignant testimony in itself, since Zettie had just been through her own ordeal—bid the

Lord Jesus and "our Father who loves us" to "console your hearts and strengthen them for every good work. *(Amen!)* . . . The Lord keeps faith! *(Amen! Yes! Thank you!)* It is *he* who will strengthen and guard you *(Al'right!)* . . . in the love of God *(Oh, yes!)* and the constancy of Christ." *(Yes! Amen!)* "God is not a God of the dead but of the living! All are alive in him!" proclaimed Father Kirk from Matthew's Gospel, recounting Jesus' retort to the Sadducees's question about the resurrection.

"Our Brother Al Winslow showed himself to be what Jesus was talking about today," Father Kirk preached minutes later, "a son of the Resurrection *(Amen!)*. Even when he was dying, the disease taking him inch by inch, he never lost hope! *(Amen!)* . . . It is in the *dark circumstances* that we come to our fullness of resurrection. . . . [The seven Maccabee brothers and their mother] knew, in the dark valley, that they saw the light, and they proclaimed it, *as we must do* in our dark moments! . . . If there is no resurrection, *everything we do* is empty! *(Amen! Amen!)* . . . But because Jesus *is* raised, and we have hope, we can face *anything* this world can offer, *(Amen!)* because we know that the Father is *pulling us, pulling us, **pulling** us* toward him! *(Yes!)* And that we shall stand, *in our bodies*, Church, *(Al'right!) in our bodies*, and *with one another, (Yes!)* before the Lord!" *(Yes!)*

The community's voices wove their own web of images, as song upon song voiced the affirmation, "God is my all and all!" "How do you recognize a child of God," we queried on the pulsing beat of the opening song, only to answer, "I'm washed in the blood of the Lamb." "God is the joy and the strength of my life," welled up in the midst of the Scripture readings; "He removes all pain, misery, and strife . . . I want to go with Him when He comes back. I've gone too far, and I'll never turn back!" "Oh, I want to see Him and look upon His face," we chorused as the altar table was prepared; "There to sing forever of His saving grace. / On the streets of glory, let me lift my voice./ My cares all past, I'm home at last, / ever to rejoice!"

*I*t was late in the service when Judy Brown signaled a "special request" for "Rough Side of the Mountain." The room still echoed the vamped sounds of "Wonderful rest! Sanctified rest! Glorious rest! Everlasting rest!!"—successive waves of climax to the stately "Near the Cross." Without hesitation, Reed Fromer fingered a few bluesy flourishes, then burst into the driving rhythms of "Rough Side of the Mountain"[13]—a traditional gospel piece that "starts intense and stays intense." Isaiah Brown was right with him. Against their insistent rhythms, Judy Brown's voice could be heard, "This is for you, Mama Winslow! All of us are comin' up on the rough side of the mountain!"

I glance out from the choir at the scene before me. Some quarter of the church house seem to be on their feet, moving, clapping, and enjoying the sheer exhilaration of getting into the song. I can see Liz Bell at the very back, both hands in the air, as if to say, I know this story! Bessie Brooks grabbed the *chekeré* from the floor beside her, striking it rhythmically against her hand—strung beads against the dried gourd adding strident accents to the alternate beats. *Sing it!* someone shouts.

"I'm comin' up," we chorus, and Judy Brown, mike in hand, begins to echo each phrase:

<blockquote>
(I'm comin' up, Lord) on the rough side (on the rough side)
of the mountain (of the mountain)
I must hold to God's, his powerful hand!
I'm coming up (I'm comin' up, Lord) on the rough side (on the rough side)
of the mountain, (and it's hard sometimes)
and I'm doin' my best to make it in!
</blockquote>

Immediately, we repeat these heartfelt lyrics. People are caught up in the song and movement, their exuberance almost drowning out the shouts of *Oh, yes!* and *Al'right!* Then, conviction etched on her voice, Judy takes up the first verse, the choir now echoing her words:

<blockquote>
Oh, Lord, (Oh, Lord) I am striving, (I am striving)
trying to make it through this barren land, Lord! *(Oh, yes!!)*
But as I go from day to day *(Al'right!)*
I can hear my Savior say,
"*Trust* me, child! Come on, and I'll hold your hand!"
</blockquote>

"I'm comin' up on the rough side . . ." we chorus again, intensity swelling from every part of the church. You can feel the passion and joy of this pulsing, singing body of people, as they proclaim once again, "and I'm doin' my best to make it in!"

Judy leans into a second verse, her body and spirit surrendered to the song's sentiments and its truth. It's clear to community members that she's feeling the power of the Spirit within her.

<blockquote>
I'm comin' up, Lord, (I'm comin' up, Lord) I'm comin' up, Lord,
(I'm comin' up Lord)
Although my burdens *(Yes!)* sometimes press me down, Lord. *(Sing it!)*
But if I can only keep the faith *(Oh, yes!)*
I'll have strength just to run this race.
Oh, I'm looking, I'm looking for my starry crown. *(Yes!!!!)*
</blockquote>

Her last words are more shouted than sung. "I'm comin' up on the rough side . . ." we chorus again, as if to feel the textures of this well-climbed hill and the fact that we "must hold to God's, his powerful hand!" Then, carried on another wave of energy—her left hand in the air now as if to say, "I know of what I sing!"— Judy launches into a last verse.

94

> This old race (this old race) will soon be over, (soon be over)
> Oh, and there'll be no more race for me to run, Lord! *(Oh, yes!)*
> But I got to stand before God's throne
> All my heartaches will be gone,
> Oh, when I hear my Savior say, *"Welcome home!"*

The whole church, it would seem, has thundered those welcoming words of God! Shouts of delight persist as Reed traces a glissando down the entire keyboard with a hymnal he's just grabbed from the pew beside him:

> I'm comin' up (I'm comin' up) on the rough side (on the rough side)
> of the mountain (of the mountain) . . .

we chant again, releasing, it would seem, the very heartaches of which Judy has just sung. Then, as if to savor those sweet words heard before the throne of God, she repeats the last verse,

> This old race (this old race) will soon be over, (soon be over)
> and there will be, there will be no more race for me to run, Lord!

Once again, as she presses into the words we will one day "hear my Savior say," clamorous shouts from all over the church complete her phrase: "Welcome home!" A final, full-throated *ritornello* brings the song full circle: "I'm comin' up on the rough side . . ." The tempo slows just enough to hear Judy's last interpolation, "and it's *hard* sometimes!" before the final phrase spreads itself broadly into a last testimony, "and I'm doin' my best to make it in!!"

"*Oh, thank you, Jesus! Thank you, Jesus!*" Judy shouts against the *Amens* and applause that well up all around. Reed and Isaiah sound a final arpeggiated chord and drum flourish, only to rejoin the spirited spill over. *Amen!!! Hallelujah!!! Amen!!!!*

When the exuberance finally subsided, and people took their seats to await Barbara McKinney's arrival at the ambo for announcements, the words rang in my ears: "Welcome home!" God's eternity imaged as home, I mused. God's future—tasted, proleptically, as a place like this one! But lest my thoughts spin off along some theological trajectory, relaxing the tension this liturgy had so clearly held in place, Barbara's words brought me back.

"Stop the new power plant!" she announced. "You're encouraged to attend a meeting to protest the building of a new plant"—the sixth in this part of San Francisco, we all knew—"that would produce 280 tons of air pollution annually for Bayview-Hunters Point and the surrounding areas! The California Energy Commission is holding a meeting to discuss their latest report, which has ignored our cries and arguments. Bayview-Hunters Point has the highest rate of breast cancer *in the world! In the world!*" she repeated, lest we had missed her last phrase "*And* the highest rate of asthma, bronchitis, and respiratory illness in San Francisco. PG&E is not shutting down any older, dirtier plants [to build this one]. So please attend the meeting!!"

*A*s I drove home to Berkeley that day, the morning's events played like dancing light on my mind. It struck me that the passion with which this community had just claimed a "home" beyond this one, a welcome waiting when "this old race" is finally over, was hardly an otherworldly fantasy but rather a means of resisting society's attempts to define them in terms that belie their true identity as God's own. It's a form of ritual resistance, I thought—a claiming of God's own promise, an imaginative anticipation of the truth that, despite the necessity of "striving to make it through this barren land," to live in freedom and with hope, the ultimate outcome, as Father Kirk had preached so eloquently, is already defined by Jesus' resurrection,[14] and by God's claiming each as "a child of God" who is "washed in the Blood of the Lamb."

*A*nd I began singing all over again. . . .

Intermezzo

SPACE

*F*rom their earliest history, Africans on American soil created spaces within which their distinctive experience of the living God could be honored, expressed, and ritualized. These spaces did not come ready-made. Nor were they reliant on architecture. Glens, forests, clearings became "found places"— ritual spheres within which to access the spiritual power of God; "created spaces" whose boundaries were fluidly defined by the outer circling of a ring shout.[1] Here, participants fused music, dance, and ecstatic prayer into a vibrant proclamation of life in the face of the death, claiming their humanity in the face of "one of the most oppressive forms of slavery the world has ever known."[2] In these "found places," the biblical God of liberation could be known—imaged in the call and response patterns of the Spirituals, felt in the rhythmic pulse of tapping feet and swaying bodies, present in the bonds of community that were forged and heard in coded messages that cloaked signals about the Underground Railroad as "stealing away to Jesus." Spaces claimed and transformed as places of resistance and hope. Arenas of grace and empowerment where everyone had a place, a role to play in the unfolding dance. These were the "architecture" of the "invisible church."

*L*ourdes is such a "found place." Its walls and windows trace an invisible "geometry of love."[3] Entering this space, one feels the imprint of generations who have prayed here, the "field" created Sunday after Sunday as people actualize this tiny church house as living, vibrant place—where one is both at home, and a "guest of the Almighty God." Some thirty years ago Brother Banks sensed "a presence" here, despite the broken windows and tattered interior. Father MacKinnon, finding the church overridden with anise weeds, cars junking the field beside it, chose to reopen its doors.[4] Flourishing now, it still remains the little church at the foot of "the hill,"[5] where "our doors remain open" to welcome all who come.

Lourdes has taught me that a worship space is neither its architecture, nor its furnishings, nor its decorative environment, although these come into play. Rather it is a "tensive construction," brought into being by how the community molds the space in its ritual action, by the cultural assumptions brought to the worship by its members, by the felt qualities they generate within the liturgy, by the other "realms of space" they evoke in the action—all of which mediate a sense of the community's identity, "who they are" and "whose they are."

Religious-cultural space / assumptions / experience / history / roots: How did it get to be this way?

*E*ntering this little mission church early on a Sunday morning, when things are still, one is immediately struck by its windows—by the presence of men and women whose faces are softly illuminated by the incoming light. A closer look and the history of the Christian church, with its roots in African soil, begins to unfold. On the left, a procession of faces: Moses the Black, fourth-century desert monk, and martyr; Felicity and Perpetua, third-century martyrs; Augustine of Hippo, fifth-century bishop; Victor I, second-century pope; and a darkly complected Virgin Mary caressing her Child. In cherishing the memory of these holy persons, the community claims that its roots are firmly planted in the church's earliest history.

But there's a humming, an unvoiced dialogue, across the space, as African faces turn toward their modern counterparts who line the right side of the church house—African American poets, musicians, orators, and freedom fighters who have helped keep the voice of faith alive in oppressive situations of the contemporary world: Frederick Douglas, Sojourner Truth, Langston Hughes, Mahalia Jackson, and Dr. Martin Luther King, Jr. These leaders gave witness to the God in whom they fiercely believed, and their testimony continues to inspire each new generation at Lourdes.

Other elements in the space are drawn into this humming. A half-life-size carved statue of Martin de Porres, seventeenth-century Black saint of Peru, stands just inside the left entryway, offering his silent welcome. A dark, carved figure of the Black Madonna of Montserrat rests in the domed niche near the left front of the church, just above Isaiah Brown's drums. An African crucifix hangs against a backdrop of richly figured African fabric on the rear sanctuary wall. A small blue banner of the Knights of St. Peter Claver is suspended above the first pews on the right, signaling the presence of "Knights" and "Ladies" of that organization within the community.

Looking around, it is clear that the church has been transformed—"reclothed," as it were, to speak of Lourdes' rich religious-cultural heritage.

Its Catholicity is evident as well. A wood carved altar table and similarly constructed ambo stand at the center of the "sanctuary" portion of the church. Behind, three chairs on an elevated platform for presider, deacon, and youthful assistant. A tabernacle in the domed niche to the right keeps the tradition of reserved Eucharist alive. Small stations of the cross line the side walls between the bright windows. A small, marble baptismal font, original to the church, now stands near the tabernacle, a large paschal candle at its side—both ready to be moved into the "open space" for baptisms.

There's an intentionality about the way the space is cared for—cleaned weekly by community members, prepared seasonally and weekly for worship. In 1995 the community added two new "windows" to the procession of holy persons who encircle the church. Portraits of two contemporary Black Catholic women, Blessed Josephine Bakita of the Sudan (d.1947) and Sister Thea Bowman (d. 1990), were commissioned and painted by a local artist and hung on either side of the sanctuary. Their treasured memory is alive here.

Action / actualizing space:
How is the space used?

*T*his heritage is set in motion each Sunday morning as members of the community arrive, filling the church house with their colorful dress, the warm sounds of their voices, and the familial feel of persons drawn close to each other. The space becomes a living reality, a sphere of action, full of a vitality that flows from community members' assumptions about worship, about themselves, about God, and about how to act in this Godly place.

Although the outer perimeter of the church house is doubly bounded by strong walls as well as a protective fence,[6] these potential barriers are transcended by "doors that remain open," welcoming all who arrive, even those who come unexpectedly. Visitors to Lourdes are frequently persons of other faith traditions and cultural backgrounds. Many return, some establishing long-term affiliations with Lourdes. As evidenced in a night of Revival, the community actively seeks out other Black Christians across ecumenical lines and provides hospitality each Sunday to the membership of Grace Baptist Church, who worship in Lourdes' church house.

Throughout the extended time of Sunday worship, the acoustic space is permeated over and again with waves of sound that well up from within the gathering—as if to burst the permeable walls and flow out into the surrounding community—and which then subside into moments of hushed reverence, only to break forth once again. The space is alive with living sound that vibrates, energizes, engages bodies, invites movement—the voices of the community resonating together and in dialogue, creating a kind of spiritual effervescence, an acoustic metaphor for the living presence of the Spirit of God. This vibrant sound is not hapless or formless but deeply personal—shaped by the cadence of Brother Banks's prayers, the unmetered embellishments of a lead singer against the choir's percussive chorusing, the gentle movements of Reed's accompaniment, the energy of Father Kirk's preaching.

The community's action within this tiny church house transforms what could be a restrictive space—pews affixed to the floor, a single central aisle with no side passageways—into a liberating space, a place of mutuality and interaction, of shared faith grounded in the One who is present here. Architecturally, the single center aisle creates a pathway to the front of the room, tracing, as in many churches, a metaphoric image of life's journey to its goal, imaged in Catholic imagination as the "sanctuary," the place of Presence.[7] Photos of the original church reveal such a schema—the center aisle led visually to the tabernacle atop an altar table against the rear wall of the sanctuary, with baldacchino above. This was clearly the focal point of the room, the "destination" of the metaphoric life-pilgrimage, both communal and personal.

Not only has the sanctuary been renovated—the tabernacle given its own place of honor just to the right—but the worship space is further "reshaped" by the community's action, its orientation transformed from linear to circular. At the outset of the liturgy, choir members, presider, deacon, and young assistant process in step toward the front of the room, only to turn and face the community for the duration of the liturgy. This creates a convergence of persons, both visually and acoustically. The goal of one's metaphoric journey has been transformed—from a "place of presence" at the end of the room to one "in the midst" of the community. Ministers and choir, together with the rest of the assembly, now surround the sacred action that takes place. The church-house-in-action becomes more circular, more labyrinthian if you will—its metaphoric destination is now in the middle. Margaret Visser comments that in this circular figure of the journey of life, we have also a "a picture of the soul," in which "the truth—God—[is] to be found at the heart of every self."[8]

What emerges in the course of worship is a room transformed as the sphere of communal and godly action that has both a "focus" and a "locus." The locus of the action remains in the entire church house. It is evident that there is no single channel for the action of God in this assembly—observable in the communicative movements of a person's hand raised in testimony, a body set in motion by syncopated musical beats, a mother or grandmother gently rocking a small child, a woman crossing to the other side of the room to comfort someone who weeps, and the familial movements throughout the space during the extended exchange of peace.

At the same time a certain "focal point" of the action, its affective center, its point of attraction, emerges as well. This affective center is focused near the front of the church, in what I describe as the "open space." (*See diagram of the space, Appendix 2.*) This area is bordered first by the front pews, then by drums and piano to the left and the tabernacle to the right,[9] and finally by the altar and ambo at the edge of the sanctuary, which complete this "open space" and are included within its sphere. This focal point is both the acoustic and visual center of the gathering, its dialogic point of convergence. It is the open and fluid space from which the pastor preaches and from which the music is generated by pianist, drummer, lead singers, and choir. Here, eucharistic bread and wine are offered to the community, baptisms are celebrated, special blessings given.[10] The affective attraction of this focal space is animated by the emotional intensity of Brother Banks's prayer, the dynamism of Father Kirk's preaching, the magnetic witness of lead singers, director, choir, pianist, and drummer. One is drawn into this space, called, invited. Like the center of the historic ring shout, it becomes the focal point of inclusion in a liturgical action that welcomes the active response of everyone. It is the center of the visual and auditory dialogue that happens continuously, as patterns of call-response structure the space and the liturgy dialogically.

Within this "open space," at the heart of the gathered assembly, there are subtle shifts in the focus of the action—from ambo, to table, to the area in front of them. The choir highlights these shifts by physically moving from place to place, assuming one of three configurations designed to support the focus of the action. (*See diagram of choir's movements, Appendix 2.*) During moments when the sung word is the primary liturgical action, the choir members arch across the sanctuary to assume their leadership. At times when music accompanies other actions, such as the reception of Communion, singers lead from the choir seating. When the presider and deacon stand at the altar table for the Eucharistic Prayer, singers converge on the sanctuary steps behind them, bearing up their spoken prayer on song. Thus, music leadership is organically and spatially related to the focal action of the worship.

As this rectangular church house is transformed by the "circularity" of the action, music orchestrates a range of movements within the circulating whole. Music is a catalyst for "celebratory movements" of stepping, clapping, swaying, praising, and testifying. It accompanies "preparatory actions" of carrying bread and wine to the altar table, "processional movements" such as receiving Eucharist, "incorporating gestures"of extended peace greetings, as well as "informal movements" that take place in the midst of a song when one community member moves to another place to comfort another. Movements throughout the liturgy, both patterned and improvised, are free, energized, and personalized. The pathways created are never one-directional, but crisscross, weaving a web of spatial relatedness. The church-house-in-motion becomes, like the historic ring shout, a place of inclusion.

Qualities of space / "force field":
What is it like to be here? How do we know how to be here?

Like all space, a worship space is never empty, but filled with "fields"— invisible, nonmaterial forces generated by those who gather within it, qualities of space that affect all who enter.[11] There's "something in the air," something "in the space"—forces created by how persons relate with each other over time, by the intentionality of their action together, which seems to inhabit the places where they have engaged.

Walking into Lourdes, one intuitively feels at home—not dwarfed or anonymous, but welcomed into a place of intimacy and peace. It seems good to be here. The energies generated by persons arriving make it clear that something is about to happen—pay attention! There's an excitement in the air, a sense of anticipation but also a sense of "at homeness" with life as it is, and with persons as they are. Everyday experience is not shed at the entranceway but generates a felt-sense of "why we are here." Familial ways of being together are welcome. There's a liberative sense that love is what matters, and love seems the centerpiece of this Godly space. Hospitality and joy well up spontaneously. Even visitors sense a freedom to be who they are, to move beyond more restricted patterns of behavior and be drawn into the embrace. One senses that Lourdes is a "safe place," where one can freely claim to be "a child of God" despite whatever demeaning, threatening forces inhabit the social environment within which one lives.

As liturgy unfolds, the space takes on a tone and texture that is lively, colorful, vibrant, and resounding, as well as quiet and reflective. There is a spiritual climate generated that feels "full"—filled up by the closeness of persons one to another, by the vibrational intensity of the vocal and instrumental sound, by the emotional ardor of the faith communication that takes place—"as if one's life depended on it," and by the bodily warmth generated as people engage prayerfully with each other. "I am filled up," "I am full" are comments one hears often at Lourdes. These are the personal counterparts of a space permeated with "livingness"—overflowing, at times, in tears that are not of sadness but of joy. Before anything is said or done, this felt-quality becomes a spatial metaphor for the vital and active presence of God as Spirit.

The force-field created within Lourdes' church house is itself tensive—layered with energies that are not uniform but multipersonal, polyphonic, diverse, even divergent. These communally generated energies interact in a continuous dialogue, never fully merging but maintaining a sense of an inter-personality that is deeply valued by members of Lourdes. This spiritual climate becomes a context for knowing a God whose manifold gifts are richly present in a diversity of persons, a variety of gifts, and a multiplicity of ministries.

"Realms" of space / cosmic geography:
To what other spatial environments does this space relate?

*I*n worship at Lourdes, "here" and "there" touch—realms of space intersect without ever losing their distinctness. This little church house, nestled in a corner of San Francisco, becomes a juncture in a cosmic geography evoked by sight and sound, singing and believing.

On his voice and in his body, Brother Banks carries the community's past "there" and present "here"—the struggles of the plantation South and the challenges of the urban North—all the while keeping his gaze turned toward the future place of God's welcome, where there will be "singin', singin', like we've never heard before!" On any given Sunday, the sounds of various songs make present the memory of family members, of beloved parents, of ancestors in the faith who have lived in other places and other times. Each time the children sing, "Oh, how I love Jesus, because He first loved me," one suspects that Brother Banks's mother is near.

The very sight of the church building at the foot of "the hill" elicits its own connections to the history of Hunters Point—the migrations of African Americans from the South during World War II; the race riots of the '60s and the subsequent rebuilding of this area in which Lourdes played a vital part. "What a Mighty God We Serve" is as readily sung by the Lourdes choir on the edge of Golden Gate Park, in protest of the city's action against the homeless, as it is from the pews of this church.

The tonality, texture, and familial style of worship brings the realm of worship and that of everyday living very close. "Sacred" and "secular" are not distinctions readily made by community members. Rather than dichotomous, these spheres intermingle and permeate each other. The community's choice of the gospel music idiom has its own way of traversing these would-be distinctions. In fact, gospel music draws its distinctive power by harnessing the rhythms and stylistic elements of a range of secular musics to speak a message of faith, once described as "good news in hard times."

The faith dimension of these intersecting spheres of space goes further. The two worlds of this community's space-time, and the space-time of God's kingdom—announced in Jesus and fulfilled in God's future promise—seem to come very close in the communal imagination. In the words of a song sung on many Sundays, "*This* is the place, *now* is the time, *we are the people* Jesus had in mind, gathered in this place at this appointed time . . ."

The action of praying and singing opens the spatial imagination to God's "home" already proleptically present within this home, while signaling the still future arrival of "God's realm." As the lyrics of songs that fill the acoustic space put it, "I want to be ready when Jesus comes!" because "I'm goin' up yonder to be with my Lord!" Performatively and lyrically, the community claims that "Soon and very soon, we're going to see the King" and "there's no more weepin' there . . ." "This old race will soon be over, and there will be no more race for me to run, Lord." Then, as "I stand before God's throne, all my heartaches will be gone as I hear my Savior say, 'Welcome home!'"

Microcosms / metaphors for space:
How does music-making image the whole?

*I*n nature, the overall shape of many living things is reflected in their smallest components—the form of a whole crown of broccoli imaged in its smallest floret, the design of an entire fern reflected in each smaller component of its lacy structure.[12] "Fractals," as named by Benoit Mandelbrot, who discovered them, reveal an intriguing dimension of the natural world—that tiny portions of our experience can serve as metaphors or microcosms for a larger system.

At Lourdes, music is a fractal reflection of the spatial aspects of the community's worship. A single song, remembered from childhood, can evoke a whole stream of religious and cultural history. The sounding of a particular vocal timbre or drummed rhythm can make present a vivid faith memory that moves people into a place of shared understandings. Gospel music, with its patterns of regenerating traditional words, phrases, and melodies, intends to awaken such consciousness, to bring those who make it into a space of memory and remembering, into a place where living faith is actively passed on from one generation to another.

Each song is an arena of action, a microcosm of the sphere of action created within the whole church house in the course of Sunday worship. Song performance holds the tension between the "focus" of the action and its "locus." Clearly, music-making has a focus, an affective center, concentrated in the lyrical and bodily praise and testimony of the musical leadership (lead singers, choir, director, and instrumentalists). But its unmistakable locus is an assembly of persons extended throughout the space who propel the music forward through their movements, responses, and vocal participation. In fact, in gospel music performance "filling in" the musical line with sung or spoken interjections and adding to the rhythmic density through percussive clapping or visual movements are expected ways of participation.[13] All aspects of the music—its rhythmic structures, melodic phraseology, and performance practice—create a "musical space" into which others are expected to enter. The music is "built up," architectonically, through a layering of voices, instruments, words that interact and overlap. The whole church house, as spatial extension of the music-making, becomes densely dialogic. Participating in music, one enters the force-field of joy, energy, welcome, and freedom, that pervades the whole spatial atmosphere. One experiences what it is to be "alive" and to be "alive in God's presence."

Identity / community mediated within space:
How do we know ourselves here?

*S*pace is a powerful element in the ritual mediation of a community's identity in worship. Spatial strategies situate people in relationship with one other and with their God, evoking a dynamic memory of "who we are" and "whose we are." By filling the acoustic space vibrationally with intense outbursts of praise, the Lourdes community images, even beyond their words, a God of great majesty and power, glorious and awe-inspiring. The reverberating waves of "Jesus, excellent is your name!" stretch beyond verbal imagery to evoke the presence of One who is matchless, admirable, and worthy of all praise. This splendid God is also One who has drawn very near, who is immanent—mediated spatially through the tender exchanges between one member of the community and another, and by the closeness of all to the faith actions of proclamation, testimony, singing, and sacramental action by which the presence of the Incarnate One is made known; and mediated sonically by the intimacy of a hushed, sung prayer, such as "Lord, give me an unwavering faith" or "Please, Lord, set my soul free."

Modes of participation in most any portion of the ritual action, but especially in music-making, create a spatial image—a "presentational symbol"[14] if you will—of a community that holds diversity and solidarity in creative tension. Individual faith expressions are woven acoustically and visually into a tapestry of communal sound and movement. Young and old, men and women, are part of this fabric, their roles different yet complementary. Bonded as family, children grow up in the space—musically, liturgically, spiritually—while older members are reverenced. In this spatial, interpersonal environment, the sacred actions of worship and those of everyday living are likewise held in creative tension, their interplay in the liturgy revealing their deep and abiding connection.

A spatial metaphor for ministry emerges as well: persons who face one other, whose interaction is marked by reciprocity, mutuality, and balance. The one who presides is never alone but is surrounded by a host of other ministers—Brother Banks and a young assistant to his side, the choir filling the adjacent areas. The energies of their shared ministry seem focused on overcoming spatial and social distance, on creating connections that unite the community in a common purpose and a shared act of praise and thanksgiving offered to the living God in their midst. At the same time, inspiration, testimony, words, and actions of faith flow freely throughout the assembly, strengthening and building up the whole body in their ministry one to another.

In sum, what emerges at Lourdes is a multigenerational community with shared leadership, all of whom actively contribute to the worship. Persons are not isolated but are known, connected, and interwoven spatially throughout the liturgy. One feels the truth of the proverb articulated by a young adult, Corey Monroe—"I am because we are." Lourdes is a centered community, affectively drawn to a spatial center by faith actions that mark their particular expression of Catholic liturgy. This experience of centeredness, of spatially surrounding the holy transaction of worship, carries a rich biblical resonance—one imaged in the closing chapters of the book of Revelation: God dwelling "in the midst" of God's holy people.

Chapter Seven

"IT'S ABOUT A MESSAGE!"

—SINGING THE GOSPEL—

"We are not performers, we are God's messengers. We are here to deliver a *message!*" declared Pat Goodall with conviction. It was a chilly Thursday evening during my first January at Lourdes. Arriving at the church house that evening, I had asked members of the choir if I could talk with them about their ministry before rehearsal got underway. Finding agreement, I pulled a chair into the open space at the front of the church so I could face choir members who were scattered across the first few pews.

It was about fifteen minutes into our conversation when Pat spoke up. "We do not perform! We sing to do God's will. . . . We are here to deliver a *message!*"

I could feel in her words, and the conviction with which she spoke them, a corrective to my questioning the choir about the "musical dimensions" of their "performance." Yet I realized intuitively that Pat had just given me a pivotal image, one that would unlock the experience I was witnessing from Sunday to Sunday—a key insight into how musicians at Lourdes understand, describe, and embody their art; an interpretive framework within which to hear the comments of others at Lourdes about the impact of the music on their lives and worship; and a potent invitation to participate fully in this primary "mission" of the music-making. It's about more than creating beautiful or even "sacred" sound. It's about *delivering a message!* It's about *singing the Gospel!*

The mood that Sunday morning had been a bit muted, at least for Lourdes. Perhaps it was the chill in the December air, or the accumulated tiredness of the days after Christmas. Late in the liturgy, Jean

Alexander stepped out in front of the choir. Microphone in her right hand, she looked intently at the community before her.

"Is everybody willing to say yes to Jesus?" she begins almost conversationally over Reed's free improvisation. Hearing some tempered *Yeses*, Jean calls out, "*Al'right!* Let's *wake up!* You act like you're *dead* this morning! *(That's right!)* We're serving a *living* God!" There's fire in her voice now, as she fuels the sparks she's igniting. "You've *got to testify! (Yes!) You can't be ashamed of it!! Let 'em know what He's done for you!!!* (Applause . . .) *Oh yes!*" Isaiah's drums are now stoking the embers as well. *"Just like we can holler for the Giants, we've got to holler for the living God! He's gonna be there for you when the Giants and the 49ers are not!!!*" Shouts of *Yes! That's right! C'mon!* are echoing back now in rapid fire, playing off Jean's every word. "Al'right!" she tapers off, aware that the community has been roused and is ready to sing. Reed and Isaiah's rhythms are emphatic as we burst into a spirited chorus,

> I'll say Yes! Lord, Yes! to your will and to your way![1]
> I'll say Yes! Lord, Yes! I will trust you and obey!
> When the Spirit speaks to me, with my whole heart I'll agree
> and my answer will be, Yes! Lord, Yes!

Jean's voice is ringing out over these voiced affirmations: "Sing out! . . . We've got to trust you, Lord and obey! . . . With my whole heart I agree! Yes, Lord, Yes!" Then, inciting another chorus, she shouts, *"C'mon, Church, wake up!"*

> I'll say Yes! Lord, Yes! to your will and to your way. . .

resounds again. Several people around the church are on their feet moving freely to the dance-like rhythms. Chorus completed, Jean's voice takes the lead. Her head back, left hand raised, you can feel the testimony in her tension-edged voice:

> Lord, I've given you the glory *(Yes!)* for which you've given me. *(C'mon!)*
> I feel my life has overflowed.
> And I will go with you *(C'mon!)* wherever you choose! *(Oh, yes!)*
> You're the Lord of life, *(Al'right!)* so how can I say no-o-o-o-o!!

Jean is all but jumping up and down, her body resonating with these words of commitment. Roused again, the community rebounds,

> I'll say Yes!, Lord, Yes! to your will and to your way! . . .

taking the song to a new level of energy, spurred on by Jean's continued shouts, "Yes, Lord!". . .

"*W*hen I choose a song," commented Jean to me once, "I have to find a message that I feel I can give to others. I pray that God will use me to help others in their struggles. . . . I pray and trust that I will be able to deliver a message to those who need it. But the reaction of the people is very important. . . . When I see them, I respond! You never know how the Spirit will move. But when the Spirit moves, the song touches people."[2]

"You know, [people sometimes say to me,] 'Why do you have to preach all the time you sing?' I say, 'I don't know, that's me.' There's something that's within, and the Spirit takes over. When I learn a song, and [even] before I learn it, I ask God to use me in *His* way, not mine. And then I will be able to reach somebody . . . who needs to come to him! . . . Whatever comes up, this is the way God uses me."[3]

"*T*he words are very powerful and have a very special meaning," observed Tina Edwards, offering the perspective of community members who receive the choir's ministry. "[But] it would not be the same if the singer didn't really believe in what they were singing. . . . You really have to have faith in God to sing a good gospel song. It's like, 'I believe in you [God], I trust you, I'm your worker, work through me!' That's the message they're relaying when they sing the song. . . . 'I've been there, I'm here to help you.' . . . You really feel like the [singer] knows what you're going through and God will help you, and you start to think about all the things you once took for granted. . . . God never gives you what you can't handle!"[4]

*I*t is Passion Sunday. Hangings of red fabric create a stark backdrop as Pat Goodall turns from directing the choir to face the congregation. Her eyes are closed, head bent slightly forward, as if attending to some inner fire, some deeply felt fervor. Already, the song's chorus has evoked a sense of communal intimacy, as we sang together the fervent words of those who have experienced deep love: "Jesus, I love you for your tender care. . . ." The measured pace of the music makes room for the message to take hold, to deepen all that has transpired since we processed into the church some half-hour earlier singing: "Ride on, King Jesus!"

"Because he first loved me," Pat begins ardently, "is why I love him so!"[5]

Her voice and body seem to be as one as she pulls the message from some inner core of her being, sending each phrase forth with mounting intensity:

> His life *(Yes!)* he gave *(Oh, yes!)* for me *(Yes He did!)*
> when no one, *(Oh, yes!)* no one seemed to care!

Isaiah is prodding the swell of her voice with his insistent drumming.

> For his life *(Yes!)* he gave so free // so free *(Thank you Jesus!)*
> And I'm yours with all // my // being!

Bursting into the lyrical line, choir and congregation take up the song:

> Je–sus! Jesus I love you!
> Oh, oh, oh, oh ye–s, I do!!
> Oh, oh, oh, ye–s, I do!
> Oh, oh, oh, yes // I do!!

"*T*o stand up there and open your mouth and let words flow out in the right key is one thing. That's not singing," Pat commented over lunch one Saturday. "You have to really *feel* a song in order to get it across. . . . In order to give a message, you've got to *believe* the message! . . . The song has to mean something to [you] in the first place. . . . [If] a song has meaning for you, when you sing it . . . that feeling comes again—seems like it rises from the pit of your stomach . . . and just comes on up and just takes over. . . . [That way] it will take on meaning for somebody else. . . . You never know what's happening in people's lives. . . . You never know what they need at that point. . . ."[6]

"*W*hen I pick a song," explained lead singer Bessie Brooks on another occasion, "it fits me! I need those songs! The songs I learn, I pick them out carefully. . . . I have to sing [them] the way I feel [them] down inside. . . . I feel the words, the Gospel, the words I want to get across to the people. . . . I feel every song within me. . . . A lot of times I know I sound like I'm preaching to everyone, but it's just the way I want to get [the message] across to the people. . . .

"Last Sunday," she continued, referring to her singing of "Mine Eyes Have Seen the Glory" the previous week, "I was feeling that I was out there trampling with God across the vintage, trampling everything. And I could just *see* him! I *see* him like he was riding a horse with wings. . . . I can just see the whole picture when I sing that song. [Or when I sing] 'Lord, let your Spirit fall on me,' I can see the dove coming down. I see it, and I'm singing about it. You have to *see* it, you have to really *feel* what you're singing, so that it comes across. . . ."[7]

"*A*ll the songs have pretty much the same message: 'Put your faith and trust in God!'" remarked Tiffany Isles, speaking of the impact of songs on members of the congregation. "We all know this, but sometimes it feels really good to hear someone *say* it to you. Not just *say* it, but *sing* it to you with all their heart, their feelings, and their soul. . . . You can feel them singing it *to* you."

"It's like, 'I've been there! I'm here for you! Come with me!'" added Tina Edwards.

"It's more than the words, then?" I asked.

"Right, it's the words and the feeling," responded Tiffany. "You can know the words to the songs . . . but it's when you hear the person sing them to you. . . . It's like their soul is flowing with their words into your ears. . . .".[8]

*I*saiah's drums are throbbing, the pulse of tapped triplets on his snare filling in the stronger accents of his metronomic bass drum, rousing people to their feet. A few measures of Reed's lusty introduction to this moderately paced favorite sets the church house in motion. Rose Isles steps out in front of the choir, the free movements of her body mirrored in the flow of her blue choir robe. Behind her, the choir is swaying rhythmically from side to side, playing off Reed's more syncopated improvisation.

Rose flings out her first free "call," inciting the choir's steady, more beat-oriented "response."

It's good to know . . .	It's good to know (*Jesus!*) Jesus![9]
Everybody ought to know . . .	It's good to know (*Jesus!*) Jesus!
He's the lily of the valley,	
my bright and morning star!	
It's good to know . . .	It's good to know the Lord!

Rose glances back at the choir, just as Pat calls out, *C'mon choir!* and they launch into another cycle of tightly entwined interplay,

It's good to know . . .	It's good to know (*Jesus!*) Jesus!. . .
Everybody ought to know . . .	It's good to know (*Jesus!*) Jesus!
Oh, he's the Alpha and Omega,	
The beginning and the end!	
It's good to know . . .	It's good to know the Lord!

Rose's left hand is in the air now, as she leans into a first verse

I came to Jesus, just as I was.
I was weary, wounded and sad!

But you know what? she calls out, her voice sailing right through the melodic line into the free space of expressive speech.

> I found in him a resting place,
> and he has made me glad!! Oh-oh, oh-oh!
> *It's good to know* . . .

she shouts, and the cycle begins again, prodded by her insistent goading, and the free flow of new lyrical images:

> | | It's good to know *(Jesus!)* Jesus! |
> | *Everybody ought to know* . . . | It's good to know *(Jesus!)* Jesus! |
> | Oh, he's joy in sorrow, | |
> | my hope for tomorrow! | |
> | *It's good to know* . . . | It's good to know the Lord! |

The message is all of a piece, Rose projecting its feeling as much through the fluid, downward movements of her body as through the vibrant tone of her impassioned voice. "I love the Lord," she sings, invoking the well-known lyrics of "Dr. Watts,"[10]

> 'cause he heard my cry,
> and he pitied, he pitied every groan!

There's no restraining the words as Rose propels them out into the church house:

> As long as I live while troubles rise,
> Oo, I hast-en to his throne. Oh-oh, oh-oh!
> *It's good to know* . . .

she shouts, and the cycle begins again. . . .

"**W**e're disciples," Rose commented one afternoon, reflecting on the choir's ministry. "We're giving a message to the people, and they're receiving it. . . . We're sending a message out . . . [so that people can get] some kind of healing, some kind of release if they're worried about something. . . . I would like them to know that God is there with them! . . . God is *really* there with them. . . . If I can get this message to them by my singing, I think I did my job! . . . A lot of people come and have different problems. . . . I think we as a choir . . . can help them get over these problems, deal with these problems. . . . I really think we are *disciples.* I don't go door to door to preach, but we are disciples in our own way because we are really getting a message over to people. . . . In every song that we sing, there's a message there if people only listen."[11]

"I get my feeling from the choir," she added on another occasion. "When the choir sings the background, that's what I feed on. If they haven't given me what I need, I can't give it to the people. So I feed off them, and if they're not singing, well, I turn around and look at them and say, 'Let's sing that again!' That's how I get my feeling. I have to get it from them, so I can give it to the people."[12]

"The drums are important, too," remarked Liz Bell in a conversation with members of Lourdes Women's Sodality. "We need something to make us move, and feel the music. . . . The instruments help. . . . The drums, the piano, they really help bring out the feeling. . . . They give more power [to the singing]."[13]

"Gospel music is like soul music. . . . It has a lot of soul and feeling," remarked Tiffany Isles. "You can almost feel [choir members] singing from their soul. You can feel it, because they put so much into it and it's coming out from the bottom of their stomach. You can feel the energy they're putting into the song and it's feeding back [to] you."

"It's very lifelike, full of life!" added Tina Edwards. "I've seen other choirs, not gospel choirs, but traditional Catholic choirs. I'm not saying they're not good, but I just don't feel the same thing. It's set—you have to sing it that way or it doesn't sound good. But with gospel, you're putting yourself into it, depending on how you're feeling that day. . . . If it's a bad day, 'I'm crying out to the Lord!'. . ."[14]

"Music is so important to my spirituality," remarked Tiffany some years later. "It's about feeling God's presence. . . . The first time that I felt God was when I was a teenager and it was during a song. . . . It was not at all like I thought it would be. I felt a peace, a profound love for everyone and everything. It was also the joy of knowing that I am loved and it made me want to share that love. It's very emotional. . . . I feel God's presence through the music from Lourdes."[15]

Sing it, Walter! shouts Shirley Valmore from the first pew as Walter Turner glides into a second verse of a well-loved Communion song, seemingly unaffected by the August heat. His high baritone voice rings out over the circulating flow of people coming forward to receive Bread and Wine and returning to their seats.

"I am lost" he begins serenely, leaving room within his carefully delivered lyrics for the abundant shouts of *Yes!* and *Sing it!* that interrupt even the spaces between his slow-forming syllables.

. . . if you take // your hand // from me
I am blind // with—out // thy light, // thy light to see.

Sing it, Walter! shouts Shirley again as he soars to the apex of the melody, her body indicating that she's not only hearing but feeling the music as well.

Lord, just al–ways let // me *(Woo!)* // thy ser—vant be, *(Sing!)*
Oh, lead me, // dear Lord, // lead me. *(Thank you, Walter!)*

Lead me, // guide me, // along the way,[16]

choruses the assembly, as Walter, with a look of quiet engagement, embellishes their lyrics;

for // if you lead me, I // just can't stray.

Choir members, seated behind Walter in the sanctuary, are rocking gently in slow duple movements against the song's extended triple meter, all the while calling out their own exclamations.

Lord, let me walk *(Yes!)* // each day with thee. *(Well . . .)*
Lead me, oh Lord, // oh, Lord lead me. *(Amen!)*

C'mon, Walter! prods Shirley from the front, as Walter, standing full stature and never losing composure, leans slightly forward toward the ambo mike. Doubling back into the first verse, he intensifies the energy ever so slightly against insistent shouts from around the church.

I am weak, // *(Yes!)* and I need // *(Oh, yes!)* Thy strength // *(Yes!)*
and power *(Al'right!)*
to help // me o-o-o-o-ver // *(Yes!)* my weak– // *(Yes! Sing it!)*
my weak—est hour.

Cresting again in a melodic swell, Walter punctuates his long, spun-out lyrics with percussive word endings that give force to his supplication:

Help me through *(Yes!)* the dark-ness, // *(Yes!)* Thy face to see, *(Well . . .)*
Oh, lead me, // *(Oh, yes!)* dear Lord, // lead me. *(Oh yes, lead me!)*

The assembly surges into the chorus with renewed fervor, carried on Reed and Isaiah's steady accompaniment:

Lead me, // guide me, // along the way,
for // if You lead me, I // just can't stray . . .

"**W**hen I sing a song," remarked Walter one evening, "[I hand it over to God]. I ask the Spirit to anoint my vocal chords."[17] Other singers echo Walter's emphasis on prayer before singing. It's common for a lead singer to preface his or her song, "Pray with me, Church, while I sing this song!" It seems that this reliance on prayer, their own and the community's, affects the musical process itself. In handing over the outcome of the song, the singer seems to relax into the song, trusting that their purpose for singing it will be effective.

"**T**he Spirit works through us," contends singer Louise Wood. "God uses us. . . . He uses each one of us in a different way. But it's all part of his ministry. There are certain songs that we sing that you will hear a distinct reaction from the choir. . . . You'll see hands raised, because the Spirit is within, coming out. . . . When the Spirit is like that, it reaches everyone. . . . [God] within, being drawn out to someone else. When you are used in that way, the same kindred spirit in another is going to be touched. I don't think you do that without the Spirit. God has to use that part of you inside to reach that part in someone else."[18]

"**S**ome Sundays," observed singer Judy Brown, "the Spirit is so thick in here you can see it! Other times you're singing but it's not getting across. There are other things on [people's] minds, and they're not really into it. . . . They don't let the music soothe. . . . They don't get the message. . . . But there are other times when the Spirit is just so thick that whatever we would do that day would go over."[19]

"**T**he music makes us let go of all the things that's torturing us on the inside," claimed Liz Bell in one conversation. "The Holy Spirit talks to us. Through that music, the Holy Spirit is talking to me, making me believe in myself. All these things I'm carrying around, all these burdens, when I hear the words and this music, I can let go of all that."[20]

"**I** had to get used to the idiom of gospel music. . . . I had to learn what it meant for my faith," commented Father Kirk over coffee one morning. "Certain songs touch me deeply. . . . [In the] years I've been here, this music has really penetrated my spirit. . . . I was weaned on classical music. I love it! . . . But I have deepened my faith by participating in music here. . . . The formula of gospel music is very simple, child-like. The message is direct. . . . Simplicity makes it powerful. . . ."[21]

❦ ❦ ❦

*Y*ou can feel the energy level elevate slightly as Reed modulates to the next highest key. "Fill my cup, let it overflow!" the choir has just sung, "let it overflow with love!" Nestled between the Scripture readings on this Sunday of the Ascension, images of being "filled" and "overflowing with love" play off the biblical announcement that "before many days you will be baptized with the Holy Spirit," the promised gift of the same Father who has "put all things under Christ's feet," the same Christ who "fills all in all."

Rita Johnson leans slightly into the microphone that rests in a silver-toned mike stand before her. Pat signals her to double back into the verse she's just sung, gesturing to her as if to tease out an intensity that breaks gradually into Rita's clear, soprano voice.

It's my desire, to live for thee![22]

she sings. "Live for Thee!" answers the choir, as people goad Rita forward with their shouts.

. . . and to always walk upright!

she responds, echoed once again by the choir, "Walk upright!" Then, like a stream bubbling up and flowing out across a downhill watercourse, she presses into the lyrics, her voice propelled forward by shouts of *Yes! Sing it, Rita!* and Reed's increasingly pulsing accompaniment.

"Give me the strength I'm gonna need to face the day!"

She's embellishing the lyrics now. Her hands, which until this time have stayed close to her tall, erect body, move gently, allowing us to glimpse the inner emotion that fuels the song. Pressing on into her last ardent plea, she implores,

Stay here with me through the night!

Choruses of *Yes!* erupt around her as the variegated vocal sound of the whole community swells once again into a last, full-voiced refrain. Rita plays off each line, overlapping it with her responsive phrases, until joining the unison as the song draws to a close:

Fill my cup let it overflow! (Just fill my cup, Lord!)
Fill my cup let it overflow! (Fill my cup, Lord!)
Fill my cup let it overflow! (Let it overflow!)
Let it overflow with love!

*J*udy Brown, who selects the songs to be sung at each Sunday's liturgy, begins with the Scripture readings of the day. "I meditate on the readings and the Responsorial Psalm," she commented as we talked about the process one Sunday. "I ask the Lord to help me to pick the right song to get the right feeling and the right meaning across to the people. I work it out with the help of the Lord."[23]

Other members of the community experience the connection between the songs and the Word of God. "The songs . . . open you up," remarked Mike Edwards. "All the songs we sing are close to the readings or the Gospel [of the day]. You can relate better to the readings and the Gospel because of the song. . . . [While the Scriptures are being read,] you might wander off. But you listen to the songs and you think back on what the reading says. . . . You understand the readings better. . . ."[24]

"When you're singing," noted Rhoda Charles, "you get more of a spiritual connection with the Word of God and the things he has done for you. . . ."[25]

"*W*hat we sing comes out of the Bible," stated Bessie Brooks emphatically in one conversation. "The words *are* the Gospel! . . . We may have our own woven into it, but the words and everything in those songs are in the Bible. So it's *Gospel.* Like [the song] 'Precious Lord, Take My Hand'—God is anxious for us to hold onto his hand. That's in the Bible. Hearing the music and listening to the words from the Gospel, that moves you and lets you know that the Lord is on your side, and you're gonna hold on to his hand, and try to be strong. . . ."

"Jesus wept, so he don't mind us being emotional! He wept for Lazarus when he was in the grave. We can cry all we want to. We can cry when we're happy, we can cry to be sad. But we praise and raise his name up, because he's worthy! . . . That's how we get our feeling. The feeling comes from the words."[26]

*I*t was late in the service on that June Sunday in '95 when Brother Banks preached about the challenges of fatherhood and the need for "unwavering faith." People had settled into their seats again after coming forward for Communion. Reed begins to weave a gentle modulation from the closing phrases of "Amazing Grace," as Jean Alexander moves out in front of the choir.

"Good morning, Church!" she begins, looking out at the crowd before her. "I'd like to dedicate this song to Alexis and Juwan." She glances over at them, seated on the left side of the church house, and continues: "You know the Lord's been carrying you! . . . It's not easy to do God's work! Especially when something's wrong with a mother's child, she's gonna worry. But the Lord is on your side!" A ripple of *Yeses* affirm her words of comfort. Reed settles into the new key, hinting at the harmonies of an old gospel favorite, "His Eye Is on the Sparrow."[27] Jean begins slowly, making room for the words to settle into our ears and hearts like a warm summer rain on thirsty soil. Each unmetered phrase is shaped by the emotion in her voice.

> Why should I feel discouraged, *(Oh, yes! Well . . .)* //
> and why should the shadows come,
> Why should my heart be lonely, *(Oh, yes!)* //
> and long for heaven and home,
> Since Je-sus is my portion? *(Oh, yes!)* // My constant friend is he.
> His eye is on that little sparrow, *(Oh, yes!)*
> and I know my God watches, *(Yes!)* he watches me. *(Yes! Amen!)*

Jean's eyes are closed now, head tipped slightly back, her raised left hand mirroring the ardor in her voice. Reed and Isaiah catch the nuance of each deliberate phrase, embellishing it with arpeggiated fingering and dramatic cymbal flourishes.

> Whenever I'm in trouble *(Yes!!!)* // and whenever doubts arise
> and song give place to sighin' *(Yes!!)* //
> and hope within me dies. *(Scattered handclaps . . .)*
> I'll draw the closer to him, *(Well. . .)*
> from care *(Yes!)* God sets me free! *(Thank you, Jesus!)*
> His eye is on that little sparrow, *(Yes!)*
> and I know *(Yes!)* my God watches, *(He does!)* he watches me. *(Amen!)*

The whole church house breaks into an impassioned, full-voiced chorus, the rhythms now steady and lilting. Jean's voice rises above the fervent sound, embellishing each phrase as she echoes the lyrics.

> I sing (I sing) because (because) I'm happy (I'm so happy!),
> I sing (and I sing) because (because) I'm free!! (God set us all free!)
> His eye (Oh, his eye) is on (is on) that sparrow, (that sparrow)
> and I know (I know) he watches (God watches) me.

Jean looks out at the church house. "God said," she calls out, then intones a new verse:

> Let not *(Yes Lord!)* your heart be troubled! *(Yes!)*

She breaks the line, crying out "Help me, Jesus! Church do you hear me?" Reed punctuates her shout with an insistent volley of repeated chords. "God said," she exclaims again, relaunching the verse,

Let not your heart be troubled *(Yes! Al'right!)* //
his tender words I hear *(Oh yes!)*
while resting on God's goodness, Hallelujah!
I lose all doubts and fears, *(Yes!!!)*
though by the path God leadeth, *(Amen!)*
and one step I may see. *(Yes! Bits of handclapping . . .)*
His eye *(Oh, yes!)* is on that little sparrow,
and I know, *(Piano punctuation . . .)* yes I know! *(Piano punctuation . . .)*
yes I know!!! *(Piano and cymbals . . .)* God watches me!! *(Yes!)*

"Thank you Jesus!" shouts Jean, as we burst into the chorus.

I sing because I'm happy, I sing because I'm free
his eye is on that sparrow and I know he's watching me.

"Oh sing out, Church" Jean shouts, "we all know God watches!" as Reed elevates the key a tone higher. A last resounding chorus breaks out.

I sing because I'm happy, I sing because I'm free,
his eye is on that sparrow—

Voices and accompaniment pause. Jean retakes her lead, playing out each last phrase as a moving testimony that she *knows* God cares for her!

And I know!!! *(Piano and cymbals . . .)* Yes, I know!!! *(Piano and drums . . .)*
God watches . . . *(Applause . . .)* He watches over . . . //
me!!!! *(Piano and cymbals . . .)*
Yes he watches me!!

"*O–h hallelujah!!*" Jean shouts over the spreading applause. "*Yes!!*" she continues, head thrown back, caught up in a moment of exultation. "*Thank you! Oh, hallelujah!!! Thank you Jesus!! . . .*"

❧

"*I*t's about a *message!* It's about *singing the Gospel!*"

Chapter Eight

"PREACH IT!"

—AN ORAL / AURAL ART—

*T*here's a porous boundary between preaching and singing at Lourdes. Listening to singers talk about their ministry, at times describing it as preaching, I began to see the connection. Preaching and singing "deliver" the Gospel in a way that people feel its power to touch, to challenge, to heal. Both require messengers who put their own faith on the line, who witness to a message that has touched them first. Both are communal events—needing the entire community for their dynamism, their resonance, their truth. Both are dependent on the action of the Holy Spirit—whom singers and preachers speak of as partner, even "co-creator" of what takes place.

"Let's pray, choir!" signals Father Kirk as people settle into their places on any given Sunday morning. Huddled in the small entranceway at the back of the church, choir members and Brother Banks join hands with him for a moment of prayer and dedication. "Father, we ask you to be here in this church house today! *(Amen!)* You know there are troubling things happening in this city, *(Oh, yes!)* in our families, in our community. But we ask you to lift our spirits, to guide us now as we minister to your people! *(Yes!)* Let your Holy Spirit be in our hearts and our voices so that your people may hear the Word of comfort, of support, of love that you want to speak to them! That they may leave this church house today with courage and readiness to return to their lives, filled with *your* power and *your* strength to live the week ahead. We ask this in Jesus name!" "Amen!"

*O*ctober 8, 1995. Three nights ago, Father Kirk slept in Golden Gate Park beside its homeless residents. The choice had not been easy. Last Sunday, preaching on the Gospel story of the rich man and Lazarus, Father Kirk wrestled aloud with Jesus' challenge.

"It's a safe bet that no one in this church house can call themselves rich. . . . [Yet] this story is a living Word, Jesus coming to us, now, with a message for *us* about the poor of San Francisco . . . today's Lazarus . . . so many of whom are being treated like trash!" Jesus speaks "an uncomfortable word. . . . The rich man doesn't *offend* the poor man, he just *ignores* him! Nor does Jesus say that Lazarus was a *good* man, he just says he was a *poor man,* that he had *nothing!* When you open up the Bible, Church, you complicate your life!"

Father Kirk was struggling with the demands Jesus might be making on his own life. Sister Bernie Galvin, spokesperson for the Religious Witness with the Homeless, had asked him to disobey the law. To sleep in the park in protest. To make this Gospel real in San Francisco. "Pray for me, Church, as I make this decision!" he pleaded. A jail term would affect not only him but the people of this church.

Fortunately, no one was arrested. The police turned a blind eye—for one night, at least. But as another Sunday morning dawned, the October air brisk and clear, and people gathered in the Lourdes church house, a sea change had taken place. The ground had shifted. O. J. Simpson had been acquitted on Tuesday, freed of charges in the murder of Nichole Brown Simpson. The country was reeling from the verdict. "We've come this far by faith!" chorused the community as the liturgy opened, affirming once again that "we can't turn around!" no matter what "trouble is in your lives." "Let us ask the Lord Jesus for mercy," invited Father Kirk minutes later, "for our nation, so broken by hatred and misunderstanding!"

That morning, compelled by readings from the prophet Habakkuk, by St. Paul's summons to "not be ashamed of testifying to the Lord, but take your share of suffering for the Gospel," and by Jesus' call to "faith the size of a mustard seed," Father Kirk ventured into the "deep wound" tearing our nation apart.

Setting the Lectionary on the piano to his right, Father Kirk—a man of moderate stature, his hair and cropped beard, once red, now muted with grey—returns to the "open space" from which he has just proclaimed the Gospel. The room is hushed.

"This is certainly the week that was," he begins conversationally, resting a hand momentarily on the first pew as he looks out at those seated before him. *Amens* fill the pause. "It's interesting that last Thursday night, as some of us who remained [in Golden Gate Park] after the prayer service slept in our sleeping bags, snugly secure, the police // drove by // and pretended we weren't there! *(Uh huh . . .)* And yet it's strange that the night before, the police were entering

120

the park and sweeping the poor and the homeless out like trash! *(Amen!)* We live in two Americas. *(Yes! Oh, yes!)* There are two Americas. And if we are tempted to deny that fact, the cover was *ripped off* last Tuesday! *(Yes! Amen!)*

"I phoned my father . . . yesterday. He's eighty-seven years old . . . a wonderful man. I love him dearly. He was angry because of the verdict. *(Well . . .)* He saw injustice in the verdict. *(Well . . .)* He saw unfairness and a lack of truth in the verdict. Most white people do. Because we live in two Americas. *(Tell it like it is, Father!* rings out Brother Banks's voice.*)* Are we ever, as a nation, going to fix our *basic wound* which is *racism?* *(Amen! Amen, Father!)*

Playing out the history of this "old, old wound," Father Kirk explores the "whole system" of racism in its many incarnations. First, the institution of slavery, which "made this nation an economic power." Then the realization, on the part of some white Americans, of the "wrongs of slavery," which ushered in the "terrible bloodshed of the Civil War." A brief "attempt to reconstruct on a political basis" followed. "But you **cannot** *reconstruct unless people want to change their hearts!*" he contends forcefully. *"You cannot* **legalize** *fairness!"* Then segregation, "a new version of how we can avoid one another," took hold; until "Rosa Parks, God bless her"—claiming, *"'My feet hurt and I'm not moving! I'm not giving my seat to* **anybody***, Black or white! (Amen! Amen!) I'm staying right here because* **I'm tired!***'"* *(That's right!)*—launched the Civil Rights Movement. "We've made some progress, haven't we, Church. . . . But the wound is still here, and it hurts just as much! And it's dividing us just as much!" *(Yes!)*

"Now what does this have to do with today's [Scripture] readings?" Father Kirk's pace has quickened, his green chasuble set in motion by the movements of his hands and arms. The words spill out. "The readings today are about *faith!* The songs that Judy picked out for the Mass today are about *faith. Faith is our understanding that God is with us. Faith is our understanding that no matter what goes wrong, God still loves us, and God is still here.* We heard from Habakkuk this morning—*and you read that so* **powerfully***, Ella Mae!*" he calls out, looking directly at Ella Mae Sims seated several rows from the front. "You read that as if you *wrote it! (Yes! Amen!)* Habakkuk looked at his times and heard his people saying, We are being *abused!* We are going through *violence!* We are being *treated like trash!* We are being *stepped upon!* **Where is God?** And so Habakkuk had to remind the people, *God sees it all!* God doesn't miss anything, Church! God doesn't miss a thing. God reads *every heart,* **every heart!** *(Yes, Lord!)* And so he reminds the people through Habakkuk, *don't lose faith in the vision!* Martin [Luther King] called it the dream. Don't lose faith in the dream. *The dream will happen,* but you must continue to believe. *(Al'right! Yes!)* We must *continue to believe, Church,* that people can *change.* Racism will only end *when people change their hearts. (Amen! Yes!)* But Church, *it is possible* for people to change their hearts! *My heart was changed!*

"I was born a racist." *(Hmm . . .)* Father Kirk's tone is conversational once again as he begins to recount his own story. "I was a little kid in Pennsylvania.

All my playmates were white! I didn't know anything but white! And early on, my loving parents, God bless them, put into me the certain 'cares' that you have to show around people who are different than you. *Those are the seeds planted right there!* (*Al'right!*) I grew up . . . in the wonderful mountains of Pennsylvania as a young, innocent racist. (*Have mercy!*)

"We moved to New York. Now New York is very different from the mountains of Pennsylvania! (*Amen!*) In New York, you at least have the advantage of rubbing shoulders with persons other than you. We met Jewish folks—I'd never met Jewish folks before. . . . I went to a high school where surprisingly enough, in the '50s, there were some Black students, Black Catholic students in that high school—the only Catholic high school in that town that did that. I was able to associate with them—notice my words, Church, 'associate' with them! (*'Yes, I got it, Father! I got it!'* calls Louise Wood from the choir.) And they *seemed all right!!!* (Laughter . . .) But *nothing really changed* in me.

"College, the same thing. Catholic college. A smattering of people who were not white. We treated them with 'respect.' (*Hmm . . .*) Into the army I went. And in the army, it's a very different world. I was associating very much with whites and with Blacks. I went to the South, went to Texas. And I dropped some of the fears, some of the anxieties, some of the misconceptions because I was there rubbing shoulders. But nothing really changed inside me. Then after the army . . . I went into seminary, and that was *all white!! **All white!!*** I was being *prepared in a white seminary for a white church.* (*Have mercy!*) Thank God that was changed when my first assignment after ordination was to St. Mary's Church in Stockton, California, which is skid row! And I suddenly came face to face: If I'm to serve as a priest, I better get *over this white stuff! I better get over it!* (*Quickly!* someone responds, and Father Kirk catches the signal.) *Quickly!* But you know, *those things don't die quickly!* (*Amen!!!*) They're like the *dragon.* You cut off one head and another pops up. (*That's right!*) . . . What was happening inside still wasn't the change that was necessary. And that didn't come, Church, until—"

Father Kirk breaks off momentarily to inquire, "I hope I'm not boring you with my story?" Shouts of *No! Go ahead! Tell it like it is, Father!* urge him on. "I'm giving you my story because I really think it's possible for other people to change! (*Yes!*) . . .

"It was [only gradually, slowly] that people // broke // my white // heart." (*Have mercy!*) Speaking deliberately, Father Kirk turns full circle, looking first at the choir seated behind him, then returning his gaze to the rest of the congregation. All eyes were focused on him, the room hushed by the power of his honesty. I could feel tears welling up inside me—tears of recognition, tears of empathy, tears of healing.

"I realized that in people who are different from me, who are not like me because they are not white—people who are Black, who are Hispanic, who are Asian—*I'm carrying them inside me but I'm not allowing their voice to come out!* (*Well . . .*) *We are members of each other, **that's the way God made us!*** (*Yes!*) He made us to be brothers and sisters. *(Yes!)* But this *racism prevents it from happening! (Well . . . Yes!)* If we are really honest with each other, and I look into my heart, I can see Black, I can see Asian, I can see Hispanic. It's all there because *we're linked!! (Yes!)* God has made us *to be linked!* And when that doesn't work, we have *something demonic happening, set up to mar what God has enabled us naturally to do as human beings. Look at little children playing together. Do they see white and Black? They see each other. That's all they see! And they have to be **told,** 'Oh, he's Black. She's white.' (That's right!)*

"Yet, people can change! What Habakkuk was talking about can happen. It happened to me. You call me Father, that's the title the church gives me. *But I've told you many times, I am your **brother, Church!!!** (Amen!!!) I am your brother! (Yes!)* Now, we are *blessed,* here at Lourdes. *(Yes!)* We are *infinitely blessed! (Amen! Yes!)* We can feel the *grace of the Almighty God among us here now,* and we know that people come as visitors and they *feel it! They feel it! It's real! (Yes!!!!) You can almost put your **hands on it!** We have something to give—to give first to our local church, *(Yes!)* which suffers in many ways from racism. It's struggling hard to get away from it, but it won't happen unless people *change their hearts* and allow the way *God made them* to come forth! . . .

"Do we have faith, Church?" he asked, returning to the images of the Gospel. "Do we have the kind of faith *(Well . . .)* to get us through these next years? They're going to be hard years. The reaction of some white people is going to be horrendously ugly. *(Yes!)* The Mark Furmans[1] of the world are strong and in place, Church. *(Yes! Yes!!!!)* But it's not simply the Mark Furmans. . . . It's *good people* like my father, whom I love! *(Yes, Lord!)* It's good people who do not **see** the racism that has *enslaved, degraded, and abused* people of color *(Well . . .)* in this nation *for three hundred, four hundred years! (Have mercy, Lord!)* Habakkuk had the faith and the courage to say, **Hang on!** The *vision will happen. (Yes! Yes!)* **Church,** *let's hang on.* But let's do *more than hang on. Let's get active! Active, Church! Let's be positive. Let's **do** something* as we leave this church house. *(Yes, Lord!)* Let us *challenge* those we know are racist—challenge them *lovingly, (Amen!) not* with a gun, *not* with a hateful face, *(Oh, Lord!)* but with the face of a brother or sister to say, what's going on in your heart that you act that way? *(Yes!) Why do you **need** to find any group of people less important than you, when God has made us all equal? (Amen!)*

"Something my father said *frightened* me!! He said, You know we're going to have another civil war. (Multiple responses . . .) That's where this can lead, Church! It *can* go that far, to where we feel *so separated that no bridge can be built! (Yes!)* And we feel *so far apart* that the *only* option is **war.** . . . It could happen here. *(Yes!)* Church, we are *given something* by God. We are *given a grace,* and it's a *free grace*—we heard Jesus say, *you don't merit it! Don't say it's because you're good!* **We're useless servants!** *Just thank God that we're his servants! (Amen!!!)* **We have something to give!** *Let's give it, Church, with a **full heart!** Let's give it **courageously!** Let's give it **generously!** Because the other option is **simply unacceptable!!!**"

Amens break out, and in no time people are on their feet calling out their appreciation. Reed slips his piano improvisation beneath their applause. As Father Kirk reaches his chair at the rear of the sanctuary, Brother Banks embraces him warmly. Pausing only momentarily, Father Kirk gestures the community to stand.

"*Church*," he queries forcefully, using the oldest form of Christian faith profession,[2] "do you believe that God the Father, who is also a mother to us, has put into the heart of *every human being his image? The image of God exists in every human face, every human heart on the face of the earth! Do you believe that God has done this?*" "*I do!*"comes the resounding response.

"Do you believe that this God sent us his eternal Son Jesus to *show us how we can become brothers and sisters of each other? Do you believe that Jesus' message can work in our world? Do you truly believe in him?*" "*I do!*"

"Do you believe that no matter what, no matter how closed, how hate-filled, frightened, or distorted any human heart is, the *power of God's Spirit can transform it, and that Spirit can transform our world into the one family God intended it to be? Do you believe in the power of this Spirit?*" "*I do!*"

"Church, this is our faith, this is the faith of the church, and we are proud to profess it in Christ Jesus our Lord!" "Amen!"

"*F*ather Kirk is not just a priest, he's a preacher!" said Pat Goodall as we lunched at Mel's Diner in Berkeley one Saturday. Intrigued, I asked her to say more. "You have some priests who are homilists; you have some that give a sermon; you have some that preach," she responded. "A homilist is someone who gets up there and he just talks. It may reference something in your life, and it may not. It's strictly about what he's taking [from] the Bible. A person who gives a sermon is one who has a message but can't really get it across. He has a good message, but he just can't deliver. A preacher not only [has] a message, but he knows how to get it to you. He brings it home, makes it fit with what's happening with you right now. And you're there with him every step of the way. It's like he's looked into your soul and knows exactly what you're doing. That's a preacher!"[3]

A tall order, I thought to myself! Preaching—not only having a message and the power to communicate it, but knowing the lives of those who listen, keeping them engaged in the message, and touching soul to soul! Pat's comments came back to me some months later while talking with Tina Edwards. "In other churches," Tina remarked, "if you're a priest, you don't really go out and deal with the people. Father Kirk gets involved, he's down with the people. He doesn't just stand there and preach, he comes down to where we are and talks.

. . . [He's] not an authority figure, telling us about the Word of the Lord . . . [but] 'I'm your brother. I'm talking with you, not at you.'"[4]

It's about making connections, I mused. Overcoming distance—spatial, social, and spiritual—between those who deliver the message, be they singers or preachers, and those who receive it. Standing in the midst of the community, in the "open space," so that a dialogue of faith can happen around the Word of God. People speak back. They respond. They affirm truth when they hear it. "I love it," commented Father Kirk to me one January morning. "[People's responses] spoil me, give me an emotional platform to stand on, hold me up. . . . They affect me, guide me. [It's] crucial to learn the needs of my people. . . . I try to listen to the responses. My basic principle of preaching: understanding people [and] what God is doing. . . . In act, I *listen* to what they are saying, incorporate it in the future."[5]

"Lourdes is the seedbed of the Spirit," he added several months later, as we continued our conversation over coffee in the rectory kitchen. "It's challenging to preach at the Gospel Mass. . . . People have suffered through so much that if you don't speak honestly, they say, Come on, let's get real! . . . I pray a lot! . . . In some settings, I can get away with doing the things I learned in seminary. . . . But Lourdes is different. Lourdes is the seedbed of the Spirit. So I try to acknowledge that. . . . The Spirit is *in* these people and they're *aware* of the Spirit, they're *grateful* for the Spirit being with them. . . . They actively celebrate the fact that the Spirit is here. . . . What you say has to come out of that context, it has to reflect that."

"It strikes me," I remarked, that the "whole way you approach [your preaching assumes] that the Word is in the community, the Spirit is in the community, and you are articulating it in that context."

"I try to clarify it," Father Kirk responded, nodding, "to define it so that everybody sees it more clearly. In other places, 'Father speaks' and so we listen. It's an intellectual thing. Whereas at Lourdes, preaching is more organic to the whole person . . . to the whole community."[6]

*T*he following Sunday, tensions were still high across the country. But the mood in the church house seemed to cut through the struggles to find a place of confidence and joy. "He keeps doin' great things for me!" we sang over and again as the service began. "To God be the glory," we voiced minutes later,

> to God be the glory, to God be the glory for the things He has done!
> With his blood He has saved me, with his power He has raised me!
> To God be the glory for the things He has done!

The Gospel that morning told of ten lepers, one of whom returned to thank Jesus for his healing. "And he was a Samaritan!" proclaimed Father Kirk as he neared the story's end. "'Was no one found to return and give praise to God except this foreigner?' Jesus asked. *(Amen!)* . . . 'Rise and go your way; your faith has made you well!'" The Gospel of the Lord! . . .

"These readings we've listened to," began Father Kirk, once all were seated, his voice full of energy, "they're wonderful readings, they're beautiful readings, and of course . . . they speak of our need to be thankful to God! *(Yes!)* *Everything we have, Church, comes from God! (Yes! Amen!)* Nothing we have has not come from him! . . . And so we have these wonderful stories about individuals who *realized God has acted powerfully in their lives* and from them wells up this feeling, this desire to say, *'Thank you, Lord!' (Amen!)* . . . These are models . . . of how grateful we should be. . . . Sometimes I have to admit . . . *I've been in that nine that didn't show up! (Oh, yes! Amen!)* . . . But the Word is here to bring us up short and remind us, yes, we need to be grateful! *(Well . . .)*

"But there's something else going on in these readings, Church." I could feel the energy shift. Beginning with the story of Naaman the leper, proclaimed in the first reading, Father Kirk began to weave the strands of his preaching, unfolding the not so obvious underside of this morning's lessons.

"Naaman was a military man, a Syrian," who had "no concept of the God of Israel." But tired of being treated a leper, he set out to find the prophet Elisha, whom he heard had "power with God" to cure him. "Thinking the way the world thinks," Naaman "packed his mules and his camels with gold and treasure—all the things that make this world operate." On arrival, Naaman was put off by the simplicity of Elisha's instruction: "Bathe in the Jordan seven times and you will be healed!" Moreover, he was appalled by the paucity of water in the river Jordan. "We have powerful rivers in Syria!" Yet, convinced by his level-headed friends, Naaman bathed seven times, and his "skin was like a baby's! He was totally cured!" Elisha refused his gold and silver, "all these wonderful things" that Naaman thought everyone would admire. Instead, "Naaman, *overcome* with the changes that were going on, *not only in his skin, but in his heart, (Yes! Amen!) begged* the prophet, *'please let me take some of the soil of this nation back to my country so that when I pray, I can stand on this soil . . . and acknowledge and praise your God!' (Amen!)* It was a total transformation!"

"Now Jesus . . . takes that story and uses it in a way that he uses the story of the ten lepers today. *(Hmm . . .)* Because when Jesus came to his time, he came very often to people who were closed. They saw things as already fixed and they can't be changed. They saw things from the viewpoint of an insider—those who had arrived. . . . What Jesus was offering [them] wasn't really that important. So, preaching one day, he says, *'You know folks, you people don't have the faith that Naaman had.' (Amen!)* And he reminded them of the story of how God had worked through Naaman. . . . 'This same God is operating in your lives, but you're not opening up [to him].' The people . . .

wanted to kill him . . . to throw him off of the cliff, they were so upset by what Jesus said about Naaman.

"Jesus marveled, as well, at the outsider in today's Gospel story—the Samaritan. . . . Samaritans, remember, were *totally hated!* They were looked upon as *heretics!* They were looked upon as people who had *deserted God.* They were looked upon as faithless people by the Jewish people. *(Well . . .)* And Jesus lifts up this man and says, 'This is the one, this is the one!' . . . Jesus is reminding us that God has no favorites! *(Amen!) God has no favorites! (Amen!) We have favorites! Our society definitely has favorites! (Oh, yes!)* But God has no favorites! And so when Jesus encounters the foreigner . . . the outsider, [those who are] not in the powerful in-group [of society] . . . Jesus welcomes them and says, 'These are the ones that are ready to receive the kingdom of God and open up to God's love!' . . .

"Right now in San Francisco *(Have mercy, Lord!)* there is a story of two young men who . . . got themselves involved in fist fights. Unfortunately, the victim . . . in both cases died. Anthony hit a man . . . and two days later this man was dead. Louis hit a man and he fell to the ground, fractured his skull and died on the spot almost. Now the story is this: Anthony is a white man, Louis is a Black man. *(Yes!)* The D.A. has decided that in Anthony's case—Anthony has some friends in the San Francisco Police Force—that in Anthony's case it was really an accident. *(Uh huh . . . Hmm . . .)* Although the coroner has said in both cases it looks like a homicide. . . . In Louis's case, the judge forced a bail of $500,000 and so Louis, a Black man, is in jail. Although the circumstances of this event in both cases was very similar. . . .

"The world we live in obviously plays favorites. *(Oh, yes!)* But God does not. Now what is our reaction to this? What are we going to do with this? . . . In spite of the fact that the world does play its favorites, that the world operates in many cases on a playing field that is uneven, what can we do?

"Did you hear the reading from St. Paul this morning? Jesus has put into our hearts, yours and mine, the ability to see how much God loves us. That's a gift! That's the Good News! *(Well . . .)* That's the heart of the Good News! *God is a lover and his love is aimed at us human beings, everybody without exception! With God there is no foreigner, there is no outsider! There is no need for [Proposition] 187!*[7] . . . *[No need for the] great divisions, the great chasm between Black and white that our society has set up. (Well . . .) All of that is **nonsense** to God! (Amen!) **Nonsense!** That is what Jesus has revealed, that's the message!* And he proved it. When his enemies ganged-up on him, he still would not surrender to them nor copout in any way. He would not take the cheap way out and say, 'Oh yes, why, I think you're right.' He said, 'OK, do with me what you want!' *(Amen!)* . . .

"Now Paul is telling us this morning: Jesus is going to be faithful to us! *(Well . . .)* He has already proved his fidelity by the fact that he would not surrender to his enemies. . . . He will be faithful to us! He asks us in turn, because we have received his Spirit, Church—*everyone of us here, has received in abundance, (Well . . .) please don't doubt that, please don't doubt that, Church!* (*Amen!*) *We have received in* **abundance** *the Holy Spirit!* (*Amen! Amen!*) *Everyone of us here! We express it in a thousand different ways, but we are all recipients of that Holy Spirit of God*—and it is that Spirit which enables us, in a world which is **grossly** *unfair at times,* (*Amen!*) and cruel, and a world in which the insiders, who have great power and great wealth and great connections, can *distort and play havoc upon the children of God!* (*Amen!*) *We know that exists!* (*Well . . .*) But he asks us, this loving God who gave his life for us, to remain faithful to his ideals. (*Well . . .*)

"And his ideals are such as this: that when I look at my enemy, when I see the *one who wants to put me down,* the one *who is willing to go to court and lie to get at me,* (*Yes!*) *the one who will use the various instruments of my society so that he can bring them to bear to hurt me*—that I will not allow my heart to be *warped and hurt and wrinkled and distorted by the hatred which is in my enemy.* (*Amen!*) I will return my enemy's hatred with love. *Now, Church, that's hard!* (*Amen! Well . . .*) Our natural inclination is, *'I'll get even with you.* (*Yes!*) *I'll hurt you back and I'll hurt you hard.'* (*Yes! Well . . .*)

"Jesus asks us to be something better!" Father Kirk's words broaden momentarily, only to quicken again as he adds, "He also asks us not to allow anybody to make a *doormat* of us! (*Amen!*) *We are to be no person's doormat!* (*Yes!!*) But at the same time, // to give thanks to a God who has revealed himself in the person of Jesus Christ as *love!* (*Yes!*) As *justice!* (*Yes!*) As one who *reaches out naturally to* **every** *human being* **without exception: black, white, yellow, purple, it doesn't matter!** (*Amen!!!*) He asks us, *Please,* // *don't allow that dream of Jesus to go bad in our hearts!* (*Amen!*) *If we are to thank God as the Scriptures invite us to do, let us thank him by giving our God a heart that resembles his Son's!* (*Yes!*) *Please, Church!*

"We're entering into some rough times (*Amen!*) as a nation. (*Yes!*) The inequalities that we have striven to deal with for the last thirty years—this effort is going *awry* right now! (*Amen!!*) It's not working the way Martin dreamed it would work! (*Amen! Amen!*) Right now it's not working that way! (*Amen!*) Where are we going to be in this struggle, Church? (*Uh huh . . .*) Where are we going to be? The most important question we have to ask ourselves is, *where am I going to be before God?* (*Yes! Amen!*) What kind of heart am I going to hold as I struggle to fight for what is good in my times? That's the question! I believe that we can truly *thank God* by allowing his Spirit, // the Spirit of God which is the Spirit of *compassion,* of *mercy,* of *understanding, yes,* of **justice!** (*Amen!*) That the Spirit will *overtake* us // and we will not allow our hearts to be corrupted by the insidious pleas that the world has // to make us hate them. (*Yes! Amen, Father! Yes!*) . . . That we will go through life dealing with the problems and saying, 'Thank you,' and holding up to God, and to our brother and sister human beings, (*Have mercy!*) a heart that's pure! (*Yes, Lord!*) We've got a struggle ahead of us, Church! (*Amen!*) Let's not kid ourselves! (*Amen!*) We've got a struggle! (*Oh yes, Lord!*) But let us struggle as the *children of God,* who *believe in* *his **love** // and believe that because of him, we shall prevail!"* (*Amen! Amen! Amen, Father!* Applause . . .)

*T*here's passion in Father Kirk's voice when he preaches. There's energy. There's fire.You can't miss the power he experiences in the Word of God, and it's difficult not to be drawn in. *Amen! That's right! Go ahead!* are neither rote nor random responses, but part of an engaging "conversation" evoked by his words and the way he delivers them. The power is not only in what he says but in how he communicates. It's drama! Despite his years in the theatre, which have clearly shaped the dynamism of his preaching, Father Kirk points to the Gospel as the real source of the drama. "In the Gospels there's drama!" he commented, reflecting on the manner in which people at Lourdes participate in the preaching and the Scripture proclamation. "There's real drama! Jesus interacting as a human being with his brother and sister human beings, and there's drama there!"[8]

Listening to Father Kirk preach over time, it becomes clear that what drives his emotional, passionate delivery are deeply held values which are shared by others at Lourdes. To "clarify" the Word of God as addressed to this community, which he describes as his role, the message must be real, situated in experience, faith-filled, honest, and always full of hope. He regularly ventures into the political arena. In fact, without a rootedness in the political realm, in truth about society as it is, his preaching would fall flat, would miss the mark. Truth-telling is crucial at Lourdes. Years of resistence to those in our culture who "speak lies" have created a fierce independence in those at Lourdes, that listens for truth before following. *Amens* are honest assent.

However, "What I do is not Black preaching," Father Kirk contends, despite the affective resonance his words have with that powerful art. "Black preaching has cadence to it and a repetitive use of words. It's very effective! But I don't do that. I use my feelings, my own attitude toward things, and my own set of beliefs—that's all part of it. But my delivery is to try to build, and build, and build, and build—and then [stop]! Basically that's the structure of my style. It starts off quietly, and then . . . you have a tension, you bring in the problems, challenges, then you finish with, 'Where is our faith?'"[9]

His portrait is quite accurate. As in many of the gospel songs, the build-up—in pace, volume, emphasis—may happen more than once, allowing the very shape of his voice to convey the tensions of the faith-filled living about which he preaches. Invariably, the community is brought to a peak moment, compelling a response which ripples out, first in *Amens!* and applause, then in a profession of faith. The ancient baptismal formula, used regularly at Lourdes for this confession, corresponds in style and form to the dialogue of faith that has unfolded during the preaching. And the faith professed is not an abstract belief that "God is," but a communal conviction that "God is indeed working!" And, as more than one gospel song proclaims,"*God is able!*"

*T*he late April sun suffused the church house with a warm glow that Third Sunday of Easter, 1995. Deacon John Dupre—native of New Orleans, resident psychologist at San Quentin Prison, deacon of the Archdiocese of San Francisco, and beloved friend of Lourdes—had been invited to preach. The church house was ringing with strains of "Where God leads me I will follow," as people prepared to welcome the Gospel. Deacon Dupre turned to Father Kirk, standing beside him, to receive a blessing. Then descending the three steps from the sanctuary platform, he approached the ambo. A colored stole, draped crosswise, adorned his white alb. As he lifted the large red lectionary, you could sense people's anticipation. Nor would they be disappointed. Deacon Dupre's words were full of the verbal art of Black preaching—the turns of phrase, images, aphorisms, the rhythms and rhymes that root this oratory in Black culture. The very sound and cadence of his voice evoked rapport, a sense of shared history, shared experience. Like many songs at Lourdes, his preaching would "begin intense and stay intense."

"Oh, praise God this morning!! (*Yes! Amen!!!!*) This is *indeed* the day the Lord has made! (*Amen! Yes it is!*) Let us *rejoice* and be *glad* in it! Be glad because *God woke us up this morning* (*Amen!*) // *clothed in our right mind* // able to choose *our own prayer ground!* (*Amen!*) So we *thank God* that the rain has gone! // We can *see clearly* now! // We can see *clearly* that the *triumphant victory* // *of Christ over the grave*—well, the grave *couldn't hold him down!* (*Amen!*) We come to *magnify the name of Jesus,* (*Amen!*) where *Jesus is the reason for this season!* (*Al'right! Amen!!*) . . . The *reason* for our *joy in the **midst** of our pain* // is that *Jesus is risen! Hallelujah!* (*Amen!!*) We stand together as a *holy community of witnesses* (*Al'right!*) to the *living reality* that *Jesus is risen* // *from the dead* // and this *same Jesus is eastering in our lives* even right now! (*Al'right! Amen!*) The great singer Stevie Wonder asks the question, 'Where is your God?' (*That's right!*) *He lives within us.* (*Yes! Amen!*) *Jesus is **alive** in our hearts* today! (*Yes he is!*) I *feel **Jesus alive** in* this *place* today! (*Amen!*) So I *praise God* (*Yes!*) for the *mystery* of Easter! (*Yes!*) I *praise God* that his *spiritual body is lifted up in our hearts today!* (*Amen!*) From the *tomb of **Friday** death* // came a *womb of new **Sunday** light* that we call Easter. (*Amen!*) *Oh glory, hallelujah!* (*Amen! Al'right!*) . . .

"Now pray with me this morning . . . from the 21st chapter of the Good News according to John verses 1-14. . . . The setting is plainly at the Sea of Tiberius. Simon Peter had said to the other six disciples. . . . 'I'm going fishing.' Marvin Gaye, in a popular album in the early '70s asked the question 'What's going on?' *(Al'right!!)* To put it another way, *'What's happening?' (Yes!)* What was happening was that *Jesus* had *died,* was *crucified,* and was *hung on the tree* on a hill called *Calvary. (Amen!)* But if the truth be told, his disciples were *so fearful* that they had been *locked away in the upper room for nearly two weeks. (Amen! That's right!)* Although *Jesus had appeared to them two times* before this date, they still didn't understand what was happening. *(Amen!!!)* And though *Jesus was on the shore,* / / they would not *recognize* him. . . . What was happening was that all night / / they had caught *not a single fish. (Yes! Amen!)*

"Church, we know that there are *many ways in our lives (Yes!)* that we *go fishing (Oh, yes!) and do not catch any fish! (Amen!)* As an African American people, *(Tell it!)* we're among the *first fired* and the *last hired, (Yes!) first to go to jail* and the *last to make the bail. (Amen!!)* Yes, African American people know what it means to *fish all night (Yes!)* / / and yet *catch no fish! (That's right!)* When we can *catch no fish,* we can rightly ask the question, *'What's happening? (Yes!)* What's going on?' *(What's going on? Applause . . .)*

"*What's going on in Washington (Yes!)* is that the so-called *'Contract With America'* is another name for the *'Contract On **Black** America.' (That's right!)* To let *Newt* [Gingrich] tell it, one would think that the *only African American dream is a welfare queen! (Amen!!* Shouts and applause . . .) Let *Newt* tell it, he'll turn every *social safety net into a drag net! (Yep!)* Yes, a drag net that *ensnares and imprisons so many of our talented African American men! (Yes!)* They are hauled into the *jails* and the *prisons* of this country. *(Yes!)* Indeed we are becoming a *police state! (Yes!)* Over a million men are locked behind jails and prison walls. *(Amen!)* Indeed, these are isolated, concrete structures of human degradation! *(Yes!)* What's happening? What's happening is that we *Black people are always to blame. (Yes! Amen!)* We are *blamed for the violence. (Yes!)* We are *blamed for the drugs. (Yes!)* We are *blamed for the crime. (Yes!)* Yes, **we know** what it means to *fish all night and yet catch no fish!* *(Amen!!! Applause . . .)*

"But, my sisters and brothers, *as dawn drew near for the disciples (Well . . .)*—*yes, weeping had endured for the night, (Yes!) but it is **always darkest just before the dawn** (Al'right!!)—as the dawn broke onto the disciples, Jesus stood on the shore and said, 'Children, have you caught anything to eat?' (Yes!)* But the *disciples did not recognize him (That's right!).* . . . Jesus then instructed them to *cast on the right side of the boat. (Yes!)* . . . Indeed, Church, whatever happens in our lives that has led to *pain, (Well . . .)* whatever it is in our life that has led to *agony, (Uh huh . . .)* . . . led to *despair, (Uh huh . . .)* whatever is going on in our life that has led to the frustration *(Oh, yes!)* . . . to the heartache *(Yes!)*—if we but *pray long enough, (Al'right!)* if we *pray just hard enough, (Yes! Al'right!) we can hear the voice of Jesus say,* (Applause . . .) *'**Try one more time! (Yes!) Cast your nets in the name of the Lord!** (Yes! Amen!) Cast your net on the **right side** of the boat.' (Al'right! Yes!) We* / / *will have abundance! (Alright!) We will have abundance of life! (Yes! Al'right!) More of what we need than what we can handle for ourselves! (Yes!)*

"Then John recognized Jesus and said, 'It is the Lord!' (Uh huh . . .) Peter put on some clothes and *swam with haste!* (Al'right!) But Peter also *swam with hope.* *Peter swam like a* **sprinter** (Yes!) *whose speed could only be limited by the* **measure** *of his hope!* (Yes! Amen!) By the *desire to win the race.* (Yes!) *Yes, Church, hope has a way of being its own answer to our prayers.* (Oh, yes!) Paul said a long time ago in Romans 5, (Amen!) 'We boast // in our hope!* (Al'right!) We will *boast in our hope of the glory of God,'* (Amen!) *knowing that affliction produces endurance,* (Amen!) *and endurance, proven character;* (Al'right!) *proven character, hope.* (Yes!) And *hope does not disappoint, Church!* (Amen! Applause . . .) *Because the love of God has been poured into our hearts through the Holy Spirit* that has been given to us! (Oh, yes!) *Church, I've come here today to tell you that the Holy Spirit has been given to us!* (Al'right!) *Peter swam with the hope of this very Holy Spirit!* (Yes!) . . . The **speed** *and* **urgency** *with which he swam betrayed this fervent hope!* (Well . . .)

"The other disciples, with the beloved disciple John, reached shore in the boat. They all *dined to a beautiful feast* of charcoaled fish. (Amen!) They even *broke bread with the Lord.* (Amen!) *Yes, Church, Jesus calls us to dine with him!* (Yes!) *And he calls us // from where we are,* (Amen!) // to *where* **He** *wants us to be!* (Right!) And he calls *each of us,* to be a *people of hope,* (Yes!) *to be a people of vision,* (Yes!) God calls us to be a *people of purpose,* (Amen!) a people of *conviction.* (Yes!) But *first, // but* **first,** *Church, //* we must *walk like Caliph and Joshua,* (Yes!) *'walk by faith,* (Well . . .) **not by sight!'** (Amen! Applause . . .) *Yes, Church, I believe that 'eye has not seen,* (Yes!) // nor *ear heard,* (Al'right!) // *what* **God has prepared** (Yes!) // *for those who love him!'* (Amen!) This can *only be revealed by the Holy Spirit!* (Amen!)

"*Jesus calls each one of us today //* to *walk by faith born of the hope in the risen Christ!* (Yes!) *Jesus conquered death once and for all.* (Amen!) If *today* we declare with Paul that *'death is swallowed up in victory,'* (Amen!) *because of this victory //* we *shall not all fall asleep!* (Yes!) *'We shall all be changed,'* (Amen!) yes, I believe, *'in the twinkling of an eye,* (Yes!) when the *last trumpet sounds,* (Yes!) *we shall all be raised up, incorruptible!'* (Yes!) *Somewhere I read, 'I* **am the resurrection.'** (Yes! Amen!) *Somewhere I read, 'I* **am the life.'** (Yes!) *Somewhere I read, 'I* **am the light of the world!'** (Yes!) *Jesus is* **here** *for us, Church!* (Yes!) *If our minds will just not be clouded, like the disciples,* by our lack of *understanding of our own salvation,* (Amen!) *if we'll only let the Holy Spirit enlighten this understanding* (Yes!) *with revived hope!* (Amen!) *Yes, Church, our minds have become* **entombed** *by our own fear!* (Yes!) *The Holy Spirit needs to revive the history of our salvation so that we recognize* **Jesus** *on the shores of our troubled lives!* (Yes!)

"Yes, Church, in conclusion, just as *all have died with Christ through our own baptism,* (Yes!) *we shall all rise with him in the revived hope //* as *Easter people.* (Yes!) *Let us celebrate today and break bread at the holy table* (Oh, yes!) // *with this renewed conviction that* **whatever** *happens,* **Jesus** *is on the shore!* (Al'right!) *All we need do is* **call out to him!** (Al'right! Amen!) *All we need do is call out the* **name of Jesus,** *and say* **'Thank ya' Jesus!** (Thank ya'!) **Thank ya'** *for your resurrection.* (Al'right! Applause . . .) **Thank ya'** *for the revival of our hope of our salvation.* (Yes!! Yes!) **Thank ya'** *for*

132

*the faith that has answered all of our prayers. (Amen!) Thank ya' Jesus for whatever happens! (Yes!) When it happens to us in our lives, we can rely on your love (Yes!) and compassion and understanding // and you will lift us up. (Yes!) Until that bright day when we will **see you face to face** (Amen!) // **in the new Jerusalem!** (Amen!) **We'll walk together, just like John.** (Shouts and applause . . .) **Oh glory, glory, hallelujah! Hallelujah! Amen!'"** (Hallelujah!! Amen! Amen!!! Applause . . .)*

The atmosphere is electric! People are on their feet, some shouting. Deacon Dupre's energy has not lagged for an instant, as he carried this community to this moment of celebration. *Amens!* and overflowing applause make it clear that the news this morning, for all Deacon Dupre's honesty, is only good news!

Catching the fire, and without missing a beat, Father Kirk invites this exuberant community into a profession of faith—faith in "a powerful, risen Lord Jesus who stands on the shores of our lives, of our world, of our hearts, to give us new hope and a new way of life!"

*P*reaching, like singing at Lourdes, is an oral/aural art in service of the dynamics of the Gospel. Both invite people into an experience of God's action here and now, making connections between the Scriptures and the soul-searching, often heartwrenching situations of everyday living. *How* the message is communicated is as important as what is proclaimed. The sound of the words, the "shape" of the preaching, the cadence, energy, and emotion of the delivery, are integral to the message, and fueled by the preacher's /singer's own faith. Like singing, preaching is not "score-bound"—not delivering a text but engaging in a Spirit-guided conversation. Others in the church house participate freely, even passionately. And always preaching moves toward action. The real art is in the living.

Chapter Nine

"LORD, HELP ME TO HOLD OUT!"

—MOSAICS OF SOUND AND MEANING—

Words create space. They mark time, create a place where the community can dwell for a time. At Lourdes, words—sung, preached, prayed, shouted, whispered, called, answered, chorused, accompanied, repeated, vamped— open a path *into* the words and *beyond* the words. The "message," delivered and received, becomes a place of celebration, of joy. You can't get there by yourself. It's a communal art. Within this space, they tell me, change can happen —surrender, abandon, confidence. "The words *are* the Gospel," I remember Bessie Brooks claiming. Within the words, "the Holy Spirit is talking to me, making me believe in myself," affirmed Liz Bell. The goal, it would seem, is more than either the message or the messenger. It's about discovering a place of presence.

It was the October Sunday when Father Kirk preached about racism. The "wound that divides the two Americas." The possibility that change can happen. People were just beginning to settle down again after a lengthy Exchange of Peace, sorting themselves out, returning to their places in the church house. Choir members, one by one, made their way back to the front of the church as Reed fingered a few bluesy flourishes on the well-worn keyboard, hinting at what was to ensue. Pat Goodall gestured the choir to reassemble and fan out across the sanctuary. I could see Rose Isles out in front of us, mike in hand, as I slipped into the choir line between Ernestine Harris and Jeannette Howard.

In a flash, Reed Fromer and Isaiah Brown lock into the opening measures of James Cleveland's "Lord Help Me to Hold Out" and instantly, people are "in the song," wrapped in the familiar embrace of rhythms and lyrics already in their bones. We know this place well. We've dwelt here before.

The song's pace is moderate, but the energy is driving. Isaiah steadies the undulating beat on his snare and bass drums, with cymbals throbbing beneath his pulsing taps. *"C'mon, Rose!"* calls someone from the front pew. *"It's al'right, daugh'er! Sing it!"* adds Louise Wood from the choir *"Yeah, Rose!"* shouts another, as if to summon the song out of her into this anticipated rendezvous of spirits. *"Al'right, choir, here we go!"* shouts Pat Goodall, her eyes meeting ours.

"Lo—rd" we burst forth, stretching the invocation an entire measure, only to complete the entreaty with a phrase as clipped as the holy name has been prolonged: "help me to hold out!" Shouts of delight ripple out, filling the momentary pause before we chant again, "Lo—rd, help me to hold out!" "Well. . ." I hear Brother Banks call out from behind us in the sanctuary. "Lo—rd," breaks out a third time, borne on another wave of energy, hand-clapping punctuating each alternating beat, "help me to hold out!" Then, a surge of melodic energy completes the chorus: "un—til my change // comes!" The final word rings out like a percussive point of arrival, answered by shouts of *Yes! Amen!* . . .

Once again, we implore:

> Lo—rd, help me to hold out!
> Lo—rd, help me to hold out!
> Lo—rd, help me to hold out!
> un–til my change // comes!

"*H*old Out," as it's fondly called, was a favorite before I came to Lourdes. The lyrics are simple, direct, and real. They match your life. "People often ask me to sing this song," remarked Rose Isles as we talked about her experience of singing the song one Saturday afternoon. "People really need to hear these words because the way the world is going now is crazy! And you're asking God to help you to hold out just one more day, because every day is different. . . . He said our way is not going to be easy. All you've got to do is put your trust in Him. . . . The change is going to come!"

"'Hold out,' it's an old song," she added. "Reverend Cleveland," referring to Reverend James Cleveland who composed and performed the song, "I love the way he sings this song! I really love him. He's a very spiritual man, and the way he sings, you can get that powerful feeling from him. . . ."[1]

Cleveland, minister, composer, lyricist, and a pivotal figure in the California gospel movement of the '60s and '70s, is deeply respected by singers at Lourdes. "Hold out" is a masterful fusion of driving rhythms and memorable phraseology. The lyrics, I've come to realize, are crafted of cherished images at once Biblical and rooted in the historical experience of African Americans. Beginning with the unspeakable hardships of slavery, belief that "a change is gonna come," that God's deliverance would win out over injustice, has welled up in the voiced lyrics of the Spirituals, freedom songs and gospel music, fueling the imaginative hopes of Black Americans. Coupled with the invocation "Lord, help me to hold out," which echoes St. Paul's exhortation in 2 Timothy 11:12, that if we *"hold out"* with Christ, "we shall also reign with him," the song's message holds out a promise that stirs the hearts and bodies of members of the Lourdes community.

❦ ❦ ❦

"C'mon, choir, sing it again!" chides Rose, turning toward the swaying line of blue-robed singers, as if to tease out yet more sound. She depends on the choir's intensity to energize her own singing, she's told me, assuring me that "If you're out there in front . . . you can definitely hear . . . if they're singing like they're tired. . . . It's not about what *we* want to do. We're here to do a ministry! C'mon we're going to do this together!"

"Woo-oo!" sighs someone as Reed leads us back into a spirited chorus, "Lo—rd, help me to hold out! . . ." Isaiah's drums are pulsing. Rose begins to layer the choral sound with terse invocations—"Help me to hold out, Lord!" "Sweet Jesus, help us to hold out!"—thickening the textured sound. People in various parts of the church are on their feet, their swaying bodies and clapping hands accentuating the visual and sonic rhythms. Others seem content to be carried on the waves of harmonic sound, singing along or gently rocking in their places. Everyone seems caught up in the music as we wait, jubilantly, "un–til my change // comes!"

The rapprochement is tangible. Despite the bedrock rhythm, which holds the community within a felt sense of solidarity, participation is far from unison. "It's a blessing here," commented Joan Dill in a conversation with Brother Banks and me one Sunday. "This doesn't occur in every church, but there's a freedom of expression here at Lourdes. If you feel you want to get up and clap, you can get up and clap, stomp your foot, sing the song . . . whatever the Spirit hits you to do."

"And if you can't sing, you can moan," added Brother Banks.

"When you sing some of these songs, the Spirit will hit you and you have to get up and move, clap your hands," continued Joan.

"It moves the body as well as the heart," I mused aloud.

"Yes, like a light switch," retorted Joan, "just flip it on, and you're right there, all the light! It's a wonderful feeling. It brings tears to my eyes sometimes, but they're not tears of sadness. . . . Sometimes I don't even know the tears are coming. . . . I feel the tears running down my face and it's not sadness. . . . People seem to equate crying with bad and sad, and it's not true. I'm not sad! I'm fine. I'm just feeling emotions, and they swell sometimes."[2]

Mike Edwards offered another perspective from his preferred place in the back of the church. "When Judy and Jean and Rose sing their songs, when Walter sings his songs, when the choir sings their songs, you can see how everyone stands up. . . . People get involved in the song. But you can also just be sitting down, and you can still draw in all the energy! And that keeps you going inside, and you don't even have to say anything. . . . A lot of people see us standing in the back. . . . But we pay attention! . . . We have our own way of doing it . . . but when it's time to get involved in church, we're always there. . . ."[3]

"**C**'mon, Rose!" someone shouts again. Surrounded by sound and movement, Rose launches into a verse-like variation on the chorus we've just sung. Despite the shouts of affirmation that punctuate every phrase, Rose's eyes are closed, her body leaning into the invoking lyrics:

> Lord, *(Yes!)* I need you to help me to hold out! *(Yes! Well . . .)*
> 'Cause the mountains are too high! *(Shouts . . .)*
> I need you to help me to hold out! *(Oh, yes!* Shouts *. . .)*
> Give me *(Yes!!!)* the patience *(Yes!)* that I need to hold out!

Instantly, the sound swells as fervent voices join hers,

> un–til my change comes!

A mood of jubilee transfuses the church house, holding the struggles of which she sings within a place of confident hope. It's not that the message isn't heard. Insistent shouts suggest otherwise. But troubles seem transformed in this place of joy.

"Woo-oo!!" sighs a voice from the front. *"Oh, yes!"* cries another. Never lagging for a moment, Reed and Isaiah lead Rose into a first full verse.

My way *(Yes!!)* may not be easy! *(Yes!)*

she sings, her left hand raised in testimony.

You did not say that it would be! *(Yes!)*

Then, sailing up the octave in a melodic crescendo, her body abandoned to the message, she sings through the lyrics into a shout-like affirmation:

But if it gets dark *(Yes!)* can't see my way,
you told me to put my trust in thee!
That's why I'm asking you:

she sings insistently, leading us back into a fervent chorus, all the while embellishing our steady lyrics with her free flowing, dulcet supplications:

Lo—rd, (Help me Jesus!)
help me to hold out! (I need your help right now!)
Lo—rd, (Oh, Lord) help me to hold out! (Help me, Jesus!)
Lo—rd, (Oh, Lord!) help me to hold out! (Help us to hold out!)
Un–til my change // comes!

"**W**hen my Mom sings 'Hold Out,' it's such a powerful message," remarked Tiffany Isles in a conversation with Tina Edwards and myself one Saturday. "Everybody is struggling, and she sings 'Help me to hold out until my change comes.' That's what we're all waiting for. . . . Everybody is trying to hold out until their change comes. . . . You want the Lord to help you to hold out, and you keep saying it over and over and it's like, Yes! So much emotion is involved. There's so much emotion and feeling. . . ."

"The music is very powerful," added Tina. "People really break down, the wall crumbles . . . and they give themselves to the Lord. . . . 'Here I am, Lord; before I was holding back!'" "You release, and you completely surrender yourself to God," remarked Tiffany. "You realize you have to turn it over to Jesus. . . . I don't know if that's the Holy Spirit. I'm assuming it is."[4]

"**W**henever we sing this song," I remember Sister Irma commenting, "people in the community will doubtless be experiencing struggle or difficulty. The lyrics of the song remind us that God is the only one who can provide what is needed. The act of singing the song—the movement, the rhythms, the words, the repetition, the encouragement and hope that singers and others express—can re-center us in God. A change can happen. A movement beyond. A new experience of God's presence and faithfulness."[5]

"*L*isten, Church!" Rose shouts as she doubles back into the same verse, but this time she is addressing the lyrics directly to us. Instantly, the "*my* way" of testimony is transformed into the "*our* way" of exhortation. Her voice is full of unaffected emotion, her eyes fixed on the dancing church house before her:

> *Our* way *(Yes!)* may not be easy! *(Shouts . . .)*
> God did not say that it would be!

Cries ring out from persons around the church house against a battery of drum beats that propel her almost shouted admonition:

> But if it gets dark *(Yes!)* can't see your way,
> He told you to put your trust in Him!
> That's why I'm asking you:
>
> Lo—rd, (Lord, Jesus!) help me to hold out!
> (Oh, we all need your help right now!)
> Lo—rd, (Oh, Lord!) help me to hold out!
> (We're just about to make it over Lord!)
> Lo—rd, (Oh, Lord!) help me to hold out! (Help us to hold out!)
> Un–til (un-til) my change (my change) // comes!

*L*ike most gospel songs, the unfolding of "Hold Out" is more circular than linear. There's a Western assumption, reminds Black music scholar Olly Wilson, that music has a beginning, middle, and end.[6] This is a culturally shaped premise, he claims, that comes from linear thought. Gospel songs are not structured in this way. They double back into repetitions of a refrain or verse; swirl around a reiterated word or phrase, forming places of density, intensity, and surplus. They circle down and spiral up in waves of dynamic changes, as if the melodies and rhythms are seeking a core rather than a goal, a center rather than an end point.[7]

The lyrics themselves are repetitive—"mantras," as Sister Irma Dillard likes to call them. Repetitive and redundant, like the lyrics of a Taizé chant, or the word play of Black preaching. More traditional hymn lyrics provide a "reader's text"—a linear unfolding of biblical-religious thought that can serve as the basis for meditation and reflection apart from the singing. Literature, in a true sense. But gospel lyrics are "orature"—situated in an oral-aural tradition that values the repetition of words and short phrases as a mode of memory, a way of allowing the word to enter the body and be remembered. "Mantra" is a helpful image for gospel lyrics, contends Sister Irma, since reiteration is important to the music's purpose. Repetition allows you to "*feel* the words, to *breathe* the words, to get out of your head and stop intellectualizing! The song takes over, and the [repeated] words free you up to do that."[8]

❦ ❦ ❦

*R*ounding out the chorus with a flurry of syncopated, ascending octaves, Reed executes a split-second glissando down the keyboard, then locks into the undulating rhythms of the "vamp." The dynamic level drops ever so slightly, to make room for the layering of sound that is about to ensue. Vamps are holding patterns—stalls in the rhythmic and melodic unfolding of a song, that hold a community of music-makers in a relentless build-up of energy and intensity that finally releases into a bold final chorus. Singers at Lourdes refer to the vamp as an "ad-lib" section, inferring the lead singer's freedom to send out her improvised invocations over the highly repetitive choral background.

Isaiah rides his "high-hat" cymbal with an almost mesmerizing insistence. The church is alive with movement. Pat Goodall walks, dance-like, toward the blue-robed altos, cuing the first of the choir's staggered entries into this repetitive cycle of sound: "Lord help me to hold out!" the women on the left side of the sanctuary sing percussively, leaving just enough room at the end of each phrase for baritone voices, moments later, to answer their call. "Hold out!" retort men's voices at Pat's signal, and the inner volley is launched:

//: "Lord, help me to hold out!" "Hold out!" ://

they chant, building intensity with every repeat. Rose is already dispatching her fervent pleas as if generated by an inner "prayer-wheel." "Help me Lord!" she sings. "We need your help right now!" "Lord Jesus, help me now!" Her lyric gestures are short and well placed—a difficult task she's told me, that requires her to stay deeply engaged in the song, listening carefully to the intersecting parts, "tuning" her entreaties, as it were, to the surging sound. Her eyes are closed now, as she calls out,

"Lord Jesus, help us now!" "We need your help right now!" over the relentless chanting of pulsing voices. You can't miss the building intensity
as Pat "dances" her way toward the sopranos, her whole body mirroring the rhythms that set it in motion. "Lord, we need your help to hold
out!" We sopranos sing at her cuing, joining the altos' "call" at the
melodic interval of a third, while embellishing it with our faster paced
lyrics. The baritone volley, "Hold out!" becomes more energized with
each repetition:

> //: "Lord, we need your help to hold out!"
> "Hold out!" ://
> //: "Lord,   help   me   to   hold out!"

Rose's improvised entreaties are less distinct now, caught up as it were in
a huge mosaic of contrapuntal sound, swirling in an interchange of rhap-
sodic immediacy that seems to spiral down as it scales the heights. . . .

"*R*ose is playing with the words," responded Sister Irma once when I inquired if she could make out Rose's invocations during this portion of the
song.[9] Playing with the words, I mused. Hardly a way in which most Christians would speak of the tone, feel, or intent of their worship-music. Yet play
is an insightful way to describe this moment. Being playful is a way of surrendering to a freedom from compulsion, from the need to control a situation.
Having a good time as a mode of worship signals this community's distinct
perspective on Catholic worship—on the purpose for which the community
gathers, on the kind of God who might be encountered, on how an assembly
might act, and, in acting, know itself and God. Play requires others, a joint
entry into a spirit, a place that is open-ended and not goal-oriented. To "play
with the words" is to realize that communication about the life of the spirit
and about God pushes us beyond the literal, semantic meanings of words into
the realm of the aesthetic, into a place where Word becomes event and Presence, into a place of vulnerability, where surrender and abandon are possible.

*S*uddenly, Reed "drops out" of the swirling sound. Isaiah moves in
quickly to fill the vacuum, redoubling his throbbing pedal drumming
and emphatic cymbal crashes. The choir's rapid volley of clipped phrases,
call and response, escalates and intensifies:

//: "Lord, we need your help to hold out!"
                                            "Hold out!" ://
//: "Lord,   help   me   to   hold out!"

Borne aloft in the sheer intensity of layered, percussive sound, people around the church house seem lost in this "stalled" and spiraling moment of communal "waiting"—bodies moving freely, clapping, people singing along with the choir, rocking, or just enjoying the "wash" of sound. You can't help but be in the music, the moment. It's irresistible.

Pat has returned to the center, standing now at the heart of this web of intermingling sound. Her arms are outstretched, floating at her sides as if on the oscillating waves of the frolicsome Pacific. Despite her playfulness, I can tell she's ready for what is about to happen. She glances first at Reed, and with a slight nod, signals his reentry, then turns to Rose to sense Rose's readiness to abandon her improvisatory flow of supplication. Knowing the right moment to end this escalating pile up of sound and image is always a matter of feel, she's told me, a matter of Spirit-guided intuition that the music has accomplished its spiritual goal and that singers are ready to bring the song to conclusion. Looking intently at the choir, she gestures the moment of release. As if with one voice, the whole church bursts into the final phrase:

un–til my change // comes!

The air is charged with exhilaration. "Lo—rd," we chorus one last time, "help me to hold out!" "Oh Lord, help us to hold out" pleads Rose with unmetered freedom, her voice arcing above the pulsing rhythms.

Lo—rd, (Oh, Lord!) help me to hold out!
(We all need your help right now, Lord!)
Lo—rd, (Oh, Lord!) help me to hold out! (Help me to hold out!)

Then ascending as one voice to utter our last entreaty, we chant:

un–til my change . . .

But the phase is left incomplete! The floodtide halted, abruptly! People all over the church have been moving, clapping, singing, shouting—immersed in the buildup of polyrhythmic and polyvocal sound, all the while anticipating Pat's inevitable direction: to interrupt the final cadence in mid-air, like a trapeze artist pausing just before she grabs the swinging bar. Now, caught in mid-cadence by her signal, the whole community is suspended yet pulsing with anticipation, pleasuring in the tension held within each body, as if we, together, held our common breath. All the while, the song's intensity is building—the silence densely energized by the unresolved chord waiting to be completed, the unfinished phrase waiting to be sung. A delicious, well-known interval created for the sheer pleasure of its imminent resolution. Bits of sound erupt like tiny sparks revealing the pleasure of the waiting assembly—Isaiah flashes a fanfare of brush strokes on his drums; "Lord have mercy!" cries Brother Banks from the front. "Amen!" answers Shirley Valmore from the second pew—choir and congregation surrendering their beating hearts into Pat's control, as she waits, listening to the "feel" of the moment within herself, the length of time which is just enough but not too much, lest we miss the swinging bar as it approaches us. Then, with a sudden gesture of her hand and a look of fire in her eyes, the whole assembly bursts like a crash of musical lightening into the song's final chord. "Comes!!!" we shout, as if giving birth after a long labor, the silence shattered by drums, piano, and shouts of joy. Applause spreads through the gathering like wildfire. *Amen!! Thank you, Jesus! Amen! Oh, Hallelujah! He's worthy! Amen! Oh, yes! Amen! Thank you, Jesus! . . .*

Songs like "Hold Out" are "scribbles in the sand."[10] In the eighth chapter of John's Gospel, Jesus scribbles in the sand. A woman accused of adultery has been brought to him. Asking a single question, Jesus begins to write in the sand. As he does, the situation reconfigures itself. The accusers retreat. Jesus is left alone with the woman, who is now no longer "the accused," but one who is loved, supported, challenged, and sent on her way as a disciple. What has changed is not her situation, but the woman's relationship with Jesus in the midst of the situation.

Songs like "Hold Out" mark time. Their sung lyrics create space. They fix the attention, hold the tension for a time. In the process, the struggles, challenges, problems of those making music are not alleviated, but can be redefined in relation to the action of God. Transformation is never once-for-all. Yet change and transformation are the Gospel call. At Lourdes, an exuberant moment of song holds the community in a place where change can happen. The song, and the particular way it is "shaped" in performance, creates a social-spiritual space within which a perspective may be nudged, a resistance can be unblocked, a new sense of purpose and trust can emerge.

Intermezzo

WORDS

*T*he "sounded word" is at the heart of Black music and Black worship. Deep within African American culture is a predilection for the oral and aural—for the living, sounded word, articulated in rhythmic proclamation, dramatic preaching, passionate singing; for the emotive word, expressing conviction, determination, deep feeling, and shared values; for the contextualized and personalized word, communicated through tone of voice, turn of phrase, metering of syllables, placement of accents. This predilection for the living, sounded word reaches back historically into the fertile oral traditions of Africa in which every aspect of life was permeated with the generating, sustaining, and life-giving powers of the spoken word.[1] Fueled by the antiliteracy laws of slavery, African Americans cultivated the transforming power of vocal utterance—expressed in spirituals, chants, moans, work songs, spirited preaching, testimony—to exorcize evil,[2] create alternative communication patterns, and enact a way of life not bound by the horrors of slavery. Moreover, they pursued an African-based fascination with *Nommo:* described by one author as a feel for the "subtleties, pleasures, and potentials of the spoken word";[3] or as others image it, "that singular emotional tone that defines black cultural behavior"; a "musical sensibility," an "ethos"; the "spirit of black consciousness."[4] This cultural valuing of the expressed word has been maintained even within in a highly literate society: evidenced in the rhetorical contours Martin Luther King, Jr.'s preaching as he fueled the Civil Rights Movement, and celebrated in the sophisticated literary traditions of Zora Neale Hurston, Langston Hughes, Alice Walker, and Toni Morrison.

*T*he "sounded word" is at the heart of worship at Lourdes. Words sung, preached, prayed, shouted, whispered, called, answered, chorused, accompanied, repeated, and vamped create an oral/aural flow of communication

144

within which words—alive, energized, voiced by numerous persons—set off complex rhythms of vocal interaction. Appointed biblical texts and official prayers are read from the Lectionary and Sacramentary respectively, but virtually all other spoken/sung communication takes place without the intervention of printed texts.[5] Words unfold as relational action. The bodily presence, gestural and facial communication of speakers/singers, as well as the range of emotional energy carried on their voices, heighten the immediacy, the "event" quality of the vocal action. At the same time, the sound and cadence of voices root the worship in the history of the community, contextualizing God's Word as well as the whole liturgical action within a specific cultural-religious context.

Within the complexities of this vocal interaction, several kinds of word-actions unfold. Fueled by a "faith aesthetic" that seeks to release their generative and healing power, sung lyrics, preached metaphors, and prayed images focus the community's interaction with God, with each other, and with the world in distinctive ways. Speech and song coalesce into an expressive medium of faith communication that opens to the "revelatory word," and creates a matrix within which the worship and its music can become an "event of Presence."

Words as interaction / transaction / collective action: What kinds of words are sounded?

Words sounded within a liturgical assembly are actions, interactions, transactions. At Lourdes, several kinds of word-actions unfold in the course of Sunday worship. Of these, six predominate and are key to what takes place: word-actions that (1) acknowledge the community as "Church" and invite engagement in the worship, (2) proclaim and preach the biblical Word of God, (3) profess faith commitments, (4) make intercession, (5) give thanks and praise, and (6) express personal participation in the faith-event. The first five of these vocal interactions are found in their most focused form in sequentially unfolding portions of the worship—recognizable as the vocal structuring of Catholic liturgy: Introductory rites, Liturgy of the Word, Liturgy of the Eucharist. Yet they are not limited to these portions of the worship, but are sounded redundantly throughout the service, voiced by many persons, and especially present in moments of song.[6] Giving thanks and praise, for example, focused in the praying of the Eucharistic Prayer, is the dominant thrust of songs that fill the worship—voiced to the One who "from the rising of the sun until the going down of the same" is "worthy to be praised!" Proclaiming and preaching the biblical Word of God, focused in the reading, responsive singing, and preaching of appointed Lectionary passages, spills over into songs that both reiterate and heighten the impact of the biblical word, and through which singers "preach" the Gospel. Professing faith commitments, focused in the threefold Profession of Faith that follows the homily, is redundantly present

145

in the multiple forms of testimony that well up—voiced by community members during intercessory prayer and spoken or shouted by a lead singer at the conclusion of a song. Words that acknowledge the community as "Church" and invite engagement in the worship, while focused at the outset of the liturgy in the deacon's and presider's greetings and welcome, are heard as well in the numerous greetings exchanged among community members while gathering and at specific times during the liturgy—including the extended "exchange of peace"—and sounded in the reiterated address of the community as "Church" by the presider and others.

What most transforms these sounded actions—changing them from single-directional communication, speaker to hearer, and recasting them as communal transactions—are the expressions of personal participation voiced by community members throughout the liturgy. These are the responsive sounds of Black worship[7]—*Amen! Yes! Well. . . Al'right! Yes, Lord! That's right! Hallelujah! Thank you, Jesus! Preach it! Go ahead! Thank God for the Blood! Take your time! Oh, have mercy! Praise God!*—that punctuate prayers, songs, and preaching, and through which community members communicate affirmation, support, ascent, encouragement, praise, intercession, and testimony. Setting off complex rhythms of interaction, these interjections heighten the acclamatory tone of the liturgy; propel the worship forward; acknowledge that the word is taking effect and touching one's life; encourage others to go ahead, to go all the way, to tell the truth, to witness to their faith, to sing on through tears; and weave intercession and praise throughout the textures of the whole liturgy. While often referred to as "responses" or antiphonal patterns of call-response, which indeed they are, these spoken/shouted interjections actually transform the vocal communication into a collective action—one that engages those in leadership as well as the rest of the assembly in a dialogic process that unfolds contrapuntally and polyrhythmically throughout the liturgy.[8]

Message–delivery / functional aesthetic–faith aesthetic: What is the intentionality and impact of sounded words?

Sounded words at Lourdes are meant to *do* something, to have an impact on others: to evoke response, to invite change, to elicit faith. For this reason, *how* words are sounded is as important as what is said. The *Nommo* quality of words—their affective and affecting power—is cultivated, not simply as a fascination with the subtleties of oral communication but through a heightened sense that words are meant to have a reflective and emotional impact. Words are sounded so as to release their generative power—to heal, touch, move, support, encourage, challenge, and create bonds of love and mutuality. What is often described as the "functional aesthetic" of Black rhetoric and art—never *l'art pour l'art* but always intended to affect and effect[9]—becomes the "faith aesthetic" of vocal communication at Lourdes.

146

Conversations about singing and preaching, explored in the preceding chapters, reveal this faith aesthetic at work. They offer insight into the intentionality and impact of words sounded throughout the worship. Singers intend to *deliver* a God-given message through their song. This message is rooted in the Gospel ["The words *are* the Gospel"], and has touched the one who sings, connected with his/her faith ["Words are powerful" but the singer "must really believe what they are singing"]. It is sung with deep feeling ["You can feel them singing from their soul"], "delivered" by a singer who allows his/her whole body and vocal range to carry the inner message ["The feeling rises from the pit of your stomach . . . and just takes over"], and sung to a community that has been prepared to hear the message ["Wake up, Church! You act like you're dead this morning! We're serving a living God!" "Let 'em know what he's done for you!"]. The message, to be effective, must be actively received by the community [*"Amen! Sing it, Rose!" Thank you, Jesus!*] and ultimately is enabled by the Holy Spirit at work in all the participants ["The Spirit takes over." "The Holy Spirit talks to me, making me believe in myself"]. The fruit of this process is clear: "I've been fed!" "I have what I need!" "All those burdens I've been carrying around, I can let go of them."

A similar pattern is evident in comments about preaching. The task described by Father Kirk is to "clarify the Word of God," to bring alive the "drama of the Gospels: Jesus interacting with real people," healing, challenging, comforting, inviting them to change and to live the Word. To do this, the message must be timely and truthful [*"Go ahead, Father. Tell it like it is!"*], able to touch one's life ["he makes it fit with what's happening with you right now"], and delivered with passion, energy, and a fire that is fueled by faith ["He's a preacher! . . . He not only has a message but knows how to get it to you"]. The preached word can then evoke a response ["People respond!" "They affect me, guide me"], and open toward godly possibilities that are yet to be realized ["The power of God's Spirit can transform our world into the one family God intended it to be!"]. Ultimately, the preached message is effective because the Holy Spirit, active in the preacher's voiced faith, is already at work within the community ["Lourdes is a seedbed of the Spirit! The Spirit is in these people" "They actively celebrate that the Spirit is here"].

Perhaps the most striking aspect of this process of delivering and receiving the message is the emotional intensity involved in both. A question is sometimes raised about the reliability of feeling as vessel for the communication of faith. Do feelings impede the word/Word and its purpose or foster it? Although it is beyond the scope of this intermezzo to explore these questions in depth, several perspectives might shape such an inquiry. Walter Ong, for example, in his classic work on orality, recalls that the first type of communication between a mother and her child is the language of feeling—the language of love and bonding.[10] Within a community such as Lourdes, where there is a shared receptivity to the emotional impact of words, the affective quality of spoken/sung words seems to foster communal interrelatedness and solidarity. In addition, there seems a foundational belief at Lourdes that, since a primary purpose of words sounded is to enable the Word of God to be active, emotion is essential to the message. Nathan Mitchell concurs, positing that "Feeling and emotion are an intrinsic part of revelation itself. God's word to us is not only cognitive and rational; it is incarnate and emotional."[11] Moreover, as reported by members at Lourdes, the emotion-filled word has power to invite reflection, to put one's life in perspective. Martha Nussbaum, in her lengthy and highly nuanced exploration of emotion as "upheavals of thought," describes emotions as "judgements of value"; as energies "suffused with intelligence and discernment" that are an integral part of our systems of ethical judgement.[12] Shaped in the dialogic process of faith communication that we have seen at Lourdes, emotion-laden word-interactions might be viewed as formative of what Toinette Eugene describes as "orthopathy"—"righteous heart or feeling"—that can mediate between orthodoxy, "right teaching" and orthopraxis, "right action."[13] From this perspective, the faith-aesthetic we see operative at Lourdes has implications beyond the worship itself.

Sung lyrics / preached metaphors / prayed images: How do sounded words focus the community's interaction with God, each other, and the world?

*T*he "faith-aesthetic" we've just explored makes clear that words spoken and sung at Lourdes are meant to create a dialogue of faith around the Word of God—a participation *in* the words as addressed to this community. Within this context, images and metaphors invoked by those who sing, pray, and preach focus the community's interaction with God, with each other, and with the world, in particular ways, and invite participation in the very relationships they image. Moreover, sung lyrics, preached metaphors, and freely-improvised prayed images converge to set the whole range of words sounded, including the official texts of Catholic liturgy, in distinctive relief, allowing them to be heard in a new way.

Lyrics of the gospel songs sung at Lourdes have much in common with biblical psalms. They address God simply, directly, humanly, powerfully, at times tearfully, but always hopefully; expressing boldly the joys, struggles, heartaches, and fears of human-living-before-God. In tone, they are more like love songs than theological exposés: not romantic love, but life-giving and soul-committing love. Like biblical psalms, they intermingle praise, thanksgiving, supplication, and testimony, often in the same song. Like their scriptural counterparts, they often speak in the voice of testimony, the first person singular, assuming, like the communities from which the psalms emerged, that the "I" of song lyrics is deeply rooted in a communal identity of "we."

148

Images of God in these gospel songs are relational, participative, experiential, celebrative ["God of our weary years," of "our silent tears"; "a mighty, peaceful, loving God" who stirs "awesome wonder," and who is "worthy to be praised"; who is "my today and tomorrow," "my all and all"]. Metaphors are often "verbal,"[14] describing God with verbs that reveal how God acts in and for us and for the whole human community [God "has set me free," "has smiled on me," "keeps doing great things for me," "is blessing me right now," watches over even the smallest of creatures, keeping an "eye on that little sparrow"]. In response, "I say yes, Lord!" "I love you!" "I praise you!" "I lift you up!" "I thank you!" "I'll never stop praising him!" "To God be the glory!" As the memory of this God is actualized in responsive singing, lyrics focus the community's supplication ["Lead me, guide me," "Touch me," "heal me," "help me to hold out," "keep me near the Cross," "make me what you want me to be," "show me the way," "give me unwavering faith," and "let your Spirit fall on me"]. At the heart of this relational process is Jesus—God revealed as one who is involved in people's lives, destiny, struggles, pain, and joy ["Alpha and Omega," "my bright and morning star"; who is "good to know," has "never failed me yet"; whose name "is excellent," who "is everything to me," because "I have touched the hem of his garment and his love has made me whole."]. All of this is contextualized, even spurred on by a world that is a "barren land," where "heartaches" and "burdens press me down"; a world that "has forgotten about You" and "needs a word from You," and where "I must hold to God's powerful hand." Despite these expressed difficulties, sung lyrics become testimonies of the community's strong hope—that "Victory is mine!" "We've come this far by faith" and "can't turn around"; we stand "facing the rising sun of a new day begun!" continuing to be "on the battlefield for my Lord," following "where God leads me," because God is working, and "God is able!"

The metaphors of Father Kirk's preaching are likewise richly biblical. His words, rooted in the biblical texts of each Sunday's liturgy, situate God's revelation to this community in the concrete socio-political world in which they live. Like the prophetic thrust of the Gospel and many books of the Hebrew Scriptures, he images a God who is on the side of those who are the least in the eyes of the "world"—the outsider, the homeless, those "treated like trash," the poor, those who have experienced "centuries of oppression." This is a God who is deeply involved in the human struggle—who "has no favorites"; who is "revealed in Jesus as love, as justice," and who is ultimately *"pulling us, pulling us, pulling us toward himself"* so that we might share the resurrection of Jesus. The challenges that Jesus faced are ours as well. His Word "complicates our lives." We struggle with the demands of his passionate and self-giving love. Because of him, we are *"radical* people": proclaiming life in the face of death; addressing the "old, old wound of racism"; challenging others with love; and transforming society with the fairness and justice of Jesus. Jesus' Spirit makes this possible—the Spirit who is a "powerful force" that "draws us together," transforms our fear, gives gifts abundantly, brings Jesus alive in us, so that, in a "nation broken by hatred and misunderstanding" we can "keep alive the vision," believing that "people can change" with God's help; that life is stronger than death; and trusting that *"everything is possible"* if we believe in God's love.

The distinctive images of Brother Banks's improvised prayer, which complement these sung lyrics and preached metaphors, awaken the community's memory, speak truthfully about their present situation, and invite an imaginative entry into a future filled with hope. Over and again, he recalls Jesus' promise to be "with us," to "bring us together." He rekindles the memory of God's faithfulness in the past—"in the cotton fields when they didn't have nothin'"—and the lived experience that Jesus "never comes short of his word!" In a world filled with "trials and tribulations," where "everythin' else is failin'," where people are "down and out" and leaders build more jails, we need to "get close to Jesus," to be his "guest," because without him we "cannot make it," cannot endure what we "have to go through," nor come "together as brothers and sisters." But this life, as Brother Banks images it, opens out into a future: when that "old ship of Zion will come over," opening to us a world without sorrow, pain, or suffering; where peace will prevail; where we will be "free at last!" as we "walk around the throne" of God, singing and crying, *"Holy, holy God almighty!"*

Pace / rhythm/ shape / interaction:
How are speech and song integrally related?

Speech and song are integrally related in how the words of worship become effective at Lourdes, and in how a dialogue of faith is created, evoked, and sustained by those who take leadership as they interact with other members of the community. In the vocal communication that takes place throughout the liturgy, speech and song prepare for each other, frame each other, give way to each other, intersect and punctuate each other, overlap, undergird, and create an ongoing counterpoint of voiced sound.

It is striking that much of the spoken communication that takes place inhabits the realm of musicality: the cadence, rhythms, emotional flow of Brother Banks's praying, often undergirded with Reed's free piano improvisation; the pacing, emphasis, build-up of Father Kirk's preaching; the rhythm, rhyme, intensity of Deacon Dupres's or Sister Renee's preaching; and the percussive, polyrhythmic shouted interventions of community members that are a constant part of the vocal fabric. At the same time, sung words give way to expressive speech: a singer's voice "sailing through the melodic line into the realm of expressive speech" in order to address the community directly and forcefully; the spoken words of a singer preparing the community for a song, or the overflow of praise she might shout at the conclusion of a song. Not only are the boundaries between the community's speech and song fluid, but together they seem to create a "single expressive pattern"[15] with a common intent and complementary strategies.

Musicians and preachers at Lourdes, for example, "shape" their voiced interaction with the community in similar ways. The deliberate pacing and extended duration of Father Kirk's preaching, like that of a slow gospel song led by the choir, create time and space for people to be drawn into an unfolding process. Both begin "conversationally," then move to levels of greater intensity, acceleration, and emphasis, reaching peak moments that signal the crux of the message. As Father Kirk describes it, "I build, and build, and build—and then I stop!" Community members become progressively engaged, but they also participate in shaping the song or preaching through their spoken/shouted responses and acclamations. As this dialogue of faith unfolds at various times over the course of a lengthy liturgy, sung and spoken words have a cumulative impact on all who participate.

What seems to motivate this interdependence between speech and song is the very nature of the sounded words that fill the liturgy at Lourdes—communication about the life of the spirit, about God, about human bondedness and Gospel mission. The rhythms and musical inflection of Brother Banks's voice increases the persuasiveness of his language. The "sound of words," the textures and rhythms of shouted responses ["*Thank ya' Jesus!*"] awaken memory and association—a sense of "home," of roots, of purpose. The melody, rhythms, repetitive "mantras" of songs, as we have seen, not only unlock the emotional power of words but push beyond the semantic meanings into an aesthetic realm of surplus and mystery; moving people "out of the head," beyond intellectual engagement, into the realm of the heart; opening places of vulnerability where surrender and abandon are possible, and where the imagination can envision what does not yet exist. Moreover, singing enables the gathered community to experience its common voice of faith. Speech and song at Lourdes seem to require each other: the musical dimensions of sounded words opening into the realm of the Spirit, of unseen and transcendent mystery, while always remaining rooted in the "revelatory word"—revealed in human flesh and human words as incarnate Word—as source of the godly power that is tapped.

Incarnate word / enfleshed revelation:
How do sounded words / collective action / become an event of Presence? of the Word?

Sounded words, as we saw in the previous chapter, are meant to give way to a deeper process—the action of God. Rose Isles, speaking as a lead singer, sums this up: "When I sing, I want them to know that God is with them; that God is *really* there with them!" All dimensions of the dialogue of faith—the collective vocal interaction of the community—that we have explored so far coalesce, creating a resonant space where people can touch, taste, sense the mysterious presence of God—can *know* that God is really there with them—and surrender. At Lourdes, the whole manner in which this space is created through speech and song attests to a belief that the God whom the community seeks to know is a God who "cannot be *thought* but can only be *met*."[16] Word-interactions become a place of that meeting, a place of God's free and revelatory activity, an event of presence.

Commentary by members of Lourdes suggests that this "place of meeting," this "event of presence" that unfolds within the dynamic interchange of sung and spoken words, has certain distinctive contours. First, while "knowing" God in this vibrant process is deeply personal—feeling moved, strengthened, reoriented—it is inseparable from its communal context: God acting in the community, in the person beside you, in the singer before you in whom the Spirit acts. This "communal art"—creating a space where abandon, confidence, and surrender are enabled—is fostered by people's willingness to give witness to the tenderness and ardor of their faith through heartfelt words and passionate singing. What is created is a communal faith intimacy in which members can "savor the Word in the arms of a loving community."[17] A second characteristic of the faith "knowing" experienced within the vocal transactions of the worship is that it is rooted in the history of God's faithfulness. Memory actualized through song and prayer—that God has always been there for us—awakens hope for both present and future. The sounded words invite *anamnesis*—dynamic memory. Third, intimations of God's presence and nearness in the worship are activated through the very processes by which bonds of communal affection, mutuality, and solidarity are deepened. Shared words of faith, which reveal a supportive, believing community, can evoke a God-given strength to struggle against all that might diminish or threaten the community or its children. Finally, as sounded words that "deliver the Gospel" become effective—as healing, encouragement, challenge, and deeper love—through the power and action of the Holy Spirit, the Word becomes more deeply incarnate, enabling community members to enflesh a Gospel way of being in their daily lives, living as leaven in the world.

Chapter Ten

"HAVING CHURCH"

—BEING CHURCH—

*T*he energy had been building all morning, but it was Deacon John Dupre's preaching that set the gathering on fire.[1] Preaching on that Third Sunday of Easter, he declared, *"I feel Jesus alive in this place today!"* (*Amen!*) Then, bringing us to the very shores of Tibereas to witness the disciple Peter swimming toward the Risen Jesus *"like a sprinter* (*Yes!*) *whose speed could only be limited by the measure of his hope!"* he charged us to swim with that same urgency toward the Risen One who stands on the shores of our lives, never losing hope *"until that bright day when we will see God face to face* (*Amen!*) *in the new Jerusalem!* (*Amen!*) Oh glory, glory, Hallelujah! (*Hallelujah!*) Hallelujah! Amen!" (*Amen! Amen!!! Hallelujah!*)

"I do!" rang out with special resilience that morning as Father Kirk summoned us to profess our faith in this *"powerful Risen Lord"* who will "bring us through . . . *no matter how dark this world becomes!"* The music sparkled with an Easter freshness as Reed's fingers graced the keyboard again after a two week absence. After Communion, the community's singing of "Perfect Praise" spiraled to such intensity that Pat Goodall signaled an extra repeat, sending one more volley of "Jesus, excellent is your name!" soaring to the rafters, and sparking an overflow of shouted praise. As wave after wave of *Thank you, Jesus! Hallelujah! Glory to you!* spilled over, Barbara McKinney walked from the back of the church toward the ambo to make announcements. A petite woman, smartly dressed in a gray suit set off by a single string of pearls, Barbara paused briefly as she neared the ambo, waiting for stillness to settle in once again. Then stepping onto a small wooden box behind the ambo so as to see out to the congregation, she exclaimed, "Brothers and sisters, *have we had church today?"* A burst of applause and shouts of *Amen!* broke out again.

While each Sunday gathering carries its own exhilaration, occasions like this one release a unique and communally felt energy, an intensity of shared experience, that is described at Lourdes as "having church." People leaving the church house that morning confirmed Barbara's perception. "I'm *ready* for the week ahead!" commented Jeannette Howard. "Oh yes, we've *had church!*" affirmed Liz Bell. "I've been *fed!*" exclaimed Pat Goodall.

"**H**aving church" is a startling concept. "Church" as verb—something done. Our English language gives us away. "Church," like "music," is a noun but never a verb. As noun, "church" is a concept, a building, even a community, but never an activity in which we engage. At Lourdes, "having church" supplies more than the missing verb. It describes a pervasive attitude, a deeply valued quality of human relatedness, that transcends occasions like this Third Sunday of Easter when people are deeply stirred. Having church is a cultivated way of *being* church, one to another and before God, in season and out. It is a commitment to being together on the journey of faith, and to kindling the fire of that faith when the community gathers for worship. It is a recognition that each one present is an actor in the great drama of worship, giving voice to its prayer and enacting its sacramentality.

"What I mean by having church," commented Sister Irma Dillard to me one evening, "is that people have the freedom to be who they are. For us church is like a second home. We *are* the church! . . . People come to pray. . . . Some may sit in the back and be quiet, others may stand up and shout. If something is really heavy, if they need to pray out loud, the church prays with them. . . . The church is a community. We can pray, we can laugh, we can cry together, we can celebrate the joys, the strengths, and we do it all together. It's in song, in music, and within the liturgy."[2]

There's a wisdom here, added Father Kirk in another conversation. "When I came to Lourdes, [a whole way of doing the liturgy] was in place, and of course I didn't interfere." The leaders who initiated and fostered this "showed a great deal of courage and insight. They understood that liturgy is truly the work of the people! The priest is part of the community, and there are roles to be carried out. . . ."[3]

Having church, being church, is an apt way to describe what took place at the midpoint of that April liturgy in 1995. The vibrant images of Deacon Dupre's preaching still rang in our ears, and the power of the community's "I do!" to Father Kirk's query—"Do you believe that just as Peter and John saw Jesus because they loved Him, so we too, in our love for Jesus, can see him in our world, in our hearts?"—still echoed in the church house. As a hush settles over the church house again, Brother Banks takes the lead.

"We come now to the prayer of the faithful," he begins, his hands folded against his white alb, moving now and then to the rhythms of his prayer. "After that great sermon, *(Amen!)* we come to thank God for givin' us this day our daily bread. *(Yes!)* So many things happ'nin' in our lives, *(Oh, yes!)* many things happ'nin' in our country. *(Yes! Lord Jesus!)* But we must *thank God* . . . and depend on him, for he said he would not leave us alone, *(Yes! Amen!)* no matter how hard it may be. . . . We ask Almighty God to bless Deacon Dupre, as he speaks the truth, *(Amen!)* our pastor, Father Kirk, all those who represent the Holy God. *(Amen!)* . . . Today, so many people are *tryin' to blot out God!* . . . But those of us who *hold up his name must* **keep faith in God!** *(Amen!)* Bless our choir, *(Oh yes, Lord!)* choir leaders, musicians . . . our little children *(Yes, Jesus!)* . . . the old people who are sufferin' so much *(Oh yes, Lord!)* . . . all of you who are here this mornin', *(Yes!)* who come to *praise his name! (Amen!!)* . . . We ask him to *forgive us all our sins (If you please, Lord!)* . . . so that we will *recognize him (Al'right!) and say,* **I know that he is my God for he lives in my soul!** *(Amen!!!) That we'll come to love one another, (Oh yes, Lord!) praise him and give thanks! (Yes!)* We ask him to *lead us and guide us (Yes!)* in times like these . . . that we will not give up, we will *not weaken* but we will say *Thank you, Lord* for giving us this day our daily bread! *(Amen!)* . . . We ask a blessing on everyone." *(Yes, Lord Jesus!)* Brother Banks's voice has come to rest again as he concludes, "Now we invite your prayers, in Jesus' name." *(Amen!)*

As on all Sundays, prayers are voiced from every part of the church house. "I'd like to ask the Church to pray with me . . ." they often begin—for loved ones who are ill or facing death; for friends suffering from cancer, AIDS, or dealing with a loss of family members, at times tragically—the truth of people's lives, the web of sorrow and joy, now spoken openly to God in the hearing of the whole community.

"Let us pray for addicts and alcoholics who suffer and are dying today," *(Yes, Lord!)* came Victoria Stith's voice from the back of the church, "for their families and their children, who suffer as well, *(Yes!)* and so do our communities. Let us pray to the Lord. . . ."

"I want to pray for my cousin Shirley, who is grieving the loss of her mother," *(Have mercy!)* prayed a woman whom I could not see, "and for all those who are grieving the loss of family members; that God will help them to have peace in their hearts *(Yes!)* . . . and deal with the loneliness that is left behind. *(Yes!)* Let us pray. . . ."

"Let us continue to pray for the poor people of Oklahoma City, their relatives and friends," *(Have mercy, Lord!)* prayed Bessie Brooks. "And that God will bring our country together again," added another. "For the hungry, *(Yes!)* the homeless, those in prison, *(Yes!)* those who are depressed and lonely," *(Oh, yes!)* beseeched a visitor; "that they experience in the most appropriate way your love, O Lord! . . ."

155

I've become aware that prayers prayed with deep emotion have a way of etching themselves on my heart, nudging me over and again to pray, to remember. Only a week ago, Louise Wood prayed "for Charlotte Ann." *(Oh yes, Lord!)* You could hear an empathy in Louise's voice that only another mother might feel. "Lord, you're hearing the moanings and groanings of a husband and children. *(Have mercy, Lord!)* We don't know what your will is, but I ask you to have mercy this morning!" *(Oh, yes!)* "I ask you to look down on her as she suffers and give her peace. I ask you Lord, in the name of St. Benedict, *in the name of your Mother,* and all the saints, to look down on her give her peace, Lord if it is your will, just give her peace. *(Yes!) Have mercy on her,* on her *husband—her mate for all of these years! (Oh, have mercy!)* Let him, help him, to accept your will. *Look on her children,* let them know that they're not going to be motherless. *Help them Lord! (Yes!)* If it be your will, have mercy. *(Oh, yes!)* For this and all things, in the name of Jesus, I pray to the Lord. . . ."

Faced with the tragic murder of a woman by her own son several months ago, Jean Alexander voiced the prayer of those in this community who had known and loved her: "I want to thank the Lord for giving me strength, for giving me courage, *for giving me patience* to face last week. I thank him so much! *(Yes!)* I ask the Church to join me . . . to pray for Ira, her sisters and brothers, her nieces and nephews, the whole family. We ask you Lord to *touch them this morning. (Yes, Lord!)* Give them the *serenity* to accept what they can't change. It was so tragic, but *the Lord knows* what they need. I ask him to enter them, *move the devil out of their way! (Yes!)* They're gonna need a lot of prayers to get through this. And we have to depend on the Lord *to give us the courage* to pray for them. We ask this in the name of Jesus! Let us pray to the Lord. . . ."

"I lift up my Uncle Joe, first his cancer and now the pneumonia," prayed Charlene Edwards on another occasion. "Father, that your hand of mercy will be on him, and that he will know in such an intimate way your love and your presence to him, that you will strengthen him and all those afflicted with cancer. Let us pray to the Lord. . . ."

Prayers are intimate and honest. Faced with seemingly impossible situations, people implore God for strength, direction, the "comfort of the Holy Spirit"— and a deeper love among those who must deal with the situations. Last week, in the aftermath of the bombing in Oklahoma, Brother Banks's prayer caught this wisdom. ". . . We wonder why God lets things like this happen. But *he knows* what he's doin'. He has a way of bringin' us together in the hardship. *(Amen!)* . . . His son *died* to show us how to love one another. . . . We need to come together with *Jesus* as our leader. . . ."

As Brother Banks said so well, struggle invites deeper commitment. Responding to President Clinton's initiative to increase police presence in large urban areas, Louise Wood prayed, "I'd like to offer a prayer for those in authority. That goes for Mr. Clinton on down! That the Lord will *change their hearts. (Oh, yes!)* That he will make them *see the pain and the suffering they are caus-*

156

ing—and that more police are not necessarily the solution to our problem. *(Amen!)* I ask you Lord to hold us together as a nation, as a city, as a community —that we too might *change where change is needed*. For this let us pray to the Lord. . . ."

Another woman in the assembly continued, "I would like to pray for the children . . . who are going through a real tough time right now, not knowing why the police need to be there to 'save them.' I talked to two young girls the other night and they were just frightened to death. They need our help! *(Yes, Lord!)* The police have to do their job but they also have to know that [it's hard for these kids to] get through life. Their parents are doing the best they can, and obviously it's not a very good example. So I really want to go out for those children. Let us pray . . ."

No matter how difficult the struggle, prayers of thanksgiving are always abundant. "I would like to offer a prayer of thanks from Lea and myself," prayed David Shermerhorn as he and his wife celebrated their thirtieth wedding anniversary last Sunday. "I thank God and thank this church that we are here in joy this morning. *(Amen!)* . . . It's been said that it takes a village to raise a child. *(Amen!)* It certainly takes a whole village to support a marriage! This is our village. *(Amen!)* Let us continue to give back what we have taken from this village. Let this village stay strong, for the children, the mothers and fathers, the grandmothers and grandfathers, the great-great grandmothers that are here taking care of babies. *(Amen!)* That's a village. And what's happening in the world with the mutilations, the massacres, the killings *(Oh, Lord!)*—only a village can protect us. Let's maintain the village, let's maintain each other. Be strong, and only with God's help can we do that. *Thank God for Lourdes! (Yes!) Thank God for all of you. (Amen!) Praise be to God!* Let us pray to the Lord. . . ."

"I'd like to offer a prayer of thanksgiving," prayed Judy Brown the week before. "I thank the Lord for the blessings he bestowed on me and my family last week. Because you ask the Lord for things, and he doesn't give them to you right away, and you figure he's not going to answer my prayer. But it's always said that the Lord comes 'right on time.' *(Amen!)* And *he was right there for me and my family! (Amen! Oh, yes!)* Yes, Lord, and 'thank you' doesn't seem to be enough. Just two words doesn't seem to be enough. But all I can say is *thank you, Lord!* The *glory belongs to you and only to you! (Amen!)* For all of these things let us pray to the Lord. . . ."

"I offer a prayer of thanks to God for continuing to give me strength," *(Oh, have mercy!)* prayed Jean Alexander recently. "And I continue to pray for Brother Banks, who *prays so hard*." Indeed, the emotion of Brother Banks's prayer that morning had caused some concern, given the weakness of his heart. "He's *such a man of prayer! (Amen!)* If anybody's ever known or seen a child of God, *he is one! (Amen!!!) There's no doubt in my mind!* I'd like to let him know now while he can smell the flowers, when he can see it and feel it, that we *truly love him (Amen!) and respect him for the man he is. (Amen!) He's not ashamed of God!* And *he testifies to that everywhere he goes.* And if anybody knows him they know that. I ask the Lord's blessing on him, to give him the courage to stand each day, because *I know it's not easy!*" I could hear Brother Banks responding, "Oh, have mercy!" "But *he has that faith* to keep on keepin' on." concluded Jean. "For all of this, let us pray to the Lord. . . ."

Thanksgiving to God mingles with thanks to others who have shared the struggle: "I'd like to thank the Lord for Our Lady of Lourdes church, and especially the choir, who brought consolation to so many of my family members last Thursday night! *(Thank you, Jesus!)* And that the Lord give you strength to keep on! That this church remain here *(Yes!)* to give people courage and consolation. Let us pray . . ."

"I want to offer a prayer of thanksgiving to God," prayed a visitor to Lourdes, "who has led me through a really bad time of crisis, and healed every need—mental, emotional, and, today, spiritual. I want to thank him, and I want to thank this body of people that I've been allowed to come into today. Thank you Lord! . . ."

"Let us all pray and give thanks to the Lord, that he *never gives up on us!*" Liz Bell's voice from the back of the church seems to sum it all up. "He *never gives up!* As long as we call on him, *he will answer our prayers,* not in the way we want, but he *always answers!*"

Gathering up this morning's prayers and perhaps the cumulative praying of weeks and months, Brother Banks concludes, "Our Father who art in heaven and everyplace, we ask you to hear these petitions. You know what's in the hearts of everyone; you know what they're goin' through. Take them, Almighty God, to your throne of grace! *(Yes!)* Let your will be done. Help us, Father, to accept whatever your answer may be *(Amen!)* and say, 'Yes!' as the holy Mother did. Let thy will be done! *(Amen!)*

"We go now to the holy Mother. She didn't go away when Jesus was on the cross! *(Oh yes!)* She stood there and faced it, tears running down her face, to let him know that she loved him. We go to her *(Yes!)* and ask her to help us come closer to her Son *(Yes, Lord!)* in that great prayer, prayed from our hearts, Hail Mary. . . ."

*P*rayer shapes believing—so the ancient adage goes. It is striking that these prayers "of the faithful" are addressed to God, but always in the hearing of the community. Intercessions are woven with testimony, with words of encouragement or admonition, with expressions of concern. Those who pray aloud open themselves and their faith as source of strength for others. And the church responds, not only in the formal words which close the prayer, but in the repeated *Amens!* that weave webs of understanding and solidarity as each prayer unfolds. One hears the voice of this church—a voice that in turn renews the community in its faith and its determination to stay on the journey. In that voice is an openness not only to what is prayed for, but to the unpredictable ways God may choose to answer. "If only we do the will of God," reiterates Brother Banks over and again. Prayer together becomes a school of discipleship. The church is edified, is healed and built up, sustained in times of struggle, and grounded in an all-encompassing gratitude for God's continuous care.

❦ ❦ ❦

*M*any years before I came to know them, Lourdes adopted the ancient liturgical practice of offering "the Lord's peace" immediately after the prayers.[4] The flow seems deeply natural. A "seal on the prayer" was the ancient understanding; "love radiating" seems to be the wisdom here. "*Church,*" exclaims Father Kirk, arms extended, as Brother Banks concludes the prayers, "*this is the day the Lord has made!* **The Spirit of Jesus is truly among us!** *Let's take time to spread His peace around!*"

As if moved by an unseen force, a sudden and spontaneous communitas breaks out, a burst of movement, hugs, greetings, and laughter that tests the space limits of this tiny church house. People begin flowing out of their pews, reaching over benches, walking toward the front to greet choir members, pressing their way through the crowded center aisle to reach persons in other parts of the room, embracing each other as they go.

I turn to greet others in the choir—Ernestine Harris, Rita Johnson, Rhoda Charles, Jeannette Howard, Carol Lugo, each of the sopranos in turn. "Oh, I needed that hug!" effuses Jean Alexander after a warm embrace. Then up the three steps to greet Brother Banks who's been ill these past weeks and has wisely remained at his place. Failing health has never dimmed the sparkle in his eyes or the warmth of his words. Then out toward the center aisle to embrace others in the church house. A hug for Joan Dill who's looking so elegant and upbeat this morning despite the struggle with her health. Dear Mercedes Salguero, always so gracious. "Have you ever wanted to be ordained?," she asks, but there's no time to really probe the query. Turning slightly in this press of people, I'm face to face with Father Kirk. We embrace, just as little Ebony Perriman slips between us on her way to greet a friend. Children have their way in this crush of bodies! Oh yes, Mrs. Margaret Fisher, always so buoyant and cheerful that it's hard to believe she's a great-great-grandmother! We talk briefly of Sister Helen Carroll and make plans to visit her at the retirement center where she now lives. Just then I notice a few visitors seated in the third pew, smiling as the scene unfolds before them—perhaps a bit puzzled, but drawn in as others reach out to greet them. Feeling a tug on my jacket, I turn to find Tyree McDuff looking up at me ready for a hug. Shirley Valmore is beside me now, a great-grand niece in arms—a warm double embrace! Harry Bryant and his dear wife Lillian. Walter Turner. Dallas Tillman and his wife Marie. Pressing on, I make my way toward Mama Winslow further back in the church house. "Oh, it's been a good week," she reports. "The pain is not so bad, and all the family are coming for dinner today!" Mama Levy has a similar response, "Oh, I'm making it!" And there's Betty Cooper—I've told her more than once that when the choir sings I can always feel her spirit reaching from the back of the church to the front. She tells me today of a 6:00 a.m. prayer group that she and several other school bus drivers have formed to begin their day. And thankfully she's made it through the first anniversary of her son Danny's senseless killing. What a sorrow for a mother to bear!

I can hear John Brown's voice from the front now, inviting everyone to "please return to your seats!" But it never happens quickly. No one seems in a hurry. One more hug for Mike Edwards who's standing with "little Mike" in arms at the rear of the church, and of course, a greeting for Liz Bell. Slowly, people begin making their way back to their places. As the room begins to settle again, you can't help but feel that you've tasted a bit of God's shalom, as liberative as it is chaotic. The lighthearted, familial spirit that permeates this gesture of peace-offering belies the truth that what is happening is serious business—the business of "being church," of surrounding each one with an embrace of love that can sustain them in the struggle, and lift even the heaviest heart.

It's music that will ultimately gather this dispersed community back into the rhythms of shared action and praise. Reed's fingers are tracing songlines on the keyboard as the choir moves into place and a last few people return to their pews. Then, with a sudden burst of enthusiasm that brings people around the church house to their feet, we chorus,

> You don't know what you're missing if you're not serving God!
> You don't know what you're missing if you're not serving God![5]

The challenges of "being church" in a troubled world find their way over and again into Father Kirk's preaching. And the daily discipline of the community's "serving God"—of carrying this radiating love beyond the church house—is woven back into its Sunday Eucharist on many occasions. Numerous examples come to my mind.

• *I*t was a balmy Sunday in mid-November, 1995. Father Kirk stood before the community, preaching about Jesus' confrontation with the Sadducees concerning the resurrection from the dead and his proclamation that "God is not God of the dead, but of the living!" How difficult it is, Father Kirk mused, to

160

come to faith in the resurrection of Jesus in a world that impels us to concentrate on its own goals. As believers, we come to that faith through the Word of God proclaimed. We come to it through the *"brilliant gift"* of our baptism in which *"we hold our hands in the hands of the Risen Lord,"* (*Amen!*) the same Risen Lord who was brought back to life by a God *"who would not allow his Son to remain a victim of death* (*Amen!*) *but . . . scooped him up in new life* (*Amen! Yes!*) *and brought him back to his disciples, brought him back to us!"* And this Risen Jesus says to us, *"I have new life* (*Amen!!!* Clapping . . .) *and I promise you new life!"* (*Amen!!!*)

But how does our faith in the resurrection come *"alive in our world?"* asked Father Kirk, come alive *"in the dark circumstances of our lives? . . .* What do you say, Church, to a mother who's standing by the bedside of a young man, thirty-five or thirty-six years old, (*Oh, Lord!*) who's in the last stages of AIDS? (*Have mercy!*) *What do you say?* What do you say to that woman when she asks, 'Why? Why is this happening?' (*Hmm . . .*) *There is only one answer, Church!* God *loves* this young man, and will bring *him back to you, to the world, and to the church in the resurrection!* As his eyes darken—and anybody who has seen a person in the last stages of AIDS, (*Oh, yes!*) *it's not a pretty picture;* (*Yes!*) it's an *awful picture;* (*Yes!*) it's a *dreadful way to die* (*Yes, Lord!*)—the one thing that we can say is that Christ, who is raised from the dead, is *holding this young man in his arms* and one day this young man will be restored in the *fullness and beauty* that was given to him originally by God! (*Amen!*)

"What do we say to a woman whose son is killed on Third Street? (*Have mercy!*) Twenty-one years old. What a waste! (*Yes!*) From our eyes, what an *incredible waste!* His life was *just beginning*. What do you say to that family? *Have hope!* He's gone, yes he is gone—*wasted by cruel people* (*Yes!*) in a *cruel society.* (*Yes! Well . . .*) But have hope. *God is not through with him yet.* (*Yes! Amen! Thank you, Jesus!*) *He will raise that son to new life, to new glory, to new beauty in a way that no one can take from him. That is our hope!* (*Yes!*)

"What do you say to a people who have gone through *centuries of oppression and prejudice?* (*Oh, have mercy!*) What do you say to a people—such as we have today, right here in San Francisco—to a people who are walking through a society which is *clearly unfair* toward many of its members, especially low-income members, poor people, (*Hmm . . .*) homeless people, (*Yes!*) people of color? (*Yes, Lord!*) *What do you say when the government seems to be going farther and farther away from concern* (*Yes!*) *about these people?* (*Amen! Yes!*) Well, you say two things. First of all you say, the Lord is the Lord of life! (*Yes!*) And the Lord *sees* the poor and *hears the cry* of the poor. (*Yes! Well.*) And the Lord's power of risen life will overtake this corrupt and incorrect society and bring balance, and restore order to it. *That's what the Lord will do! But in the meantime, if you believe in that, then put your energies together* (*Amen!!*) *and work together* (*Amen!*) *against that kind of injustice, Church!* (*Amen! Amen!*) God *loves us* and God *acts.* He also puts strength and spirit *in all of us* (*Yes!*) so we can act together! (*Yes! Well . . .*) . . . Church! Jesus has given us hope! (*Yes!*) And he's given us *strength*, (*Oh, yes!*) and

in that strength we can face anything! (That's right!) **Anything, Church!** *(Oh, yes! Amen!)*
Anything! . . ."

• *J*ust a few weeks ago, as we neared the close of the liturgy, Father Kirk
walked to the center of the room, his purple vestments flowing as he moved.
"Bobby and Michelle" he began, addressing a young couple seated some six
rows from the front, "tomorrow is your third anniversary. *(Yes!)* The Church
wants to give you a special blessing. *(Yes!)* We prayed for you in hard times!
(Yes! Amen!) Would you please come forward." Jean Alexander's voice could be
heard above the applause that broke out, "Bring your kids! Bring your blessings!" As I watched this young couple walk forward, each carrying one of
their two toddlers, both of whom had been baptized at Lourdes, you could
feel the community surround them with love. Reed slipped in, suffusing the
moment with the gentle sounds of his improvisation.

"Church, please rise," invited Father Kirk. "If you believe that the Holy Spirit
is in you, then you share in this blessing!" Looking out, I could see people all
over the church house stretching out their arms in blessing. "Heavenly Father,"
prayed Father Kirk, "we call down your blessing upon Bobby and Michelle
and upon their family." Little Kaelin fusses in her mother's arms, oblivious to
the prayer that envelops her. "We ask you to bless them as they continue now,
into another year *(Oh, yes!)* of joy and sorrow, *(Yes!)* the ups and downs on the
journey of married life. *(Amen! Yes!)* You've brought them through a hard year,
Father! *(Oh yes, Lord! Amen!)* You brought them through a year when they may
have wanted to give up, but they didn't! *(Yes! Thank you, Jesus!)* You brought them
through a year when they may have felt abandoned, but they weren't. *(Yes!)*
Now in the years ahead bless them more, *(Amen!)* give them strength, *(Amen!)*
make their love more complete *(Yes, Lord!)* so that they can face *anything*, knowing that you, Lord, are with them. *(Yes!)* We bless them! The Church blesses
them, Father, Son and Holy Spirit!" Applause, *Amens*, and embraces sealed
the prayer.

Then addressing the whole community, Father Kirk continued, "May our
all-loving, all-powerful God, the God who *launched us on our journey*, who walks
with us every *step of the way*, *(Yes!)* who *picks us up* when we fall, *(Amen!)* the God
who gives us strength to keep one foot ahead of the other, *(Oh, yes!)* the God
who *pulls us* toward that moment when we shall *be with him forever*, *(Yes!)* may
that loving God, the Father, Son, and Holy Spirit, bless you and be with you
forever!" *Amen!*

• *I* was startled one November morning by a phone call from Jean Alexander. Zettie Le Blanc, a pillar of the community, had been seriously burned in a
tragic accident. Prayers were released immediately on her behalf. Members of
Lourdes vigiled with her through weeks of intensive care, hoping against

hope that she would survive. Their concern never flagged through months of multiple skin grafts and medical interventions as this strong, beautiful woman made her way inch by inch through a torturous hospital stay.

One warm June Sunday the following year, as choir members were gathering in the small entryway at the back of the church and greeting people who were flowing through the doors on either side, I heard someone exclaim, "Zettie's home!" There in the doorway, cane in hand and assisted by two of her granddaughters, Zettie LeBlanc was making her way into the church house. Still quite frail and needing assistance as she walked down the center aisle, the beauty and strength of this valiant woman outshone the scarring that could be seen on the lower portion of her face. Welcome home, Zettie! recurred like a mantra throughout the liturgy. Father Kirk, preaching on Luke's Gospel account of Jesus setting his face toward Jerusalem, spoke of the tenacious faith that had brought this courageous woman through her terrible ordeal. Someone, perhaps Zettie herself, made a special request that we sing "Lord, help me to hold out!" after Communion. Just before the service ended, Zettie's granddaughters thanked those who had walked the difficult journey with their grandmother, offering each one a hand-lettered testimonial of thanks signed by Mayor Willie Brown, and invited the community to lunch in the parish hall. More than once in the weeks that followed Zettie reminded us that, despite her continued frailty, this Sunday gathering kept her going.

It was Holy Thursday evening two years later. I hurried from my car to avoid a torrential downpour and slipped through the church doors as quickly as possible. One of the first to greet me was Zettie Le Blanc. Her sculpted face seemed lovely in the muted light of the entrance way, her tall bearing full of strength. Embracing her, I could feel the love that flowed from her whole countenance. We spoke briefly about this holy night, her love for this feast, and her desire to be here despite a penetrating tiredness. She had spent the day buying bread and gathering other foodstuffs for the sandwiches she and Liz Bell would distribute tomorrow to homeless neighbors living on the streets of San Francisco. This was not a Good Friday practice but a weekly commitment to those who would otherwise want for food and care.

As I listened to the Scriptures proclaimed that evening—stories of a Passover meal celebrated in thanksgiving for the great exodus from Egypt; Paul's account of Jesus offering bread and wine to his friends on the night before he died, claiming these simple foods to be his very flesh and blood; and John's poignant description of Jesus washing the dusty feet of his beloved followers —a single image seemed fixed in my heart. Zettie had spent the day buying bread, preparing a humble feast that would be celebrated tomorrow on the streets of San Francisco.

*T*he air seems charged! Shouts of *"Hallelujah!" "Yes, Lord!" "Thank you, Jesus!" "Excellent is your name!"* are riding on Isaiah's final drum flourishes and a swell of applause that cascades through the church house. The late-April sun is well overhead now. The hours have flown by since Deacon Dupre carried us to the very shores of Tibereas and stirred us with his charge to have faith in the Risen Jesus! We have heard the church's proclamation that Jesus "has made us children of the light . . . and has opened the gates of heaven to receive his faithful people!" We have wept and prayed. We have tasted the Bread of Life.

It's now late in the service. Pat Goodall announces, "We have a special request this morning for 'Oh, it is Jesus.'"[6] But her words can hardly arrest the overflow of praise that continues to well up. *"Amen!"* exclaims Bessie Brooks,*"We praise you, Lord! Thank you, Lord!" "Hallelujah!"* answers Jean Alexander who has stepped out in front of the choir to take the lead. Reed is weaving new songlines into his unfolding modulation, setting in place the sturdy if leisurely rhythms of Andraé Crouch's "Oh it is Jesus!" ***"Feel the Spirit of the Lord!"*** shouts Jean, setting off another cycle of interlocking acclamations and bits of clapping. *"Thank God for the **blood!*** *(Oh, yes! Thank you, Lord! Oh, thank ya', Jesus!) It's not **easy** to do God's work!"* continues Jean. *(Amen!) It's not **easy** to walk that straight line! (Yes!* Clapping *. . .)* ***You've got to lean on Jesus!*** *(Amen!!!) Help me, Lord!"* Jean's voice tapers off, signaling a readiness to begin. The choir is already swaying to the undulating rhythms, and several people, one by one, rise to join the unfolding dance.

"Oh it is Jesus!" we chorus in a corporate wave of testimony. *Hallelujah!* adds Jean, as she begins to fill the interstices of our lyrics with embellishments that range from lyrical flourishes to shouted outbursts:

> Oh it is Jesus! (talkin' about Jesus!)
> It's Jesus in my soul! (He's in my soul!)
> For I have touched (all you've got to do is touch!)
> the hem of his garment (his garment!)
> And his love (his love) has made me whole.
> (It will make you whole, Church!)

The whole room seems to be in motion, carried in a flow of harmonious sound and action, and punctuating the waltz-like rhythms of the song with the swaying of their bodies and occasional handclaps.

> Oh it is Jesus! (talkin' about Jesus) Oh it is Jesus! (my sweet Jesus!)
> It's Jesus in my soul! (He's in my soul!)
> For I have touched (all we have to do is touch!) the hem of his garment
> (the hem of his garment)
> and his love (his love) has made me whole. (Oh, yes it will!)

Jean's arms and body are in motion, caught up in the passion carried on her voice as she presses into a verse:

> Lord, I've tried *(Yes!)* all I could! *(Amen!!)*
> Seems like nothing did me any good! *(Yes!)*
> Then the I heard Jesus *(Yes!)* He was passin' by, *(Yes!)*
> So I decided *(Yes!)* to give God a try! *(Oh, yes!!* Clapping . . .)*

Once again, the church house breaks into strains of "Oh, it is Jesus! Oh, it is Jesus! . . ." There's a sense of abandon that permeates the gathering, a heartfelt ardor that is matched by Jean's soulful responses, "Talking about Jesus! . . . My sweet Jesus!" "It's Jesus in my soul!" we chorus again, only to claim once more that we have "touched the hem of his garment! And his love has made me whole!"

"Oh, thank you, Jesus!" shouts Jean, her voice edged with fervor as she glides into a reprise of the verse,

> Lord, we've tried *(Yes!!)* all we could! *(Yes! Amen!!)*
> Seems like nothing *(Yes!)* did me any good! *(Yes!)*
> Then I heard Jesus *(Yes!!)* he was passin' by *(Yes!)*
> So I decided *(Amen!!)* to give God a try! *(Oh, yes!!!* Clapping . . .)*

Jean is almost jumping up and down as she sings this last phrase. Her head is back, left hand in the air in testimony, as if to claim this message as her own. Reed modulates to the next highest key, and a new wave of energy surges through the room. "Oh it is Jesus!" we chorus for the last time, "It's Jesus in my soul!" Drums, piano, and voices slow into a broad *ritard* as we declare once more,

> For I have touched (all we've got to do) the hem of his garment
> (the hem of his garment)
> and his love (yes, his love) has made me whole. (He makes us whole!)

A floodtide of applause and shouted praise suffuse the church house. *"Thank ya', Jesus!"* shouts Jean, almost drowning out the other acclamations with the ardor of her overflowing praise. *"Thank ya'* (Amen!) *Hallelujah!* (Amen!) *Praise the Lord! Glory to you! Thank you, Jesus! Thank you, Lord, for the blood that you shed for us!* (Amen!!) *Oh, thank you Jesus!"* Jean's voice tapers off a bit, but the volley of exclamations from other choir members continues to well up, spurred on by Reed's continued improvisation and Isaiah's intermittent drum flourishes. *Thank you, Jesus! Amen! Nothing but the blood! Praise the Lord! Thank you! Thank you! Amen! Praise the Lord! . . .* Jean entrusts the microphone into

Pat Goodall's hands, then walks to her seat. "Thank you, Jesus!" I hear her whisper as a calm begins to settle into the church house.

Barbara McKinney has arrived at the ambo to make announcements. But before she can begin, Jean breaks out again, *"Oh yes, Jesus!"* *(Amen!)* and a last surge of praise erupts. *"You can go to him **anytime!** (Thank you!) A friend some-times, **but God is all the time! And I thank you Jesus!** (Amen!!! Amen! Thank you, Jesus!) Ooo"*—Jean sighs, her voice trailing off. "Hallelujah!"

"Good morning, brothers and sisters!" Barbara exclaims, sensing that this last wave of praise has waned. "Have we had church this morning? . . ."

*T*here were numerous visitors in the church house that April Sunday. At Barbara's invitation, they stood to introduce themselves and were greeted with applause. A woman named Ann from Oakland thanked God "that I was able to come here to praise the Lord with a full voice!" *(Amen!)* The brother of a parishioner claimed, "It's a pleasure to be able to worship with so many fel-low believers!" *(Thank you, Jesus!)* "It's a pleasure to be here," added Deacon Dupre's wife. "I grew up in the Bayview and never knew this church was here! *(Have mercy!)* It's been wonderful!" A woman in a red dress added enthusi-astically, "First giving honor to God! It's good to be back here. I was baptized in this church! *(Al'right!)* Grew up in Hunters Point, and I came back today be-cause of my good friend Zettie LeBlanc. I just want to say that I feel so good today! *(Amen!)* I am full of the Lord!" *(Amen!)* Her voice faltered a bit, as if tears were welling up. *"It's al'right!"* responded a woman seated near her, others joining in, *"Take your time!" "It's al'right!" "Hallelujah!" "Thank you, Lord! Thank you, Jesus!"* Regaining her composure she continued, "My best friend just died *(Have mercy!)* and I feel so full. *(Yes! Al'right!)* And I thank God for everyone here!"

"My name is Pamela Sims," began a woman in her mid-twenties. "I'm Willa Sims's daughter and I grew up in Hunters Point. I thought, *I thought* I had come here to make a presentation this morning." Minutes later Pam would in-vite us to protest the city's attempt to impede a low-income housing initiative that would enable residents of Hunters Point to stay here and raise their fami-lies, rather than be forced to flee to the suburbs. "But obviously," she continued, "I *really* came to be reminded of what's important! *(Al'right!)* I have been in-spired by all of you! *(Thank you, Jesus! Applause.)* It's nice to be back home, and to see all the families together, worshiping and remembering why we're here!" *(Amen!)*

After a few more introductions, Reverend Lane's voice is heard from the back of the church. Being small of stature, Reverend Lane, pastor of Grace Baptist, walks down the center aisle just far enough for most in the church house to see him. "I'm not a visitor but I'm a witness! *(Al'right! Yes! Applause.)* I came this morning to bear *testimony* that God is good!" His voice flows with the cadence of a well-experienced preacher and storyteller. "I left here Easter Sunday burdened and heavy, because my mother was gravely ill. *(Yes Lord Jesus!)*

I went there with a mind that I would see her for the last time, *(Yes!)* in order to do what was necessary, as we give honor to those who pass on. Somehow, with your prayers and the prayers of others, she made some kind a *miraculous recovery! (Amen! Thank you, Jesus!!!)* I praise God *(Oh, yes!)* and thank you for your prayers! *(Oh yes, Lord! Thank you, Jesus! Amen!!!)* **God is still able!!** *(Yes He is!)* And He wants us to be one!" adds Reverend Lane in a gesture of ecumenical grace. Amidst the *Amens!* I can hear Father Kirk affirming, "That's right, John! That's right!" Without missing a beat, Reverend Lane exclaims, *"Let everything that has breath (Oh, yes!) give him praise!!"* Reed slips in under the applause and *Amens*, echoing these last psalmic sentiments with the strains of a favorite gospel song, "Jesus, blessed Savior! He's worthy to be praised!"

As the affirmation dies down, Barbara McKinney returns to the ambo. "We are so blessed to have so many wonderful, beautiful visitors with us this morning!" Then, as if to sum up the whole morning, she adds, "You know, Church, God keeps getting better and better!"

*I*ndeed, any Sunday morning in this church house one is compelled to agree: "God keeps getting better and better!" Having Church—tasting that deeply satisfying experience that we shared that late-April Sunday that moved people to say, "I've been *fed!*" "I'm *ready* for the week ahead!"—is more than a performative effect or a passing exhilaration. Rather, the intensity of a morning like this brings the community to a threshold—to a deeply felt sense of solidarity on the journey of faith, to a reassurance that God walks in the midst of God's people, and to a sureness that together, "we have touched the hem of his garment and his love has made us whole."

Chapter Eleven

"LORD, LET YOUR SPIRIT FALL ON ME!"

—SPIRIT-DIRECTED WORSHIP—

"*Pentecost is now!*" exclaimed Father Kirk, his red robes dancing as he swung around to face the choir seated behind him. "*Pentecost is now!*" he reiterated as he turned back toward the rest of the community, just clearing the stately paschal candle that stood beside him in the open space between the altar and the pews. "*Pentecost is in our hearts! (Amen!)* . . . The reason the paschal candle is front and center today on this final day of the Easter Season . . . is to remind us that *Jesus has given us the Spirit (Yes!)* so that *he* will be front and center *in our lives as well! (Amen!)* As we conclude today our remembrance of what the Father did in Jesus, and what the Father and the Son are continuing to do in Jesus, we focus again on the gift, the *special gift*, the *most **wonderful** gift*, the gift of the Holy Spirit, *(Yes! Amen!)* which isn't *out there* somewhere, *(That's right!)* *isn't floating around this building,* although we are going to see some effects of that Spirit in this church house today!" *(Amen!)* Father Kirk pauses. For a moment the room is hushed. "The Spirit is here," he adds gently, one hand resting on his chest as if to penetrate the folds of his red chasuble. "God within us!" *(Amen!)* . . .

Everything seemed so alive that May morning! A warm breeze blew gently inland from the bay as I drove along Evans Avenue, dancing on the rippling water of India Basin as it came into view just past the PG&E power plant, and rustling the pinnate leaves on the tall palm tree near the Lourdes church house as I greeted people at the door. The gathering inside seemed to stir with that same effervescence—a lightsomeness that dilates the heart and stretches one's soul. Many who came that morning were dressed in red, filling the church with the vibrant feel of Pentecost. As Father Kirk continued his preaching, the story of that first Pentecost, read earlier by Judy Brown, still rang in our ears.

"God has gifted each of us with the Spirit. And although the gifts of God are different in each of us, *(Yes!)* nevertheless there is this *binding force,* this *powerful force (Well . . .)* that draws us together, that *unifies us in love,* and makes us *overcome the differences,* that enables us to see each one of us with the eyes, the love, the power of the Lord Jesus, *(Amen!)* the power of the Holy Spirit. . . . Judy just read for us what happened two thousand years ago as recorded by Luke. The disciples were together, men and women, *(That's right!)* were together in the room—*they were there in fear!* They were *afraid!* They were afraid of being *hurt.* They were afraid of their *enemies. (Well . . .)* They were afraid of people who would attack them because they had said, *'We belong to Jesus, we believe in this Jesus!'* And *they had even **seen Jesus alive!** (Yes!) They had seen him coming back to them, eating with them,* after his death. He had *risen!* He was *there for them.* Yet they were *still afraid! (Amen!!!)* They were *still* **petrified** *(Amen!) of what might happen to their skins because of what they believed! (Amen!!!)* But—they were together. *(Yes!)* They weren't running off in other directions. They at least had the common sense to say, 'I'll find my strength in you. *(Uh hum . . .)* I'll find my courage in you. I'll find some kind of support in you. And let's *tremble* together. *(Amen!)* Let's *be afraid together.* But at least we are together.'

"It was at that moment that the great gift occurred. The gift they *never dreamt of! The gift that was unthinkable,* where *God* **penetrated** *their fear, walked through those closed doors, those barred windows, and entered their hearts, and changed those pussycats into* **tigers!** *(Amen!!! Laughter . . .) And from that posture of fear, from that trembling, they* **burst** *open the doors* and went out and *witnessed to the Lord Jesus, this living Lord that was not a memory any more but was living in them! (Amen!!!)* What a difference! What a difference. *(Amen!)*

"Now that's the model. That's how it works. Luke was no *fool* when he wrote the story. He wrote it for a *purpose. (Yes, Lord!)* He wrote it so that we could understand *how the Spirit works together in us. (Yes! Yes, Lord!) . . . You* have a gift, *you* have a gift, I have a gift, not for me alone, not for you alone—it's for *all of us! (Amen!) All of us! (Amen!) . . .* It's fear and ego—they're the ones that get in the way of the Spirit! *(Amen!) . . .* When we place ourselves in front of the work of the Spirit, *(Oh, Lord!)* the Spirit is removed farther and farther from us. *(Amen!) . . .* That Spirit of the Lord, the Spirit of the *Risen* Lord symbolized by this wonderful, beautiful candle, *(Yes, Lord!)* that Spirit is *in us*—first of all to *acknowledge, enjoy, in gratitude* and in *faith,* that we are *all different from one another.* **Thank God for that!** *(Yes! Amen!) . . . Each of us brings that special uniqueness (Yes!) created by God (Amen!) . . . and makes us* **richer because we're different!** *(Amen!! That's right! Amen!)* And it's the Spirit that makes us open our eyes *(Yes!)* to see the beauty, the *wonder,* the very *special gift* God has [placed in each one]. . . .

"Pentecost is now, Church! Pentecost is *in our hearts!* *(Yes, Lord!)* . . . to make us realize that the gift is *stronger than fear,* the gift is *stronger than ego.* *(Amen!)* Because of that, *we can do anything!* *(Yes, Lord!)* May his *Spirit be upon all of us,* *(Amen!)* today and forever!" *(Amen!!! **Amen! Amen!** Applause . . .)*

Not only on Pentecost is this Spirit of God a focus of worship at Lourdes. Week by week, community members profess faith in a Spirit who can transform them—in whose power, as Father Kirk reminds them so often, they can do anything! Listening over months and years, I realize that *this* is why people come—to be touched by the Spirit and be drawn closer to each other. Each time the community gathers, this Spirit seems to rest like a hidden power waiting to be tapped, invoked, awakened, and given freedom. Once stirred, a life-giving energy seems to well up, take hold, and flow through the church house.

Of course, there's nothing automatic about it. I remember Judy Brown remarking at the end of one Sunday liturgy, "I'm so glad the Spirit is alive in this church house again! For the past few weeks, it seemed that God was *dead! But I **know** the Spirit is here this morning!*" When the Spirit comes, change can happen—a new perspective, a new freedom, a new witness. Preaching can rouse this sleeping Spirit, stirring embers into flame. Embracing can release its potency. Praying can reach down into its subterranean waters or be borne aloft on its breath. Above all, music seems to stir the hearts of this community, awakening a felt-sense of the Spirit's presence and power, unleashing a wellspring of memory and praise. As one member of the community reminded me, "The Spirit does not descend without song!"

Brother Banks was one of the first to put images on this experience for me. We were well into a conversation one warm April Sunday when I inquired, "But Brother Banks, how is music related to the Holy Spirit and, for that matter, to the Spirit's role in the whole liturgy?" He looked at me wisely, his eyes dancing behind his dark rimmed glasses. "The Holy Spirit is always there," he answered. "It's like somethin' that's there, but like a little child, it's asleep. When the song comes, it wakes that Spirit up! . . . Christ is always there, but it brings him alive in you! Certain songs can do that. It wakes him up!" Brother Banks paused briefly, as if searching for an image that would help me understand. "It's like you take gasoline—you're sittin' here and you take gasoline. You throw it on a fire and see how it blooms. The same way, the fire was already burning, but that gasoline gives it a new boost. The songs give you that boost. The Spirit comes alive in you!"[1]

I remember Liz Bell's saying once, "I need these songs!" because "through that music the Holy Spirit is talking to me, making me believe in myself. All these things I'm carrying around, all these burdens, when I hear the words and this music, I can let go of all that."[2] Tina Edwards put it another way: songs we sing at Lourdes "touch your emotions" and make you realize "I'm not alone. . . . People really break down," she added, "the wall crumbles . . . and they give themselves to the Lord. . . . 'Here I am, Lord; before I was holding back.' You release and you completely surrender yourself to God. . . . You realize you have to turn it over to Jesus! *I don't know if that's the Holy Spirit,* I'm assuming it is."[3] Pat Goodall described the Spirit's action as a cleansing. "Sometimes it happens to us [in rehearsal] when the mood is not good," she commented once, "People are a little edgy, touchy. . . . There are times when we rehearse a certain song that just seems to wash that all out and everyone is great afterwards. . . . It's like a washing, a cleansing. . . . It's like God is saying, 'I've heard enough of this! It's time to move on!' And he moves us on. . . . He lets the next song that we're rehearsing, no matter what it is . . . be the song that cleanses and washes all that out."[4]

I arrived late that Thursday evening, caught in the snarl of traffic on the Bay Bridge. As I slipped into the church house, rehearsal was well underway. I was still new to Lourdes, so I took my usual place several pews from the front. The choir was working intensely on a new song. Suddenly, Pat Goodall stopped everything and exclaimed, *"It's dry! It's dead!* Let's go back to the top and start again!" I mused the next day on how striking Pat's images were for what was missing in the music—the opposite of dry is moist, fertile, refreshing. What began to change that evening, as I watched the choir rehearse, was not the tempo, the pitch or rhythm of the song, nor even the arrangement of voices—these were already well in place—but the energy they seemed to invest in the singing. Their bodies became more engaged, their voices more confident, their concentration more focused, their singing more vibrant and soulful. It was as if the song began to sing itself, as if they were tapping some inner spiritual power that infused the music with a new vitality. Sitting there in the empty church, I could feel it. "That's great! That's fine!" remarked Pat as the song came to an end, clearly satisfied. "Let's go home."

I began to listen more carefully to the images Pat and others used to describe how music sounds and feels when it's "good." A cluster emerged over time—"good" music has energy; it flows, it builds, it's alive, it's pulsing, it touches, it gives comfort, it brings joy. Certain songs "bring out the fire in me," remarked Corey Monroe in one conversation. "They touch me," "they give me energy." "You get warm inside!" "[You] can feel it!"[5] These images, I came to see, were remarkably similar to those used by members of Lourdes to describe their experience of the Holy Spirit. Music becomes Spirit-like when it stirs, when it moves with an inner potency, when it surges with life that can draw you down or raise you up—music that is not dry but moist, fertile, refreshing. Perhaps it was no accident that a few weeks later I stumbled on these words of

Hildegard von Bingen, the mystic musician, written centuries earlier: "Music has the power to soften even hard hearts, and by rendering hearts moist, it ushers in the Holy Spirit."

Singers often talk about the Holy Spirit "using them" to touch others, to "reach someone who needs to come to him." "I pray that God will use me to help others in their struggles," I recall Jean Alexander saying one evening. "You never know how the Spirit will move. But when the Spirit moves, the song touches people." "The Spirit works *through* us," added Louise Wood. "God uses us . . . [as] part of his ministry." She described how certain songs stir the hearts of choir members and you see them respond. "When you are used in that way, [others are] going to be touched. I don't think you could do that without the Spirit. God has to use . . . you . . . to reach . . . someone else."[6]

It's striking that the lyrics of many of the songs sung at Lourdes explicitly invoke the touch of God's Spirit. "Lord, let your Spirit fall on me!" we chorused that Pentecost morning. "Keep your hands on me, Lord" the same song concluded. "Use me, mold me, make me, Lord, what you want me to be—right now!" came another spirited piece. "Touch me! Touch me! Touch me, Lord, touch me!" we pleaded soulfully later that morning. "I'll never be very much until the hand of Jesus comes and touches me!" added lead singer Rose Isles, answered by Jean Alexander, "I don't know about you but I've been praying that the Lord would touch me!" The sustained passion in each of their voices brought many people in the church house to tears that morning.

"The music is related to what's happening [in people's lives]," commented Pat Goodall in a conversation over lunch one Saturday. "[We sing], 'Lord let your Spirit fall on me!' Lord, I've got these problems . . . but if you would just let your Spirit fall on us, things will be alright!" It's not only the music that invites this change, she added. "Father Kirk preaches it: open up, accept the Spirit, it's alright. That's what God wants. If you trust and believe, it will happen!" Indeed everything in worship at Lourdes seems to work to the same end and with the same inner direction. "Father Kirk's energy," she asked, "is it not the same energy the choir puts into their songs? Is it not the same energy that Brother Banks preaches? It's all the same energy. It's *got* to be the Spirit, it's *got* to be. What else can it be?"

"Does that energy have something to do with the way the Spirit feels," I inquired, "with the way God feels?"

"Yes," Pat replied emphatically, "but also with the way we open up and accept. If we were not an *accepting people,* the Spirit wouldn't have a chance. But being such an accepting people, the Spirit is able to do exactly what it needs to do for each of us, as a collective group and as individuals."[7]

*B*essie Brooks's singing is always intense. Even as she stepped out from the choir to lead us in song, her body seemed focused, her energies concentrated on the message she was about to deliver. Making her way across the front of the church to take the microphone in hand, she seemed unmindful of the lingering conversations, the bits of laughter, the movements of people slowly returning to their places, still caught in the energy of the Exchange of Peace. Reed Fromer's fingers begin to glide over the keyboard— first a blusey flourish, then free improvisation.

The church house seemed especially full that chilly November Sunday in 1995. A new "Book of Lourdes's Saints" lay open near the front of the church, awaiting a fresh influx of memories of those who have gone home to God but whose spirits linger with us. Vibrant green print fabric draped the rear wall of the sanctuary. Barbara McKinney's voice was strong as she proclaimed the first reading from the book of Wisdom: "Your immortal Spirit, O God, is in all things. You love all that exists. . ." Zacchaeus was the focus of the Gospel—Zacchaeus, the little man who climbed the sycamore tree to see Jesus; Zacchaeus, the tax-collector, the outcast, whom Jesus loved and called.

"Many of us here today go through . . . what Zacchaeus went through," preached Father Kirk that morning. "We live in a society that is unjust, unfair, where there's a growing tension over racial differences . . . where the chasm between the rich and poor is widening. . . . Yet, we have *the Spirit of God in us, Church!* (*Amen!*) The Spirit resides in us, *not like a stone at the bottom of a well, doing nothing.* The Spirit is *in us, urging* us: *Come alive! Come alive!* **Come alive people!** (*Al'right!*) *I'm giving you my breath!* That's what Spirit means. We have the *breath of God in us, Church,* (*Amen!*) *the Spirit of God* . . . so that we can **transform** this society of ours . . . so that we can *bring to our world the* **fairness** *and* **justice** *of Jesus Christ!"* (*Amen! Amen!*)

No doubt these words are moving in Bessie's heart as she readies herself to invoke the Spirit of God once again, to invite the Spirit to "fall on me," to fall on us—to settle once again not only on us but on all those "who need you, Lord," as Bessie will sing and for whom she will intercede. As the music gets underway, Pat Goodall invites three youngsters to carry forward the "Gifts" of bread and wine so the altar table can be prepared. Then, addressing community and visitors, she adds, "It's our offertory time. You know we are a loving church, but we have to pay the bills also. So *please* be as generous as possible so we can *keep on loving under this roof!*" Reed's fingers move freely over the keyboard, sensing the appropriate time to bring the song into focus, listening for the moment when Bessie and the community are ready to engage.

"One thing that I've always appreciated in music," Reed explained to me over lunch one day, "is chaos coming into order . . . going from something nebulous to something that's recognizable. . . . I didn't do this before . . . but I've taken to playing intros that are not as recognizable as they used to be. . . . Instead of just starting [at the beginning of a song], I tend to start at the "bridge" or somewhere else. Once I'm sure that the children have brought the Gifts forward and everyone is ready to go, then all right! The song arrives!"

Arrive it does! Reed shifts to the steady rhythms of "Lord, Let Your Spirit Fall on Me"[8] and Isaiah's bass and snare drum begin to pulse with the relentless beat of the song's duple meter. Pat motions those of us in the choir to fall into place behind Bessie. Then with the gentle rocking of her own body, Pat draws us into the undulating movement, our blue robes swaying from side to side. I can feel an energy begin to flow among us. Spontaneously, people pick up the contagious rhythms and punctuate the swirling sound with their measured handclaps. "Well . . ." comes Brother Banks's voice from behind us. "O.K. choir!" comes an expectant voice from the front row as energies around the room begin to coalesce. Then in a flash, a burst of lyrics spill through the gathering.

"Lord let your Spirit fall on me!" we sing. "Oh, let it fall on me, Lord!" Bessie implores, weaving her freely voiced pleas around the steady flow of our chorused phrases.

> Lord, let your Spirit fall on me (Oh, let it fall on me!)
> As I go (as I go) my way (on my way) from day to day,
> Lord let your Spirit fall on me!

As Pat Goodall signals us back into the chorus, and once again we entreat the Spirit to "fall on me," Bessie's left hand is raised in a gesture of invocation, her head back as if to look out over the heads of the congregation toward something beyond. I remember her saying to me once that when she sings this song, she can see the Spirit coming down like a dove. "I can see it!" she reiterated. Now, as the choir yields its chorusing to her lead, you can feel her concentration. There's tension in her voice, a deeply-felt fervor that seems to well up from within her and fuel the free flow of her lyrics.

> Lord, how can I forget // all the things you've done for me! *(Oh, yes!)*
> One day you shook my dungeon // and set me free! *(Yes!!!)*
> You're a heart-fixer, *(Yes!)* and I've got a made-up-mind; *(Well . . .)*
> I'm ready to shout about it, *(Yes!)* 'cause you're with me all the ti—me.
> Lord, just walk in front of me and hold my hand,
> Lord, let your Spirit fall on me!

Pat Goodall's movements are dance-like as she leads us back into another burst of "Lord, let your Spirit fall on me!"—her arms in full motion as if riding on the surge of musical energy. Father Kirk is on his feet behind us, his green vestments set in motion by his rhythmic swaying. The church house seems filled with a sense of luminous freedom as Bessie once again takes the lead:

> So much confusion over the land, yes there is! *(Oh, yes!)*
> So many things *(Yes!)* // I just don't understand! *(Oh, Yes!)*
> But you told us in your word *(Yes!)* that if we hold on to your hand *(Oh, yes!)*
> that you would lead us day by day *(Yes!)* and brighten up our way-ay-ay-ay,
> Lord, just walk in front of me, and I won't stray, *(Yes!)*
> Lord, let your Spirit fall on me.

The insistent rhythms have brought people in almost every part of the church house to their feet. Reed's fingers trace a swift glissando down the keyboard and he and Isaiah propel us into a new refrain.

"Lord, keep your hands on me," we sing, changing the lyrics of our chorus-ing as if to invite the intimacy and guidance of the Spirit's touch:

> Lord, keep your hands on me! (Oh, keep your hands on me, Lord!)
> As I go my way (on my way) from day to day, Lord keep your hands on me!

Immediately, the dynamic level of the piece softens, the intensity of our singing relaxes, and we center down to voice over and again a single supplication:

> //: Keep your hands on me! Keep your hands on me!
> Keep your ha——nds on me! ://

Reed and Isaiah join the vamped "stall" as we circle around this mantric cen-ter. Even our clapping becomes muted as Bessie embarks on a wave of chanted invocations which she ad-libs above the swirling sound.

"Not only me," she implores freely. "Somebody else needs you Lord." Her melodies unfold freely in syncopated counterpoint to the steady pulse of the choir's repeated chanting, "Keep your hands on me!"

> There's a mother // that needs you Lord!
> And a father // that needs you Lord!
> There's a brother // that needs you Lord!
> And a sister // who needs you Lord!
> And there's children // that need you Lord!

Bessie's eyes are closed now as if to tap some inner stream of prayer. Her left hand moves freely in a gesture of pleading, then reaches out as if to gather in the widening circle of people for whom she intercedes:

Children in America *(Yes!)* // need you Lord!
Children in Africa *(Oh, yes!)* // need you Lord!
Children in El Salvador // need you Lord!
Children in the Philippines // need you Lord!
Children in Mexico // need you Lord!
Children all over the wor—ld // they need you Lord!

Pat's eyes are fixed on Bessie as she signals the choir to swell its chanting into a broad crescendo:

//: Keep your hands on me! Keep your hands on me!
Keep your ha——nds on me! ://

But realizing that Bessie is still deeply engaged in her unfolding intercessions, Pat softens the sound again, watching for signs from Bessie that it's time to bring the song to a close.

The people // they need you Lord! [Bessie is leaning into each supplication.]
The homeless // they need you, Lord!
The people in prison // they need you, Lord!
And the clergy // they need you, Lord!
And the nations // they need you, Lord!
Jesus, we're waiting on you.
Jesus, we need you!
Jesus, the children need you.
Jesus, the people need you.
Jesus, keep your hands on us!
Jesus, keep your hands on us!
We need you, Lord!

Sensing that Bessie is ready to move on, Pat gestures a dramatic crescendo and the relentless vamp gives way to an exuberant final refrain. "Lord, let your Spirit fall on me!" we sing with abandon.

Lord, let your Spirit fall on me! (Oh, let it fall on me!)
As I go (as I go) my way (my way), from day to day,
Lord, let your Spirit, (Let it! Let it! Let it!)
Lord, let your Spirit, (Let it! Let it! Let it!)
Lord, let your Spirit fall on me!

The song bounds to a close with only the slightest *ritard* and the syncopated cadence of Isaiah's drum and cymbal strokes. Applause swells from around the church house. *Amen!! Oh, let your Spirit fall! Yes, Lord!* Reed pauses momentarily on the final chord, then continues to play freely. Isaiah sounds a few drum and cymbal flourishes as Bessie, a bit flushed, returns the mike to Pat Goodall, pausing for a brief embrace before returning to her seat. *Amen! Yes, Lord! Amen!*

The overflowing *Amens* taper off gradually and the church house begins to settle once again. The release, the exuberance of our singing seems to have prepared the way for a growing stillness. I remember Pat Goodall commenting that it's so important that the song chosen for this time in the liturgy be upbeat "because we're getting people ready to celebrate the life and death of Christ."

Father Kirk waits momentarily at his chair, then moves to the altar-table. Brother Banks takes his place just to his left, and choir members begin to walk from either side of the sanctuary to take their places on the three steps directly behind them. As we move toward the center, I can feel a convergence—not only a movement of people but a gathering of forces, a focusing, a centering down into this moment of prayer. A calm has spread out over the church house, a readiness.

A brief prayer and people are on their feet. "The Lord be with you!" exclaims Father Kirk, arms extended wide to the community. Spontaneously, people mirror his gesture as they respond, "And also with you!" "Lift up our hearts!" "Let us give thanks to the Lord our God!" The room is hushed as Father Kirk begins the great prayer,[9]

> Father, all-powerful and ever-living God, we do well always and everywhere to give you thanks through Jesus Christ our Lord. *(Oh yes, Lord!)*

Father Kirk's voice is strong and deliberate. The voiced acclamations of those standing around me begin to well up—a gentle mummer that grows stronger as the prayer unfolds.

> Through his cross and resurrection he *freed us* from sin and death *(Yes!)*
> and called us to the *glory* that has made us a *chosen* race, *(Yes! Amen!)*
> a *royal* priesthood, *(Al'right!)* a *holy nation, (Oh, yes!)* a people set apart. *(Amen!)*

There's a rhythm in the exchange. I remember Father Kirk saying, "I never rush [this prayer]. . . . I try to make it my prayer . . . to consciously place myself before the Father . . . to speak for this community and to bring them with me. So it becomes my prayer . . . it becomes our prayer."

> *Everywhere* we proclaim your mighty works, *(Amen!)* for you have called us *out of darkness (Well . . .)* into your own *wonderful light! (Amen!)*

Invited to join with all the choir of angels in heaven in a song of joy, the community breaks into jubilant song, people swaying to the steady 6/8 rhythms as they sing, 'Holy, holy! Holy, holy! Holy Lord God of hosts! Heaven and earth are full of your glory, Hosanna in the highest! . . ." The hymning continues, filling the church house with *Hosannas* before giving way once again to stillness.

> Father, from the beginning of time you have *always* done what is good for us, *(Yes, Lord!)* so that we may be holy as you are holy. *(Amen!)* Look with *kindness* on your people gathered here before you: *(If you please, Lord!)*

Indeed, it is a beautiful sight to look out over this gathered community—little ones in the front pew caught up in the moment; adults, some with children in arms, standing row upon row in the hushed church house. Father Kirk's extended hands rest above the bread and wine as he continues,

> send forth the power of your Spirit *(Yes, Lord!)* so that these gifts may become for us the body and blood of your beloved Son, Jesus the Christ, *(Yes! Amen!)* in whom we have become your sons and daughters.

The image is striking—that by the Spirit's power these humble gifts will become "holy things for holy people." Standing in this flow of prayer week after week, images of the Spirit's action, which might have slipped past my ears, take on a new resonance. Transform not only the bread and wine, I hear Father Kirk implore the Spirit over and again, but this gathering of people into "a living sacrifice of praise." Sunday after Sunday, the Spirit is asked to change, to fill, to gather, to empower, to make us one body and one spirit. The "Spirit changes our hearts," I remember him praying last week; enemies now "speak to one another, those . . . estranged join hands in friendship," nations seek ways of peace. Bessie's song seems to echo still, "Lord, let your Spirit fall on me!" . . .

"When we were lost and could not find the way to you" Father Kirk recalls now, God loved us "more than ever."

> Jesus, . . . innocent and without sin,
> gave himself into our hands and was nailed to a cross.
> Yet before he stretched out his arms between heaven and earth,
> in the everlasting sign of your covenant, *(Yes!)*
> he desired to celebrate the Paschal feast in the company of his disciples.

Taking the bread before him in hand, Father Kirk recalls that on that holy night, Jesus gave thanks and praise, breaking and giving the bread to his disciples: "Take this, all of you. . . . this is my body. . . ." The words seem held in the hush of the room, as people join in a gentle bow. Then lifting the cup which only minutes before the children carried to this altar table, Father Kirk remembers how Jesus, "knowing that he was to reconcile all things in himself by the blood of his cross," *(Yes, Lord!)* gave thanks, and "handed the cup to his friends,"

Take this, all of you, and drink from it: this is the cup of my blood, the blood of the new and everlasting covenant. *(Yes, Lord!)* It will be shed for you and for all so that sins may be forgiven. *(Yes!)* Do this in memory of me.

The community bows again. Father Kirk invites us to proclaim this great "mystery of faith" and the plaintive lyrics of a beloved spiritual begin to wash through the church house.

> I want Jesus // to walk with me!

Jean Alexander's voice can be heard embellishing each entreaty. "Just to walk with us," she sings.

> I want Jesus (We need you!) to walk with me (Just walk with me!)
> All along (Yes, along) my pilgrim journey (our journey)
> Lord, I want my Jesus (Lord, we want Jesus)
> to walk with me! (Oh, yes, Lord!)

The singing spills over into a gentle humming, as if to entreat Jesus over and again to walk this journey with us. Above the sustained humming, Father Kirk proclaims that we do all this "in memory of Jesus Christ, our Passover and our lasting peace," celebrating "his death and resurrection" and awaiting that great day when "he will return to give us the fullness of joy!" *(Yes, Lord!)* The images seem to ride on the undulating rhythms of the community's voiced but wordless sound. "Look with love on those you have called to share the one sacrifice of Christ," Father Kirk continues, so that "by the power of your Holy Spirit" *(Yes!)* we may become "one body, healed of all division." *(Amen!)*

> Keep us all in communion of mind and heart with John Paul, our pope,
> John, our archbishop, and William, our future archbishop.
> Help us to work together *(Oh yes, Lord!)* for the coming of your kingdom,
> until at last we stand in your presence to share the life of the saints,
> in the company of the Virgin Mary,
>   the mother of God, who is the loving patron of our parish, *(Amen!)*
> with all the apostles and martyrs,
>   with all the holy ones of Africa, *(Yes!)*

You can almost feel that great company of holy ones drawn into this circle of prayer as he continues,

> with Monica and Augustine, Perpetua and Felicity, Victor and Moses,
> with Blessed Josephine of the Sudan, with Martin de Porres, with
>   Joseph and Francis—

and with our departed brothers and sisters whom we commend to your mercy. *(Yes, Lord!)*

> We ask you to look with a special love on those whose names
> have been included in our Book of Saints, *(Yes!)*
> and those whose names we have placed on your altar.
Then, freed from every shadow of death, we shall take our place in the
new creation and give you thanks with Christ our risen Lord.

Humming gives way, as Reed modulates into the energetic rhythms of a closing doxology: "Through him, with him, in him" we sing, the pace lively, the energy flowing—"all glory and honor are yours, almighty Father . . ." The song is hardly on our lips when, one by one, six of the youngest members of the community slip out of their seats in various parts of the church and cluster in front of the altar table . . . "for ever and ever!" we conclude. A bit of prompting from Pat and these little ones are ready to spur us on as we break into the familiar cadences from the "Lilies of the Field." "Amen!" we chorus. "Sing it over!" they answer, their little voices less than timid as smiles break out on the faces of everyone around them. "Amen!" we sing again, catching the flow of energy from this little band of choristers. "Praise the Father!" they retort. "Amen," comes the next wave, only to be met by their guileless "Hallelujah!" "Amen!" we sing, "Amen! Amen!" Yes, indeed: *Amen!*

The moment is suffused with joy, as the children slip away once again into their pews and into the waiting arms of smiling parents and grandparents. *Amen!*

Brother Banks invites us to "reach out across the aisle," to "join our hearts and our hands" as "we pray that great prayer that Jesus taught us." There seems no hesitation. People spill into the center aisle, grasping each other's hands, reaching across the pews to join as one body. The Spirit, it would seem, has given us a taste of the unity for which we have just prayed. . . .

Chapter Twelve

"OH, LORD, HOW EXCELLENT!"

—MOVEMENT TOWARD COMMUNION—

"*B*y then, enough has happened. . . ." "We've been through something together. . . .""I feel so connected to everyone in the church. . . ." "Something has happened—we're ready to receive a new message . . ." "By Communion time, people have gone through an internal process. . . ." "Something emerges from and through us. . . ."

Fragments of conversation, bits of insight offered by members of Lourdes at various times, converge on a single perception: at Lourdes, everything moves toward Communion. The whole way the community engages in liturgy seems calibrated to bring us to this moment, to this time of Communion, to this point of arrival—and then to hold us in this place of intimacy and solidarity, to engage us in this rich human-divine exchange.

But there's nothing automatic about it. Communion is the fruit of a process. It requires a readiness. It takes time. You can't rush it. It needs to be prepared. You don't arrive at the doors of the church ready for its fullness. But by now, late in the Sunday worship, "we've been through something. . . ." By now, the cumulative affect of our praying and singing makes us "ready to receive a new message. . . ."

"Look what happens here at Lourdes on Sunday mornings," I remember Father Kirk remarking in a Pentecost homily. "We come from our different places, different residences, different localities, different locations, and we greet one another. *(Yes!)* We're always *very happy* to see one another before the service starts. *(Amen!)* And as we move on through this *wonderful act of communion together in the Lord, something emerges from and through us. (Yes!)* And you notice that it generally happens by *Communion time*. That's when the *Spirit really kicks in.* *(Amen!!)* It is because we're so *united.* *(Yes, Lord!)* We have assembled in *Jesus' name!* *(Yes!)* We are here because of *Him!* We are here to thank the Father in *his* name, and the Spirit comes. . . ." *(Yes, Lord! Amen!)*

❦ ❦ ❦

*P*eople are converging on the center aisle, making their way toward those who are ministering the Eucharistic Bread and Wine at either end of this central passageway. The words we've heard just a moment ago ring in the air. "Happy are those who are called to this supper." There's a press of bodies, a somewhat free-form, organic movement forward—"processional" if you will. It's clear that we're all in this together. There's a feel of "Church." Persons inexorably bound up in a common life and a common destiny.

Sun streams through the windows on the left side of the church—a welcome touch during the coldest, darkest November I have known in the Bay Area. Many came this morning with heavy hearts. Dear Lenora Rutherford is in intensive care, her family waiting with her through this time of suffering. Joan Dill and other parishoners are ill as well. But as Brother Banks welcomed us to this feast of Christ the King, he thanked God for "another day in the land of the living!" That ray of hope and gratitude seemed to spread through the church house as songs, prayers, and readings reframed these hardships in God's faithfulness and power. Jesus is "the Alpha and Omega, the beginning and the end," read Tina Edwards a bit later from the book of Revelation, conviction in her voice. He is the "faithful witness" who has made us "a kingdom of priests" to the "glory of God!" This same Jesus will come again "on the clouds of heaven!" As we hymned our response to these images of promise, something seemed to take hold. You could hear it in people's voices as we chorused,

To God be the glory, to God be the glory!
to *God* be the glory for the things he has done!
With his blood he has saved me, with his power he has raised me,
to God be the glory for the things he has done!!

Suffering seemed drawn more and more into a place of praise and confidence.

I make my way from the sanctuary with other choir members to join the front of the line that's forming in the center aisle. A few youngsters hold back the flood-tide of persons spilling out of the pews to make room for us. The gentle strains of "Blessed Assurance" encompass us as we move forward. "The Body of Christ, Pat," I hear Father Kirk say as he presses a small wafer of bread into her hand. I notice that Jawana Stith is next to me in line. Her serious face

1.

1, 2. Mission style tower of Our Lady of Lourdes can be seen behind Brother Jesse Banks, who pauses on the church steps before people begin to arrive for Sunday Liturgy.

3. Original sign welcoming visitors and parishioners to Lourdes.

2.

3.

2.   3.   4.

1. Father Kirk Ullery greets the Lourdes community at the opening of Sunday Liturgy, while Brother Banks gestures his assent.

5.   6.   7.

2–7. Images of African and African American holy persons—St. Augustine, Pope St. Victor, the Black Madonna and Child, Sts. Felicity and Perpetua, Mahalia Jackson, and Dr. Martin Luther King, Jr.—surround the community gathered for prayer.

8, 9. Brother Banks, arms aloft, joins in the music-making.

10. Brother Banks leads the community in the Prayer of the Faithful.

8.

"He's the soul of the community."

10.

9.

1.

1. Choir members arch across the sanctuary to assume their leadership.

2–4. Lead singers Judy Brown, Pat Goodall, and Walter Turner animate the community.

2.

3.

4.

"It's about a message!"

5.

5. Lead singer Ernestine Harris.

6, 7. Gospel Choir sopranos Ernestine Harris, Carol Lugo, Rhoda Charles, and Jean Alexander, "in motion," along with altos Bessie Brooks (with *chekeré*), Darlene Molina, Charlene Edwards, and Louise Wood.

6.

7.

1.

2.

1. Father Kirk proclaims the Gospel from the "open space."

2, 3. Members of the community listen attentively to the preaching.

3.

4. Father Kirk proclaims the Gospel.

5–7. Father Kirk's dynamic preaching engages the community.

8. Jean Alexander preaches about motherhood on Mother's Day.

4.

5.

6.

7.

8.

"Preach it!"

"Having church."

1.

1–4. Members of the community exchange a sign of the Lord's peace.

5–11. One by one, people stand to join in the music-making.

2.

3.

4.

5.

6.

7.

8.

9.

10.

11.

1.

"Lord, Let Your
Spirit Fall on Me."

1–3. Lead singer Bessie
Brooks.

2.

3.

4.

4–8. Pat Goodall directs the Gospel Choir.

5.

6.   7.   8.

1–3. Drummer Isaiah Brown:
ages 5, 7, and 18.

2.

3.

4. Pianist Reed Fromer.

"Lord, Help Me to Hold Out!"

5.

6.

7.

8.

5–9. Lead singer Rose Isles.

9.

1.

"Growing up in the church."

2.

3.

1. Tyree McDuff with his grandmother, Jean Alexander.

2. Children carry gifts of bread and wine to the altar table.

3. Ebony Baxter leads the final "Amen" of the Eucharistic Prayer.

4. Lourdes' Miracles.

4.

5.

5, 6. Tina Edwards and Betty Cooper receive from the Cup while Father Kirk distributes the Eucharistic Bread.

7. "Happy are those who are called to His supper . . ."

6.

7.

The author joins other women of the Lourdes community on the church steps after Sunday Liturgy. From top to bottom: Sister Irma Dillard, Shirley Valmore, the author, Judy Brown, Pat Goodall, Rose Isles, and Jean Alexander.

breaks into a smile as our glances meet. We embrace, her tiny body enfolded in my arms. I missed hugging her during the "peace." "The Body of Christ, Mary," says Father Kirk to me with a warm smile. No strangers here. The pastor knows each of us and calls us by name. I notice Jeannette Howard standing just to the side of Father Kirk as Minister of the Cup. I'm struck by her beauty—tall, reserved, quiet, strong—a young version of the woman who portrayed Maya Angelou's mother in "I Know Why the Caged Bird Sings." She smiles as I approach her, kisses me, then offers me the Cup.

I am moved by the delicacy and tenderness of this not uncommon gesture. To kiss before offering the Cup. There's a freedom, here, to *be* the Body while receiving it. On another occasion, Tina Edwards, noticing that I had been weeping, reached out to embrace me before saying, "The Blood of Christ." Judy Brown offered me the cup one Sunday with the words, "The Blood of Christ, my sister." I was touched to be addressed as "sister," as family member; to feel her reach across the chasm of racial division harbored for centuries within this nation and too often within our churches, to address me as kin. Only the Blood that she offered me that morning could have "broken down the enmity between us," could have enabled this sisterhood. "Enough has happened. . . ."

People continue to press forward, engaging with each other as they move—a hand held out, a word, an embrace. Reverence, I've come to realize, is a cultural sensitivity. At Lourdes, reverencing the "Body of Christ" seems inseparable from reverencing the body we are. Saying "Amen!" to the living body. Like Jesus, it's very incarnational, very fleshy, very holy. "Communion" seems richer, deeper, because it is communally mediated. As one woman remarked, "I can read my Bible at home, it's true. I can listen to gospel music. But I *need* to be here!" "Holy gifts for holy people!"[1] they say in the Eastern churches.

"Blessed assurance, Jesus is mine! . . ." Reed's gentle improvisation gives way to singing, as Rose Isles takes up the familiar lyrics of this beloved hymn,[2] allowing the images to spill over us. "Oh what a foretaste of glory divine!" I return to the sanctuary, pausing for a moment to kneel beside other choir members beneath the African-carved image of the crucified Jesus that hangs high on the rear wall of the sanctuary. The stately black figure above us, dressed in a white robe, instills peace, confidence, deep trust. "Heir of salvation," I hear Rose singing, "purchase of God, born of his Spirit, washed in his Blood . . ."

Returning to my seat among the choir, the scene continues to unfold before my eyes. Children are being led forward by adults, smaller ones carried in arms, and Father Kirk rests a hand on each of the little ones. As Cameron Isles approaches, Father Kirk stoops down, as if to meet him eye-to-eye, offering a word of recognition. Ebony Perryman seems poised and radiant in her black velvet dress, followed close behind by her grandmother, Shirley Browning. A swell of musical energy now and people around the church house join the song's refrain: "This is my story, this is my song!" we sing with abandon, as if voicing a common testimony. "Praising my savior all the day long . . ." People are returning to their places. Some kneel and pray. Others sit and gently rock with the music. I notice Richard Olive leaving his seat to cross the center aisle and sit beside a woman who is in tears. He rests a hand on her shoulder to offer comfort. Tyree has fallen asleep in Shirley Valmore's arms, content in her embrace. Gradually the aisle clears. Communion ministers place the remaining Bread in the tabernacle and return to their places. We rest here, "filled with his goodness," as Rose is singing, "lost in his love." A swell of sound from piano and drums and choir members stand to join in a last ardent chorus,

> This is my story, this is my song
> Praising my Savior all the day long!
> This is my story, this is my song,
> Praising my Savior all the day long . . .

My sense of reverence has indeed been stretched. Sharing this moment over weeks and months, I've realized that the disciplined or "proper" ways of doing things that have shaped my liturgical imagination are only one pathway to reverence. Orderliness and decorum, of themselves, are not synonymous with Godliness. Reverence is about presence. About mutual presence. Communion is about being fed, about giving and receiving, about being both host and guest. To eat is to know. To drink is to know. To kiss is to know. . . . No one seems ready to leave. . . .

Communion time unfolds at Lourdes like a symphony in three movements, a drama in three acts—a protracted and musically orchestrated time of intimacy and solidarity. Eating and drinking the "Bread of Life and Cup of Salvation" are but its first episode. No one seems anxious to hurry on. I recall Sister Irma Dillard remarking that if you've been to a dinner party and you've enjoyed it, you don't rush away, you linger. "We've been through something. . . ." "We're ready for a new message. . . ." "I feel so connected with everyone in the church. . . ." To rest now in this communion is to appropriate it more fully, to "taste and see" that the Lord is good. To rest here, praying and singing—first a weekly "Communion Meditation," then, on most Sundays, a song specially requested by a member of the community. To linger here, embracing and praising, is to be held in a human-divine exchange that heals and reorders, that fills and overflows.

The choir spreads out across the sanctuary to lead the community in a "Communion Meditation"—this morning, a song with such power that it's never sung before this moment in the liturgy. Enough needs to have happened.

From the moment Reed's fingers begin to trace the slow, stately harmonies of "Perfect Praise," there seems an electricity in the air.

>Oh, Lord, how excellent! How excellent!

we begin in hushed tones, layering praises over Reed's gentle accompaniment, only to spiral through ascending intervals and a building crescendo into a surge of jubilant praise,

>Jesus excellent is thy name!

Amens, even shouts, are evoked from other members of the community as we spiral down once again into hushed, sustained praises: "Oh, Lord, how excellent!" Memories flood my mind, memories of being welcomed into the choir just two months ago as this canticle was unleashed for the first time.

>There is none like you! None like you! None like you!
>Jesus, excellent is your name!

Surges of devotion are released with each reiteration of "Oh Lord, how excellent is your name!!!"—people around the church house voicing their own words of praise and engagement: *Amen! Excellent! He's worthy!* Then tenors, altos, sopranos, each in turn, take up St. Paul's exhortation to the Philippians:

>Every knee shall bow, and every tongue proclaim that he is Lord!
>In all the earth! In all the earth! In all the earth! In all the earth!

issuing in a burst of praise: "Jesus, excellent!!!" and an final resurgence of the stately refrain:

>Oh Lord, how excellent! How excellent! How excellent is your name!

The community seems galvanized by the intensity of the sound, emotions tuned to praise. Common praise. Shared ecstacy. The moment spills over. . . . "Something emerges in and through us. . . ." A strength to go on. A reorientation. An inner release.

Still, no one seems ready to leave. "Something has happened. . . ."

*C*ommunion meditation songs at Lourdes are usually slow and reflective—and often old. Each evokes and deepens communion in its own way: communion born of a shared history, a common spirituality, of personal and collective memories. "Near the Cross" for example, sung on Easter Sunday, 1994. This "old, old gospel song," beloved of many at Lourdes, awakens memories of family, of struggle, of finding a way through hardship by drinking of that "precious fountain" that is "free to all, a healing stream," and that "flows from Calvary's mountain." I recall Joan Dill remarking, "That's such an old spiritual! I remember that my mother would sing it all the time. . . . It brings back memories of my childhood. . . . It brings back emotional feelings about my life."[3] Singing "Near the Cross," this community is plunged into a living stream of faith that has coursed through generations of fathers and mothers, a collective memory that wells up fresh with each retelling. "Jesus keep me near the cross, there's a precious fountain!"

*E*aster dawned as bright as the voices of the children who swarmed the church house that April morning and as radiant as Jeannette Howard's smile as she declared, "I feel like a new person!" Last evening, in the midst of a smaller, more intimate gathering of the Lourdes community keeping vigil, Jeannette was confirmed, and Joan Dill and her daughter Alexis Alexander were welcomed into full communion with the Roman Catholic Church. Dressed this morning in soft yellow and still aglow with the memory of that event, Jeannette wears over her right shoulder the "garment" she'd been given last evening—a white stole lined with Kente cloth.

Indeed, we've been through something these past few days. I recall Bishop Carlos Sevilla[4] washing the feet of little Coy Lacy on Holy Thursday evening as he sat amid a row of young and old parishioners in the front pew. "This is to remind you that God loves us beyond our imagining," the bishop told him, just loud enough to be overheard by those in the adjacent pews who leaned forward to witness the touching scene. Good Friday afternoon was filled with three hours of prayer, readings, unaccompanied song and testimony—the white hydrangea plants still resting near the small "altar of repose" at the rear of the church as Father Kirk proclaimed, "Behold the wood of the cross . . ." "The blood that Jesus shed for me," we chorused on Holy Saturday evening as Joan and Alexis joined us for the first time at the "supper of the Lamb"—"it will never lose its power!'

Today as we gathered in the morning light, Father Kirk's voice rang out, *"Christ is risen!* (Amen!) *Jesus lives!* (Amen!) *He lives in us!* (Amen!) *Hallelujah!"* (Hallelujah!) Despite the wiggles of an overflow of children dressed in Easter finery, which has kept this morning's liturgy blessedly ragged,[5] and the occasional yawns of those who had untiringly led us through three days of prayer, the church house seemed filled with a sense of peace, of freshness. Indeed, we've been through something. . . . But the challenge remains before us, as Father Kirk put it so well—"that we go out these doors in a few hours and say to the world, *He lives! He lives in us!"* (Amen!)

186

"We are *a radical people because of Jesus!*" he continued later in the service. "**Radical!** Which means that we must *go into the world* with a *new way of looking at life. . . .* The challenge of this feast . . . *the challenge Jesus places before us as he comes into our midst* **alive** . . . is this: *if you and I don't* **act** *as if we really believe* **with all our hearts** *that He is alive—which means that . . . no matter how bad things are, he's going to pull life out of death in our lives—if we don't* **act** *that way, no one's going to believe it! . . .* If we don't *act as if he is alive,* **alive in us,** *where is he? Where is he?* We have a big job to do, you and I, as we go out these doors: *to proclaim his* **life**—not his history, not his greatness, not simply his love— that's all very important. . . . *But do I believe that he is alive in me?* That is the question!"

We are nearing the end of the Easter celebration now—the church house settling once again after Communion has been ministered and Reed modulating to the familiar harmonies of a Communion meditation. Despite the waves of exuberant sound and movement that have coursed through the gathering several times over the past two hours, people seem ready to center down just one more time, to rest here just a little longer, to drink of that "precious fountain" once again, to be here "near the cross." Enough has happened. . . .

Walter Turner steps out from the choir. "Take your time!" someone urges. *"In the* **cross**!" echoes Brother Banks, repeating the phrase several times, as if the very sound of Reed's unhurried piano phrasings were stirring his memory. As Walter's silken voice in high falsetto permeates the room, people immediately begin to punctuate his tarrying syllables with insistent acclamations— weaving their sentiments so tightly with his sung lyrics as to make every phrase a communal invocation.

> Je–sus, keep *(Oh, hallelujah! Sing your song, Walter!)* me near the cross *(Oh, yes!)*
> There's a pre—, a pre–cious fount—ain, *(Oh, yes!)*
> And it's free *(Oh yes, it's free!)* to all, *(Thank you, Jesus!)* a heal—ing stream, *(Yes!)*
> And it flows *(Oh, yes! Amen!)* from Cal—, from Calvary's mount—ain.
> *(Oh, yes! Al'right!)*

Reaching this last line, Walter descends momentarily into the full resonance of his rich baritone voice—sending a ripple of energy coursing through the congregation—only to return once again to begin his second verse in high, fluid falsetto.

> In the cross *(Oh, hallelujah!)* I'll watch *(Yes!)* and wait, *(Oh, yeah!)*
> And I'll be hop–*(Yes!)*–ing, trust–*(Yes, Lord!)*–ing, e–*(Oh, yes!)*–ver! *(Oh, hallelujah!)*
> Till I reach *(Yes!! Oh, yes!)* that gold—en strand *(Well . . . Oh, yes! C'mon!)*
> And it's just *(Yes!!* Multiple shouts . . .*)* beyond, *(Oh, yes!)*
> it's over the ri—*(Yes!!!* Clapping . . .*)*–ver.

The whole church house takes up the chorus, singing with full-voiced intensely, while Walter incites each hasteless line with anticipatory embellishments:

> (In) In the cross, (In) In the cross,
> (Woo, woo, woo, Be) Be my glo—ry e—ver!
> [Walter:] Till my rap–*(Oh, yes!)*–tured soul *(Yes!* Clapping . . .*)* shall find *(Yes!)*
> [All:] (I want to find) Rest beyond the ri—ver!

We circle once again through these chorused words of testimony, only to break forth into wave after unhurried wave of vamped affirmation:

> // : He'll give me wonderful rest! He'll give me sanctified rest!
> He'll give me glorious rest! He'll give me everlasting rest! : //

Ernestine Harris laces the choral sound with intermittent soprano flourishes while Walter prods us on with spoken reiterations of "wonderful rest! sanctified rest! everlasting rest!" until Pat draws us from vamped repetitions to final affirmation:

> Re—st! He'll give me rest!
> Re—st! Won—der—ful rest!

The chorused sound stops abruptly at Pat's signal, allowing Walter's falsetto tone to soar once again before our final cadence gives way to an outburst of applause:

> [Walter:] He'll give me — [All:] won-der-ful rest!!

Amen!!! Amen!!! Wonderful rest!! Near the cross! Thank God for the blood! Yes, Lord! Glorious rest! Amidst the overflow of praise, drum and piano flourishes, Brother Banks's voice can be heard: *"The Lord's gonna give us wonderful rest! There won't be no more pain! No more trouble! No more heartache! . . ."* Thank you, Jesus! Thank you, Jesus! . . .

Gospel music makes one truth clear: Christ is the center. Lyrics of song upon song at Lourdes reiterate this perception. "Christ is all." "Christ is everything." "Christ is my 'all and all.'" "It is Jesus in my soul!" "It's good to know Jesus!" "He's the Alpha and Omega, the beginning and the end!" "I want Jesus to walk with me." " Blessed assurance, Jesus is mine!" "In Jesus Christ I have everything!" There's a feeling of intimacy, of companionship. Jesus, it would seem, has leapt the barrier of God's transcendence to dwell here among us;[6] to rest here in our midst at this focal point of Sunday worship. His presence and passion seem humanly perceptible. Singing stretches the sacramentality of the moment, as words of faith are ministered one to another. To eat is to know. To weep is to know. To embrace is to know. To sing is to know. "Something has happened. . . ." "I feel so connected to everyone in the church. . . ."

*E*lsie Edwards, the great matriarch of the Edwards family, "went home to God" one brisk Tuesday morning that same April. "Many members of our church, many strong-voiced members of our church have returned to Louisiana to celebrate her victory, her going home to God," noted Father Kirk the following Sunday as we gathered in the church house for worship. You could feel their absence—Jean Alexander, Judy Brown, Rose Isles, John Brown, Shirley Valmore, and Isaiah Brown. Isaiah's drums lay silent through most of the liturgy, as if to remind us of the loss of a great woman who was deeply loved and respected by her extended family. "Sometimes it feels like we have to go through things all alone," remarked Brother Banks as he welcomed us that morning, "but *Jesus* is here to help us go through our trials and tribulations! . . . We're so glad to see so many here today. We hope that when it is over you'll say, '*I'm glad I came,* I have something to carry me through!'"

By the time we reached Communion that morning, many in the church house were no doubt feeling as Brother Banks had hoped—glad they'd come. We'd been through something together. . . .

"Now keep that same spirit!" shouted Louise Wood as we concluded our Communion song. *"Keep that same spirit!"* she reiterates as she walked out in front of the choir to lead the Communion Meditation song—"Christ is All"—an "old gospel song" cherished by generations at Lourdes. The lyrics, penned by Kenneth Morris in the 1940s, contrast the hardships of urban life—the fare of many African Americans, including members of this community, who at that time had recently migrated from the rural South to northen cities—with the irrevocable gift of Christ's love. *"C'mon, daugh'er,"* shouts Pat Goodall to Louise, *"tell us what Christ is all about!"* Blessedly, Dirk Isles has seated himself at Isaiah's drums. . . .

Just a few weeks ago, amidst the panoply of Passion-Palm Sunday celebration, Louise had testified at length that she's *"been on the Lord's journey!"*—that despite any hardship, *"God is able!"* Now, despite the song's slow, gentle pace, the ardor in Louise's voice arouses a flow of acknowledgment, people filling every momentary break in the unfolding lyrics with ripples of assent.

I don't possess *(Well . . .)* houses or lands, fine clothes or jew'lry,
(Al'right! Oh, yes!)

Sorrows and cares *(Well . . . Yes!)* in this old world my lot seems to be,
(O—h, yes Lord!)
But I have a Christ *(Yes I have! Oh, yes!)* who paid the price
(C'mon daugh'er! Yes!)
way back on Calv'ry, *(Woo!! Yes! It's al'right!)*
And my Christ is all, *(Yes! Yes he is!)* He's all and all *(Oh, yes he is!)*
this world to me. *(Oh, yes!)*

Oh, yes! C'mon! calls Pat, prodding Louise into the next verse:

There are some folks // who look and long *(Take your time! Take your time!)*
for this world's riches *(Ye—s!)*
There are some folks *(Yes, Lord!)* who look for power, position too!
(Well . . . O—h, yes!)
But I have a Christ *(Excited responses . . .)* who's all in my life *(Hallelujah!)*
and this makes me happy! *(Oh, yes it does!)*
And my Christ is all, *(Yes he is!)* he's all and all this world to me! *(Oh, yes indeed!)*

Liz Bell is on her feet in the back of the church, both arms stretched with abandon toward the low ceiling of the loft above her. "Christ is all! Sing it everyone!" shouts Louise as her verse ends, urging us into a full-throated refrain
and unleashing a surge of communal passion. "Yes, Christ is all!" comes the
wave of chorused sound, "He's everything to me!"

Yes, Christ is all, (he) rules the land and the sea!
(Christ is all!) Yes, Christ is all, (without him) nothing would be!
Christ is all, he's all in all this world to me!

"*Oh yes!*" Louise exclaims, launching into the next verse:

Yes, Christ is all, *(Yes, he is!)* means more to me *(Yes!)* than this world's riches,
(Oh, yes, Lord!! Sing your song now!)
He is my sight, *(Yes, Lord!!)* my guiding light *(Yes!)* through pathless seas!
(O—h, yes, he is!)
Yes, it's mighty nice *(Yes!)* to have a Christ *(Yes!)* who will my friend be!
(O—h yes, Lord!)
And my Christ is all *(He is!)* he's all and all this world to me! *(Oh, yes!)*

"*Oh yes, you can sing it!*" shouts Louise, urging us into another chorused proclamation that "Christ is all! He's everything to me!" Each surge of affirmation
seems to take deeper hold, each confession winding a surer path into our communal soul. Then as if to tarry with us just a bit more, Louise doubles back
into a reprise of her last verse—eliciting even stronger shouts of *Sing your*

190

song, daugh'er! and *Oh, yes!!*—only to lead us into a final, double reiteration of the treasured message,

> (Christ is all!) Yes, Christ is all, (he's) everything to me!
> Yes, Christ is all, (he) rules the land and the sea!
> (Christ is all) Yes, Christ is all, (without him) nothing would be!
> Christ is all, he's all in all this world to me! *(Amen! Hallelujah!)*

"Oh, yes!" cries Louise as the song comes to a full stop, then breaks into shouted testimony over Reed's continued improvisation, ***"Oh, yes!"*** *(Amen! Yes, Lord!)* she reiterates, her blue robe set in motion by the movements of her left hand raised in testimony. *"I know, **I know,** Mother, you're suffering about your son,"* she cries, addressing an unnamed woman in the community. *"But I know this: I know the **Lord will take you through!** (Amen!) I know the Lord will **be there with ya'** when the rest of us won't! (Amen!) Keep on prayin', Mother, (Amen!) because he's gonna be there with you! (Amen!) **I know the Lord!** (Amen!) I may not **seem like I know him, but I know him in here!** I wanna tell you, I **know** the Lord! (Amen!) I know him!!! Oh, yes!! When I sing that song, that's my testimony. I want you to know that today, because **I know** // when everybody's gone, when it's late at night and early in the morning, (Yes, Lord!!) he's gonna be there!! (That's right!) Oh, yes! (Al'right!) Oh, yes! (Al'right!) Oh, yes!!! (Yes, Lord!) Yes, Lord!!! (Thank you, Jesus!) Thank you Lord! Thank you Lord!! Oh, yes!! (Praise Him!)* . . .

Gradually, Louise's voice trails off as do people's shouted responses. Reed winds into a gentle cadence, allowing a few last improvised sounds to carry the lingering acclamations to shore. No one seems in a hurry to leave. . . .

Most every Sunday, the Communion meditation is followed by a "special request," a spontaneous appeal from one member of the community that the choir minister a song to them. "When people *need* something," commented Pat Goodall one Sunday, "no matter how often [we've sung a song,] we have to give it, for the *soul.*" In the intimacy of this Communion time, singing ministers heart to heart. Tears, embraces, and outbursts of praise are as much a part of the music as Isaiah's persistent drumbeat, as healing as the touch of a hand resting reassuringly on one's shoulder. Sorrow or joy spill over.

The custom of incorporating a special request developed some years ago, narrates Jean Alexander. She and other women of the parish were assisting families to plan funerals for loved ones who had died. Often, family members asked that a particular song, a favorite of the deceased, be sung at the funeral. Listening to these requests, Jean found herself asking, Why wait for a person's funeral? Sing to them while they are alive! Minister this soothing balm when they feel the hurt! Surround those struggling with words of encouragement!

Lift up those who are discouraged on the community's song! Rejoice with them in moments of thanksgiving. Walk with them along the path of discernment, recalling the truth that "in Jesus Christ, I have everything!"

It all happens in the context of Communion. "I feel so connected to everyone in the church [at this time]," explains Sister Irma Dillard. "[Including] the ones who are not here. . . . [Even if I] don't know who asked for the special request . . . I can feel the pain. . . . I sense it. I feel it. . . . It's kind of scary sometimes. The first time, I said 'Whoa!' But when you allow the Spirit to work, you let go and the Spirit takes over. It's not about me but about being community. About being in tune with the Spirit." About being church.

Seated next to me in the pew on that cold, March Sunday in 1994 was a slender young Bosnian woman from Sarajevo, Rajna Klaser. Months before, Rajna had arrived in the States to pursue a degree in ethnomusicology at the University of California. Today she'd come to Lourdes as my guest. Sensing the poignancy of her being here, separated from family and homeland at the height of the struggle between Serbs and Croats that was tearing Sarajevo apart, member after member of the community expressed their concern. Louise Wood embraced her reassuringly shortly after we arrived. "If there's anything we can do, please ask!" Little did she know the ministry they would extend, the healing they would midwife, the deep inner response they would evoke. . . .

It's late in the liturgy now. Emotions spill over as freely as the exclamations of praise. *"We need you to come by here, Lord!"* cries Jean Alexander. "We *need* you, Lord!" "Oh yes indeed!" answers Pat, embracing Jean who is in tears. Reed continues to play as the successive waves of feeling unleashed by the Communion Meditation song subside. Moments ago, Jean dedicated the song to her sister Shirley, "that God will give her the strength to do what she's got to do! Remember," she added, "*he* has the power! Oh, thank you Jesus!" Words of faith have been ministered. Shirley sits weeping now in the pew behind us, comforted by Denise Alexander.

I notice that Rajna, seated at my side is now in tears as well. I rest my hand on her shoulder, hoping that my concern will penetrate the dense cloth of her denim jacket, as Pat announces a "special request" for "The Power." Reed weaves a gentle modulation as Cameron Isles, pleased to be asked, carries the microphone to where Reed is seated at the piano.[7] Isaiah's drums are still for the moment. Reed begins to sing lyrically:

It's hard to have faith *(Well . . .)* when your world is crumbling. *(Oh, yes!)*
It's hard to see light *(Oh, yes it is!)* when you're lying in the dark. *(Yes!!!)*

There's a stir of recognition. The words touch. Brother Banks's responses are the first to be heard. Other voices join in affirmation. Ripples of resonance move through the listening community. The steady whish of Isaiah's brush strokes can be heard as Reed continues,

> But don't you give up, *(Can't give up!)* 'cause a change is coming. *(Yes! Al'right!)*
> Remember these words and take them to your heart. *(Yes! Oh, yes!)*

There's a gentle swell of energy. Ernestine picks up the vocal dialogue from her place near the ambo, reiterating each of Reed's sung phrases:

> There'll come a time, (there'll come a time) when you will find
> (when you will find)
> That you are free of the troubles *(Yes!)* of today! *(Oh, yes!)*
> There will be light, (there will be light) things will be right,
> (things will be right)
> There is a power that will set you free some day! *(Oh, yes!)*

I move closer to Rajna, aware of her weeping. She's not alone. The lyrics evoke tears. Tears of release. Tears of empathy. Tears of healing. These words are true. They name experience. They offer hope. They touch. I reach into my purse, hoping to find a tissue to offer Rajna.

Reed's accompaniment becomes more syncopated, his voice more animated. You can feel the buildup, the swell:

> You're out in the storm, *(Oh, yes!)* and the thunder's rolling, *(Yes!!!)*
> Alone and afraid, you just don't know where to run. *(Yes, Lord!!!)*

Brother Banks is on his feet now, his hands moving with the music. "C'mon Reed," someone calls out, as a wave of clapping erupts.

> But just you hold on, *(Hold on!)* till the wind stops blowing. *(Yes!!!)*
> The end of the storm you know is bound to come!

The singing overflows. Ardent voices around the church join in a deeply-felt refrain:

> There'll come a time, (there'll come a time) when you will find
> (when you will find)
> That you are free of the troubles *(Yes!)* of today! *(Oh, yes!)*
> There will be light, (there will be light) things will be right,
> (things will be right)
> There is a power that will set you free some day! *(Oh, yes!)*

The music is pulsing now, spurred on by Isaiah's insistent bass drum, propelled forward by Reed's highly syncopated improvisation. His voice is free and full of feeling, his whole body in motion as he leans into the microphone:

You're out in the storm, *(Oh, yes!)* and the thunder's rolling, *(C'mon! Yes!)*
Alone and afraid, you just don't know where to run. *(Yes, Lord!! Clapping . . .)*
But just you hold on, *(Hold on!)* till the wind stops blowing. *(Yes!!)*
The end of the storm you know is bound to come!

It is as if the song has become a great vessel, carrying this gathered community out into the turbulent waters, out into the storm, navigating a sea of tears, allowing the truth of struggle and pain to wash over, all the while holding them in a deep commingling of spirits, a shared space of hope and reassurance, until "the wind stops blowing," until the "end of the storm" is in sight, until change and healing can come, until God's liberating intentions can be experienced. To sing is to know. To weep is to know. Voices join in words of hope, words of promise, ministered heart to heart:

There'll come a time, (there'll come a time) when you will find
(when you will find)
That you are free of the troubles of today! *(Oh, yes!)*
There will be light, (there will be light) things will be right,
(things will be right)
There is a power that will set you free some day! *(Oh, yes!)*

As if to allow energies to subside, emotions to ebb, a vessel to reach port, the last phrase spills over into a gentle, hummed reprise. "Oo-o-o-o . . ." Brother Banks can be heard over the lingering *Amens!* "Oh yes, there's a *power* that will set you free some day! Thank you, Brother Reed."

*R*eflecting on her visit to Lourdes as we drove home across the Bay Bridge that Sunday, Rajna expressed amazement. How could she have been touched so deeply? A community she did not know. Music she had never heard before. How was it that she found herself in tears by what she encountered here? Lyrics so general, communicated so personally. Across cultures and continents, the intensity and sincerity of the feelings expressed by the Lourdes community had enabled her to know her pain and find release. Seven years later, she would write me that her morning at Lourdes had played a significant role in the healing of her memories of war in Sarajevo.

*E*nough *had* happened. . . . Something *had* emerged from and through us. . . .

Intermezzo

FLOW

*T*he most distinguishing characteristic of Black music-making, claims Father Clarence Rivers, "is the attribute of being free."[1] "Notice," he invites us, "how freely a good jazz instrumentalist revels and rhapsodizes even within the confines of a set rhythm. Notice how a good blues, gospel, or jazz singer can liberate the words of a text from the imprisonment of a given notation. When music is free, it is soulful at its source, and soul-stirring in its effect. . . . When music is free, it is alive, and communicates life. Without this freedom, this soul, music is dead."[2]

The freedom of which Father Rivers speaks is not an absence of musical form or structure—those necessary components such as rhythm, harmony, pitch and meter—but is rather a musician's ability to allow spiritual power to move *through* the music, to *inspirit* it from within: in his words, to "rhapsodize and revel *within* the confines of a set rhythm"; to "liberate the words of the text from the imprisonment of a given notation." The goal of this performative freedom, Rivers suggests, is the communication of life, resilience, vitality, spirit, and "soul," so as to quicken, touch, and fill the human spirit.

Rivers's images underscore that to access what is most essential to Black music we must attend not only to the music's *form* but to the manner in which it *unfolds in performance*—that is, to the music's *flow.* Likewise, to recognize what is most distinctive about worship and music-making at Lourdes, we must explore more than the form and content of the rite and its music—the sequence of elements, the content of its proclamations, songs and actions. Rather, we must attend to how the music and worship unfold in performance, to how they are *inspirited* from within—to the qualities of the community's action, the strategies, assumptions, expectations, predilections that set the liturgy and its music in motion on any occasion. We must, in sum, heed their *flow.*

Tapping into the flow of music and worship at Lourdes—which is readily characterized as alive, spirit-filled, moving, emotion-filled, flowing, changing, overflowing—we touch an underlying spirituality, at once receptive and self-giving; a religious-cultural expectation that worship will be filled with the living, rhythmic breath of the divine Spirit, who will draw participants into a dynamic connectedness one with another, and carry them more deeply into the mystery of their communion with God. Cultivating this mode of worship at Lourdes requires of all participants, and especially those in leadership, the musical, social, and spiritual skills, as well as the mutuality and trust, that enable them to "tune" the worship to the free and liberating movements of the Spirit.

Improvisation / indeterminacy / personal initiative: What assumptions / predilections affect how people engage in the flow of the music / worship?

*S*everal assumptions seem to be at work in the way people at Lourdes engage in the flow of their music-making and in the worship event as a whole. First, the foundational premise: worship is meant to be enjoyed. As we have seen, people come to "have a good time in the Lord!" They relax. They expect to be drawn in, to be moved by what will take place, to participate freely. Second, each one present is understood to be "a child of God," to have the Spirit of God within them, and therefore to have something to contribute to what takes place. Being oneself and expressing one's faith are expected. Children learn at an early age to let their voice be heard in a way that harmonizes with the community's purpose. Within the well-known patterns of doing worship and making music, there's room for personal initiative—for speaking out in prayer and testimony, for engaging in the dynamic call-response of singing and preaching, for showing support and care for one another. Third, those in leadership are committed to evoking and promoting the participation of others rather than silencing it. "Wake up, Church! We're here to praise the living God!" shouts singer Jean Alexander when participation seems hesitant or weak. Father Kirk's comment expresses the attitude well: "Liturgy is the work of the people; the priest is part of the community and there are roles to be carried out." Moreover, there's a strong sense of shared ownership of what takes place, expressed in numerous comments such as "We are the church!" "This is the people's church." "We're part of this liturgy." Ownership poises people to be more action oriented than passively reflective. All are co-creators of what transpires.

Participating with the Lourdes community, one experiences the worship and its music as an organic life form—an interactive and living system—rather than as a text, script, or musical score waiting to be enacted. Within the community's oral/aural practice, people come to know the patterns of Catholic worship through participation rather than through visual representations (books, texts, scores). Over time, this participation yields an internalized sense of the order and progression of the ritual in which variability, changeability, expandability are not "exceptions" to "the liturgy" but how worship is done. Liturgy is known as a "field of action and meaning"[3] that is not rigidly bounded or fixed, but living and dynamic—the sum of experience stored in consciousness, stored bodily and psychically, a memory of changing textures and qualities of time. Moreover, cultural models for how people participate in worship and music—as well as the social, liturgical, musical skills and the inner resources to engage in this way—are inseparable from how people know the tradition and hand it on from generation to generation.

Given these factors, liturgy at Lourdes might be described as a communal, improvisatory[4] art— more like the responsive fluidity of a jazz ensemble than the precise synchronization of a symphony orchestra. Within the conventional patterns of Catholic liturgy, the community values a certain indeterminacy in how they will unfold. The action, musical or liturgical, has an open-ended quality about it that seems to foster responsiveness, cooperation, and partnership among those participating, that places emphasis on unfolding relationships rather than conforming to an external norm.[5] Waiting, listening, and yielding to others are as much part of the discipline of this art as speaking, singing, or giving testimony. Likewise a willingness to surrender one's isolation, although not one's individuality, to the communal prayer.

Flowing / overflowing / spilling over: How do these qualities shape the music / worship event?

*D*escriptions of what takes place each Sunday at Lourdes require words such as flowing, ebbing, overflowing, spilling over. Songs overflow into acclamations of praise, allowing the emotion of the singers, the energy of the lyrics, and the movements of the soul to flow beyond the boundaries of the song itself. Preaching spills over into a profession of faith which springs directly from the challenges and consolations of the Scripture readings of the occasion. Singing overflows into bodily rhythms that mark the undulations of pulse and syncopation. Prayers of the faithful well up from people's lives and spill through the porous boundaries that might otherwise distinguish intercessions, thanksgivings, and admonitions. Prayers overflow into embraces and exchanges of the Lord's peace, which then take their own course, their own time. There's a sense of fullness, of abundance, of life welling up like a great river coursing into its tributaries.

Moreover, the flow from one moment in the worship to another is often made articulate through spoken words or musical sound. Brother Banks's words of welcome make a verbal, dynamic, and emotional transition from the opening song to Father Kirk's first greetings. Reed's piano improvisations trace the flow from the proclamation of a Scripture reading to the song that follows, or from a song to another portion of the rite, thus making audible the underlying currents of prayer and faith response that connect these elements. Lead singers, offering spoken introductions to songs they are about to sing, make connections between the lyrics of a song and people's lives, or between the spiritual thrust of the song and what is taking place in the worship. Transitions-made-articulate in this way create a sense of inner connectedness among various aspects of the worship, a perceived sense of movement from one to another that is organic and natural rather than imposed.

Most significantly, flowing, overflowing, and spilling over characterize the spirited interchange that happens among persons—an exchange that actually propels the worship forward dialogically. At most any moment in the liturgy, there's an explicit flow of energy among people, an exchange of words and gestures. People enter the flow of songs, preaching, prayers, infusing them with a communal energy that envelops, quickens, carries, and enlarges the action. The flow of energy is visual, auditory, and kinesthetic.

At the heart of this interchange is a regular, patterned flow of leadership from one "dynamic center" to another. Each of those who assume major leadership—Father Kirk, Brother Banks, Pat Goodall, Reed Fromer, lead singers, the choir as a whole—is dynamic and skilled, able to animate, engage and hold people's attention. Yet each is willing to yield, to allow the leadership to flow regularly to another "center," creating interest and variety and drawing others into the action.[5] This is particularly evident during times of music-making, as the constant flow of interaction among lead singers, choir, instrumentalists, choir director, and the rest of the assembly—connecting, layering, receiving energy from one another and returning it—dynamically shapes the song: its timing, duration, and affective force. It is likewise true of the whole worship. Those in leadership assume that others are intentional co-creators of what takes place, and interact with the community in a way that unleashes, releases, fosters and evokes their participation. Through this interchange, the worship and the music are shaped as a living event overflowing with a vitality that spills over into the community's everyday lives, giving them "something to feast on all week."

Àshe / breath / living Spirit:
What fuels/generates the flow of this river, of this worship?

*F*rom an African perspective, one that has deeply affected African American religious culture, *àshe* [pron. Ä-shay] is the life force, the spiritual power that surges through the universe, that animates creation and resides in human persons.[7] *Àshe* is God's animating spirit given to everything that exists. "Existence . . . is dependent upon it; it is the power to make things happen and change."[8] As Joseph A. Brown points out, *àshe* "is defined in a manner sur-

198

prisingly similar to the traditional Catholic understanding of grace. . . . 'God's own enabling light rendered accessible to men and women.'"[9]

Àshe, Brown continues, "is the same force found in the Genesis account of creation. It is given to all of creation by the touch of the Creator."[10] It is the animation of God who infuses life, energy, and power into all created beings through God's own Spirit. It is the action of a God who, in the words of Father Clarence Rivers, "breathed that Spirit into motionless clay and made it a moving, living soul"; who "could stir the waters and make [them] capable of sustaining and renewing life"; and who "turned a stagnant sprawl of lifeless bones into a moving dance of life."[11] This Spirit of God, from a Christian perspective, is a living breath, the *ruach* of God, divinity itself poured out, "overflowing all boundaries, propelled by its own fierce fullness," and filling creatures with this same "ecstatic drive" which propels "them to return . . . back to the source from which they came."[12] Thus, "the cosmos, and human beings within it, express and participate in divinity's own ecstatic life: fullness that brims over, desire that explodes its own boundaries."[13]

Rivers contends that in African American religious culture, communities sense the presence of Spirit of God when worship and music are intensely expressive and moving, when spiritual power is released and newness is created.[14] Through this felt-action of the Spirit, a community touches the living, divine source of worship: the impulse to flow beyond oneself, to give oneself over in dedication and surrender.

These understandings shape a spirituality that is deeply embedded in the assumptions and expectations operative at Lourdes and that fuels the flow of the community's liturgy and music. The gifts of God entrusted to each one—which, as Father Kirk preached, are the presence of "the living Spirit, the breath of God"—are meant for others. They must overflow and be manifest so that others in turn can be touched by this Spirit. As Sister Thea Bowman queried on one occasion, "If I keep my faith locked up inside myself, what good is it to you?"

In African understandings of *àshe,* any part of creation touched by this potency can bestow its power upon others. *Àshe,* spiritual power, "is sought for the benefit of all. *To dance for the community is to be generous.* The gifts one receives are bestowed upon all."[15] What generates the flow of worship at Lourdes is a spirituality that requires generosity, self-giving, and a willingness to be a vessel of the Spirit whose life flows out to others and returns in praise to the Creator.

Tension – resolution / motion – emotion / storms-at-sea – arrivals-at-port: How do the music/worship move toward a destination? fulfill their purpose?

Within this flowing and overflowing event of worship, there is a sense of movement toward a destination, toward deeper communion, as we have seen.

It is striking that this perceived movement is not simply a linear progression of events towards an end point. Rather it is more like a *flow between opposites* which are always being held in tension—outbursts of praise and moments of quiet reflection; upbeat songs that surge through the gathering and reflective, slower songs that quiet the spirit and restore calm; "centralized" moments of focused prayer and "decentralized" moments of free exchange among people— all of which give the worship a deeply rhythmic character.[16] From an African perspective, rhythm intimates the presence of the divine spirit. Rhythm, it is said, "is the property of the dieties."[17] The forces that well up and sustain life, which display divine action surging through creation, are essentially rhythmic—involving growth and change, ebb and flow. Moreover, living systems regulate themselves and grow through this natural flow between opposites in rhythmic alternation—"[d]ay turns to night, winter into summer, the in-breath into the out-breath."[18] Like the swinging pendulum, this alternation of opposites in living things never returns to the same place but *progresses forward, spiral-like*.

Rhythmic progression—a spiral-like flow between opposites—becomes evident at Lourdes in the contrasting dynamics of a song like "Perfect Praise," in which hushed words of praise give way over and again to surges of energy that spiral into outbursts of "Excellent is your name!" only to return once again to calm moments of quiet acclamation. The overall effect is less a linear movement from the start of the song to its final chord and more a dynamic ebb and flow of energy that leaves the community in a new place, at a deeper level of co-action and mutuality. The same rhythmic progression is felt when a period of worship marked by one modality of engagement—a focused, "centralized" time of preaching and prayers—gives way to another that is markedly different—the highly "decentralized" engagement of an exchange of peace; or when the exuberant singing of "Lord, let your Spirit fall on me!" yields to the more gentle, attentive, focused praying of the Eucharistic Prayer. Movement from one type of action to another, like inhalation and exhalation, allows the community's worship to breathe and to move rhythmically forward toward a destination.[19]

Within this overall flow between opposites, individual songs, preaching, prayer, and the liturgy as a whole are propelled forward through a recurring buildup and release of tension—musical, dramatic, emotional. A slow gospel song, for example, begins gently with a gradual layering of sound—first a piano introduction, then choral voices, then embellishing lead singing— allowing time for people to enter the flow, the mood, and the message of the song before the dynamics gear up; then moves through a gradual buildup of sound, a growing intensification of emotional and musical energy, creating a tension that is often heightened by the "stalled" harmonies and lyrics of a vamp, only to explode into a moment of release in which energies spill over and reverberate until the emotional and spiritual feelings that have been generated subside. This same buildup and release of tension can be heard in the cadence of Brother Banks's voice as he leads the community in prayer. It can likewise be experienced in Father Kirk's preaching. Like singers who describe the musical process as "building a song," Father Kirk depicts his framework and dynamics in a similar manner: "I try to build, and build, and build, and build—and then [stop]! Basically that's the structure of my [preaching] style. It starts off quietly, and then . . . you have a tension, you bring in the problems, challenges, then you finish with, 'Where is our faith?'"[20]

Emotions are set in motion by this buildup of tension and release, emotions that draw members of the community beyond their personal realms of thought and self-awareness into a space of shared feeling and engagement. E-motion, Clarence Rivers reminds us, is precisely that: a moving out of oneself, a movement toward the other, a way of knowing and relating to others, an intuitive sharing of life.[21] As emotions are evoked through the buildup and release of tension, people are drawn more deeply into an active and affective engagement with each other and a corporate involvement in the action of the liturgy which is sustained not only in moments of peak intensity but in times of quiet prayer. Shared emotion becomes the basis of union and communion with each other and with the Other who is the heart and "destination" of the worship.

Moreover, emotional engagement in patterns of tension and release situates the community's music and liturgy "close to life," connected to the ebb and flow of the life of feeling, to the rhythmic textures of everyday living. In African American music, including songs in the Lourdes' repertoire, life, with all its struggles and hopes, is often imaged metaphorically as "being out in a storm." As Reed Fromer sang that March Sunday when Rajna Klaser visited Lourdes, "You're out in the storm // and the thunder's rolling, // alone and afraid, you just don't know where to run! // But just you hold on, // till the wind stops blowing, // The end of the storm you know is bound to come!" Release, freedom, liberation come not in an avoidance of struggle but in finding a way *through* it: "There is a Power that will set you free some day." Engaging musically and liturgically in patterns of emotional tension and release at Lourdes allows people to ground their everyday struggles in the faith perspective of the worship. Participating in a communion of shared feeling that mirrors life, people engage not as passive voyagers but active pathfinders seeking together a way through life's challenges to the Power that will set them free.

Order / chaos / and the "paradox of control": What keeps this worship from coming apart at the center?

*T*here's a wisdom at work in all of this about the relationship of order, chaos, and control. Allowing emotionally charged moments to unfold and take their course, taking time for highly decentralized moments like the exchange of peace, which might appear to persons outside the community as chaotic and "out of control," seems to fly in the face of the normal assumptions about liturgy—that control brings order out of chaos, and that this type of order (i.e., control) is essential to good liturgy. Things should not come un-raveled, lest something of the "weight of the mystery" be lost. In the words of the poet Yeats, "Things fall apart; the center cannot hold, mere anarchy is loosed upon the world."[22]

Yet this fear—that things fall apart—may have more to do with culturally shaped values of decorum, control, and time-management than with lessons about order that can be learned from an "orderly" universe. What transpires in a free-fall, decentralized moment like the peace-greeting at Lourdes is actu-ally truer to the nature of the universe as perceived by quantum physics—that within chaos there *is* order, that chaos is always seeking its own higher order, which cannot exist without the chaos. Order and chaos are actually "mirror images, one containing the other, a continual process where a system can leap into chaos and unpredictability, yet within the state be held within parame-ters that are well-ordered and predictable."[23] "In life," writes Erich Jantsch, "the issue is not control, but *dynamic connectedness*."[24]

It is here that we touch something of the wisdom operative at Lourdes: dy-namic connectedness—a cultivated way of being together, of being-in-rela-tionship, that thrives when the action remains open-ended. Renato Rosaldo proposes that if we are to understand the full spectrum of human action, we must look beyond our dichotomous ways of distinguishing order and chaos—which usually assume some normative notion of order and relegate every-thing else to "undifferentiated chaos"—to "the less explored realm of 'non-order.'"[25] Non-order is a social space within which people can develop culturally valued qualities of human relations. Within this more improvisatory space of non-order, which of its nature requires a certain level of indetermi-nancy and variability, people develop "positive qualities of social being" such as "timing, coordination, and a knack for responding to contingencies." These qualities, Rosaldo contends, "constitute *social grace*."

What is mediated at Lourdes, and particularly evident in "blessedly ragged" times of non-order, is a particular *aesthetic of engagement*—one that highlights the rich diversity among members of the community, that values personal ini-tiative, individual gifts, and personal skills for participating. In contrast to an aesthetic that prizes precision and greater efficiency of action—which in turn requires more control, in the hands of fewer persons, perhaps even one—Lourdes values an aesthetic of engagement that is communal and consensual, and which assumes that freedom to engage interpersonally is essential to the efficacy of the ritual and its music.

"Dynamic connectedness," "social grace," and a communal aesthetic of en-gagement, all of which thrive at Lourdes, are deeply connected to one more factor: an implicit realization that a community can only taste transcendence when it abandons the fear of losing control—when it recognizes what Mihaly Csikszentmihalyi describes as the "paradox of control."[26] Exploring the deep enjoyment that pervades human experiences "in which people are so involved in an activity that nothing else seems to matter"—a description which might characterize Lourdes' "having a good time in the Lord"—Csikszentmihalyi proposes that it is the lack of "a sense of worry about losing control" that frees persons to engage fully.[27] We see this freedom in the abandon of a lead singer transported on the mounting intensity of an extended vamp, and hear it in the building emotion of Brother Banks's voice when he prays expectantly for that time when "there will be no more tears, no more sorrow," when we will be "free at last, free at last!" We feel this lack of worry about losing control in the threshold moments of emotion-filled singing as well as in the more taken-for-granted manner in which leadership is shared. In such unselfconscious, at times passionate moments, Csikszentmihalyi contends, persons experience the "*possibility* rather than the *actuality* of control"—they touch the "power to effect something of grace and beauty."[28] In these joy-filled experiences at Lourdes, the community opens beyond itself to taste transcendence. No longer is it a question of the worship "coming apart at the center." Rather than breaking apart, what opens up is the possibility of *breaking through* into what the community believes to be the center of its worship, the living Spirit of God alive and operative in the community, which can only happen when worship is free.

Tuning / attuning / tuning in: How are the flow of music and worship "tuned" to the Spirit's action?

*T*he question remains: How are the flow of music and worship at Lourdes tuned to the Spirit's action? What enables Spirit-directed worship? The musical metaphor of "tuning" is useful here. Tuning is always a relational process.[29] To tune is to adjust, to align, to bring into harmonious resonance with another sound, another voice. Tuning to the Spirit's action is likewise a relational process that begins with *tuning in* to other members of the community as locus of the Spirit's action—through the interactive communication of singing, preaching, praying, and embracing. Mutuality, reciprocity, and an openness to the witness of others become the basis for the shared communion that only the Spirit can effect.

While people come to Sunday liturgy expecting that the Spirit will be present, acting in ways that they can perceive, effecting change—a visitation, a reorientation, an experience of being touched, brought to tears, filled, given strength to "keep on keep in' on"—there's a keen awareness that the Spirit's action can never be marshaled by the sheer efforts of the community. The Spirit moves freely and acts in unpredictable ways. So keeping the situation free enough, the structures and timing supple enough, the praying, singing, and speaking responsive enough, are all part of enabling individuals and the community as a whole to sense the Spirit's presence and respond appropriately.

Since the Spirit is given to all and not only to a few, taking everyone's rhythms into consideration is important. Whoever is leading at a given moment must wait on, listen for, a consensus, a shared sense about when to linger and when to move on. Learning to lead in this situation is learning to "feel" with the community—to read their unfolding experience, to tune into the delicate partnership between members of the community and the Holy Spirit.

"Tuning to the Spirit" invokes a logic that is more biblical than rubrical. Whereas a rubrical logic seeks the "right way" of performing conventional patterns, biblical logic opens to what will infuse these patterns with living breath. It seeks a deeper organizing and ordering principle which is not to be found in the "law" but in the action of God's Spirit as depicted in the Scriptures. Biblical images of the Spirit of God reveal an animating force poured out on old and young, infusing them with life and courage, energy and power; that can move them "to dream divine dreams and speak in the name of God"; and that can transform timid disciples—"pussycats" as Father Kirk described them—"into tigers!" Invoking a biblical logic at Lourdes is to expect the Spirit to accomplish these liberating intentions within the actual worship event— freeing, transforming, releasing, comforting, enlivening both individuals and the community, praying within each one in sighs too deep for words.

Discerning the action of God's Spirit on any given occasion is a communal art that is more implicit than self-conscious. It begins with tuning of the music and the worship to Spirit-like qualities such as warmth, fire, energy, and joy. Singing, praying, preaching that are Spirit-like—that stir and move with an inner potency, that surge with life that can draw you down or raise you up, that are not "dry and dead" but moist and refreshing—can open the community to the Spirit's free action and enable those who sing, pray, and preach to become vessels of the Spirit's presence one to another. When people are moved to tears or testimony or outbursts of praise; when individuals reach out to each other in love and affection; when faith is deepened and burdens lifted; when new strength to meet the challenges of life is tasted, the Spirit's presence is felt. Moreover, tasting what the Spirit is like in worship that flows out, spills over, overflows into people's everyday lives becomes a basis for discerning the Spirit's action. One Ascension Sunday, Richard Olive, who was new to the community at that time, thanked God that he has come to know the Spirit in this community because, he claimed, this experience has enabled him to recognize and embrace the Spirit leading him in the rest of his life.

Chapter Thirteen

RHYTHMS OF THE BODY, RHYTHMS OF THE SPIRIT

—A GOD WHO LOVES SINGING AND DANCING—

"**M**usic is a gift of God," remarked Tina Edwards breaking into a youthful smile. Tina, Tiffany Isles and I were conversing about how music at Lourdes affects one's experience of prayer. "Music is natural," she continued. "Hear the birds! Hum a tune! [Feel it as you're] walking down the street! It's the rhythm, it's the pace, it's always there! Music is a gift of God, a gift he gave us so that we can worship better, so that we can worship in his house."

It seemed she'd touched the core, the heart of all that we'd been exploring that April afternoon. The song doesn't begin with us. It's a gift of God, to be received and returned in praise to the One from whom it comes. It's a godly presence that makes our worship fuller, richer, more precious to the One who offers the gift. To receive this gift, explained Tina and Tiffany that afternoon, is to allow the sound, the energy, the truth, the vibrations, the message of the music to fill your body, to stir your soul, and to shake the dust off your praises; to tap into your fears, to flood you with consolation, to break down your inner barriers and enable you to surrender to God. In the rhythms of the body, [they seemed to say,] you discover the rhythms of the Spirit. "'Here I am, Lord . . . before I was holding back.'" Tina concluded. "You release and completely surrender yourself to God."[1]

As Pat Goodall and I turned off Haight St. onto Clayton Avenue, Pat's voice was full of animation. Returning from a Day of Prayer for the San Francisco School of Pastoral Leadership, at which the Lourdes choir had sung, we were discussing the importance of people worshiping God according to their own distinctive styles and sensitivities. I pulled the car near the curb across from Pat's home so as to finish the conversation. "We at Lourdes need to make a *joyful* noise," claimed Pat. "We need to worship God as *we know and feel God to be!* Our God is *happy, joyful,* not depressing, sad, or uptight. *God's shoes don't pinch!*"[2]

The image lodged in my mind as I continued my drive home. A God whose "shoes don't pinch," I mused, is no doubt a God who is at home amidst our singing and dancing; a God who delights in a creation that is rich with rhythm, movement, color and diversity—all of which is the work of God's own hand; a God whose Wisdom is at play in the universe, delighting to be at large in "God's playhouse."[3] The very *way* we worship and make music, Pat seemed to say, reveals how we know God, how God reveals Godself to us.

*C*onversation flowed easily among the women of the Lourdes Sodality huddled around a long table in the church hall that May morning. Margaret Fisher was seated across from me, her head nodding as various women spoke about their experience of music in the Lourdes liturgy. Margaret, a slender great-grandmother with wisdom in her eyes and dignity in her bearing, was dressed that morning in a tailored navy suit set off by the ruffled color of a crimson blouse. A gentle woman, she waited patiently to join the flow of words and images. Then, as if too full to hold back any longer, she remarked, "Well in the *Bible* it says that we should praise God with *cymbals and drums!* Let *everything* praise God. . . ." Her comments were swept along in the flow of conversation, but her reference to Psalm 150 was clear. She might well have continued to claim a biblical warrant for praising God with clanging cymbals, with loud crashing cymbals, with drumming and dancing! "Clap your hands all you peoples, shout to God with cries of joy!" Liz Bell returned to Margaret's theme moments later. "The instruments—the drums, the piano [we use here at Lourdes]— help bring out the *feeling* of the music, the *power*. . . . Like we're praising the Lord in a lot of ways and with a lot of voices!"[4]

Instruments, these women seemed to say, stretch our ability to praise God. Drums, piano, crashing and clanging cymbals amplify the sound, the energy, the feeling, and the power of the music so as to awaken our bodies and enable our spirits to resonate with God's gift of song. They expand the "voices" of our praise, enabling us to express the "unsayable"—those dimensions of our praise that go beyond our words.

"*M*any of the songs we sing at Lourdes come from the greater Black church," remarked Father Kirk from across a small kitchen table in the parish rectory as we talked about how this community claims a musical tradition that is both Black and Catholic. "We make them our own. They enrich our Catholicity. But that's not the point for people at Lourdes. . . .

"The *main* priority is to praise God. . . . It's all about praising God. And there are many ways of praising God. Clapping, for example—we clap to praise the Lord, that's the basic reason, not to keep the choir in rhythm. To make sound before the Lord. . . . The priority here is to praise God."[5]

Father Kirk's words are borne out in conversations with others at Lourdes. No matter what the message of a song—be it thanksgiving, supplication, or testimony—the act of singing is understood to be one of praise. Indeed, singers often use "singing" and "praising" interchangeably. "I love singing to God and praising his name," commented Judy Brown. "I love praising God. That's why I sing—for the grace of God, all the blessings he's given me—singing is just giving back. . . . It's giving back to him what he's given me in my life."[6]

At Lourdes, singing and praising are never timid or hesitant. A God who "is worthy to be praised," as song after song reiterates, deserves colorful praise, embodied praise, dancing praise, and at times, ecstatic praise.

These conversations weave a perception that at Lourdes, music-making is revelatory—revelatory of the community's experience of who God is, of what it is like to be in God's presence, of what it means to be created in God's image, and of what it is like to experience God as living Presence at the heart of the community's prayer. In the rhythms of the body one discovers the rhythms of God's Spirit—a God who loves singing and dancing.[7]

Music as gift "of God" carries the imprint of the Giver—a Giver whose life is refracted in sound and movement, in dress and dance, in timbre and gesture. At Lourdes, to sing and praise God is to become a vessel of that life, to be moved by that life, allowing it to fill one's mind, to touch one's emotions and liberate one's body. It is to realize that "the world and time are the dance of the Lord."[8] It is to join the "cosmic dance" which, as the great contemplative Thomas Merton once wrote, "beats in our very blood. . . ."[9]

*I*t was the only time I saw Brother Banks dance. The "holy dance" that is, a dance recognized by the community as the impulse of the Holy Spirit. A dance that reaches back into the tradition of Black worship. A dance he no doubt first experienced in his youth on a Louisiana plantation, in the gatherings for praise and worship which he so beautifully described in our conversations.

It was June of '94—a challenging time for the parish, a time of uncertainty. Just a week before the archdiocese had announced the closure of All Hallows, Lourdes's neighboring parish, and Lourdes was faced with an influx of new members into its tiny church house. What would become of this parish, Father Kirk would ask as he preached that morning. How would he and members of the community welcome another community in grief, mourning over the loss of their beloved parish—including a large Samoan community with its own distinctive style of worship and life together?

Before the liturgy began that morning, Father Kirk sensed a heaviness in people's hearts and requested that someone in the choir sing "Unwavering Faith"—a song that could capture the sentiments and prayer of the community, their plea for "faith to climb those mountains" which inevitably lay before them. Yet after a day of rehearsing for a gospel concert in Santa Clara, neither Ernestine Harris nor Pat Goodall felt ready for the vocal challenge.

Just then, like a miracle, Charlene Edwards arrived unexpectedly all the way from Stockton, and was pressed into service. Many times before, during her years as choir director, Charlene's resonant contralto voice had gathered the Lourdes community into a fervent plea for "unwavering faith," for "faith to climb that old, old rugged hill"; for "faith to ensure God will answer if we only do his will." This morning would be no different.

It is late in the service and people are settling into their pews after receiving the Body and Blood of Christ, when Charlene moves to the microphone.

Lord // give me // that un-wav-er-ing faith! *(Yes, Lord!)*

she begins freely, in unmetered rhythm, the fullness of her voice drawing us into a communion of spirits. As each unhurried line flows out into the community, the ardor in Charlene's voice swells ever so gently, the responses of *Yes, Lord!* and *Amen!* from around the church became more insistent. By the time she reaches the end of the song, a final soaring invocation for "unwavering faith," many are in tears.

But then, a sudden sea change washed the church house. As the final cadence of Charlene's song sounded, with arpeggiated piano flourish and a swell of Isaiah's cymbals, Charlene glances at Pat Goodall. Their eyes meet. A brief word is exchanged. Then a hushed word to Reed and Isaiah, who know all the songs by heart, and Reed segues into a jubilant "old, old gospel song," recognized immediately as "I've Got Jesus and That's Enough!"[10] Isaiah is right behind, tapping into its rollicking duple meter with cymbals swinging and drums pulsing. Even before Charlene begins to sing, people around the church house are on their feet. Rhythmic clapping echoes off the walls. Charlene launches into a first verse, her voice spirited against Reed and Isaiah's infectious syncopations:

There's always somebody talking about me // really I don't mind!
They try their best to block my progress // most all the time.
The mean things they say don't make me feel sad;
I can't lose a friend that I never had.
I've got Je—sus and that's enough!

The entire church house seems to have joined Charlene on this last affirmation: *"I've got Jesus and that's enough!"* *Yes!* calls someone from the first pew. *Amen!* shouts another from further back.

The song has hardly begun when Brother Banks rises to his full stature behind the choir. Cautiously, now, he begins to descend the three steps from where he was seated beside Father Kirk. Parting the choir line with a gentle nudge, he slowly walks out in front of the singers, and there, in the midst of the sanctuary, like the center of a ring shout, Brother Banks begins to sway with the gently percussive movements of an elderly dancer. Whatever has seized his soul is likewise stirring his body!

To my amazement, he sways as if lost in the music. His movements are halting but never constrained. His white alb and red print stole shift from side to side with the gentle oscillation of his body, his arms, elbows bent, set in motion as if to an inner dance. "I've got Jesus and that's enough!" rings another pulsing chorus. Joy, it seems, has taken hold, not only of Brother Banks but of the whole church house.

The lyrics are tripping off Charlene's tongue as she sets up a rapid call-response:

> He's a Great Emancipator! A Heart-Regulator!
> All: *Jesus is! Jesus is!*
> He makes my burdens lighter, my pathway brighter!
> All: *Yes he will! Yes he will!*
> You break me down and God picks me up.
> Stays right by me when the going gets tough!
> *I've got Je–sus, and that's enough!*

Brother Banks, leaning ever so slightly forward, rocks rhythmically with each rapid phrase. Shifting weight from one foot to another, as if walking in place, his shoulders undulate in rapid waves of motion that echo through his arms and torso. Then, his feet shuffling, he turns in place. It seems Brother Banks is doing what we all wish to do. He dances at the center of the gathering, dances in our name! We've come into a clearing with him, a place of trust and celebration. It's not that we've escaped the challenge of "climbing those rugged mountains" about which Charlene just sang, nor the "unwavering faith" necessary to make that ascent—but that we've broken through into a place of assurance, of security that God will be there with us. Behind Brother Banks, the choir is swaying with a jubilant sense of "victory" as Charlene invites us to declare over and again, "I've got Je–sus, and that's enough!" It's a moment of grace, a moment of reassurance. The Incarnate One, who knows our struggles and offers us hope, seems to be dancing in the very rhythms of Brother Banks's elderly body.

Bishops in full regalia usually stand out in a crowd. But when Bishop Patrick McGrath[11] arrived at Lourdes that chilly March morning in '95 to celebrate Confirmation, the church house was already ablaze with color—colors more intense and diverse than those that meet the eye most any Sunday at Lourdes.

Members of the Gospel Choir, assembling near the entryway of the church, were dressed in a full spectrum of African prints: Ernestine Harris in a striped tunic redolent with hues of purple and blue, a matching swath of fabric wrapped stylishly around her head; Rose Isles in a handsome black and gold dress; Jean Alexander and her daughter Denise garbed in matching orange and green print tunics; John and Judy Brown wearing contrasting tunics, each replete with red, black and white designs; and Pat Goodall in a long flowing garment in gold and purple print set off by a gold necklace and matching shoes.

Sprinkled among the gathering assembly were other outbursts of African color, as well as a sampling of bright Polynesian designs worn by members of the Samoan community who had come to honor relatives who would be confirmed. Clearly, *adorning oneself with gladness* is important in this house of God—allowing the inner rejoicing, the inner worship to find an outward expression.

Already the seven *confirmandi* and their sponsors filled the front rows on the right side of the church house. Marina Lugo and her mother Carol—a choir member who is herself from South Africa— were bedecked in African dress. Beside them sat Teresa Veronica Julio adorned in a fragrant *lei* of purple and white flowers prepared by members of the Samoan community. Later that morning, as the altar table would be prepared for Eucharist, similar leis would be placed on the bishop and other ministers, wreathing them in fragrance and color.

Filling the rows behind the *confirmandi* were a band of "women in white"—identifiable by their gold-trimmed cross-sashes as the Ladies' Auxiliary of the Knights of St. Peter Claver who meet on the second Sunday of every month. Another group of mature Samoan women in long white dresses, each wearing a gold medal suspended by red ribbon around her neck, converged near the rear of the church. Dress, I've learned, is not incidental or simply ornamental to worship at Lourdes, but a way of expressing one's dignity and identity in the presence of God and the community. Moreover, *festive dress becomes one of the many "voices" of praise.*

Gathering with the choir in the rear of the church, his assisting deacon, Ricarco Viray, at his side, Bishop McGrath seemed at home in this festive gathering. A tall, gracious man with a touch of Irish accent in his voice, he was dressed in a two-toned red chasuble, a white miter on his head, a carved wood crosier grasped with his right hand. Three young Samoan boys, candles in hand, in white cassocks set off by red cummerbunds and red fringed yokes, stood beside two young African American girls holding the Lectionary and the Sacramentary that would be used for the liturgy.

210

I glanced out into the church house. Indeed it seemed, to my imagining eye, the throng of "tribes and nations" gathered before God's "throne of grace!" Although the triadic Polynesian harmonies of the Samoan community, which now fill this church each Sunday at 8:30, would remain unsung that morning, their music seemed implicit in the festive garments of Samoan members present.[12] We seemed a miniature of the church—*color, dress, adornments juxtaposed,* struggling to learn the ways of understanding and mutuality, of maintaining the identities so evident in the panoply of garments while receiving each other's gifts with reverence.

*T*he African dress I was wearing that morning was a gift of friendship and of deepening hospitality. On other festive occasions, I'd been content to echo the bright African garb of my fellow singers with a swath of Kente cloth draped over my right shoulder. But for this occasion, Pat insisted, and offered to help me find an appropriate garment. Her insistence, I realized, was not about conformity but about participation— an invitation to enter the community's experience more fully; to taste something of their dignity as persons of African origin; and to savor our shared spiritual identity as children of God. Moreover, it was an invitation to enter the music more fully—to put on garments of festivity and service, to enter the praise.

We'd spent the day before searching several African markets in Oakland for the right dress. As we wandered through aisles of brightly colored garments, scanning racks of hats, dresses, tunics and pants in bold and subtle designs, stopping to try on an attractive piece here and there, I realized that my pale skin was no match for most. I lacked the rich complexion that could set off their brilliance, their boldness. Finally we settled on a long and flowing tunic and matching draped trousers, with intricate patterns in subtle shades of brown, rose, turquoise and gold, giving off an overall hue of rich plum.

*A*s we processed down the center aisle that Sunday morning to the rhythmic pulsing of "Lord, let your Spirit fall on me," I could feel the music in my heart inhabiting this new garment, spilling through its folds of brown, its circles of gold, with each progressive "step." Margaret Fisher reached out a reassuring hand as we passed, smiling her approval. "Lord, let your Spirit fall on me," we chorused again, the repetitive lyrics and energetic rhythms inviting everyone to join the music-making—bodies swaying, hands sounding clapped praises—all the while Bessie Brooks overlapping our invocations with her ad-libbed interpolations. *"O-oh, let it fall on me!"* she chanted. "Let it fall on me!" *Color, sound, movement* seemed to conspire, to flow from person to person, joining us as one resonant body. As we reached the sanctuary, the bishop took his place atop the three-stepped platform. The church house pulsed now with the insistent plea, "Lord, keep your hands on me! Keep your hands on me!" The only voice missing from the jubilant music-making that morning was Brother Banks, hospitalized once again because of his ailing heart.

"Let us rise for the reading of the Gospel!" called Pat Goodall a bit later, filling in for Brother Banks. The Gospel that Lenten Sunday was the familiar account of Jesus' transfiguration. As I listened to Deacon Ricardo Viray proclaim the story, the Lukan imagery came alive in a new way—Jesus' divinity revealed to his disciples through garments as brilliant as the sun! Human signs of his resplendent identity, confirmed by a voice from the cloud that proclaimed, "This is my Son, my Chosen: listen to him!"

Jesus is the Light, Light of the World!

we chorused as we welcomed that "good news," reiterating that truth over and again.

Jesus is the Light, Light of the World!
Jesus is the Light, Light of the World!
He's forever shining in my soul![13]

Carried aloft by Reed's modulation, we launched a second time into that vivid proclamation that "Jesus is the Light, Light of the World!" Everyone seemed swept into the flow. *"He's forever shining in my soul!"*

Indeed, that Light of the World shining in the soul of each one present, especially the *confirmandi*, was key to the bishop's message. Jesus calls us to be "unlikely heroes," he claimed, standing now in the open space just in front of the altar. Jesus calls us, as he called his own disciples, to be precisely that— unlikely heroes.

"Jesus the Christ, walking through the dusty streets of Jerusalem and along the shores of that lovely lake of Galilee, called forth, from darkness into light, men and women—and they were very, very ordinary people. *(Yes! Amen!)* They weren't the wealthy of the day, *(Yes!)* they weren't the politicians of the day, *(Amen! Yes, Lord!)* and they weren't even the *clergy* of the day. *(Amen!!! That's right!)* They were tax collectors, prostitutes *(Yes!)* and fishermen *(Amen!)*—very ordinary people. . . . They were with the Lord for three years and still they didn't understand him. *(Yes! Amen! Yes!)* When he died . . . they ran away. *(Yes!)* . . . They were cowards, *(Yes!)* and not even the events of Easter could change that! . . . They were afraid! *(Amen!)*

"What happened to turn these cowards into heroes? . . . The answer is very simple but terribly profound. The answer is love. *(Yes!)* They experienced the love of God. *(Yes!)* They experienced that love at Pentecost, when God came to live not beside them, next door or down the street from them, *(Uh huh . . .)*

212

but *in* them. *(Yes! Yes!)* They were now the house, the home, the dwelling place, the *temple* of God on earth. And they thought that was good news *(Yes!)* . . . and set out to bring that good news to the ends of the earth. . . . The love of God had changed their lives forever. *(Amen!)*

"God continues to call unlikely heros," the bishop concluded. "He called all of you, *(Yes!)* and he called me. *(Yes!)* He called us individually, *by name,* in baptism. *(Amen!)* . . . And this is the faith that you who will be confirmed are confirming today. You are saying to me and to the community that you believe . . . that you have been called by God, by name, . . . that this is good news, and that you are going to bring that good news to your world. *(Amen!!)* . . . Our world needs to hear that message of love, *(Yes! Amen!)* to know that we are not alone, that God is with us. *(Yes!)* . . . God has placed that message of love into your wonderful hands. Our world will never receive that message unless it receives it from you. *(Amen!)* . . . Our world needs every one of you, *(Yes!)* no exceptions!"

I glanced around the room—a church house full of "unlikely heros," bedecked in garments that in some small measure allowed that "light of the world . . . shining in my soul" to glisten, to be refracted in so many hues and colors, ages and dispositions. The bishop had come to confirm seven members of the parish. But late in the liturgy—the church house having been filled over and again with the rhythms of the Spirit, with a panoply of sound and movement, drumming and praising—he confirmed this little community of unlikely heroes and their place in the archdiocese. Congratulating the *confirmandi,* thanking all for their welcome, Bishop McGrath concluded:

"My special and sincere thanks to the choir, the director, soloists, pianist, drummer for a sterling job! *(Amen!)* All of you added prayerful beauty, and I mean *prayerful* beauty to the liturgy! *(Yes!)* . . . The archdiocese, our local church, is so blessed in this community, because you add so much vibrance and life to the church of San Francisco. You are indeed an important part of the mosaic that makes up the family of our church. I am grateful to all of you and ask God to bless you and the archdiocese through you. . . ."

*L*ast night was a jubilant night! From the first singing of "We've come to praise the Lord, our King!" by the combined choirs gathered for a night of Revival, to the closing "Victory is mine!" the evening was replete with singing, praying, preaching, and testifying. The church house was full to capacity. Four choirs were present to offer their musical ministry—Zion Hill Baptist, St. Patrick's, Rose Olivet, and Emmanuel Baptist, and of course, the Lourdes Gospel Choir. Colorful choir robes filled the first eight pews on the right side of the church, while a row of youngsters, eyes wide in anticipation, assumed their regular places in the front pew to the left. Father Kenneth Crowe-Hamilton, S.V.D., was revivalist for the evening.[14] Although Father Ken had not previously met the Lourdes community, there was immediate rapport—a shared cultural heritage, a reservoir of common songs, a set of ritual strategies, a warmth and a welcome. From the beginning, a mood of hospitality and festivity prevailed—a sense of freedom, relaxation, enthusiasm, honesty, and sheer joy.

As the evening progressed, it was clear that people were touched. During the "altar call" for the laying on of hands, Mary Fields shouted her praises after Father Ken prayed with her. Only weeks before, Mary testified to the church that, through three years of an unidentified illness, only faith had kept her going. This community "brought her back to life" with their love, faith, support and prayer. Now the memory of God's healing seemed to envelop her body and find a voice in her *Hallelujahs!* Carlos Hernandez was in tears as well, hugged by a choir member after Father Kirk laid hands on him in prayer. Carlos's mother died of colon cancer in December, he told me later that evening. His father, recently hospitalized, came close to death three times in the past week. The press of Father Kirk's hands on his head, the prayer, the song encircling him, had comforted his weary heart.

Throughout much of the evening, the four choirs wove a tapestry of praise and testimony. Reed remained on the piano bench through most, catching even the least-known tune and fashioning an inventive accompaniment on the spot, rich with syncopations and embellishments. Isaiah Brown never left his drum set. The first time the Lourdes choir spread out across the front of the church to sing, Pat Goodall invited the other choirs to join us in the sanctuary, expecting they would know the song we were about to sing. Colorful robes filled the front of the church house—blue and gold, black and white, tan and green—Lourdes' blue robes set off by a new drape of Kente cloth.

"He's blessing me!"[15] we chorused exuberantly. Indeed, the other choirs knew the tune, the lyrics, *and* the dance-like "turn in place" that would erupt several times during the song.

> He's blessing me, over and over again!
> He's blessing me, right here where I stand!
> Every time I turn around he's making a way somehow!
> Over and over again, he's blessing me!

Nearly half of those who fill the church house seem to be on their feet, punctuating the upbeat phrases with handclapping, swaying with abandon.

"He's in my mouth!" sings Rose Isles, evoking our response:"Oh, yes, the Lord is blessing me!"

He's in my feet!	All: Oh, yes, the Lord is blessing me!
He's in my hands!	All: Oh, yes, the Lord is blessing me!
He's in my heart!	All: Oh, yes, the Lord is blessing me!

The repartee flows into a new chorus. This time, however, the singing will be arrested midstream:

> He's blessing me, over and over again!
> He's blessing me, right here where I stand!
> Every time I turn around . . .

Halfway through the phrase, lyrics give way to a few bars of syncopated "dance music," as piano and drums send the colorful amalgam of singers into a full 360-degree turn-in-place, arms waving in the air, bodies swaying from side to side as we circle round.

> Every time I turn around . . .

Once again, robes swirl as songsters turn in place, enjoying every step of our danced testimony. The rhythmic pivoting reverberates through the church, mirrored by circling bodies in various parts of the room as dancing congregants negotiate the hemmed in spaces between the pews with aplomb.

> Every time I turn around . . .

Set in motion once again, savoring the delicious beat and the feeling of shared joy, we swirl once again before completing the testimony:

> . . . he's making a way somehow!
> Over and over again, he's blessing me![16]

I could feel my spirit rise, my body relax, the burdens of the day lift from my shoulders—chased to the winds by the sheer exhilaration of this spirited affirmation of God's provident love.

When the time for preaching came, Father Ken's message was clear. Taking John 20:19-23 as his text, he proclaimed that Jesus is *breaking into our lives tonight,* just as he broke through the locked doors behind which the disciples huddled that first Easter evening.

But knowing well that hearts are opened by song, Father Ken began his preaching with a medley of "old gospel songs"—among them the favorite spirituals, "I'll fly away, O glory!" and "This little light of mine!"as well as Aretha Franklin's spirited version of Clara Ward's "How I Got Over." Nary a songbook in sight, yet voices swelled from the entire church house. Reed never missed a beat, matching Father Ken's pirouetting from one song to the next with his consummate art of improvisation.

"How I got over," we chorused exuberantly at Father Ken's lead, people rising to their feet, joining spirited bodies to sounds of remembrance and trust. A member of the St. Patrick's choir, seated in the fifth pew, grabbed her tambourine and the tiny metal disks began to sizzle. "How I got over," we repeated.

> Well my soul looks back and wonders how I got over
> How I got over, how I got over!
> You know my soul looks back and wonders how I got over!

> Just as soon as I see Jesus *(Oh, yes!)* the man who set me free, *(Oh, yes!)*
> He's the man who bled and suffered, *(Oh, yes!)*
> you know he died for you and me. *(Oh, yes!)*
> I want to thank him because he brought me, *(Oh, yes!)*
> I want to thank you Jesus because you taught me, *(Yes!)*
> I want to thank you because you kept me, *(Oh, yes!)*
> I want to thank you because you never left me. *(Oh, yes!)*
> I want to sing hallelujah!! *(Oh, yes!) I just might shout this evening! (Oh, yes!)*
> Well my soul looks back and wonders how I got over!
> // : How I got over, how I got over!
> You know my soul looks back and wonders how I got over. . //

As verse after verse unfolds, hands wave in testimony above the pulsing vibrations that fill the church house. These old-time songs, with their repetitive lyrics and simple harmonies, evoke layers of accumulated meaning, rekindling an experience of God's faithfulness. The sibilant sound of tambourine, the exhilarating throb of the drum, the movements of people's bodies all prepare a way for the cool refreshing words of the Gospel.

"Despite rumors of Jesus' resurrection," continues Father Ken, his voice animated as he walks around the left side of the sanctuary, free of the ambo and his prepared text, "the disciples huddled in fear. *Can I hear an Amen?*" he asks rhetorically, since the *Amens* have been flowing ever since he began his preaching. "On that Easter evening, Jesus came *through* the doors, as he does in our midst this evening, and says, 'Peace // be with you!' *(Amen!)* 'Peace // be with you!' See my wounds. . . . *Touch* my wounds // so that you will know that *I know yours* as well. *(Yes!)* . . . That I suffer with you. *(Yes!)* // I *feel* with you! *(Yes!)* // I *experience your pain,* // so that now I can *heal* you. // Now I can show you the way. // Now I can bring you to greater life. 'Peace // *be with you!*' *(Amen!)* //. . . And Jesus *breathes* on us, as he did on his disciples, . . . *breathes his very life* into us . . . saying 'Whose sins you shall forgive, they are forgiven. // Whose sins you shall retain, they are retained.' // *You* have the

216

freedom to bind others or free them. *(Amen!)* // *You* can be a minister of healing. . . . *You, too,* // can offer that peace // can offer the peace of Jesus." *(Amen!! Hallelujah!)* . . .

Amens continued for some time after Father Ken concluded his preaching. *Amens* rang out again as the Lourdes choir moved into place. In fact, the evening seemed to peak, to reach a climax, an apex that gathered up all the prayer and preaching, song and testimony, as Reed sounded the opening measures of a song that begins gently, only to soar into a torrent of invocation. Mike in hand, Ernestine Harris steps out in front, her tall graceful body erect and calm. The choir is already swaying to the slow pulse of Isaiah's drums. Then, in hushed but rhythmic throbbing, choir and congregation sound the first entreaty:

> Order my steps in your Word, dear Lord![17]
> Lead me, guide me, every day.
> Send your anointing, Father, I pray.
> Order my steps in your Word.
> Ple–ee–ase order my steps in your Word.

Ernestine takes the lead, matching our gentle tones with her silvery plea.

> Humbly I ask thee, teach me your will,
> while you are working, help me be still.
> Though Satan is busy, God is near.
> Order my steps in your Word.
> Ple–ee–ase, order my steps in your Word.

Suddenly breaking into full volume, her head thrust back, Ernestine implores that "the words of my mouth be acceptable in thy sight! Take charge of my thoughts both day and night! Order my steps in your Word, Ple–ee–ase, order my steps in your Word."

A burst of energy from the choir, like a dam breaking, a shout to the Almighty—

> I want to walk wor–thy!! *(Yes!)*

we exclaim, cutting off the last syllable with percussive intensity. *Yes!* and *Amen!* ring out, filling the musical space. People in various parts of the church house have risen to their feet.

> My calling to fulfill,
> Please order my steps, Lord, // and I'll do your blessed will.

I can see Liz Bell standing behind the last pew, hands waving in the air in affirmation.

The world is full of changes! *(Yes!)* / / but you are still the same
if you order my steps, I'll praise your name!!

Isaiah's bass drum and hi-hat cymbal are throbbing, now, as we chorus:

Show me how to *walk* / / in your Word!

The swaying line of blue-robed choristers on either side of me breaks into a
rhythmic walk, stepping in place, arms in motion, as we implore:

Show me how to *talk,* in your Word!
Find me a brand new song to sing!
Show me how to let your praises ring,
in your Wo—rd!

The sound is intense, the energy of voices straining to capture the deep feeling
that sends each invocation soaring through the gathering. "In your Wo—rd!"
we sing again, in a final burst of fervor before spiraling down once again into
the hushed tones with which we began the song, cooling down the fires enkin-
dled, the feelings unleashed. With each closing entreaty, energies come to rest
a bit more.

Ple–ee–ase, order my steps in your Word!
Ple–ee–ase, order my steps in your Word!
Ple–ee–ase, order my steps in your. . . .

The phrase breaks off. Piano, drums, and voices pause, as Ernestine leads us
lyrically into the final cadence:

. . . in yo—ur
[All:] Word!

The sound swells dramatically again, crescendoing into an emphatic *Amen!* as
applause rises to meet it. *Thank you Jesus! Amen!! Please, Lord! Amen! Amen!
Amen!*

*L*ast night was indeed a jubilant night! I sit at my writing desk this morning, musing on the events of the evening. There's a wise and holy psychology,
I realize, that seems to permeate an evening of revival and that seeps into all
liturgies at Lourdes—an assumption that to engage in *metanoia,* that change of
heart by which we "let go" into the work of God, one's body needs to move so
as to release the burdens that so easily take up residence in our muscles and

sinews. One needs to *feel* a surge of deep joy—indeed a godly joy—that releases the tensions, the restrictions of body and spirit that so often hold us bound. One needs a community, a shared understanding that conversion is something of the total person, that singing and dancing are pathways of faith. There needs to be preaching—truthful preaching that heals the soul and sends one out to bring that same truth to others; preaching laced with song, the old songs that "lift up the praises," that carry the resonance of generations who have journeyed before us.

There's a mysticism here—not the solitary inner quest for a still center,[18] but a self-forgetfulness that is communally generated—a moving into one's whole being, releasing both the thoughts that tyrannize the imagination and the hurts and struggles that lodge in our muscles and flesh. It's a mysticism that is musically invited, the repetitive rhythms and lyrics releasing the mind and allowing the whole mind-body-spirit to move as one into the Other—an Other who is already intimately bound up with this faith-filled assembly who journey together.

On an evening like this, conversion and praise, healing and thanksgiving are deeply interwoven— ordering our steps, ordering our tongues, enabling us to "walk in your word," to find "a brand new song to sing," learning how to "let your praises ring," to return the gift of song to the Giver who dwells among us, amidst our singing and dancing. Last evening it seemed we entered the "cosmic dance," realizing together that

> . . . no despair of ours can alter the reality of things, or stain the joy of the cosmic dance which is always there. Indeed we are in the midst of it, and it is in the midst of us, for it beats in our very blood whether we want it to or not. . . . [W]e are invited to forget ourselves on purpose, cast our awful solemnity to the winds and join the general dance.[19]

*I*ndeed, we were in the midst of that godly dance . . . and it was in the midst of us. . . .

Chapter Fourteen

"DIG DOWN DEEP!"

—WOMEN LEADERS—

"*T*here's a woman who speaks to my soul," remarked Louise Wood as she stood at the ambo to the left of the sanctuary. Her eyes danced above the folds of her blue choir robe. It was a cold January morning in 1995, the fourth week of Kwanzaa. Louise—a mother, grandmother, business woman, member of the Lourdes choir and director of the Lourdes "School of Religion"—was addressing the Lourdes community, gathered for Sunday worship, about what it means to "build the kingdom of God on earth," to offer him "our *total service.*"

"This woman," Louise continued as she opened a small book resting on the ambo, "says it so much better than I can. You know, there are some people who have a way of putting things that brings out something in you *(Yes!)* that you didn't know you had!" *(Amen!)* The author of these words was Sister Thea Bowman. The occasion, Sister Thea's testimony to the U.S. Catholic Bishops in July 1989. The room is hushed as Louise begins to read:

> What does it mean to be black and Catholic? *(Well . . .)* It means that I come to my church *fully* functioning! *(Al'right! Amen!)* That doesn't frighten you, does it? *(Hum . . .)*

Louise glances up at the community with a smile, catching their response.

> I come to my church *fully functioning. (Oh, yes!)* I bring **myself,** // my **Black** self, // all that I am, *(Yes!)* // all that I have, *(Well . . .)* // all that I hope to become. *(Al'right!)* // I bring my *whole* history, *(Yes!)* // my *traditions,* my *experience,* my *culture,* my *African American song* and *dance* and *gesture* and

movement // and *teaching* and *preaching* and *healing* and *responsibility* // *as gift* to the church. *(Al'right! Oh, yes!)*

"Did you hear what she said," asked Louise, looking out again at the community. *(Uh huh . . .)* "She brings *everything*! *(Amen! Yes, Lord!)* That's how *we* have to be. *(Yes!)* If we want to build the kingdom of God on earth, we have to bring *everything*!" *(That's right!)* Then glancing down at the text, Louise continues,

> I bring a spirituality that is *contemplative* and *biblical* and *holistic*, *(Yes!)* // bringing to religion a *totality* of mind and imagination, // of *memory*, of *feeling* and *passion* and *emotion* and *intensity*, // of *faith* that is *embodied*, // *incarnate praise*. . . .[1]

As I listened to Louise, these words of Sister Thea seemed to capture the leadership of women musicians at Lourdes. Indeed, these women bring the fullness of their womanly experience as gift to this community. They bring their African American culture and traditions; their song, their dance, their gesture, movement, teaching and healing. They engage imagination, memory, emotion and intensity in expressing a *faith that is embodied, incarnate praise.*

Women musicians[2] at Lourdes are liturgical leaders. They play a central role in Sunday liturgy, leading the community in worship—in praise and thanksgiving, in beseeching God for mercy and strength. They give testimony, in word and song, to what God has done in their lives. Moreover, through this liturgical ministry, their spiritual authority is both expressed and affirmed by the community—an authority that is rooted first in their deep faith and their sense of God-given mission. Women singers describe themselves as "disciples," as "messengers," even "preachers," who have been entrusted by God with a message that can bring healing and consolation, as well as challenge, faith, hope and an experience of God's love. The community, in turn, by "receiving" their song and responding to their ministry, attests to the strength of their witness and confirms their spiritual authority. "We've watched them grow in the Spirit!" commented Liz Bell. "We know they've experienced what they sing about!"

As the liturgy drew to a close that January morning, Louise Wood stepped out to lead the closing song—a rousing "old, old gospel" tune that reiterates her commitment to "bring everything" to the work of building the kingdom of God on earth, to serve the Lord "till I die!"

> I'm on the battlefield for my Lord!
> Yes, I'm on the battlefield for my Lord!
> And I promised him that I // will serve him till I die!
> Yes, I'm on the battlefield for my Lord![3]

A few weeks later, Louise met me as I arrived at Lourdes. She looked radiant that morning, dressed in a long, bold-print African tunic in brown, white, red, orange and black. Five rows of beads in similar shades of orange, brown and white and a large gold chain with pendant hung gracefully from her neck, and a scarf in matching print encircled her head, setting off her face and cascading down the left side of her head. "Here!" she said to me, pressing a small paperback into my hands. "Read the section on music and spirituality. I think you'll like it." I glanced down at the cover, recognizing immediately the luminous face of Sister Thea Bowman garbed in brilliant African attire. "This woman describes what I feel," remarked Louise. "I come to the church with my *whole person*. Service, *service*," she reiterated, "is very important to me—anywhere, but especially in the church. I'm working to go *home!*"

❦ ❦ ❦

*I*t's not easy to sing a gospel song—to engage deeply enough with the message that others can feel "your soul flowing out with your words." Women musicians at Lourdes invest great energy in discovering that place of "soul" within themselves, in finding the inner authority from which to witness to God's action, in touching that place deep within themselves where faith gives birth to song, and in learning to capture in voice and body *"a faith that is embodied, incarnate praise."* At times, they hand on what they've learned, woman-to-woman—as in the process that unfolded during a choir rehearsal early in my time at Lourdes.

A question arose that Thursday evening as to who would sing lead on Andraé Crouch's "The Blood will never lose its power," a song already familiar to the Lourdes community. Rhoda Charles offers to try, although leading the community in song is still somewhat new to her. A gentle, soft-spoken woman, with loose buoyant curls encircling her rounded face, Rhoda is a medical assistant at a local hospital, preparing to be a community health worker. This song, with its images of blood, of power and strength, will no doubt be a challenge to her gentle spirit.

Rhoda clasps the mike in one hand and a xeroxed copy of the song's lyrics in the other as she steps out in front of the other choir members who stand in loose formation across the sanctuary. Even in an empty church, one's sense of ministry to the community is important. Reed's improvisation leads Rhoda into the first verse. Her body rocks gently as she begins deliberately.

The blood that Jesus shed for me,
way back, // way back // on Cal–va–ry,

> the blood that gives me strength // from day to da-a-y,
> it will ne–e–ver lo-o-o-o-ose its power!

Midway through the verse, Pat Goodall moves near Rhoda and rests a hand on her shoulder. "Dig down," Pat exclaims, and with the movements of her own body, prompts Rhoda to release more energy into the song. "Dig *down*," she calls again, as she signals Reed to circle back into the same verse. *"Dig down to your **toes**!"* Pat cries. Rhoda, with a look of determination in her eyes, begins again, "The blood that Jesus shed for me. . . ." Pat's movements become more animated. Her back is bent slightly forward now, her arms reaching down, pulling up, pulling up, gesturing Rhoda to find the sound deep in her body, deep within her own soul. Pat seems to be shaping, with her own body, the inner space, the inner authority, she wants Rhoda's voice to claim.

It's not easy to sing about the blood of Jesus "that gives me strength from day to day." It's not easy to tap into the depth of feeling that surrounds that image, especially at Lourdes. The blood of Jesus, in the words of one writer, carries a "massive concentration of Black [experiential] energy."[4] Early in my time at Lourdes, I asked Sister Irma Dillard about its potency. She looked at me with a look of truth-telling—reminding me of the powerful memory of blood shed by Black Africans on the American continent; blood shed through lynching, beating, assassination; blood shed for the sake of liberating a people yoked by slavery and racism. Moreover, she added, the blood of Jesus *is* the guarantee that the liberation they died for is already accomplished. Rhoda's challenge is clear.

By now Rhoda is stretching into the space that Pat is creating with her movements, struggling to discover a deeper resonance, a richer vocal timbre. Chest forward, shoulders slightly back, she breathes deeply and presses into the message. Someone calls out to her, "Rhoda, you can do it!"

> . . . the blood that sets me free // from day to da-a-y,
> it will ne–e–ver lo-o-o-o-ose its power!

Releasing the phrase into the almost empty church, Rhoda sighs, relieved to have the choir join her in chorusing:

> It reaches from the highest mountain,
> it flows to the lowest valley.
> The blood that gives me strength // from day to da-a-y,
> it will ne–e–ver lo-o-o-o-ose its power!

It's like giving birth, this singing—releasing from oneself an energy, an authority that lies deep in one's experience and that gathers force around each word, each musical line, each embellishment. One "delivers" a song, breathes it forth as richly personal, born anew in this moment, invested with womanly power to touch another, to meet another on the level of truth, lived truth, embodied experience, communal wisdom. One must know the blood of which one sings.

❧ ❧ ❧

*E*aster morning, 1996, dawned bright. The stories of resurrection and deliverance proclaimed, sung, embraced in our vigiling the night before seemed to linger as fragrance in the church house now filled to capacity with community members and visitors, young and old, all in their Easter finery. Lourdes' Easter hanging—portraying Mary Magdalene, her arms outstretched, reaching toward the risen Jesus as he makes himself known to her in a garden near the tomb of his burial—hung gracefully at the focal point of the church.

"The Lord be with you!" exclaimed Father Kirk as he lifted the Lectionary to proclaim the Gospel that April morning. Echoes of "every knee shall bow, every tongue confess that Jesus Christ is Lord!" which had just welled up from the entire church house, still hung in the air. We were now well into the liturgy, and Father Kirk was about to recount for us the events of that first Easter morning as recorded in the Gospel of John. The story begins with Mary Magdalene, who came to the tomb on the first day of the week searching for her beloved Jesus. Finding the stone rolled away, she ran to Peter and the "other disciple" to tell them the news. They came with her to the tomb and saw that it was empty. The "other disciple," finding the grave cloths, believed. But Jesus was not seen. "As yet they did not understand the Scripture that he must rise from the dead." "The Gospel of the Lord!" concluded Father Kirk. "Thanks be to God!" came the shouted response.

How distressing, I mused as the narrative came to a close. Mary Magdalene would be first to see the risen Lord and be sent by him as "apostle to the apostles." Yet the story of her encounter with Jesus, which follows immediately in the Johanine Gospel, remains untold this morning. Why is it, I reflected, that the women disciples to whom the Easter message was entrusted appear so little in the Sunday Scriptures assigned to Eastertide?

But at Lourdes that morning, there was no shortage of women witnesses, each of whom had their own good news to proclaim in song. "It's good to know Jesus!" declared Rose Isles with passion in her voice; "He's the Alpha and Omega, the beginning and the end, It's good to know the Lord!" Bessie Brooks felt such power rising in her as she led us in singing "Worship him, Jesus Christ our Lord" that upon reaching the last verse—"Let's just lift up holy hands, magnify his name and worship him!!"—her hands and body were in full motion, her feet seeming to lift off the floor in a slight jump as she proclaimed, *"He's all my righteousness! I stand complete in Him!"* Rhoda Charles, gathering all her inner strength as she stood now, not at rehearsal but in the presence of the community, announced that "the blood of Jesus will *never* lose its power!"

Among these "witnesses," Judy Brown was first to claim the Easter miracle as her own, and in so doing, to invite the community into a common testimony that "With his blood he has saved me! With his power he has raised me!" Moments after John Brown proclaimed the appointed passage from the Acts of the Apostles to the *Amens* of several in the church house, Reed begins to weave a gentle, fluid introduction, freely arpeggiating each of the song's first phrases. Two measures later, Isaiah's foot sets his bass drum resonating with a rhythmic pulse that sets the bodies of several members of the assembly swaying. "Oh yes!" Brother Banks calls out, as Judy moves out into the open space between choir and congregation, the tall white Easter candle just to her left. Concluding their introduction, Reed and Isaiah pause momentarily.

"How // can I say thanks,"[5] Judy begins freely, her voice unfettered by steady beat or metered measures. Reed begins to weave gentle arpeggios around her every phrase: ". . . for the things *(Oh, yes!)* he has done *(Yes, Lord!)* for me!" "*Yes, Lord!*" calls Louise Wood from the alto section, already moved by the message. Her shouts of *"Oh, yes!"* and intermittent handclaps become more insistent as Judy continues:

> Things *(Oh, yes, Lord!)* // so undeserved, *(Well . . .)*
> yet he died // to prove his love for me!" *(Oh yes!)*

As I glance to the rear of the church, I notice that Liz Bell is already on her feet, both hands waving in the air. Others, seated in the pews, are likewise nodding, rocking gently, a few hands raised in testimony. The emotion in Judy's voice intensifies. Despite an edge of tiredness—the fruit of three days of intense singing—she soars, pushing to reach the crest of the melodic line, infusing the lyrics with affective intensity, as Isaiah, rapidly stroking his cymbal, prods her along.

> The voices of a million angels // could not express // my gratitude! *(Well . . .)*
> All that I am *(Yes! Oh, yes!)* // and ever hope to be–e–e, //
> I owe it all *(Yes! Oh, yes!)* to thee!" *(Yes! Oh, yes!!!)*

Judy's words of gratitude ring true. So many times in this church house she's prayed in thanksgiving "for all the blessings he's given me and my family!" "You have to feel the words" I remember her saying, "before someone else can feel them, before they can touch somebody's soul and lift their spirit!" Members of the community discern the difference. "If the singer isn't really sincere," one noted to me, "no matter how powerful the words are, it's not the same."

Suddenly, the song settles into a strong, stately duple meter. Choir members on either side of me begin to sway rhythmically as the church house is swept into a full chorus, people singing with abandon, moving with the fervor of jubilant praise, while Judy echoes and embellishes each half-phrase.

> To God (to God) be the Glory! (be the glory!)
> To God (to God) be the glory! (the glory!)
> To God (to God) be the glory (be the glory) for the things (for the things)
> he has done!
> With his blood (with his blood) he has saved me! (has saved me!)
> With his power (with his power) he has raised me!
> To God (to God) be the glory for the things (for the things) he has done!

Without a moment's hesitation, Judy launches into a new verse, nudging the rhythm ever so slightly, and transforming the lyrics into personalized words of invocation and testimony. People seated in the pews call out their ascent, making her testimony their own with shouts of *Yes!* and *Yes, Lord!*

> Just let me live my life, *(Oh, yes! Yes Lord!)* may it be pleasing Lord to thee,
> *(Yes!! Oh, yes!)*
> and should I gain any prai—se, let it come from Cal—vary! *(Yes!!)*

A wave of full-throated sound spreads out across the church, gathering old and young alike in a steady-pulsed affirmation that "With his blood he has saved me! With his power he has raised me!" Isaiah's drums throb as we mount the last spirited acclamation, "To *God* be the glory for the things he has done!"

Judy presses into a reprise of her last verse. Rhythmic clapping breaks out among the choir members and spreads quickly to other parts of the church house, thickening the rhythm and layering a new wave of energy. Judy's voice is almost raspy now, but the strain in no way inhibits the power of her testimony, which seems to flow through her from some deeper source. I recall her telling me once that sometimes, when she's singing, a feeling comes over her. "I can feel the hand of God on my shoulder. I can feel him there, and when he touches you there's nothing you can do. You just have to let go and let God. You can't hold it in. The Spirit is there. God is more powerful than we are and we cannot hold that Spirit in. We have to let it go and spread it out so that everybody else can feel the Spirit."

Shouts from the community make clear that they are receiving the message she proclaims, accepting her as a reliable witness to this good news and affirming her spiritual authority to proclaim the truth that she has experienced.

She in turn, by giving voice to her own faith experience, is attesting to what *community* knows to be true as well. The overlapping dialogue between lead singer and persons around the church house seems to merge into a resonant whole, into a common voice of testimony. *"Sing it, Judy!"* someone prods from the first row.

> Just let me live *(Yes!)* my life, *(Oh, yes!)*
> may it be pleasing Lord to thee, *(Al'right!)*
> and should I gain any prai—se, let it come from Cal—vary! *(Yes! Thank ya'!)*

A surge of chorused voices rings out, proclaiming for a last time that "With his blood he has saved me! With his power he has raised me!" Judy's voice infuses each phrase with her own response, claiming an alternating melodic foreground as she reiterates that indeed the Lord has both "saved me" and "raised me!" Reaching the song's final acclamation, Reed and Isaiah slow the rhythm into a broad *ritard*, swelling beneath a final, harmonious acknowledgment, "To *God* be the glory, for the things he has done!"

Even before we've stopped singing, the church is ringing with handclaps and cries of *Amen! Thank God for the blood!"* shouts Jean Alexander from the far end of the soprano line. *Amen!* someone answers from the pews. *Amen!* calls Louise Wood from the altos. *Thank you, Lord! Praise you, Lord!* answers Brother Banks over the lingering sounds of Reed's final arpeggiated flourish. *Yes, Lord Jesus!* murmurs Jean Alexander as choir members return to their seats. *Yes, Lord!* comes one last response as the church house stills to a hush.

I asked Judy Brown one Sunday how she, a woman in the Catholic church, a Black woman in the Catholic church, came to take this kind of leadership— not only in her musical ministry but through the other roles of leadership she takes at Lourdes. She immediately credited Father Don MacKinnon and Father Gary Pometta, Redemptorist priests who reopened Lourdes in the late '60s. "They empowered us . . . they taught us that this is our church and we have to run it. . . . Things were totally different in Louisiana, where I came from. But here, it all started with the Redemptorists [who said to us] 'It's your church! We're here as spiritual leaders. . . . We're here to help you . . . but it's your church.' So we took it from there. . . . All of our pastors that have come after the Redemptorists have continued in this mode. This is your church and you're the leaders of the church, regardless if you're women or men. . . . Sometimes it's hard, but . . . God wants us all to work. . . . The women here are more in tune [with this]. We're finally getting the men in tune as well. . . .

"I think women hold the church together," she added, referring now to the whole Catholic church, "they hold the church together. It's the women who bring their families to church; they bring their husbands, they bring their children. It's the women, regardless of what [others] say, that hold the church together."

227

I inquired what difference it makes that women are so much in leadership at Lourdes. "It's more inviting," Judy responded. "There's more warmth here. . . . In most of the churches that are run by men, things go by the book. . . . [We've learned that] wherever the Spirit leads us, that's how we need to go. . . . We've been truly blessed by pastors [who affirm:] 'This is your church and you're the leaders of the church.' . . . It allows us to be free. . . ."[6]

Women singers at Lourdes are part of a legacy of women musicians who, by handing on the faith in song, have had a powerful influence in the Black community. In the words of Cheryl Townsend Gilkes, "Black women are largely responsible for shaping what is distinctive and defining in the black sacred music tradition."[7] They have been central to the gospel song tradition from its inception. As composers, publishers, evangelists, and most especially as singers of gospel, women have been carriers of religious knowledge and soulful faith through their music-making. "The crystallization of the image of God as 'a Mother to the motherless and a Father to the fatherless,'" fixed in Black expressive culture through a gospel song made famous by Clara Ward and the Ward Singers, "is but one important indication of their importance."[8]

It's striking that the face of gospel singer Mahalia Jackson, known as the "queen of gospel," appears among the saints and holy witnesses whose images surround this church house. Her mouth open in song, her eyes directed upward, Mahalia takes her place here among other women of powerful faith—Sojourner Truth, Sister Thea Bowman, Sister Josephine Bakita of the Sudan, and the early Christian martyrs Perpetua and Felicity. Mahalia represents a legacy of women gospel singers revered by the Black community as spiritual leaders. Her voice epitomizes the soulful sound that women singers at Lourdes emulate. Lyrics of the songs she popularized have shaped the religious vocabulary and theological imagination of generations who have heard and experienced her gospel singing.

But the tradition of sung faith handed on by women extends beyond those artists whose names are numbered in the annals of gospel history. The humming, "moaning," singing of so many mothers and grandmothers, aunties and friends, human mothers and spiritual mothers lingers in the minds and hearts of their children. I remember Brother Banks saying that his mother could talk about Jesus! She could sing about Jesus, because *she knew* what he had done for her! The spiritual authority of lead singers at Lourdes is rooted in this tradition as well—a legacy of faith that's reliable because these women are reliable. "We know they've experienced what they sing about!" "We've watched them grow in the Spirit!"

*I*t began as a tribute to the women. A few weeks before Mother's Day, 1995, nine men of the parish, including five who sing regularly with the Gospel Choir, joined forces *and* their voices to honor the women on "their day." Mothers, after all, play a central role in the community and are held in great esteem. After two rehearsals, this little band of men—who six years later would become the Lourdes Men's Choir—felt ready for the occasion.

As we gathered that May morning there was a note of expectation in the air. Women musicians had abandoned their blue choir robes and were seated around the church house amidst families and children, claiming their roles as mothers and grandmothers, and clearly enjoying this tribute, this affirmation, this expression of gratitude for who they are and all they contribute to the community.

Looking handsome in their dark suits, and to the great delight of those gathered, especially the women, the little retinue of men processed through the church house as the liturgy opened singing,

> This is the place, now is the time, we are the people // Jesus had in mind,
> gathered in this place // at this appointed time!
> We've come to pray, Let's get Jesus on our minds!⁹

Brother Banks was the first to wish the women a "Happy Mother's Day! (*Amen!*) We thank *God* for giving us mothers!" he added, "for turning that job over to the ladies! Because if he had given it to the men, we would *really have been in a mess!! (Amen!* Laughter . . .*)* God loves the mothers!" he continued, his voice animated." That's why he asked the Holy Mother to be the mother of his Son. Her answer was Yes! (*Amen!*) Many of these mothers have said yes, too. They've had to go through trials and tribulations (*Oh, yes!*) but they *should be honored and praised,* in the name of Jesus. The men are going to be singing today. Wait until you hear them sing! (Appreciative laughter . . .) *The angels in heaven are gonna shout today!* We're gonna *enjoy ourselves, thanking Him for **all** his blessings*—for all the mothers, mothers who've passed, mothers who are here, and for *all his blessings,* in Jesus' name."

"Nobody could put it better than Brother Banks has done," added Father Kirk. "We honor those women chosen by God to be mothers. In our community especially, that role is *central, **absolutely the center** of holding us all together*. We thank God and we *lift up all these women* as we begin in the name of the Father, and of the Son, and of the Holy Spirit." *Amen!!*

Claiming that he had no experience of motherhood, Father Kirk invited Jean Alexander to come forward, after he proclaimed the Gospel, to offer reflections on the Scriptures. An attractive woman, looking handsome this morning in a white silk suit rather than her usual blue robe, Jean walked to the open space in front of the altar, the very place she stands so often to lead the community in song. Today her message would be of love; of a mother's love for her children, despite the challenges; and of the strength she finds in a woman known here at Lourdes as "the Holy Mother."

"I didn't come here by myself this morning," Jean began, gesturing out to those seated in the pews. "I sought out some of the mothers whom God has *filled with the Holy Spirit* and with faith, and who have built a family. *(Amen!)* I got their . . . blessing to stand here before you to talk about the love of mothers.

"The readings this morning talk about love. And we know, as mothers, what love is all about! *(Amen!)* We have to love ourselves first in order to give love. We were taught that by our mothers. *(Oh, yes!)* . . . Yes, we thank the Lord for giving us mothers. He knew what he was doing when he made mothers, because mothers are there *all the time*, just like Jesus! *Jesus is there **all the time***. Mothers are there all the time, no matter what her child might do, they are still her child! Our kids do wrong . . ." [you could feel the experience in Jean's voice . . .] "but *they are still ours!* They are our gift from God. *And he didn't say our way would be easy!* *(That's right!)* . . . We have to be patient, we have to sacrifice! . . .

Jean talked about being raised with those "old time values" of love and respect, learned from the example of a mother, a father, sisters and brothers, in the closely-knit village in Louisiana where she grew up. The "old folks" taught their children to listen. Our children need these old-time values today. They need the courage to do right. But we can't give up on them. We must pray for them. We must pray for love. "Jesus gave it to us. He didn't just say, 'Go love!' He gave us himself. *(Amen!)* That's what the old people did. *(Amen!)* . . . They took time and patience to love and nurture us."

Then lifting up the "Holy Mother" as source of strength, Jean concluded, "God gave us his mother *(Yes!)* to pray to, love, and respect. We pray to Mary *(Yes!)* and ask her to give us the *courage* she had *(Well . . .)* when she had to stand and see her child nailed to the cross. *(Oh, yes!)* . . . She *stayed there* when others left, *(Yes!)* she and the rest of her women friends. They prayed *(Yes, Lord!)* and they cried. . . . Mary was blessed from day one with the Holy Spirit. *(Amen!)* And I feel God does that to every woman mother. He gives us that *courage* that we need when *things get so hard we don't know which way to go!* We say, 'Lord, have mercy!' . . . I talk to other women and they go through the same thing. *(Amen!)* . . . But we have to put God first! *(Amen!!)* . . . We have to take time to pray *(Amen!)* and say, *Lord have mercy!* *(Amen!)* [We have to be] a witness for God! . . . We have to *proclaim the word!* *(Amen! Yes!)* . . . *You can't be ashamed about Jesus!*" *(Yes, Lord!)* . . .

Then, abandoning her preacher's voice for song, Jean broke into a free interpretation of the lyrical strains which the little band of men had sung earlier this morning. "This is the place! *(Well . . .)* Now is the time! *(Yes!)* We are the people *(Oh, yes!)* Jesus had in mind. // We gather in this place *(Well . . .)* // at this appointed time *(Yes! Well . . .)* // we gather here to pray // we come to pray // so let's get Jesus, // let's get Jesus, // on our mind!" *(Amen!!! Amen!* Applause . . .)

Corey Monroe was among the men who sang that morning, lending his voice in tribute. As we reached the Prayer of the Faithful, a youthful smile broke out on Corey's face. He prayed his thanks to God for his own mother, who died ten years ago. He prayed for his two sisters, present this morning, who are "strong mothers" to their kids. He prayed for his Auntie, and so many other women who are going through difficult things with their kids. Corey knows these stories well from counseling young men. "We're losing our kids every day!"

Then glancing out at Jean, seated once again in the third pew, he offered thanks for "Mrs. Alexander, [who] filled in so many spots my mother wasn't here to fill. . . ."

"We're makin' it," he concluded. "We're makin' it, because of the *strong mothers!*"

*I*t was late in the liturgy on a cloudy March Sunday in '94. The hours we had spent together that morning, gathered around the word of God and the Lord's table, had been full of song. One by one, women musicians had brought their distinctive voices to the message of faith.

The liturgy opened with the rousing sung testimony, "You don't know what you're missing if you're not serving God!" with Judy Brown, Louise Wood, Pat Goodall and Rose Isles sharing the lead. Jean Alexander summoned us a bit later to respond, "I'll say *Yes!* Lord, *Yes!* to your will and to your way!" and chiding us, as she does often, to*"Sing out, Church! We're here to praise the Lord!"* Denise Alexander electrified the church after the Exchange of Peace, arousing us to proclaim that *"He's worthy! He's worthy! He's worthy! The Lord is worthy! He is worthy to be praised!!"* Rita Johnson's voice carried a special poignancy as she implored God in our name, "We need to hear from you! We need a word from you! If we don't hear from you, what shall we do?"

As we lingered after Communion, one song flowed into the next, prompting Judy Brown to come to the ambo and exclaim, *"It's so good to feel the Spirit in this church today!"* (*Amen!*) Then releasing the microphone from it stand, she continued, "Bear with us, Church! A lot of people have asked for special requests! Today I want to dedicate a song to my mother and grandmother. These women have played strong and positive roles in my life! (*Amen!!*) Pray for me, Church!"

Judy steps out into the open space as Reed weaves a gentle introduction to her song. Already, you can sense in the church house that she has tapped into some deep feeling, some experiential knowledge—a legacy of "strong mothers" and grandmothers who have been positive role models, who have been, in the words Judy is about to sing, the "wind beneath my wings."[10]

"It must have been you there in my shadow," Judy begins, "drawing me closer into your reign . . ." I notice Denise Alexander walking across the sanctuary from the alto section. She slips in behind her mother, Jean, who is seated among the sopranos, softly wrapping her arms around Jean's shoulders. Jean's eyes close and they begin to rock gently as Judy continues,

> You have always been there with love divine
> waiting for my life to shine.
> I was the one seeking for glory
> While you were there offering your strength
> but all of the glory was in your name
> There's not been once you put me to shame.

"Why is Niecie crying?" I hear little Tyree ask from the front pew. Shirley Valmore, who is holding him on her lap, wraps her arms a bit tighter around him. Judy herself is visibly moved, prompting Rose Isles and Pat Goodall to walk toward her, standing to either side of her in support. Rose rests a hand on Judy's shoulder as she catches a quick breath, then soars toward the apex of the song:

> Did you ever know that you're my hero
> and everything I'd like to be.
> I can fly higher than an eagle
> But you are the wind beneath my wings!

Al'right, daugh'er! Take your time! calls someone from the front as Judy struggles to continue on through tears that now moisten her cheeks.

> I may have appeared to go unnoticed
> but I've got it all here in my heart
> and I want you to know, I know the truth *(Take your time! Take your time!)*
> that I would be nothing without you!
> Did you ever know that you're my hero
> and everything I'd like to be
> I can fly higher than an eagle *(Yes!)*
> But you are the wind beneath my wings!
> And you'll always be, you'll always be my hero!

Pausing momentarily, her left hand waving in the air as if to testify to these great women on whose shoulders she stands, Judy slows into a final declaration:

> You are the wind beneath my // wings!

Shouts of *Oh yes! Amen!! Amen!!* and a rebound of applause fill the room, as Judy breaks down in tears of gratitude. Pat and Rose, standing beside her, enfold her in their arms. *Amen!!*

*W*omen musicians . . . liturgical leaders . . .
"strong mothers," grandmothers, teachers and role models . . .
women whom "God has filled with the Holy Spirit and with faith"
. . . credible witnesses . . . bearers of an African American tradition
of sung faith . . . bringing "song, dance, movement, teaching and healing
as gift to the community" . . . engaging "memory, feeling and passion,
emotion and intensity" . . .
expressing a *"faith that is embodied . . . incarnate praise."*

Chapter Fifteen

"THE SPIRIT INCORPORATES THE BODY"

—A VISION OF COMMUNAL LIFE—

*I*t was but a small fire built of twigs and scraps of wood that John Brown had gathered earlier that day. In the chill evening air, as we huddled in the dark courtyard just beside the church house, John was tending the fire, stoking it a bit here and there as it crackled in our midst. Suddenly, a strong March wind blew in from the bay, invigorating the dancing flames, fanning them into a blaze of amber light that reflected in the faces of those huddled around it for warmth. Just then, Father Tom Hamilton[1]—a friend of Lourdes who was replacing Father Kirk during his sabbatical in Rome—walked through the church doors and down the several steps into the courtyard. A large white candle rested against his broad shoulder. It was Easter night. Faces glowed in the firelight, as he traced a large cross on the white candle. Then taking a spark from the fire, Father Tom ignited the candle and, lifting it high, walked toward the church house. Still shivering a bit from the cold, we followed him up the steps into the dark church. "Christ, our Light!" he chanted, his voice full and resonant. "Thanks be to God!" came the exuberant reply. A few children scurried through the little cluster of people still halted at the rear of the church, anxious to be the first to light their tiny white tapers from the large Easter candle. Tiny flames began to spread, passed from hand to hand, candle to candle. A soft glow of light filled the rear of the church house, readying us for a few hours of vigiling. . . .

Warmth still permeated the room long after the candles were extinguished and the church house had been restored to full light—a warmth, an energy that now seemed to travel from heart to heart. By the time we reached the Gospel proclamation, there seemed an electricity in the air. For some forty-five minutes we had been awash in stories, prayer and song—tales of God's creation and Abraham's faith; chronicles of the great exodus and God's promise of an everlasting covenant; songs of deliverance, of "coming this far by faith *leaning* on the Lord!" and of "telling ol' Pharaoh to *'Let my people go!'*" With each progressive song, the prayer affections of those present became more translucent—carried like sparks on *Amens* that rippled through the room and made evident in a head nodding, a hand waving gently. As Judy Brown led us in "To God be the glory!" the sparks seemed to catch fire. Each phrase of her sung lyrics seemed to draw her more passionately into the words she proclaimed, while members of the choir punctuated her lines with *Yes, Lord! Thank you, Jesus! Oh, yes!* A last, ardent chorus of "To *God* be the glory!" ignited a wave of *Amens!* that rippled through the church house.

"Let us rise for the reading of the Gospel!" shouts Pat Goodall as Reed Fromer segues seamlessly into the slowly paced, hymn-like harmonies of "He is Lord!" Father Tom, standing at the ambo, takes the Lectionary in hand, raising it gently as a surge of chorused sound bursts forth:

> He is Lord!! He is Lord!
> He is risen from the dead and he is Lord! *(Amen!)*
> Every knee shall bow, every tongue confess
> that Jesus Christ is Lord!

I notice tears welling up in Pat's eyes as she signals the choir into each successive phrase, her gestures intense and animated, her eyes closing now as if to hold in the swell of emotion that fills her body. My own heart is stirred.

"Thank God for the blood!" shouts Jean Alexander as Reed weaves a facile modulation to the next highest key, lifting the reverberating praises to another level of intensity. I can feel each slow repeat of *"He is Lord!"* move through the blue-robed line of singers like a swelling wave that finally crests in a last ardent confession that "Jesus Christ is Lord!" There's no stopping the cries of *Hallelujah! Amen!* and *He is Lord!* that seem to bounce off Isaiah's final drum flourish and Reed's last chordings, each acclamation evoking another shout of *Amen!* or *Hallelujah!* from elsewhere in the gathering in a regenerating cycle of praise. "Are we ready to hear the Good News?" asks Father Tom gently as the shouts continue, knowing full well that the gospel is already coursing through people's minds and hearts: "He is risen from the dead and he is Lord!!!"

*P*erhaps it's the shared vibrations, the participatory rhythms, the diverse voices sounding together. Perhaps it's the feeling of freedom and abandon that seems to overtake the community as we sing, ignited first like tiny sparks, then fanned into flame by a seeming March wind that moves silently but powerfully through the church house. In moments of song like the one we experienced that Easter night, something seems to take hold, to move within and through the singing, to travel from person to person, to catch fire. You feel drawn in, connected, touched by what is happening to others, joined by some inner force.

People at Lourdes claim that the Holy Spirit is at work, "circulating with power," drawing them into an experience of being one body; enabling them to be channels of life, vessels of spirit and of grace one to another; bonding them in a way that honors the giftedness of each one while effecting a deep sense of unity. What emerges, in these moments of song, is an experience of the "body incorporated"—a vision of communal life, of "what church is all about," not just when we sing and gather for worship, "but all the time."

*M*embers of the community describe this experience of "incorporation" from different vantage points—that is, from where they find themselves in the music-making. From her perspective as choir director, Pat Goodall recounted how the process unfolds as we spoke one Saturday.

"Sometimes we start a song and it's not quite flowing the way I'd like it to flow. Some sort of energy gets charged in me. . . . I get an inner feeling that just drives me. . . . I can't really explain it. . . . My hands get to flyin' and my body gets to wigglin'. . . . The choir picks it up and comes with me. . . . I bring them up by the gestures of my body [and it seems that they become] part of my body . . . I'm part of them and they're a part of me. . . . It's like our bodies all become one. . . . The Spirit really takes over and joins us all as one . . . as one energy, one big gigantic energy. . . . It's not individual energies. . . . It's not about the lead singer. . . . It's an energy that comes from us as a group. . . . We're emerging as one large spirit rather than as individual spirits . . . or voices. As a choir, we hope that the spirit in which we bring forth the song will somehow reach others, will draw them in.

"And sometimes, there's a feeling that comes over the whole church . . . and people just get into it. . . . They get up out of their seats! . . . When the spirit is strong, it touches everybody, not just a few. . . . It often starts off with the choir . . . but once the spirit starts to rise, it's so strong that it reaches out and just pulls people in, like magnets. . . . Pretty soon everybody's in it. . . ."

I looked up at Pat. "You seem to say that something is unleashed that is beyond the capacities of the group. . . ."

"And that everybody feels," she replied.

"That creates something that wasn't there before?" I asked.

"There's a surge of the Spirit," Pat affirmed, nodding. "We're giving and the Spirit comes over, reaching from one to another and combining us in the one Lord. . . . It's spontaneous, and it flows out into the community at large. . . . [It may begin] with the lead singer, the energy of the singer flows out, first to Father Kirk and then to Mr. Banks and then to the whole community. This is what it means when the Spirit incorporates the body. . . .

236

"It's what church is all about . . . not just at this time but *all* the time, even though it's hard to maintain. . . . It's a healing, it's an awareness, it's a life style . . . what life should really be all about. . . ."

*S*peaking as those who make music from the pews, Tina Edwards and Tiffany Isles describe the "incorporation" as the "whole community walking up the hill. . . ."

"When a singer *really* believes what she is singing," began Tiffany, "you can feel her soul flowing with her words into your ears. . . . We feel the emotion [that's coming] from her, and we feed back to her the strength and energy [she needs] to sing the song." "It's like you see one person walking up the hill," added Tina, "and we're standing outside looking at her. Someone just takes her hand and starts walking and pretty soon the whole community is walking up the hill. . . ."

*L*ead singer Judy Brown offers her own perspective. "It's hard to sing to people that are not showing any emotion. But when you look around and see the faces of people, you see them rocking with you, perhaps a hand waving, you see that they are listening to the words you're singing, that they're in tune with you and not just sitting there like statues, it encourages you to go on. It helps a lot when the church is with you."

"And sometimes it seems that something catches on," I prodded, "something catches fire."

"There are times when the Spirit is so high," Judy responded, "it touches everybody, not just the choir—everybody. The whole church, the whole community, has to be into the song, into the worship. It's not just about the choir, it's about the whole community. We minister to them. . . . But the whole church has to be in one communion, like we sang this morning 'One bread, one body, one Lord of all.' If we continue to be one body then we will continue to grow. . . . We have to keep in mind that God loves us. There are different spirits, different gifts, but there's only one body. And that body is God. We're all working for that one body. . . . We all have to be in tune with it. When the church as a whole participates, you know that the Spirit is here in this church. There's a 'sweet, sweet Spirit' and it's the Spirit of the Lord."

*T*he "incorporation" that takes place musically, the "vision of communal life" that emerges in the song and the singing, are a *lived metaphor* for the Spirit's work in the community all the time. Preaching on Pentecost 2003, Father Kirk describes the Spirit's work and its impact on the community's mission in the world.

"Today, as we remember the first Pentecost, we have to remember what the Spirit invites us to do in *our own* community. *(Yes!) Every one of us* is a better person, is a better *Christian,* is a better *disciple of Jesus* precisely because we *belong to this community. (Yes!)* And the Spirit works *powerfully among us,* **circulating with power,** with *gifts,* with *insight,* with *love,* with *determination,* with the ability to *keep on going* even when we want to say, 'I quit!' *(Yes!)* . . . We get that in the strength of our community. The community is very, very important for an understanding of the fullness of what the Spirit means. Because all the gifts [we have] are given to us so that we can make the community *come alive! (Al'right! Amen!)* The gifts that I receive are not just for *me. (Amen!)* I can't say, 'Lord, thank you for giving me this' and forget my brothers and sisters! *(Al'right! Yes!)* . . . The gifts that each one of us has—and we *all have gifts! (Yes!)* **Nobody was left out, Church!** *(Amen!!!)* **Nobody was left out!** *(Amen! Thank God!)* Sometimes we don't want to *use* our gifts! *(Amen!)*—these gifts are for others. . . . We spend our lives looking inside and saying, 'Lord, *(Yes!)* what else is there *(Yes!)* that you have given me?' So as we continue our journey, it's a journey of self-discovery in light of God's *Spirit. (Yes!)* We *all* have these gifts! But they're given *not just to us* as individuals. *(Uh huh . . .)* They're given primarily to enrich our community. Because when the community is weak, the members are weak, and the ability of that community to serve in the world is very narrow and small! *(Yes! Amen!)* But when the *community is strong, (Yes!)* **the power of God is strong!** *(Amen! Amen!)*

*T*estimonies—personal accounts of God's action in *my* life—are another occasion at Lourdes when the Spirit can "circulate with power," enabling individuals to be vessels of life and hope one to another. Like song, testimonies given and received can open the channels of grace, deepening communal bonds, allowing people to taste what it's like to be "incorporated" into one body, in faith and the Spirit.

You could see this process unfolding one chilly February evening, the closing night of Revival 2002. For three nights now, people have filled the church house, singing, praying, "enjoying themselves in the Lord!" Visiting choirs clad in colorful robes have taken their turns engaging us in song—treasured spirituals, newer gospel songs. Revivalist Sister Beatrice Jeffries, S.B.S., standing each night in the mist of the gathering, has developed the theme of her preaching: "Our God is a *healing* God!" The cadence in her voice resonates with the Louisiana roots of many in the community. The warmth and conviction in her stories, poems, and parables have evoked delight and knowing *Amens.*

Halfway into in her preaching on the first night, Sister Bea's voice modulated into song. "Your grace and mercy . . ." she sang, and a wave of recognition sprang from voices around the church house. ". . . brought me through!"[2] came the answering swell of lyrics and the song was launched. In no time, Reed was back on the piano bench and people are standing, somewhat spontaneously, to join their rhythmic swaying to the chorused lyrics.

> I'm living this moment because of you! *(Oh, yes!)*
> I want to thank you *(Hallelujah!)* and praise you too!
> Your grace and mercy brought me through! *(Amen!)*

"Your grace and mercy!' shouts Sister Bea, inciting us to reprise the song, and we begin again, yielding to another wave of sung testimony: "Your grace and mercy // brought me through!" Yet again, as the chorus comes to a close, Sister Bea urges us once more into this river of song that now courses through the gathering, drawing us into a common voice of remembrance and thanksgiving.

As applause swells to cap the song's last phrase, Sister Bea cries out, *"I'm gonna praise you Lord!"* Her words fly rapidly now, carried on waves of feeling, holding us in the immediacy of the moment. Spurred on by handclapping and shouts from around the room, she continues, "I'm living *this moment* right here, right now, Lord, not because of *myself,* not because of any *good I have done, (Yes!) but because of what you have done for me! (Yes! Al'right!) God, your grace and mercy brought me through! (Yes!) When I didn't think there was a way! (Al'right!) When there was darkness in that tunnel! When I couldn't see a light (Yes!) you showed me a way out of no way! (Yes!!* Clapping erupts again. . .) *Your grace and mercy (Yes it did!) brought me through! (Yes it did!)* And I'm living *this moment, (Yes!)* // right now! // right now!" *(Yes!)* Sister Bea's voice drops suddenly, her tone hushed as she concludes, "because of you!" *(Amen! Amen! Thank you, Jesus! Amen!)*

Now, as we gather for the concluding night of the Revival, that moment of communal testimony will be refracted in the stories of God's deliverance told by members of the community.[3] At Sister Bea's invitation, several persons come forward, one after another, to tell how God has met them in the midst of their struggles— "making a way when there seemed no way"—and inviting others to know God's provident hand resting on them as well. As each one revisits the contours of God's love, they seem to hold out tiny tapers, offering sparks of faith to others who might wish to light their own. You can feel a resonance open up within the community—filled with supportive *Amens* and reassuring calls of *That's al'right!* with laugher and applause.

Victoria Stith, a choir member of five years, is first to come to the ambo. Standing tall before the community, she tells of the many years when "my life was in shambles. About seven-and-a-half years ago, I really called on God! *(Amen!)* My heart was in a lot of pain and confusion." But despite the turmoil, "God was watching over me. *(Amen!)* . . . He's done great things in me!" *(Amen!)* she proclaims "making me a better woman, mother, daughter, friend. . . . So if you or someone in your family is suffering, especially from alcohol or substance abuse, surrender to God! *Talk* to God! . . . *He is there,* but you've got to truly, *truly* call on him!" *(Amen! Amen!)* Applause swells, a wave of support and affirmation. . . .

Ralph Galloway is next to the mike. First "giving all glory and honor to God," Ralph recounts a lengthy tale, detailing the physical sufferings that brought him close to death on several occasions. A serious accident left his face crushed in, unable to talk. "They told me I would never walk again, *(Uh huh . . . .)* nor see out of this eye," he recalls. "But by the grace of God, *(Yes!)* I'm doing these things today!" *(Amen!)* More than once, tears well up *(That's al'right! Take your time!)* as Ralph describes his seven months of rehabilitation. *(Have mercy!)* Then double pneumonia. Three hospital stays left him in intensive care hanging on by a thread. Father Kirk anointed him, preparing him to go home to God. Yet "I kept praying *(Amen!)* . . . and one day they took me out of there." *(Thank you, Jesus!)* Slowly, he learned to walk again, to talk and reclaim the other skills he'd lost. One Sunday, Father Kirk spotted him in the entryway of Lourdes church house. "He called me Lazarus!" Ralph exclaims. *"Oh, thank you Jesus! (Amen!) I am nothing without him!"* adds Ralph. Then addressing "each and every one of you sitting here tonight," he reminds us, "You are an extension of one another." *(Amen!)* Be careful what you say and do, because "you never know who you are going to touch. *(That's right! Amen!)* . . . I say 'Thank you Jesus!' for the opportunity to speak to you the words that God has put within me, because without him, I am nothing!" *(Amen!!!)* Applause rings out again as Ralph concludes, "By the grace of God, we've *all* come a long way!" *(Amen!)*

Liz Bell, a gracious "elder" and pillar of the church, who spearheads much of its outreach to the neighborhood and city, is waiting near the front of the church house as Ralph finishes, anxious to add her witness to "what God can do!" *(Yes!)* "Years ago, when I first came to this church, I came with my head low," Liz recalls. "'*Old Slewfoot*' had hold of me! *(Laughter . . .)* . . . Tonight, I stand here to give you testimony: alcohol is just as bad as drugs! *(Yes! That's right!)* . . . One day I got down on my knees and I said, I'm tired! *(Amen!)* I'm turning it over to you! *(Amen!)* . . . Now I count the years! *(Al'right!)* . . . My prayers were truly answered!" *(Amen!! Amen!)* As on other occasions when Liz has witnessed to how God turned her life around, the wave of applause that rises speaks of the admiration and esteem of this community.

Carlos Hernandez, a young friend of the parish, is next to the ambo. Telling of the loss of both his parents during the previous fourteen months, *(Have mercy!)* both to cancer, he claims: "They were not cured, but they were healed!" *(Thank you, Jesus!)* Carlos recounts the story of his parents' bitter divorce, and of his father's visit to his mother during her illness, joined by Carlos and his brother. It was their first encounter in twenty-seven years! "I didn't even pray for that and it happened!" Carlos exclaims. "God is good!" shouts someone from the choir in response. "There is a God!" answers Carlos. "We don't get cured,

Church, but we definitely get healed!" As *Amens* ring out and applause swells, Reed weaves a musical commentary around Carlos's story, setting some of the choir to humming, "There is a power that will set you free some day!"

Two young members of the community are next to speak. Avery Collins, a lanky teenage boy, thanks Sister Bea, claiming that she "has really inspired me. *(Yes!)* . . . I've been through three foster homes, and I feel like a grown man because I had to take care of my little sister and brother." *(Yes!)* But because of "this woman . . . I've been feeling really good about myself this week. *(Al'right!)* . . . I've read the poems [she's given us] a million times, brought them to school. [They've help me understand and accept] my life and what I've been through." Avery's thanks to Sister Bea spills over into gratitude to all "those of you who have been there for me, like my 'Uncle' Reed[4] who always tells me what I can do and how to do it and how far I can get. . . . You are my family *(Amen!)* and I love you all from my heart." *(Amen! Amen!)* Once again, Reed improvises a gentle accompaniment beneath the appreciative applause.

Isaiah Brown, leaving his trap set to come to the ambo, reminds us that he's "been the church's drummer for more than a decade, and this church has been my family. *(Amen!)* . . . Each and every one of the church members is like a brother, sister, cousin, a mother, father or grandmother to me. *(Amen!* Handclaps . . .) . . . The two most important people in my life are my mother and father. *(Al'right!)* . . . Thanks to my parents I'm here today, because I lost two friends to [the violence of] Third Street." Unabashed by tears that well up, he continues: "I thank the Lord that I will be graduating this year from McAteer High School. *(Amen!!)* And Sister Bea, you truly are a messenger from God, because every night I've listened to every word you said, and I usually don't do that!" "*Amen!*" exclaims his mother, Judy, knowingly, from the alto section, as people surround Isaiah's words with applause.

Waiting her turn is Péla Tuimavave, a member of the Samoan community. "God is good!" she exclaims, and immediately the volley returns from around the church house, "All the time!" Péla tells us that she took part in last evening's Revival, bringing with her the youth choir of the Samoan community known as the "Young Prophets." She was so moved by what took place, she tells us, that she returned tonight bringing her sick husband, *(Amen!)* telling him of Sister Bea's message: "Our God is a *healing* God!" *(Yes!!* Applause. . . Reed begins to play gently . . .) "I just want to let Sister Bea know that the Lord works in mysterious ways! *(Yes he does!)* . . . I have been through some very tough times. Two weeks ago I had to bury my cousin who was like a brother to me . . . shot four times *(Have mercy!)* by another Samoan brother. *(Have mercy!)* . . . But we pray for that brother and forgive him. *(Amen!)* . . . Last Sunday, when I heard the Lourdes Miracles singing, I just cried and cried and cried! My brother loved to sing, he loved to lift his voice to God. *(Yes!)* . . . It touched my heart that he was gone, but then I smiled because I knew that he is now with the biggest and best choir in the whole world! *(Amen!* Applause . . .) . . .

"When we left [the church house] last evening," Péla continues, "a friend said to me, 'Girl you needed this!' *(Laughter . . .)* I did, and I'm blessed! I thank God! *(Yes!)* All day at work I said to myself, I am *blessed! (Yes!)* . . . I want to tell all of you, my sisters and brothers here tonight, *I love you all! (Amen!)* And Sister Bea. . . ." Tears well up as Péla continues. "I just want you to know that you're a *messenger! (Amen!)* . . . *The Lord works in mysterious ways! (Yes!)* . . . I want to end my testimony by inviting the Young Prophets to come up here to sing, "Surely the Presence." Because *the Lord is **truly** in this place! (Amen! Amen!)*

Slowly, a bit shyly, some twelve young men and women come forward, arrange themselves in the front of the church house, then fill the room with their strong, full-voiced harmonies:

> Surely the presence of the Lord is in this place! *(Amen!)*
> I can feel his mighty power and his grace.
> I can feel the brush of angels wings as his glory passes by.
> Surely the presence of the Lord is in this place.

A number of people are on their feet now, standing in support and appreciation, swaying with the undulating lyrics, and calling out words of encouragement, as the Young Prophets sing a second verse in Samoan.

Indeed, a sense of oneness seemed to envelop the church house. As each one spoke to us tonight, you could sense the deeper "grammar" of the struggle and faith they shared openly and freely. You could almost hear the music of God running through their lives, bringing change, turning them around, creating a new path. And you could feel something open out underneath us as we listened, sense it moving among us. "Surely the presence of the Lord is in this place," you could feel God's power and God's grace.

*M*any who have come to Lourdes over the years, who have sensed the "presence of the Lord in this place" and felt themselves "incorporated" into the community and its worship, do not share the African American heritage of the majority of the community. The vibrancy of Lourdes' music has been a powerful attraction. But as their stories reveal, music is inseparable from the whole process by which they have experienced themselves drawn into a community of faith, discovering within themselves new ways of worshiping God and a new spiritual rootedness.

• *L*ea and David Schermerhorn stumbled on Lourdes while on a bike ride through Hunters Point one Sunday in 1991. Passing the church, they heard singing coming from within, and realized it was the home of the Lourdes Gospel Choir whom they had heard some weeks before at a Union rally at Longshoreman's Hall. A few Sundays later, recounts Lea, when they returned to worship with the community, they were struck by "the spirituality of the people. . . . That's what attracted us. . . . I was raised Catholic, but I'd never before met people with so much spirituality that they openly exhibited! . . . When you meet them individually, they're ordinary people. But when they're all together, acting collectively, it's very powerful! It's their openness and spirituality. Other people talk about it, here they do it!" Lea and David, who both sing in a Slavonic choral group, found the music "very moving, very exciting. It's moving because the people are so moved by it themselves! That adds to the power. . . . The music and the songs enable me to pray!" comments Lea. "I find myself during the week singing the songs they sang on Sunday!"

For most of a decade, Lea and David arrived each week with at least one grandchild in arms. When celebrating their 30th wedding anniversary, their extended family filled two pews. Only recently, given family and other obligations, have Lea and David been unable to participate regularly.

• "*T*he first one I met was Brother Banks," recalls George Biniek describing a chance visit to Lourdes some years ago. It was a time of transition in his life. Arriving at the church that day,"I knew I was home!" The music, the warmth, the sense of community. . . . "I love to sing," George explains, "and despite the limitations of my voice, I realized, after I was here a while, that the choir would welcome me. I've sung with them now for six years. . . . I love all kinds of music . . . but when I sing gospel music, my *heart is in it!*" The week before our Easter "vigiling" on that chilly night in March, George's apartment burned, leaving him without possessions or a place to live. Members of the community offered assistance—including a bundle of household items which Mama Winslow had tucked in the trunk of her car that Easter evening—helping him get settled in his new home at the Catholic Worker. "I tell my friends," adds George: "If you ever want to find me on Sunday morning, I'll be at Lourdes."

•*A*mong those more recently "incorporated" into the family of Lourdes are Susan Wootton and her daughter Lynn Gardiner. Late in the liturgy one Sunday in 1998, as visitors introduced themselves to the community, Lynn and Susan were among them. Week after week they returned, often sitting near the front of the gathering, clearly engaged by what was happening. When the music was especially vibrant, Lynn, a slender blonde teenager, would stand to join others who were on their feet moving to the music.

One Sunday, as Reed wove an introduction to "Order My Steps" and the choir began to sway with the slow, pulsing rhythms of the song, Lynn walked from her seat in the third pew and stood beside Ernestine Harris who had just moved out in front of the choir to lead the song. Not knowing Lynn's pre-arrangement with Ernestine, I was startled to watch Ernestine put her arm around Lynn's shoulder and the two begin to alternate the lines of the song. I decided it was time to inquire about the story of their coming to Lourdes—why they came and why they have stayed.

When Lynn was in tenth grade at Marin Academy, a prep school across the Golden Gate Bridge from San Francisco, she heard about Lourdes from Reed, an alum returning as a guest arranger for their high school chorus. Her mother Susan, a bit reluctantly, agreed to accompany her to Sunday liturgy, checking first with Reed to make sure it was a safe environment. She'd heard rumors of the dangers of Hunters Point and wanted to ensure her daughter's safety.

"I was warmly greeted by everyone in the congregation!" she recounts with surprise. "Late in the liturgy, when Barbara McKinney thanked visitors for coming, she looked right at us and said, 'Our doors are always open.' Some churches *say* that but don't make you feel welcome." Lourdes was different.

Susan and her daughter are not Catholic. Susan was raised Methodist, and brought her children to the Arlington Community Church where her husband is a member. "One thing that draws me to Lourdes is the music," Susan noted. "It's inspiring music that reaches deep within you and makes you feel great happiness. . . . Every Sunday I count the choir. There are seldom more than thirteen, but they always sound like more! . . . They draw us into the singing. . . . But it's more than the music. It's the warmth, openness, interaction of the people; how the Word and Christianity come alive in a very interactive way. . . . Everyone is engaged from the time you arrive until you go home. It's the spirit, the culture, the music, the people. . . . Communication and love are going on every minute of the time. Love and friendship are just being bounced off the walls! . . . People call me by name! . . . They want to include us in their family. Rhoda calls me 'sister.' Among friends of mine, families are so exclusive. Family comes first. Here, how little I know them, still they embrace and talk about me as family."

I asked Susan if Lourdes has changed her perception of church and worship. "Indeed it has," she replied. "I'm no longer content to just sit in a pew and listen to someone. Interaction is key. I realize that it's key to Black culture as well. I was a teacher in the Richmond School District for seven years. I realize now why that school system doesn't work for Black students. There's no interaction! They get reprimanded for talking back! Here, it's so supportive to have someone say '*Amen!*' When I go back to my community church, I find I've embraced new ways. I'm currently in a period of religious growth. I'm reading with a friend about how to put faith into practice. I've started studying the Gospels. All of these I attribute to the energy, foundation, spirit I've found at Lourdes. It's a church that brings the Spirit and the Gospel alive so that I have the energy and desire to put Christ's love into practice!"

Susan's daughter Lynn, now an undergraduate at Cal State Hayward, tells of jumping at the opportunity when Reed invited her class to a Black Catholic church where gospel music is sung. "Everyone else wrinkled their noses. They're stuck in that world," she added, referring to the culture of Marin

County. "But although I wasn't raised to know African American people, I liked the way they worship. . . . The first Sunday we came, Louise Wood introduced herself to us and asked our names! . . . I was nervous being in that part of the city. I'd heard it was a bad part of town. But we came back and we've been here almost every week for five years. . . . The difference I find at Lourdes is that people worship and they're not shy to show it. In other churches, they keep it all inside. You don't know if they're thinking about God or not. . . .

"I was scared when I first came, but now I have a family," Lynn comments. "I've made friends with Isaiah. We went to my senior prom together! . . . It brought my new world to my old world! . . . Danielle Mackey—she and I have a nice bond. The first time I met her she hugged me with love and with no sense of competition. We're dear friends now. . . . I've adopted Juwan as my younger brother. He comes over to my house. I love to hear what his dreams are. . . . And I've adopted Harry Bryant as my grandpa. We always hugged at the exchange of peace, and I asked him one day, 'Do you want to be my grandpa?' I feel a family closeness to him. He brags about me and says, 'This is my granddaughter!'

"At Lourdes, I feel music move through my body. . . . I'm a dancer and a singer. Music moves me. I love to participate in the music, to stand up, clap, and move to the music. . . . [And the music stays with me.] I'm twenty, but still scared of the dark. The world seems unsafe. So when I find myself in the dark, I sing gospel songs and I feel strong! . . .

"I try now to be spiritually conscious all the time. . . . Two lines from the songs we sing at Lourdes stay with me all the time. 'Fill my cup, let it over-flow with love.' I can picture it in myself, in this church, in the whole world. I know that's idealistic, but you have to look for what you want to find. The other line, 'His praises shall continually be in my mouth.' When I'm walking, whatever I'm doing, I say 'Thank you!' All the time. Every single day. That's how the church has influenced me. That mantra is in my head. No matter what happens, I say 'Thank you.'

"When I leave Lourdes each week, I feel love bouncing off the walls. . . . The room is emitting love, love molecules, like heat molecules, are bouncing around! That's what I feel. When I invite my friends to come, I know they won't be bored, and that they'll feel the love. *People don't really know what love feels like!*"

*T*he crisp October air sparkled as people converged on Lourdes that Sunday morning in 1995. Archbishop John Quinn, no stranger to Lourdes, was among them. This was a significant moment for the parish. Weeks before, Archbishop Quinn had announced his retirement as leader of the San Francisco Archdiocese, and Father Kirk had invited him to preside and preach at Sunday liturgy in gratitude for his kindness to them. Archbishop Quinn, a gracious and unassuming man, who had been Lourdes' staunch advocate and supporter over the years, delighted in greeting members of the community as he arrived that morning.

It's now late in the service. Archbishop Quinn just has returned to his presider's chair after distributing Communion. His emerald vestments and white miter stand out against the African print draping the rear wall. Brother Banks is seated to his right and Father Kirk to his left, while blue-robed choir members surround them on either side of the sanctuary. A last surge of "Worship him, Jesus Christ our Lord. . . ." flows through the church as Communion ministers return to their places.

Reed is fingering the closing arpeggiated measures of "Worship Him," when Brother Banks, seizing the moment, rises to his feet and turns toward the archbishop. His voice full of animation, his head and torso bowing ever so gently as he speaks, Brother Banks begins to thank Archbishop Quinn—first, for allowing him to serve as deacon to this community; then, for enabling Lourdes to remain open when other parishes were being closed. Others voices chime in as a litany of thanks unfolds.

Never losing a beat, Reed modulates to a new key, and as Brother Banks's words of gratitude begin to taper off, Walter Turner steps out to intone "Jesus, keep me near the cross . . ." There's much more singing to be done. The thanks that Brother Banks has unleashed will erupt in song a few minutes later.

After two special requests, Judy Brown comes to the ambo. "Archbishop Quinn, this next song is for you from Our Lady of Lourdes Catholic Church. (Amen!) Take it with you wherever you go, because we will *always* be there with you!" (That's right!) The signal is clear. Choir members close in on either side of the archbishop and people from the front of the church come forward from their pews, ringing the sanctuary and spilling over into the center aisle, as Reed intones a familiar popular tune, a song the Lourdes community sings to persons who hold a special place in their hearts.[5]

No doubt this is a first for an archbishop, I muse to myself as Denise Alexander takes the mike in hand, even for one who has served his people for thirty-five years! Denise, standing now in the midst of the encircling community, turns toward the archbishop and begins gently,

And I never thought I'd feel this way,
and as far as I'm concerned I'm glad I got the chance to say
that I do believe I love you.

The lead shifts to Reed, seated at the piano, who continues to weave his piano harmonies beneath the unfolding lyrics.

246

> And if I should ever go away,
> well then close your eyes and try to feel the way we do today
> and then if you can remember. . . .

The song swells as people throughout the church house take up the chorus:

> Keep smiling, keep shining
> knowing you can always count on us, for sure.
> That's what friends are for!
> In good times and bad times
> I'll be on your side forevermore.
> That's what friends are for.

A smile has broken out on Archbishop Quinn's face as he glances around in amazement at what is unfolding! The circle of choristers are swaying gently from side to side as Denise eases into a second verse:

> Well, you came and opened me
> and now there's so much more I see!
> So by the way we thank you!
> [Reed:] And then, in those times when we're apart
> then just close your eyes and know these words are coming from my
> heart
> and then if you can remember. . . .

"Keep smiling," we chorus again, as if to ensure that the archbishop has tucked this scene deep in his memory.

> . . . keep smiling, knowing you can always count on us, for sure.
> That's what friends are for!
> In good times and bad times
> I'll be on your side for ever more.
> That's what friends are for.

"Archbishop Quinn," says Denise above the humming that ensues, "we'd like to thank you for all you've done for Our Lady of Lourdes." Then singing, she concludes, "Count on us for sure!" A last swell of sound from the community assures him, "That's what friends are for!" Applause and *Amens* erupt, the community encircling the archbishop with the sound of their tribute.

When the *Amens* finally subside, and Isaiah Brown's last drum flourishes taper off, Father Kirk turns to the archbishop and sums up what has just transpired. "Archbishop, Our Lady of Lourdes gives you its heart!" (*Amen! Amen!* Applause. . .)

Archbishop Quinn stands. "I don't know how to express the feelings my heart feels! But I am more grateful than I could ever put into words for the great kindness you have shown me, and especially for that beautiful song you dedicated to me this morning!

"You know," the archbishop continues, "I don't know all of you. And I don't know how you keep the commandments. *(Laughter . . .)* But I know *one* thing. You certainly keep that commandment that says, *Sing a joyful song to the Lord!* *(Amen!!! Applause . . .)* This has been a wonderful morning for me to be with you. I've experienced the depths of your goodness and your faith, and the depths of your vision and hope. *(Yes, Lord! Yes!)* God will bless that, *(Yes!)* and he will be with you, *(Amen!)* and *we will be with you! (Amen! Amen!)* I know of Father Kirk's great love and devotion to all of you. And we want to walk the journey with you! *(Yes! Oh, have mercy!) We're here to stay! (Amen! Amen!)*

I'm sure the archbishop felt the love and gratitude captured in the swell of applause that continued for what seemed several minutes. He, too, had opened his heart to us. As we stood there, still encircling the archbishop, hands and voices acknowledging our thanks and affection, I couldn't help but feel: ". . . *this* is what it's like when the Spirit incorporates the body."

"Lourdes is *indeed* a precious fountain . . . it keeps overflowing, overflowing. . . ."[6]

"No matter how many times we come to the well, it's always there for us.
We can come to the table and the food is there for the taking.
The well never runs dry.
The Spirit is there. The Spirit greets you at the door and says,
'Come on in my brother, my sister!
You're at home. Come on in.'
The circle is there. We can keep coming back.
God has put himself right in the midst of our song.
The circle closes. God holds us all—and we can feel the vibrations of his heartbeat. . . ."[7]

Intermezzo

EMBODIMENT

*T*raditions of Black music-making are holistic and embodied. They strive to encompass and express the whole gamut of human experience—to celebrate its fullness, to embody its integrity, to express its pluriformity, and to tap the outreaches of the human spirit. A gospel singer, for example, engages a broad canvas of vocal timbres so as to make audible the expansiveness of human thought and emotion. A jazz instrumentalist stretches the range and "vocality" of his respective instrument to articulate human feeling, memory, and desire in all their freshness and spontaneity. Moreover, Black music-making is replete with musical tensions that mirror the struggle-longing-fulfillment pattern of lived, human experience[1]—tensions that hold opposites in tensive dialogue: steady beat and syncopation; personal expressiveness and group solidarity; cross-rhythms and metric complexity.

Communicating this plentitude requires that the one making music, in all her bodiliness, remain at the expressive center of the music: to be first a listening ear, who can feel, "hear," intuit this range of human experience; and then a sounding body, who can channel these intuitions into sound, rhythm, movement, art. In fact, full engagement of the body as an expressive instrument is integral to the very definition of Black music, necessary for its existence.[2] Gesture and movement are never incidental nor simply an embellishment of the musical sound, but an essential part of the communicative art.

These holistic and embodied dimensions of Black music are especially evident in the gospel tradition and in the worship contexts within which it emerged and is practiced. Gospel music, writes Pearl Williams Jones, marshals all the Black arts—music, drama, movement, dance, and poetry—into one great synthesis[3] through which to express its life-giving and soul-stirring message. Spirituality, she comments, is the most potent force within this highly expressive medium—a spirituality to which the body is integral. Moreover, gospel performance style has been shaped by the dynamic interplay of persons that marks the Black worship contexts in which it has flourished—the "free-style impro-visations of the Black church congregations and the solo style of the black preacher."[4]

Worship and music-making at Lourdes are likewise holistic and embod-ied. The human body—that is the human person, body, mind, spirit as one in-dissoluble whole—is at the center of how the music and liturgy unfold. Bodily engagement is integral to how individual persons participate—musically, ritu-ally, spiritually; to how they communicate with others, and in so doing, shape the unfolding musical-liturgical event. In the course of the worship, and most especially when making music, the community as an "embodied whole" ex-presses itself in diverse ways, through changing patterns of how relationships are actualized and how persons experience themselves to be related to the whole. Bodily participation, both personal and communal, becomes a way of knowing God and the world, and of shaping and handing on a communal spirituality. Moreover, in the course of music- and ritual-making, the commu-nity "reorders" the ecclesial body, while storing the memory of this commu-nal transaction as a source of empowerment beyond the worship event.

Bodiliness / inspirited flesh / person-in-community: How is the human body integral to participation and communication?

At Lourdes, the human body is understood to be an instrument of praise and participation—a sounding, resonant instrument with the capacity to "me-diate spiritual experience."[5] In contrast to situations in which the body is sus-pect, a source of losing one's path to God, full expressive engagement in music and the gestures of worship "tunes" the body-spirit to praise and thanksgiving, to testimony and love. An expressive body is essential to the dynamism of preaching, the ardor of singing, the elan of participatory engagement. The body fully alive becomes an epiphany of the Spirit, an icon of a deeper life force that wells up within an individual and therefore within the gathered community.

Given this valuing, bodily engagement becomes pivotal to how community members deepen and personalize their participation; to how liturgical/musical leaders minister, and to how the worship becomes a living "event." Moreover, it is an essential way in which people weave webs of communication with each other, creating together a sense of "resonant community."[6]

From the time people arrive for worship until they leave the church house, they create together a strong kinesthetic base that grounds all other interaction —communicated through hugs, embraces, and kisses; through a hand resting on another's shoulder, or the arms of a grandmother around a child in her lap;

through a supportive standing beside a singer who is deeply moved by her song's message; and through rhythmic movement in harmony with others. These bodily modes of communication are ways of establishing relatedness, mutuality, and trust among members of the community. They become a context for healing, for growing into the godly qualities of self-possession and self-esteem. They communicate a sense of nearness and of presence, a metaphor-in-action, if you will, for the incarnate nearness of the God revealed in Jesus. Human touch becomes a way of acknowledging, blessing, and affirming the God-given beauty and dignity of each one; of establishing a felt-sense of the importance of each one to the whole. Moreover, this human communication creates a "resonant community": a sensitive and open relationship within the communal body, a sense of interdependence, a common readiness for those moments when something stirs within the whole gathering—those "gift" moments when people experience a deeper bond, a common "knowing," a taste of the Spirit's incorporation.

Within this framework, people engage in the worship, surrender themselves to the power and message of the music, and appropriate the impact of the preached word or sacramental action through a whole range of gesture and movement: rhythmic swaying, handclapping, gentle rocking, foot tapping, hands uplifted or waved in testimony, tears, head nodding. These gestures externalize the inner world of one's devotion, making it evident to others, while deepening one's participation in the joy of praise or the ardor of thanksgiving. What is important to note is that this repertoire of gestures, this idiom of bodily engagement, is culturally shaped—a ritualized pattern of participation, a vernacular, a kind of "mother tongue" that is cultivated within the larger African American worship tradition. While people's bodily ways of participating at Lourdes are varied and personalized, they are not primarily impromptu or self-styled; nor are they the purview of more extroverted members. Rather, these gestures are rooted in the practice of Black worship, a tradition that establishes them as a medium of prayer and a mode of spiritual participation.

For ministers at Lourdes, the whole human body becomes an expressive medium for proclaiming the Gospel and leading the community in liturgical prayer. The free movements and gestures of Father Kirk's preaching, for example, amplify the expressive range of his voice. Pat Goodall's body, set in motion as she directs the choir, communicates both the musical dimensions of a song—its rhythm, timing, and voicing—as well as the "feel," the intensity, the "dance" of the song. Each communicate bodily the surplus of meaning that eludes the spoken/sung word[7]—the aliveness of the "living Word," and the emotion, conviction, and enthusiasm it creates within their own spirits. Their gestures set off a reciprocal engagement within the whole community, an interplay of gesture which, like the verbal responses of *Amen! That's right, Yes, Lord!* transform the singing and preaching into a dialogic "conversation." As lead singer Judy Brown points out, seeing others nodding their heads, waving their hands, indicating they are receiving the message and "not just sitting there like statues," is crucial to evoking the fervor and dynamism of her song. Ministers do not minister alone but in mutuality with others.

Finally, music at Lourdes, with its strong rhythmic base, is pivotal to evoking people's responsive, holistic participation. "Music," writes Susan McClary, "has an uncanny way of making us experience our bodies in accordance with its gestures, its rhythms."[8] The complex syncopations, polyrhythms, overlapping voice parts, and vocal intensity of gospel music evoke reciprocal movements in the human body. Drums and piano are catalysts for movement; they "bring out the feeling and the power of the music." They are valued because they invite people to discover the rhythms of the Spirit within the felt rhythmic participation of the body. Moreover, this musically evoked participation— the whole church house caught up in rhythmic movement and dance—creates a sense of vitality, aliveness, vividness that bring the worship into its own as an "event" of God's active presence.[9] They create a "living space," dynamic and resonant, within which the community invites the presence of God's Spirit.

Polyrhythmic / contrapuntal / harmonious whole / sounding together: What experiences of communal embodiment emerge in the course of music-making?

Music-making actualizes relationships.[10] At Lourdes, music is a primary way people experience themselves to be a social "body," an ecclesial body, a faith community, a human community in solidarity with each other. As music sets relationships in motion, each song brings to expression a particular embodied experience of how the community is interrelated.[11] In the course of worship, differing experiences of communal "embodiment" come into being, are experienced, and impress themselves on those who participate as a "vision" of "what church is all about."[12]

Engaged in the unison singing of a repeated chorus like "Jesus is the Light, light of the world!" [Confirmation] or "He is Lord! He is Lord!" [Easter night], participants are drawn into a first mode of communal embodiment: a collective, unified action. This common and strongly united prayer gesture is grounded in the repetitive verse structure of the song, the recurring harmonies of its accompaniment, the regular pulse of the drum, and the common, rhythmic movements of those singing as they sway and clap. What emerges is a community acting, both gesturally and sonically, as *one harmonious whole*. Within this collective action there is always room for personalized elements—the lead singer improvising, and various expressions of bodily participation—but these are gathered up into the more pervasive sense of unified action.

In contrast, during gospel songs such as "Lord let your Spirit fall on me" or "Order my steps," which alternate between verses sung by a lead singer and chorused refrains, a second mode of communal embodiment emerges: personal expressiveness held in creative tension with strong unified action. Within this musical experience of "being-in-community," the personal contribution, initiative, and giftedness of individual members are highlighted, while at the same time, a strong sense of the community's unified action is maintained. Choral refrains provide the communal touchstone: vocal/instrumental harmonies and rhythms are coordinated; the voices of choir and congregation blend into one; and, on spirited, upbeat songs, rhythmic swaying and hand-clapping accentuate the corporateness of the action. In contrast to this unified action are many individual contributions to the song's unfolding: the solo singing of a lead singer on the song's verses; her melodic/lyrical embellishments and expressive gestures throughout the song; the creative instrumental improvisation of pianist and drummer; and the personalized movements, verbal responses, and diverse forms of participation by community members. In this highly interactive mode of communal embodiment, *solidarity and individuality are held in creative tension*.

During the Eucharist Prayer at Sunday worship, when music intervenes in differing ways as the prayer unfolds, a third form of communal interrelatedness is actualized. The whole community assumes the common posture of standing, with persons arranged in such a way as to "surround" the altar and the presider who leads the prayer—the choir standing behind the altar/presider facing the rest of the community. Within this centralized focus, a vocal interplay unfolds—the presider speaking most of the prayer and the community entering with periods of song. This interplay is not only an alternation of speech and song—as when the presider's proclamation of the opening of the prayer gives way to the hymning of the "Holy, Holy"—but speech, song and bodily movement are simultaneous and contrapuntal as well—as when the humming and gentle swaying of the choir undergirds the latter portion of the spoken prayer. The interaction becomes polyvocal and polyrhythmic: the free speech rhythms of the presider's voiced prayer create a counterpoint to the regular visual/auditory rhythms of movement, humming, and instrumental accompaniment. Music enables the community to participate in the action of the prayer in ways that are shared yet varied—*a unified body with diverse roles*—while maintaining a general postural expression of corporateness.

A fourth mode of communal embodiment unfolds during the Exchange of Peace, a period in the worship when music, at times, accompanies the free interaction of community members—weaving a sonic backdrop for the complex action. In contrast to the three forms of embodiment just described, the community's action during the peace greeting is centered in the initiative of each participant. Although people engage in a similar mode of action—moving through the church, embracing, engaging in conversation—the action is expressed in multiple and diverse ways by individuals with great latitude for personal initiative. In this final mode, the *communal body, in all its pluriformity*, comes to expression.

Thus, the communal embodiment evidenced at Lourdes—the felt-experience of being a social/ecclesial body—is not static but changing and dynamic; not a state so much as an action. The musically-mediated body-at-worship is an organic whole, changing and in motion—less a "being" and more a "becoming"—which defies any single "model," metaphor or "vision" of "what church is all about."

Mysticism / liberation / discipleship: How does the community, engaged as musical-ritual body, disclose a communal spirituality?

Caught up in the rhythmic movements and ardent singing of "To God be the glory!" witnessing the abandon of Brother Banks's dancing at the center of the worship gathering, experiencing a singer's "digging down" within herself to tap the core of her aliveness and passion, the Lourdes community discloses certain dimensions of a shared, embodied spirituality.

Among the most evident is the *pervasiveness of joy*—a joy that transcends words, that stirs the body as it fills the heart; a joy that erupts even in times of struggle and hardship, that is expressed in tears as well as laughter; a joy that springs from an assurance that the Spirit of God is present here, and that "God can make a way out of no way!" Indeed songs acknowledge the community's pain and sorrow, but are also a way of singing through the tears into a place of joy and reassurance that God's victory is already at work. Communicating that joy is a way of building up the body. Delight, exhilaration, jubilation, animation catch fire in the singing and circulate through the gathered community. Worship at Lourdes becomes celebration, festivity, rooted in the contemplative freedom to move beyond the "burdens that weigh me down," and experience a godly joy.

A second quality is the *centrality of demonstrative love*. Love "radiates," it "bounces off the walls," as members and visitors report, set in motion through kinesthetic, gestural communication that conveys acceptance, commitment, solidarity. Demonstrative love gathers all into a "family," while not requiring that those acknowledged as sister or brother be "intimates," persons who know each other well. People belong here; even newcomers and visitors have a place within this network of affirmative communication, simply because they are part of God's family.

A third dimension of this spirituality is a *non-dualistic embrace of God's created universe*. Spirit, soul and body, working as one animated, "inspirited" whole, are necessary for worship. Movements and gestures that might be excluded as "secular" in other settings of liturgical prayer— such as "danced," rhythmic, bodily participation in making music—are integral to how the Spirit is anticipated, welcomed, and "felt." Emotion and intellect, thought and feeling, are tightly intertwined in how the Gospel is proclaimed and received,

254

and how it impacts people's lives. A great latitude for personalized ways of engaging in the worship are held in creative tension with an embodied sense of collective action, creating a strong sense of person-in-community. In the adage voiced by Corey Monroe, "I am because we are."

A fourth aspect is the lived belief that *mystical experience of God's Spirit* is not reserved for a few "initiates" but available to all.[13] The Spirit is given to each one—no one is left out, as Father Kirk preaches. The performance dynamic of worship is intended to awaken participants to the vibrations of this Spirit within them—the living presence of God that pervades the created universe. This participatory mysticism involves full human engagement—mind-soul-spirit-body—in discovering and attuning oneself to that godly presence. It is a mysticism that, in the intense resonance of sung praise—*"Je-sus **excellent** is your name!"*—opens to the magnificence of God's transcendent power, while tasting the reassuring nearness of Jesus. It is an asceticism cultivated through regular, prolonged immersion in the community's prayer—tuning into how the Spirit moves others, experiencing the self-forgetfulness of giving oneself over to the communal dance.

All of these are related to a fifth dimension—the *realization of God's liberating intentions here and now,* not as an outcome of worship but as lived experience within the liturgical event. This expectation springs from a biblical perspective on God's liberation that has shaped the religious-cultural history of Black Americans.[14] At Lourdes, inner healing and renewal are integrally related to an expressive participation that releases one's burdens and lifts one's spirit. Interior liberation and renewal of the whole person are part of discovering Jesus to be the "Great Emancipator," as Charlene Edwards addressed him in song while Brother Banks danced. Webs of affective support and love woven at Lourdes enable individuals to experience themselves as a "child of God," as God's unique and intentional creation.

Inclusion / wholeness / power / authority:
How does this musical-liturgical practice "reorder" the ecclesial body?

*T*he embodied patterns of worship at Lourdes "order" relationships among members of this ecclesial body, and in so doing, "reorder" some commonly held expectations of Catholic practice. What becomes evident within the performance dynamic of Lourdes' worship is that the participating assembly as a whole—ministers and congregants together—is the base of all that happens.[15] As we have just seen, music-making, as an "experienced metaphor" of what the social/ecclesial body is like, actualizes relationships in such a way that makes room for all, holding personalized, inspirational, even charismatic expression, including that of those in leadership, in creative interplay with the interaction of others.

This in no way diminishes the crucial role of dynamic leaders—the pastor, deacon, singers, musicians—who are often catalysts of the animated participation of others. But leadership, as practiced by these persons, is reciprocal and dialogic, not over-against but engaged with the whole body. Pastors at Lourdes have empowered others to "be the church," to assume their appropriate leadership within the body—an affirmation that is demonstrated each time the community worships together. Beyond expected roles, children and elders take their place among those who serve within the performing assembly. Emerging leadership, such as the beginnings of a Men's Gospel Choir, is encouraged and fostered. Newcomers soon feel integrated into the whole.

What guides this "ordering" is a model of wholeness—what Judy Brown describes as "working for the one body," and Father Kirk images as the Spirit of God "circulating with power," giving gifts to all, with no one left out. Wholeness, as disclosed in the community's action, does not imply homogeneity or conformity but interdependence. A sensitivity to wholeness becomes a basis for discerning the Spirit's presence. As Judy Brown phrased it, "When the church as a whole participates, you know the Spirit is here."

Perhaps the most striking aspect of this reordering of the ecclesial body is the leadership of women, and the affirmation of their spiritual authority, of their "capacity for public spiritual leadership."[16] Inclusion, at Lourdes, is not so much a matter of language as it is one of action. "Inclusive language," a deep and very important concern in the American Catholic church and in all Christian liturgical practice, is not the primary preoccupation here. What is enacted instead is a "creative actualization" of an inclusive tradition,[17] with women taking liturgical-spiritual leadership—a fitting liturgical analog of the perception that "strong mothers"[18] are the center of this community, "holding us all together."

Women leaders at Lourdes, assuming their full Black heritage, come to their ministry "fully functioning," bringing, in the words of Sister Thea, their "African American song, dance, gesture, imagination, memory, intensity, emotion." Their ministry is potent and compelling, their leadership undertaken with dignity and grace. The roles they assume in leading the community's prayer evidence an historical "negotiation of power,"[19] an ongoing process of empowerment and mutuality that enables women to exercise their spiritual authority without others feeling threatened by their ministry. Indeed, the whole community is built up through their leadership.

Finally, in two instances of the community gathered around their bishops, we catch a glimpse of Lourdes' role in "reordering," in some measure, the "local church." What transpired during the visits of Bishop McGrath and Archbishop Quinn was replete with mutuality and support, as well as an affirmation of the contribution of this community to the "vibrance" of the church of San Francisco. Perhaps the most telling experience took place as the Lourdes community "encircled" Archbishop Quinn, committing themselves in song to an enduring "friendship"—"that's what friends are for"—and, as Father Kirk summed it all up, "offering him their heart." The archbishop's heartfelt words of thanks and appreciation seemed to seal a bond of reciprocity and solidarity—a "vision" of communal, ecclesial life.

Storing experience in the imagination / embodiment and empowerment: How does a musically experienced "vision of communal life" extend beyond the worship?

*J*oseph A. Brown—commenting on a scene from Toni Morison's novel *Beloved* in which "Baby Suggs holy" liberates a small band of women, men, and children who have gathered around her in a clearing, telling them to laugh, dance, and cry until a contagious joy erupts and envelops them in an ecstatic feast—paraphrases Baby Suggs's words to those gathered in the clearing: "If you are to keep the taste of this moment alive . . . then you must store up the power you have felt for the inevitable moment when you are challenged with destruction and annihilation. . . . She told them that the only grace they could have was the grace they could imagine. . . . Those gathered around the rock in the clearing," Brown comments, "are told to use their imaginations to see a world where they are whole, are valued, are completely at ease, and are joined in a circle of honesty and acceptance."[20]

Comments from several members make clear that at Lourdes "storing experience in the imagination" is intimately bound up with the power of their worship to impress itself on muscle and bone, to wind its way into spirit-soul-body, becoming a source of nourishment and faith, a strategy of empowerment in situations beyond the ritual. Recall Joan Dill's comment after one Sunday liturgy, "All the beauty I experienced this morning! I have something to feast on all week!"

This is especially true of music-making. The beat, the feel, the power of the music gets inside the body, continues to "play" itself in one's imagination—pulsing rhythms stored in muscles, mantras running through the mind. These rhythms and mantras, reawakened, provide avenues of faith, patterns of prayer, biblical wisdom and strategies for living to those who have embodied them. As Tiffany Isles comments, "Whenever I'm alone, or just need to be reminded why I'm 'torturing' myself in medical school, I always remember the songs I've sung at Lourdes: 'Lord, don't move that mountain, but give me the strength to climb it!' 'My way may not be easy, you did not say that it would be!' and 'Thank you Lord for all you've done for me!'"[21] Lynn Gardiner, newer to the community, describes two song lines—"Fill my cup, let it overflow with love," and "His praises shall continually be in my mouth"—as shaping her everyday "spiritual consciousness."

It's not only the rhythms and mantras that sustain and nourish but the memory of an interconnected and healing community, rooted in God's design for the human family. The experience can replace old memories and motivations. A striking comment from a member bears this out: "Lourdes has a way of making you forget who you tried to be and where you came from, and of making you realize who God intended you to be—one of his children."[22]

Storing in one's imagination this felt-experience of acceptance and "incorporation"—this embodied "vision of communal life," Spirit-given, never static but always needing to be striven for—creates an "awareness . . . of what life is really all about." Ritual action, writes Catherine Bell, impresses the very strategies a community enacts on those who participate, and in so doing, empowers them to live in the world in particular ways.[23] Impressed on one's imagination, the memory of an interconnected and healing community enables those who have participated at Lourdes to act in corresponding ways in their everyday lives. "If we continue to be the one body, we will continue to grow." "When the community is strong, the power of God is strong in them, and their ability to serve in the world is strong."

Finally, the strategies of Lourdes's worship, impressed on the imagination, cultivate a taste for the future, a future with God. Recall the community's engagement in an exuberant moment of song, chorusing with lead singer Judy Brown the heartfelt anticipation:

> This old race will soon be over,
> and there will be no race for me to run.
> And when I stand before God's throne,
> all my heartaches will be gone,
> when I hear my savior say, "Welcome home!"

Or, as Brother Banks expressed it at the opening of one Sunday liturgy, "What we do here, they're doin' in heaven!" And when we reach that realm of light, "there'll be singin', singin' . . . like we've never heard before. . . ."

SPEAKING THEOLOGICALLY

From the outset of this book, we have been "speaking theologically." Throughout the narrative chapters, we have experienced a theological discourse voiced in the experiential vocabulary of Lourdes' prayer and praise, in the affective vocabulary of their discipleship and commitment. We have witnessed a "theological assembly"[1] engaged in the encounter with the divine, which is at the heart of all theology. We have listened to "theologians"[2] reflect on that encounter, employing interpretive categories that spring from their religious-cultural heritage as Black Catholics. In the intervening *intermezzi* I have extended this reflective process, exploring from a more analytic perspective the ritual/musical dimensions of the community's lived practice. In so doing, I have anticipated some of the motifs of this chapter. Our purpose now is to harvest these riches: to highlight some of the distinctive liturgical and theological understandings and intuitions embodied within Lourdes' worship practice, noting their contribution to the life of the church and to the work of liturgical scholarship.

In the companion volume to this book, *Exploring Music as Worship and Theology,* I have begun this process.[3] Focusing specifically on the pivotal role of music—*as* worship and *as* theology—I have illustrated how the Lourdes community's music-making is integral to their worship; to the processes of liturgical change and inculturation they set in motion; to the manner in which ecclesial relationships are mediated in their worship; to their perceptions of liturgical aesthetics and creativity; and to how their worship becomes sacred time and sacred space. I have explored as well how this community's embodied theology, mediated in musical performance, addresses current understandings of the theological character of worship—as theological-trinitarian, pneumatological, sacramental, biblical, ecclesiological, and eschatological.

My purpose here is complementary: to extend these reflections by highlighting specific liturgical-theological understandings that have emerged in this volume, organizing them around five images: a sacramental world-view;

a biblical pneumatology; an ecclesiology of the Body of Christ; a Gospel Christology; and an historical/socio-political eschatology. In each image, the adjec-
tive suggests the area of newness offered by Lourdes' worship-music, becoming
a bridge between the lived experience of the community and current theological descriptions of Christian worship. In touching on each theme, I will
again underscore the pivotal role of music in the worship and lived theology
of the Lourdes community.

These reflections are not exhaustive; nor do they offer a complete "theology
of worship." Rather, they are starting points for continued conversation and
reflection. My goal is simply to highlight distinctive characteristics that I find
in Lourdes' practice, which I believe are given as both challenge and gift to
the church. I will conclude in that vein, suggesting that within the practice of
African American communities such as Lourdes, there is a rich treasury of insight, a living source of renewal, a "precious fountain" that still awaits the
church's full appropriation and welcome.

Sacramental worldview. Pervading and undergirding Lourdes' worship-
music practice, we find a particularly sacramental worldview[4]—a perception
that God who is the dynamic source of life, whose creative action in the universe is ever unfolding, is alive and active within the whole fabric of life,
present in the rhythms of life and death, joy and sorrow, growth and change.
Despite hardships and suffering, life is graced. God's created universe is good,
and God's "livingness" is expressed in all that is moving, alive, dynamic, and
filled with energy.

This sacramental worldview is distinctively African in its roots, writes Father
Clarence Rivers; grounded in an African vision of the wholeness of life and of
a God who delights in God's creation just as it is.[5] At Lourdes, this perception
of life and creation has a decisive impact on the community's Catholic worship, distinguishing their sacramental encounter with the living God as

- worship that employs a broad "sensorium" as revelatory of God's active
  presence
- worship that is rhythmic
- worship rooted in a holistic /non-dualistic spirituality
- worship that radically reclaims the beauty and goodness of their
  African American heritage.

Lourdes' worship, as we have seen, employs a broad sensorium[6] of human
engagement—at once visual, auditory, kinesthetic, and tactile—all of which
are avenues of attending to the living God and of returning praise and thanksgiving. Movement, color, sound, dress, singing and dancing are understood
to delight the One who creates and sustains the universe. Embraced in worship, they are integral to the whole sacramental process by which the commu-

nity encounters the self-disclosing God, and grows in godly ways of being. Music—as gift of God—brings alive God's vibrant universe, gives voice to its silent praise. A full spectrum of drums, piano, tambourine, movement and voices allow the creating God to be imaged, revealed, encountered and welcomed within the worship. To enjoy oneself in the presence of the living God, to be recreated within the vibrant rhythms of worship, is to realize more fully the ever-present grace of God that permeates all life: "The Lord is blessing me *right now!* Every time I turn around, he's making a way somehow!"

Rhythm, often eschewed in Catholic worship, is here reclaimed in all its vibrancy. Rhythms and polyrhythms, as generative source of gospel music, pulse through the community's music-making, giving shape and definition to the lyrics, the phraseology, indeed the whole Gospel message communicated through song. Rhythm is here perceived as godly—as revelatory of God's life-bestowing *kenosis* that pulses through the universe, inviting us into the "cosmic dance" that "beats in our very blood." It is therefore a fitting catalyst for the community's praise and thanksgiving. Moreover, worship at Lourdes is rhythmic on many levels—in the rhythmic progression of its flow; in the changing patterns of leadership; and most especially in the manner in which life and worship intersect, fuse, and flow into each other. The genius of Black rhythm—generated through two divergent impulses, regular beat and syncopated unpredictability, held in creative tension—becomes a metaphor for a worship practice that holds the tensions of everyday living close, while remaining faithful to the liturgical patterns of its Catholic tradition. The cross-rhythms, polyrhythms, metrical ambiguity that emerge in the community's music-making reflect the tensions and ambiguities of life as received from the creative hands of God, as well as the pulsing promise of God's future. In Pauline terms, they reveal God's created universe struggling in "one great act of giving birth; and not only creation, but we too," who await our full freedom as children of God (Rom 8:22-23).

The holistic, non-dualistic spirituality that permeates Lourdes' worship and music-making resonates with Christian understandings of incarnation—God's embrace of the whole of human life in the *kenosis* of Jesus. What are often deemed the sacred and secular domains of life infuse and enspirit each other. The human body is perceived as an instrument of praise, and epiphany of Spirit. Emotion is embraced as integral to perceiving and receiving the godly life and to expressing one's discipleship. Individuality, personal initiative, and creativity are fostered as building up the whole body, enabling individuals to be persons-in-community. Order and "non-order" are welcomed as complementary, as a necessary context within which persons create a dynamic sense of connectedness, and within which they cultivate social grace—life together before and because of God. Life, in all its manifestations, is perceived as an unbroken circle, connecting the community's past with its present and expected future with God—in that "better home awaiting . . ." where, in

Brother Banks's words, there will be "singin', singin' like we've never heard before."

Central to this sacramental worldview is the community's radical reclaiming of the beauty and goodness of their own African/African American heritage. As God's intentional creations, they are children of God and disciples of Jesus Christ. Their distinctive cultural roots, their distinctive ways of honoring the living God through generations of oppression and suffering—which have historically been marginalized, ignored, rejected within the larger society and within Catholic church practice—are reclaimed as an integral part of God's design for humankind, as revelatory of God's own beauty, as avenues of God's redemption, and as worthy vehicles through which to worship the transcendent God. In a striking way, their embrace of the "treasury" of their Black sacred music tradition has released a wellspring of vibrant, lived faith, that echoes, in its dynamic unfolding, the rhythmic forces of God's created universe, and the tender, caring presence of an ever-present, ever-active Creator.

Biblical Pneumatology. As noted over and again, one of the striking aspects of worship and music-making at Lourdes is the community's pervasive sense of the action of the Holy Spirit—animating individuals, gifting persons for their ministry, bringing Jesus alive in the midst of the community, enlivening the whole action of worship, and bonding community members as a living body of faith. This lived pneumatology and the discourse that articulates it, is in marked contrast to what liturgical theologians acknowledge as the paucity of understandings of the dynamic role of the Spirit that has characterized Western liturgical theology for centuries.[7] It is also rare in how Catholic assemblies perceive their worship.

What distinguishes Lourdes' embodied pneumatology and the manner in which it shapes the community's worship is that

- it is biblical in character
- its historical roots can be found in the Black religious tradition
- it envisions the "epicletic" action of the Holy Spirit as inclusive of the whole worship
- it requires the co-action of the whole community.

At Lourdes, perceptions of the Spirit's action reflect numerous images of the Spirit that permeate the Scriptures.[8] Like the breath of God envisioned in Genesis, transforming motionless clay into a moving, living soul, the Spirit's action is recognized in persons who speak, proclaim, pray, testify, adulate, sing, and preach from the living core of their being—from their very "soul." Like the life-giving energy of God that transformed Ezekiel's dry, dusty field of bones into living, dancing beings, the Spirit's presence is tasted in rhythmic movement, resonant clapping, pulsing drums. Like the Spirit imaged in Joel as poured out on all people in a great *kenosis,* that gifts and emboldens both young and old, enabling them to see visions and dream dreams, the living presence of God is welcomed here in the giftedness of all members, be they dynamic leaders or shy participants. Most especially, the pentecostal Spirit of the Risen Jesus, poured out on fear-filled disciples gathered in Jerusalem, transforming them into courageous witnesses, is welcomed at Lourdes in the faith testimony of any of its members, expressed in song, prayer, gestures, or courageous deeds. Biblical stories of the Spirit's action are not simply historical accounts, but in the preached image of Father Kirk, "Pentecost is now!" Lourdes, in his words, is a "seedbed" of this Spirit.

The roots of this biblical pneumatology, claims Father Clarence Rivers—a perspective Lourdes shares with the larger Black church—reach back beyond the arrival of enslaved Africans on American soil, beyond their encounter with Christianity and therefore with the biblical narratives. In traditional African religion, "the heritage of our foreparents," he posits, "the main thrust of religious practices is to achieve harmony with the spirits [of the High God] and empowerment by the spirits."[9] This cultural orientation, Rivers contends, prepared Black communities to recognize in the Bible a God whose life, energy, and power are released in the world through God's Spirit. It prepared them as well, in the midst of the brutal sufferings of slavery, to recognize an "unconventional God" by whose Spirit persons were "commissioned to prophesy, even in the name of and for the benefit of the poor and the dispossessed." These perceptions of the Holy Spirit as animating presence, who empowers worshipers, moving them to speak out against all forms of injustice, have been cultivated historically within African American religious culture and specifically within the Black church tradition. At Lourdes, this pneumatological perspective is integral to the community's Catholic worship.

The lived pneumatology we find at Lourdes envisions the "epicletic," transformative action of the Holy Spirit as inclusive of the whole worship. Stretching the particular *epiclesis* voiced in the Eucharistic Prayer—invoking the Spirit's power to transform gifts of bread and wine into the Body and blood of Christ—the entire worship at Lourdes seems to voice a single plea: "Lord, let your Spirit fall on me!" What is striking at Lourdes is that this epicletic invocation, and the expectation of its fulfillment, *requires* the co-action of the community, who actively receive the Spirit's power and are unafraid of its manifestations. We have seen how this epicletic co-action affects the performed structures and strategies of music-making: how aspects of performance are kept intentionally indeterminate so that musicians can shape a song in response to the movement of the Spirit. It grounds singers' expectation that God will "use them" to move, touch, and evoke the faith-response of others. It affects the manner in which musicians "tune" their song to the Spirit-like qualities of warmth, fire, energy, joy. It shapes the attitudes and practices of those who take leadership, so that yielding, attending, and listening to others become important vehicles for the Spirit's impulse. It is evident in how the worship space is infused with the felt-qualities of warmth, hospitality, and "livingness," filled with vital sound that awakens the heart and moves the soul.

Expecting the Spirit of God to permeate their worship, to dispose bodies, minds and spirits to receive the vital power of God, the Lourdes community welcomes the essential "synergy" of spirits that empowers them for discipleship and conforms them to Christ.[10]

Gospel Christology. The Christology embedded in music-making and the whole worship event at Lourdes is rooted in the Gospel revelation of Jesus— who came as the Incarnate One to accomplish God's liberating intentions; to suffer the full spectrum of human struggle and death; and to pour out his Spirit, making disciples of all who believe his message. This lived Christology sets in distinct relief the larger church's understanding that liturgy accomplishes the redemptive action of Christ[11]—stretching what may at times be a more narrow focus on Jesus' death and resurrection to include his entire ministry. Here the paschal mystery, lived out in the community's faith encounter of the Risen Jesus, is refracted in the prophetic announcement of Jesus' mission: to bring good news to the poor, to give sight to the blind, to proclaim liberty to captives, and to set the downtrodden free. (Luke 4:16-22)

This Gospel Christology is evident in Lourdes' worship as ministers and others

- proclaim a Christ who is on the side of the poor/outcast/those whom the world discounts
- enact the liberating aspects of Jesus' Gospel ministry
- engage together in the intimacy and companionship of Jesus' friendship
- transform the worship into a "Gospel event."

Within this community's worship, Jesus is vividly imaged and experienced as the inbreaking nearness of a God who is on the side of the poor, the needy, the outcast, the marginalized; revealed as the biblical God of history who freed the Hebrew people from slavery, and who desires the healing and wholeness of all persons. Those who preach at Lourdes proclaims this Jesus, "alive on the shores our troubled lives," breaking through sealed doors to show us his wounds, inviting us to "see my wounds, touch my wounds" so that you know that "I suffer with you, feel with you, experience your pain so that I can heal you." The words of Jesus both heal and "complicate our lives." They call the community to be "radical people," "prophets and prophetesses," who, once healed, proclaim life in the face of death; who wrestle with the "old wound of racism"; who "challenge others with love"; who remain children "of the resurrection," never losing hope, but committing themselves "totally to the way of Jesus," the way of discipleship. In the witness of Brother Banks, "No matter how poor I am, I have a friend in Jesus. . . . He brought me through. . . . In times like these, when everythin' else is failin', our only hope is in Jesus!" With a resounding, "I do!" the community seals its belief that "Jesus' message can work in this world!" despite the struggles, the exclusion, the racism that seem to threaten their lives and their well-being.

The experience of liberation, claims James Cone, is key to Black worship—the "power of God's Spirit invading the lives of the people, "buildin' them up where they are torn down and proppin' them up on every leanin' side."[12] Enacting the liberating aspects of Jesus' gospel ministry becomes a primary motivation for how the Lourdes community engages in worship. Time is placed at the service of people's spiritual needs, enabling them to be strengthened, nourished, and refreshed. Space is reoriented performatively as a place of Incarnate presence "in-the-midst" of the community. Familial embrace becomes a metaphor-in-act of the incarnate nearness of God in Jesus, affirming the presence and giftedness of others, building their self-esteem. Vocal-verbal communication is guided by a "faith aesthetic" that aims to release the generative power of words—to heal, touch, move, support, encourage, challenge, create bonds among those who participate; to convince them that "God is really with them!" Sounded words open to the realm of the unseen, transcendent God, while remaining rooted in the "revelatory Word." Intended by singers, preachers, and prayers to evoke a response, to invite change, to elicit faith, the affective power of words is released through the emotion, conviction, and enthusiasm with which they are sung/spoken. The whole worship becomes a "school of discipleship." within which faith attitudes are mutually shaped.

Music-making plays a unique role in enabling the community to engage together in the intimacy and companionship of Jesus' friendship. His message, announced in song by "disciples" who believe its power to touch and heal, is embraced by the community as they dwell together in the unfolding music, professing together the ardor of their love for a Jesus who "gave his life for me when no one else seemed to care;" who is the "Great Emancipator," and who ultimately is "my all and all"—my sight, guiding light, my joy in sorrow, my hope for tomorrow. This shared musical action becomes an active faith encounter with the saving, healing, life-giving presence of the Risen Jesus. It deepens the community's experience of being the "beloved community of Jesus."[13] It is a vivid liturgical, communal context for eucharistic "communion" in the Risen Lord. It is also sustenance to live and proclaim Jesus' message beyond worship—to bring to the church and society not only Jesus' word of hope, but his "radical and revolutionary praxis that announced the tearing down of the religious, social, and political status quo of his day and its replacement with a new world of justice, righteousness, and empowerment for the lowest of the low."[14]

In his commentary on Luke's Gospel, Eugene LaVerdiere[15] notes that we cannot understand Jesus' eucharistic action at the "last" supper without contextualizing it in the meal fellowship that pervades the whole of Luke's account—a table fellowship marked by Jesus' inclusive, hospitable, healing, teaching, reconciling ministry. Understood in this light, Jesus' eucharistic action at table on the eve of his life-giving death and resurrection becomes a "compendium of the whole gospel"—a summation of Jesus' entire mission of "announcing good news to the poor, sight to the blind, freedom to captives, and a time of God's favor," all of which are "fulfilled in your hearing." At Lourdes, worship becomes such a "Gospel event."

Ecclesiology of the Body of Christ. The Lourdes community, acting together in worship, reveals an ecclesiology that resonates strongly with Pauline images of the "body of Christ"—an interdependent community, marked by reciprocity and mutuality, in which each one's gifts are necessary to the working of the whole. St. Paul's image of the body of Christ is certainly not new to Catholic understandings of church. Yet the urgency of its realization in the contemporary world, after centuries of emphasis on the almost exclusive role of the hierarchy, was signaled by Vatican II's declaration of the "universal call to holiness"[16]—an ideal that has yet been only partially realized within the church's life and worship.

What emerges at Lourdes, as worship reveals Christ-being-in-his-Body in this local *ecclesia,* is a "redemptive reordering of relationships"[17]—the fashioning of an inclusive community of disciples, guided by the Spirit. We have seen this ecclesiology operative as the worshiping community

- orders persons and the community to wholeness and *diakonia*
- acknowledges and honors multiple channels for the action of God
- realigns the relationship of the *mystical* and the *real* presence of Christ
- anticipates a new order of relationships within the church and society.

Within Lourdes' worship, persons and the community as a body are "ordered" to wholeness—not homogeneity, but reciprocal engagement and dialogic conversation. Diversity and solidarity are held in creative tension—the "I" of testimony grounded in the communal "we." "Having" church—a metaphor for effective, Spirit-filled worship—implies a commitment to *being* church: to engaging with others within worship and beyond; to creating a spiritual climate within which individual gifts are expressed in manifold forms of service, of *diakonia*. Gifts-still-maturing, as well as those more fully developed, are welcomed—embraced as necessary to both the worship of God and the building up of the body. Words, songs, prayers, and gestures are transformed into collective action, communal transactions, by the flow of acclamations spoken/ shouted by members of the assembly. The community-ordered-to-wholeness is especially evident in moments of music-making, as diverse modes of participation are held in creative tension with ecclesial solidarity in the act of giving praise. In the words of Judy Brown, "There's only one body. . . . We're all working for that one body. . . . We have to be in tune with it. When the church as a whole participates, you know the Spirit is here in this church. There's a 'sweet, sweet Spirit' and it's the Spirit of the Lord."

Within this worshiping body, multiple channels for the action of God are acknowledged and honored. Each member, as bearer of the Spirit, has something to contribute. Women as well as men assume major roles of prayer leadership and their spiritual authority is affirmed—known to be an authority grounded in their faith-filled lives and the power of their message. Ordained and lay leaders assume differing but interactive ministries. The faith-gifts of elders and children are welcomed. Young adults are encouraged to address the community about their hopes, fears, and struggles, and are constantly supported and encouraged. Musical leadership is shared, enabling the voices of both children and adults to proclaim the gospel message in song. Together, the community gives witness to its faith and attends to God's action within the body.

At the heart of their eucharistic worship, as Lourdes engages in the reception of Communion, reverencing the sacramental "body of Christ" seems inseparable from reverencing the community of faith—saying "Amen" to the living body of Christ, accepting the challenge of mutual presence. Implicit in this practice is a realignment of the *mystical* and the *real* presence of Christ—a realization of their indivisibility—a recognition that counteracts what Henri de Lubac describes as "a 'deadly dichotomy' between the eucharistic body and the ecclesial body" that became firmly rooted in the church's practice in the late twelfth century.[18] Prior to that time, the *real* presence of Christ was assumed to be the community of believers as body of the Risen Lord. At Lourdes, as we have seen, the whole worship seems to flow toward communion—toward a receptive communing in the body of Christ, at once eucharistic and ecclesial. Sustained in song, this moment of communion becomes a celebration of "who we are and whose we are"—a lingering in the divine-human exchange that heals and reorders, fills and overflows; a tarrying with Christ, abiding in and for his church, within the faith-filled assembly.

Finally, Lourdes' embodied ecclesiology becomes a new flourishing of the historical active, lay participation of Black Catholics in the life of the church—a history rarely acknowledged in the annals of American faith—and of the role of women as spiritual faith-leaders within the Black community.[19] Moreover, the community's actualization as the body of Christ—interdependent and reciprocally engaged in worship and music-making; joined in praise, thanksgiving, and doxology of the living God—anticipates a new order of relationships that has yet to be realized within either church or society—a redemptive reordering, based on mutuality and the reverencing of the gifts of all, and on a bold inclusion of Black Catholics as integral to the life of the whole church.

Historical/social-political eschatology. Finally, the eschatology present within the dynamic exchange of song, preaching, and prayer at Lourdes, is situated in the concrete social-political world in which the community lives and in their historical journey as an African American people.[20] This eschatological vision, born of God's faithful presence to Black Americans in the most demeaning of historical circumstances, awakens an expectation that God's desires for this community, and for the whole human race, will ultimately be victorious. The "God of our weary years," who has "brought us thus far on the way," enkindles hope, and enables the community to face "the rising sun of a new day begun."

This eschatological vision, this dynamic memory of God's faithfulness, is evident in Lourdes' worship as the community

- claims a past of unspeakable hardship as arena of God's grace
- embraces God's action within the present struggle
- is emboldened/empowered to participate in realizing God's reign, present and future
- keeps alive a transcendent vision of God's future.

In preaching, prayer, and song, the community's history is recalled as both a journey of faith and an arena of God's grace. In the words of one member, "Faith was all we had as African Americans. It was our only treasure—the one thing they couldn't take from us." As members of the community recount the unspeakable horrors of slavery, segregation, economic oppression, and persistent racism, they make the striking claim: that their enslaved and oppressed forebears were actors in their own history and subjects of God's redemptive designs. In the words of Walter Turner, "There was faith on those [slave] ships. We brought it here, brought it with us!" Or as Brother Banks claimed: "Lincoln freed the slaves, but not alone. It was the old people prayin', goin' to God, having faith in God." Jesus was central to this faith vision—a Jesus who identified with their struggle and "made a way out of no way." In song, the community celebrates "How I got over!"—rekindling the fearless faith that "brought us safe this far" and that one day will "lead us home." "We've come this far by faith // leaning on the Lord! Trusting in his holy Word. He never failed me yet!"

This historical memory urges the community to expect God's action in their current struggles, while naming and lamenting all that thwarts human life and threatens their existence. Longing, lamenting, and truth-telling are thus integral to their worship: a truth-telling that names injustice, societal, political, and religious; a lamenting that decries the pervasiveness of violence while praying for its victims; a longing that cries out in song to God: "We need to hear from you, we need a word from you," because "this world has forgotten about you." It moves them to plead for an "unwavering faith" so as to live in a society that disregards and marginalizes them; to believe in a God "revealed

268

in Jesus as love, as justice," who is deeply involved in their struggle, who is "pulling us, pulling us, toward himself to share the resurrection of Jesus," if only the community "keep alive the vision, keep alive the dream." It urges them to receive the power of Jesus—mediated in word, song, and sacramental action—to live as children of God and not be defined by this world.[21] And it compels them to realize, within the relationships that unfold in worship, a vision of God's commonwealth, an alternate vision of society, in which persons are loved, honored and cherished as God's own.

Storing up this experience, in body and heart, muscle and bone, mind and imagination, emboldens and empowers community members to struggle in a world still marked by racism, oppression, and violence. The memory of an interconnected, healing community, rooted in God's design for the human family, sustains their commitment to the coming of God's reign—striving with others to protest, resist, speak out against those forces that threaten the safety and well-being of their neighborhoods, families, and children; and most especially, living with hope amidst the contrarieties of daily life.

At the same time, the community's worship keeps alive a transcendent vision of God's future—"a better home awaiting," an eschatological fulfillment assured because of Jesus' victory—that goes beyond what can be imagined or realized in this world. This vision, nurtured and sustained within the community's music-making, enables them to declare that "soon and very soon" "I'm goin' up yonder to be with my Lord," to claim a future where there will be "no more weepin',. . . no more dyin.'" In worship and especially in song, this vision becomes a "realized eschatology," as the community proleptically anticipates God's future. Though burdens still "press me down,"

> This old race will soon be over,
> and there will be no race for me to run, Lord.
> But as I stand before God's throne, all my heartaches will be gone,
> when I hear my Savior say, *"Welcome home!"*[22]

Joined in communal exuberance and joy, the community anticipates eschatological fulfillment as "home" and "welcome."

The music-worship practice of Our Lady of Lourdes that we have witnessed in this book offers the church both challenge and gift. Two challenges stand out. First, Lourdes' radical reclaiming of their Black religious-cultural heritage, and the fusion of this legacy with the community's Catholic sacramental practice, challenges the church to wholeheartedly embrace its cultural diversity as a necessary manifestation of its catholic wholeness. In this first decade of the third millennium, when efforts at inculturation have grown more hesitant and cautious, Lourdes' worship-music practice makes abundantly clear that a generous God's free gifts are meant to be embraced. By releasing the beauty and vibrancy of their religious-cultural heritage within Catholic worship, Lourdes invites others to do the same, and assures those who are fearful that God's praise and the church's sanctification will be the richer for having fully embraced these gifts.

At the same time, Lourdes' music and worship practice release in the church a subversive memory—a memory of exclusion and discrimination, a memory of disregard and prejudice. As the images that grace the stained-glass windows in the Lourdes church house remind us, African American Catholics share the tradition of the church from its earliest African beginnings. Yet they critique that tradition as well—releasing, in their embrace of Catholic life and worship, a memory that

> can arguably be seen as "subversive," one which is paradoxical, turning all of the accepted reality upside down to present a new reality, that of the last being called forth . . . as bearers of a vital, healing vision . . . from their experience of both racial and religious persecution. They reflect the memory of a Church that has preached equality while practicing discrimination and segregation, a Church that has preached a God of love while practicing racial hatred and division.[23]

Insofar as Lourdes' practice releases this subversive memory, it calls the church, and in a particular way liturgical scholars, to a "hermeneutic of suspicion" regarding the historical evolution and the current practice of Christian worship. It calls attention to how the liturgical patterns fostered by the church have excluded and silenced the gifts of some of its members; it questions whose voices have been missing from the church's theologizing about its worship; and it invites a more inclusive mode of reflective theology that flows from the revelatory center which is the whole church's worship.

These challenges, implicit in the "precious gift of Blackness" that Lourdes has released in worship and song, are doubtless the work of God's life-bestowing Spirit who invites the church to "widen the space of its tent." To those who have met the Lourdes community on these pages, the summons is the same—to continue to drink deeply from wellsprings that God has provided for the enrichment of the church. The Black Catholic worship we have met at Lourdes—its compelling faith-testimony in song and preaching, its holistic performance aesthetic, it's attentiveness to the Spirit's movements—can only be learned through participation. Lourdes and other Black Catholic communities invite such participation—to come, to "taste and see," to enter with them into the "cosmic dance that beats in our very blood." Father Clarence Rivers once preached:

> The church must not allow the brilliant glory of her traditional and familiar worship forms to blind her to other possibilities, to prevent her from appro-

priating with appreciation a new vitality within her midst; a vitality, a life, new to her, but conceived long ago in the ancient and fertile womb of Mother Africa. . . . Even so, a people who were once enslaved are now the channels of the freeing and renewing Spirit. . . . But let not the Black presence within the church become wrapped up in itself, but continue to press the offering of that dimension of the abundant life with which it has been particularly endowed."[24]

Lourdes is indeed a witness to that abundant life. It holds out to the church an invitation to learn . . . a particular endowment that is "authentically Black and truly Catholic" . . . indeed, a precious fountain.

Epilogue

OUR LADY OF LOURDES—2003

"*H*ow can I say thanks," intoned Judy Brown one crisp Autumn morning in 2003, "for the things God has done for me!" This song, reiterated so often in the worship of the Lourdes community, touched the heart of my gratitude. For over ten years, I have tasted the vibrant faith of this little community and been enriched by their spirited worship. This book is a tribute to all that I have learned from them.

Much growth and change has taken place in the five years that have followed most of the events recorded in this book. Yet despite change, the spirit and core values inscribed in these chapters remain strong, carrying the Lourdes community into a future yet uncharted.

*P*arish growth and change. Since 1991, Father Kirk Ullery has pastored Our Lady of Lourdes parish with strong, dynamic, and inclusive leadership. Reaching retirement age for priests of the archdiocese in the Spring of 2003, Father Kirk asked to remain at Lourdes. With relief and joy, the community applauded his reassignment in June, affirming the essential contribution of his gifts to the vibrancy of this community and its worship.

Two years earlier, the archdiocese assigned Father Gaudence Milambo, A.L.C.P., a priest from Tanzania, to assist Father Kirk as parochial vicar of the parish. Father Gaudence brings to Lourdes his African Catholic experience, training, and spirit, as well as his participation in an emerging dialogue between African and African American leaders. During the Summer of 2002, he shared his heritage with several parishioners who traveled with him to Tanzania and other surrounding African countries.

Since March of 1997, when All Hallows was reopened by the archdiocese as a chapel of the parish, Lourdes has continued as two interrelated communities—worshiping regularly in two church houses, joined by a network of friendships, parish committee work, and combined outreach. Four times a year, the two communities unite liturgically to celebrate the feasts of Our Lady of Lourdes (Lourdes Day), St. Peter Chanel (patron of Samoa), All Saints (All Hallows), and the Sunday before Labor Day (followed by a parish picnic), with joint musical leadership from the Samoan and Gospel Choirs.

Elders. Perhaps the most significant change in the life and worship of the community was signaled by a phone call from Jean Alexander on June 5, 1999. Earlier that day, Brother Jesse Lee Banks had slipped quietly "home to God," leaving our company with as little fanfare as he had lived his life. As we gathered on two successive days to celebrate Jesus' death-resurrection lived out in this man of faith, the Lourdes and All Hallows church houses were filled to overflowing with family, friends, neighbors, and representatives of the surrounding community. The services were lengthy, stretched by the tributes of numerous persons, young and old, who acknowledged Brother Banks's service to the Lourdes family, to the Bayview-Hunters Point community, and most especially his dedicated service to the children of the area. But the community's greatest tribute took the lyric voice of song, reflecting in a mosaic of sound and imagery the faith attitudes that marked Brother Banks's life—"Lord, give me that unwavering faith!"; "God has smiled on me, he has set me free!"; "His eye is on that little sparrow, and I know God's watching over me!"; "God is my today and my tomorrow . . . yes, God is my all and all!" As Judy Brown gave voice to his heavenward journey—"I'm goin' up yonder to be with my Lord!"—we could only pray that Brother Banks is now standing near God's "throne of grace," "Free at last! Free at last!" and filled with the joy of that "singin', singin' like we've never heard before."

For Lourdes, Brother Banks's passing to "a better home awaiting" was more than the loss of a great man of faith. It meant a significant shift in the rhythmic flow of their worship, a loss of the musicality of his voice and the oral history it carried on its cadence, and the silencing of his remarkable ability to improvise prayer and to lift the prayers of the whole community to the throne of God. These gifts are irreplaceable.

But people needed to be welcomed to Lourdes each Sunday, and John Brown stepped up immediately to fill that role. A bit shy at first, John's gracious presence spoke the community's hospitality. Over four years of this leadership, John's welcome has become far more animated, his voice erupting now into acclamations of praise and enthusiastic testimonies to God's goodness. "I feel God working in me," he commented to me one Sunday. "Something is coming out of me, and it feels good!"

In the intervening years other key elders have, with Brother Banks, gone home to God: Sister Helen Carroll, R.S.C.J. (+October 6, 1998), whose indefatigable service on the Lourdes staff spanned 1972–1986; Margaret Fisher (+January 4, 2000), woman of prayer and faith, beloved of several generations of family and parishioners; Zettie LeBlanc (+June 27, 2002), a valiant woman, remembered by a church house filled to overflowing with persons whom she had inspired and loved. In May of 1999, Reverend John Lane, pastor of Grace Baptist Church, "passed over to glory" as well. Given the years of friendship between the congregations of Grace Baptist and Lourdes, Reverend Lane's wife chose not to call another minister for Grace Baptist. Instead, she and others continue to make Lourdes a home and to worship with the community from time to time.

> +Eternal rest grant unto them, O Lord,
> and let perpetual light shine upon them.+

Other elders remain strong. Among them, Mama Amanda Winslow—still seated each Sunday beneath the image of Sojourner Truth, lap-robe over her knees as she receives the kisses and hugs of various members of the community —who turned ninety in October 2003, claiming that she is now the oldest member of the community. On a warm October Sunday in 2001, Elizabeth Norman Bell—our beloved "Liz Bell"—was honored with a "Liz Bell Day," celebrating her presence among us as "A true servant of God and of God's poor."

Young members. Growth and change is most evident in Lourdes' youngest members. Tyree McDuff, Naja Turner, and so many others who grew up in the choir and inhabited the front pew at the Sunday liturgies recorded in this book are now in their early teens.

For five years the Our Lady of Lourdes Miracles—growing in age, musical ability, and dedication under the able leadership of Judy Brown and Reed Fromer—made a remarkable musical and spiritual contribution both to Lourdes' liturgy and to various other groups who invited them to sing. An outstanding CD of nine of their songs inscribes their musical vitality and makes it available well beyond the Lourdes church house. But as the Miracles grew from tots to teens, new activities and commitments made coordinating hours of rehearsal more problematic. In Fall 2002, Judy Brown decided it was time to let them move on.

But Lourdes has never been short on miracles. Before our eyes, a new set of petite choristers, two to five years of age, are forming quite spontaneously— emerging from their pews each Sunday as the Doxology concluding the Eucharistic Prayer is sounded, walking one-by-one or two-by-two down the center aisle, clustering just in front of the altar, ready to lead the community in the final *Amen!* of that great prayer of Thanksgiving. A new youth choir is waiting to be born.

Young adults who grew up in the music at Lourdes make their impressive contributions as well. A few examples suffice. On June 25, 2001, Corey Monroe appeared in the taped coverage of the Omega Boys Club, San Francisco, when Oprah Winfrey honored its founder, Joe Marshall. Corey continues to counsel young Black men who come to Omega seeking support and role models for their lives. Tiffany Isles has realized her dream of studying at Howard Medical School. Moreover, she experiences it as a true vocation. "[Thinking] about my journey to medical school and through medical school," she recounts, "I never for one moment believed that I was doing this alone and that God was not with me every step of the way. [But recently, in conversation with a classmate,] I realized that God is truly calling me to be a doctor and that he is molding me for some purpose that will be revealed to me later in life."

*M*usic at Lourdes continues to be the vibrant soul of the community's worship. Over the past five years, the Gospel Choir has lost two enthusiastic members—Louise Wood and Jeannette Howard—both of whom have moved to neighboring cities, and at the same time welcomed Victoria Stith, Jackie Banks, Reginald Stephenson, Harry Bryant, and George Biniek. Most noticeably, the swell in the number of male singers has brought new vitality and strength to the baritone section, who delight in three-part contrapuntal vamps that the choir now undertakes.

Reed Fromer, who came to Lourdes as pianist in 1987 through the chance invitation of an associate, and whose skilled, sensitive accompaniments and imaginative improvisations are an indispensable part of the musical fabric of worship here, declared to the community in March 2001—on a day set aside as "Reed Fromer Day"—that his coming to Lourdes was the "life-altering move" of his adult years. "Here I've met some of the people that have had the biggest influence in my life. . . . And over the past three years, the defining transition in my life would not have come about if it weren't for this community. And she's right there," he added, gesturing to his new wife, Gina Gra'Ves. Gina and Reed met at Miracles' rehearsals where Gina was supervising her niece and nephew. "No matter what dreams I may once have had about my career, [about heading to Europe or touring the country for a year with my band,] I know now that my place is here, (Applause breaks out . . .) with my wife, my family, and with my church family. . . . This is what matters to me," he concluded, referring to Lourdes, "knowing that I can play a role in something as beautiful as this; something that has made so many people feel that they have a home, an extended family; something that has taken in so many people and changed their lives. . . ." In September 2003, Gina and Reed's first child, Devon, was born.

Isaiah Brown, on the other hand, is navigating new worlds. Having grown up in this church, loved and supported by a community who "helped raise him," Isaiah made the sad announcement as he reached his high school graduation in June 2002 that he would be leaving as the church's drummer. A career in the Navy was calling, and Isaiah, who still hopes to be a professional drummer some day, yielded to the invitation. Already we knew that his potent contribution to our sung prayer would be deeply missed. Over his thirteen years of playing at Lourdes, Isaiah had become masterful in his ability to sustain the intensity of a deeply felt moment of song on the versatile fluency of his drumming. But life was opening before him.

Over the eleven months prior to his departure, Isaiah invited another young drummer from the parish, Alva Cosey—an erstwhile member of Lourdes' Miracles—to understudy him. More than once during this time, a glance at Isaiah at his trap set revealed Alva seated just beside him, observing every stroke of his drum-sticks, each swish of his brushes. Then on an overcast Sunday in November, the community blessed, prayed over, and sent Isaiah to his new life. Indeed, there wasn't a dry eye in the house as we gathered around him that morning singing, "In good times, in bad times, I'll be on your side forevermore: That's what friends are for!" Fortunately, Alva has taken his own seat at the trap set, growing into a new and invaluable ministry to the community.

What began as a tribute to the women on Mother's Day, 1995—an emergent men's choir formed for the occasion and re-formed each May for that same occasion—took a new turn in 2001. Over six years, this ad hoc "choir" had truly found their own voice. Moreover, at the Mother's Day liturgy that year, eleven-year-old Tyree McDuff stood before the assembled men directing their singing. As the liturgy concluded that day, Father Kirk urged them strongly to remain together as a group. Taking up his challenge, this new group of songsters became the Men's Choir of Our Lady of Lourdes, the only Catholic men's gospel choir in San Francisco. Ten men, five of whom sing with the Gospel Choir—George Biniek, John Brown (President), Harry Bryant, Reginald Stephenson, and Walter Turner—and five new voices—Duke Bryant, Ralph Galloway, Michael Kirtman, Claudell LeBlanc, and David Camilli—now take their place in the monthly rotation of musical leadership, witnessing their faith in song on the fourth Sunday of each month.

Sister Martin de Porres Coleman, S.N.D.deN., founder of Lourdes's first Youth and Gospel Choirs in the early 1970s, was honored at the Lourdes Gospel Concert in October 2002. Her legacy continues.

Social context. There continues to be "no safe place for children in Hunters Point." Despite the efforts of many, including parents at Lourdes, the social fabric of the surrounding Bayview-Hunters Point area is marked by a continued violence that has visited heartache on several community members. In June 2001, Bessie Brooks's grandson Kyree Butler was shot on "the hill" behind Lourdes—another senseless killing. Two months later, Bessie and others from Lourdes joined "hundreds of hymn-singing African American members of the Bayview-Hunters Point community" as they "marched down Third Street in a stand against the violence that has claimed dozens of young black men's lives"[1] in recent years.

The social climate of Hunters Point, as Brother Banks predicted in his Father's Day homily in 1995, has continued to be riddled with challenge. Ever since the Hunters Point naval shipyard closed in 1974, the area's population, mostly African American, has plummeted.[2] Hundreds of toxic waste sites and several energy plants continue to pollute the area, while rates of asthma, breast cancer, crime and poverty exceed the norm for San Francisco.

"Save our school!" read the signs, as members of Lourdes joined other Catholic residents of the Bayview in April 2003 to protest the Archdiocese of San Francisco's closure of four Catholic schools, all in Black neighborhoods.[3] St. Paul of the Shipwreck, where many youngsters from Lourdes were enrolled, was among them. Despite the protest, representatives of the archdiocese claimed that pressing financial concerns made it imperative that the school close, leaving these students without Catholic education.

In spite of persistent hardships, Lourdes' outreach to others in the city continues. It is to Liz Bell that many turn when their pantries are bare, knowing that she will have something tucked away in the kitchen of the parish hall. Be it St. Vincent de Paul clothing drives or sandwiches for the homeless, Liz's *diaconia* is constant. On another front, Walter Turner's commitment to the kids of the area brings him to Juvenile Hall most Sundays. There he assists a deacon of the archdiocese in offering a Communion Service for kids in solitary confinement. My goal, he tells the kids, is to put this place out of business. They're good kids, he comments. We just have to work with them, one by one, helping them believe in themselves.

*V*isitors continue to flow into the Lourdes church house, tasting the community's hospitality and vibrant worship. One bright Sunday in October 2001, Patrick Naumes, teacher at a small Catholic high school near Ashland, Oregon, arrived in a yellow school bus with twenty of his students. Lourdes, he felt, was an important part of a weekend "world religions tour" he provides for his students, only some of whom are Catholic. The visit has become an annual event, and thank you notes from participating students make clear that Lourdes has expanded and enriched their perception of Catholic worship. Their recurring question: "Why can't liturgies at home be like this?"

That same October, Sister Bernadette Okure from Nigeria, a student of mine from the Franciscan School of Theology, came to Lourdes for Sunday liturgy. As the liturgy ended, she exclaimed, "My heart is dancing again! My heart is dancing again!" Indeed all of our hearts were dancing that day.

In each of our lives, we meet persons or groups that we perceive as "bushes aflame"—and like Moses in the book of Exodus, we take off our shoes knowing that we are on holy ground. For the past ten years, I have stood on holy ground.

To God be the glory,
To God be the glory,
To God be the glory, for the things he has done!

APPENDICES

Appendix One

TABLE OF "CODED SPEECH"
TO INDICATE THE INFLECTION
OF AURAL SOUND

The following patterns of transcription of spoken words will be used to indicate the aural sound of the transaction:

- regular speech
- *emphatic speech*
- ***emphatic, stressed speech, with high level of emotional content . . .***
- // — inserted in spoken words or sung lyrics indicates a break in the flow of words to create rhythmic units

The following customs will be followed to indicate the verbal interaction among participants in worship events:

(Amen!) *(Thank you, Jesus!)* *(Yes!)* — Responses from community members interpolated in prayers, Scripture readings, preaching, and singing

(Amen!!!) — Multiple exclamation points indicate that the response is voiced by several persons simultaneously or in sequence.

(Applause . . .) — Indicates other non-verbal responses to the spoken or sung word.

Appendix Two

DIAGRAMS OF THE WORSHIP SPACE

<u>Key</u>
Figure 1 = Our Lady of Lourdes Church
Figures 2–4 = Arrangements of the Gospel Choir
at various times in the Liturgy
Figure 2 = During the Responsorial Psalm, Offertory Song,
Communion Meditation
Figure 3 = During Communion Song
Figure 4 = During Eucharistic Prayer

FIGURE 1: Our Lady of Lourdes Church

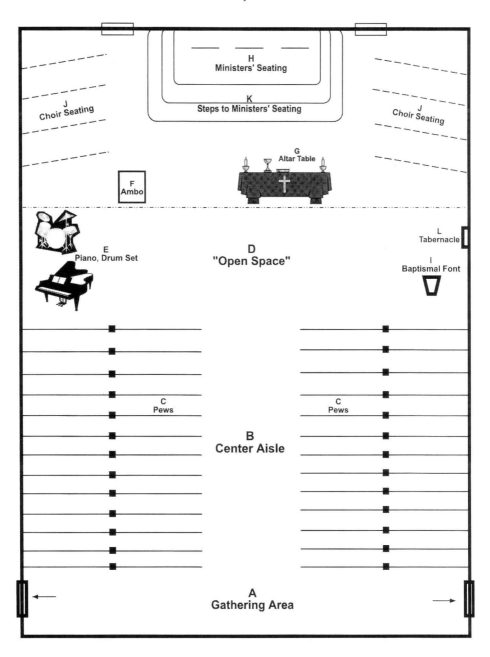

FIGURES 2–4: Arrangements of the Gospel Choir at Various Times in the Liturgy

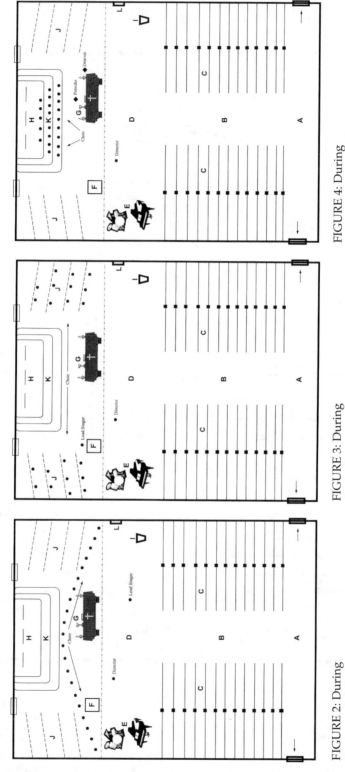

FIGURE 2: During
Responsorial Psalm,
Offertory Song,
Communion Meditation

FIGURE 3: During
Communion Song

FIGURE 4: During
Eucharistic Prayer

Appendix Three

ORDER OF THE SUNDAY LITURGY: OUR LADY OF LOURDES

	Columns* A	B	C	D	E
1. Informal Gathering		x			(x)
2. Prayer: Presider, Choir, Others		x			x
3. Deacon's Invitation to Worship		x			x
4. Entrance Song + Entrance of Choir / Ministers	x			V	
5. Deacon's Welcome	x				
6. Presider's Greeting + Welcome	x				
7. Lord Have Mercy	x			I	
8. Glory, Glory, Hallelujah	x			I	
9. Prayer	x				
10. First Scripture Reading	x				
11. Psalm Response	x			V	
12. Second Scripture Reading	x				
13. Gospel Acclamation	x			V	
14. Gospel Proclamation	x				
15. Homily (or Presentation by Community Member)	x	(x)			
16. (Baptism; Special Blessings)	(x)	(x)	x		x
17. Profession of Faith	x				
18. Prayer of the Faithful	x				
19. Exchange of Peace	x				x
20. Offertory Song + Collection	x			V	

	Columns* A	B	C	D	E
21. + Preparation of Gifts, Altar	x				
22. Prayer	x				
23. Eucharistic Prayer: (Opening Section)	x				
24. Holy, Holy	x			I	
25. (Prayer continues)	x				
26. Memorial Acclamation	x			V	
27. (Prayer continues)	x				x
28. Doxology – "Through Him . . ."	x			I	
29. Amen	x			I	
30. Our Father—Lord's Prayer	x				
31. Breaking of Bread—Pouring of Cups	x				
32. + "Lamb of God"	x			I	
33. Distribution of Communion	x				x
34. + Communion Song	x			V	
35. Communion Meditation Song		x		V	
36. (Special Request Song)		x	x	V	
37. Welcome of Visitors		x			(x)
38. + Announcements		x			(x)
39. Prayer	x				
40. Blessing + Dismissal	x				
41. Closing Song	x			V	
42. Informal Fellowship		x			
43. (Coffee and donuts—monthly) (Parish Celebration)		x	x		

Key: Column A: Elements customary in all Roman Catholic Worship
Column B: Additional elements, customary at Our Lady of Lourdes
Column C: Occasional elements
Column D: Elements performed musically
    V = Variable selection   I = Invariable selection
Column E: Improvised piano accompaniment

Appendix Four

GLOSSARY OF MUSICAL TERMS

• *Definitions included in this glossary are drawn from the following sources:*

Wili Apel, *Harvard Dictionary of Music,* 2nd ed. (Cambridge: Harvard University Press, 1977); Samuel A. Floyd, Jr., *The Power of Black Music* (New York: Oxford, 1995); H. Wiley Hitchcock and Stanley Sadie, *The New Grove Dictionary of American Music* (New York: Macmillian, 1986); Cheryl Kirk-Duggan, *Exorcizing Evil* (Maryknoll, N.Y.: Orbis, 1997); Eileen Southern, *The Music of Black Americans,* 2nd ed., (New York: W. W. Norton & Co., 1983); and the "Music Glossary" of the *All Music Guide,* (http://www.allmusic.com/mus_Glossary.html).

Cross-references are noted by an asterisk before cross-referenced entry: e.g., *syncopation.

Accent. Emphasis placed on a musical note or chord through one of several musical choices, such as sounding the note or chord louder or higher than others, or by sustaining it for a longer period of time.

Ad lib. A singer's *improvised invocations and/or embellished lyrics sung against an often repetitive choral background, as in a *vamp.

Arpeggio. Literally, "to play the harp." A manner of playing the notes of a chord in rapid succession rather than simultaneously. Arpeggios can be played in descending or ascending manner and can extend the range of a chord over the full extent of a keyboard instrument.

Beat. A sounded pulse within musical time. In Western *metered music, emphasis is often given to the first beat of each measure, designated the "downbeat." In African American music, a strong, *metronomic beat, sustained throughout a piece, is often contrasted by *syncopated beats that displace the emphasis from the downbeat to other shifting points in the unfolding musical time.

Bent notes. *Embellishments, used for expressive purposes, produced by changing the pitch of a note by raising or lowering it slightly.

Blue notes. *Embellishments to a melodic line, characteristic of the *blues, produced by flatting the third, fifth, or seventh notes of a major scale.

Blues. A genre of Black music, introduced in the first decade of the 20th century, characterized by solo singing in a slow, expressive style, with guitar accompaniment. Blues singing and accompaniment is often embellished with *blue notes and other devises used to express a melancholic state of mind.

Cadence. A series of *chords and/or a melodic formula that bring a piece of music (or section thereof) to completion by resolving musical *dissonance into the *consonance of the piece's/section's primary key.

Call and response. An antiphonal process by which one group or person performs a unit of music and another group or person copies, mimics, varies, contrasts, or "answers" in some manner the original passage. In call-and-response singing, alternating voices may overlap or remain distinct.

Chekerē. An African instrument made with strung beads attached to a dried gourd.

Chord. See *Harmony.

Chorus. *n.* A repeated portion of a song—a refrain. *n.* A group of singers and/or dancers. *v.* To sing together, often in *unison.

Consonance. Musical tones that sound well together. Various cultures determine consonant intervals differently, based on mathematical ratios (such as intervals of an octave, third, fourth, or fifth in Western music), and a listener's or performer's sense of consonance is derived primarily from the cultural context of the music s/he performs.

Counterpoint. Two or more independent lines of music sounding simultaneously.

Crescendo. A gradual increase in volume.

Crossrhythms. Contrasting *rhythms used simultaneously; may result in a conflict of *meter or *accents.

Dissonance. The effect of musical sounds that create tension or unrest in the hearers/performers. Within the harmonic unfolding of a musical piece, disso-

288

nance is generally resolved in *consonance and repose. What constitutes musical dissonance or consonance varies from culture to culture and from one historic period to another.

Drum set. A collection of percussive instruments, also named a "trap set," composed of bass drum, snare drum, tom-toms, and cymbals (high-hat, crash, and ride cymbals), played by a single player who provides both a rhythmic "ground" and nuance to the music. Drums and cymbals are played with either sticks, pedals, or brushes, creating different percussive effects. High-hat cymbals are comprised of two cymbals of the same size suspended one above the other on a spindle stand. When activated by a floor pedal, the upper cymbal sounds against its counterpart.

Duple meter. Any *meter that gives a feeling of "two" (regular alternation between a strong and a weak beat) such as 2/4 or 4/4.

Dynamics. Changing degrees of volume and intensity in the unfolding of a musical piece.

Embellishments. Musical sounds intended to ornament or enhance a musical piece, its melody, harmony, and/or sung lyrics. In gospel music, embellishments such as *glissandos, *arpeggios, or *blue notes may ornament a song's accompaniment, while a range of *vocal embellishments may be used by a singer to enhance the dynamism of the song's message.

Falsetto. Primarily a male-voiced phenomenon, falsetto situates the voice in a higher register than one's normal singing range, creating lighter *timbre and less vocal power.

Form. The overall musical structure of a piece—its temporal tonal design—which most often includes contrasting elements, such as chorus and verses. In many gospel songs, the alternation between a recurring chorus and changing verses creates a sense of unity and difference.

Glissando. A rapid, sliding scale executed by running one's finger or thumbnail up or down the white or black keys of a piano.

Gospel music. A central genre of the African American sacred music tradition that emerged in the first quarter of the twentieth century, gospel is characterized by lyrics rooted in the Christian Scriptures; by vocal and instrumental styles that draw on secular genres of blues, R & B, ragtime, jazz, etc.; and by a highly expressive performance style that includes *vocal embellishment, a broad range of *vocal timbres, energized and "soulful" singing styles, *improvised accompaniments, hand-clapping, foot tapping, and other expressive body movements. Gospel music, in its broadest sense, incorporates other genres such as *spirituals and *hymns, which are performed in the stylistic framework of gospel performance.

Harmony. The vertical combination of tones, sounding simultaneously, that structures a musical piece. Chordal harmony involves the successive unfolding of chords (three or more notes sounding simultaneously) according to certain rules, regulations, expectations, and conventions operative within a particular culture and historical period.

Heterogeneous sound. A tendency in African American music to combine dramatically contrasting qualities of sound (*timbres) into a densely textured vocal/instrumental fabric.

Heterophony. More than one simultaneous interpretation of the same melody by singers and/or instrumentalists.

High-hat cymbal. See *Drum set.

Hymns. Strophic poetry set to music, most often intended for worship. Incorporated into the *gospel tradition, hymns, often Euro-American in origin, are performed in a gospelized style, with improvised accompaniment, slower *tempos, and embellished lyrics.

Improvisation. The extemporaneous composition, variation, or *embellishment of the lyrics, *melody and/or *harmony of a musical piece by a performer.

Intervals. The tonal distance between two musical *pitches. Within a Western scale, intervals are named to indicate their respective distance from the first or tonic pitch of the scale: e.g., a second, third, fourth, fifth, sixth, seventh, and octave.

Key. The tonal center of a composition; the fundamental *pitch that gives its name to the scale or set of pitches that are the basis of the piece's *melody and *harmony—e.g., the key of G indicates a scale of pitches in which G serves as tonal center.

Lead singer. In gospel music, a soloist who both sings the verses of a song and improvises on the melodies of sections of the piece sung chorally.

Lining out. The practice of a leader intoning (singing, speaking, shouting) the next line of a song before it is sung by a choir or congregation. Common in African American oral/aural performance practice.

Melody. The contour of successive pitches that comprise the "tune" of a piece of music.

Meter. The particular arrangement of strong and weak *beats or *pulses that marks the musical units (measures) of a piece. Meter is represented by time signatures, such as 2/4 or 3/4, in which the top number indicates how many beats comprise one measure and the bottom number indicates which kind of note (4 = a quarter note) receives one beat. In 2/4 meter, the first beat is accented while the second beat is unaccented. In 3/4 meter, the first beat is accented while the second and third are unaccented. Given *improvisatory and *syncopated nature of gospel music performance, the regular arrangement of strong and weak beats may shift into complex patterns that defy a single meter.

Metronomic *pulse. The regular, insistent, at times driving *beat that typifies much of African American music.

Modulation. A change from one *key or tonal center to another. Modulation may be a temporary movement into an alternate key (for example to create contrast between the chorus and verses of a song) or the piece may remain in the new key.

Octave. See *intervals.

Performance practice. Particular conventions or assumptions, developed within a cultural context, regarding how a piece of music will be performed.

Pitch. The location of a particular musical tone within a scale or other range of higher and lower sounds.

Polyphony. Music comprised of several simultaneous voice parts that unfold independently of each other. In contrast to *harmony, which most often has a primary melody carried in one voice to which the harmonies conform, polyphony involves independent musical lines.

Polyrhythms. The simultaneous use of contrasting *rhythms within the musical fabric of a piece.

Polyvocal. Many voices sounding simultaneously but distinctly.

Pulse. Like the rhythmic flow of blood through the human body, pulse indicates a regular flow of musical *beats.

Ragtime. A genre of instrumental music, developed by Black musicians primarily for piano performance, characterized by syncopated melodies, moderate to quick *tempos, *duple meters, and contrasts between the melodic line and the "oom-pah" feel of the bass patterns.

Rhythm. The ordering of weak and strong impulses, of unaccented and accented *beats or *pulses, so as to create a sense of movement in time by dividing time into units of sound and silence. Rhythm is dynamically related to both the *meter and the *tempo of a musical piece which determine the sequence of pulses and how quickly these beats unfold.

Rhythm and blues (R & B). A genre of African American popular music, emerging in the 1940s, which grew out of such other genres as *blues, jazz, swing, and early rock and roll. Rhythm and blues is generally performed by an ensemble [voice(s), a rhythm unit (guitar, string bass, piano, drums), and additional instruments such as saxophone] and is performed in an expressive style similar to *blues and *gospel.

Riffs. Repeated, rhythmic phrases against which a soloist performs.

Ritard (Ritardando). The gradual slowing of musical *tempo.

Ritornello. Return to an already sounded section of a musical piece, such as a chorus.

Shout / jubilee spirituals. Up-tempo *spirituals that express present jubilation and the joyful expectation of a future filled with blessing.

Solfège. A system of reading or transcribing the notes of a melody using a set of syllables (do, re, mi, etc.) or numbers (1, 2, 3, etc.).

Sorrow songs. *Spirituals that focus on the trials and tribulations, both past and present, experienced by slaves and their Savior.

Spirituals. A body of African American religious songs cultivated within Black congregations of the deep South, and within the earlier, less formal, and at times clandestine gatherings of Blacks in the "hush harbors," "praise houses," and ring shout gatherings of slavery.

Syncopation. A deliberate interruption of the normal pulse of a piece's *meter, *accent, and *rhythm, through such musical choices as temporary shifts in meter, accenting weak beats rather than strong beats, accenting a different beat in each measure, making weak beats into strong beats. The effect is to destabilize and complexify the rhythm of the piece creating musical interest and vibrancy.

Tempo. The rate of speed at which a musical piece, or a section of a piece, unfolds, ranging from very slow to very fast.

Timbre. The characteristic tone color or quality of a voice or instrument. In gospel music, where vocal timbre is a primary carrier of emotion or spiritual feeling, singers engage a range of timbres as carriers of their message: *falsetto; moaning and groaning; a range of *vocal embellishments; as well as rough, foggy, or raspy singing.

Tonality. Tendency within a set of musical pitches toward a central pitch or tonic. In Western music, tonality makes reference to two types of scales (a set of eight pitches built on a characteristic set of *intervals), namely the major and minor scales. Within each scale, preference is given to one tone (tonic) as the point of greatest rest and to which the other pitches tend.

Triad. A chord comprised of three pitches, including a "root" pitch and the third and fifth above it.

Triple meter. Any *meter that gives a feeling of "three" (regular alternation between one strong beat followed by two weak beats) such as 3/4.

Triplet. A group of three notes. Triplet may refer to a group of three notes sounded in place of two, or to the subdivision of a single beat into three smaller units (as in a "triplet subdivision" of the slow beat of a gospel song).

Unison. Simultaneous playing or singing of the same notes.

Unmetered. A free rendering of *melody, *harmony, and lyrics of a song in which accented and unaccented *beats do not flow in any regular pattern but at the musical discretion of the performer.

Up-tempo. Music played with a lively *beat and a quick *tempo.

Vamps. Short rhythmic/harmonic phrases repeated multiple times to create a build-up of energy and against which a soloist *ad libs. Vamps are often incorporated before the final *chorus of a song, creating an intensity that resolves into the final statement of the song's message.

Vocables. Non-linguistic sounds used in the singing of a melody, song, or part of a song.

Vocal *embellishments. Enhancement of a song's musical and textual impact by a singer's use of *bent notes, *blue notes, slides, glides, and anticipations of / lagging behind the beat.

Vocal *timbre. See *Timbre.

Appendix Five

OUR LADY OF LOURDES—SONGS SUNG AT SUNDAY LITURGY

AUGUST, 1993–AUGUST, 1997

<u>Key</u>
Column 1: # – Number of times sung:
• = 5 times or more
•• = 10 times or more
••• = 15 times or more

Column 2: Song titles

Column 3: Composer/ source
(when known)

Column 4: Hymnals in which songs appear
(for reference only)

LMGM = *Lead Me, Guide Me* (Chicago: GIA Publications, 1987)
LEV = *Lift Every Voice and Sing II* (New York:The Church Hymnal Corporation, 1993)
SOZ = *Songs of Zion* (Nashville: Abingdon Press, 1981)
BH = *The New National Baptist Hymnal* (Nashville: National Baptist Publishing Board, 1977)
YL = *Yes, Lord! Church of God in Christ Hymnal* (Memphis: COGIC Pub. Board, 1982)
HH = *African American Heritage Hymnal* (Chicago: GIA Publications, 2001)
TFF = *This Far By Faith* (Minneapolis: Augsburg Fortress, 1999)

Column 5: Where song appears in *A Precious Fountain*

This list does not include many songs that have come into the Lourdes repertoire between September of 1997 and the present.

#	Song Title	Source (when known)	Hymnals (for reference only)	Appears in chapter:
•	All things Work Together			
•	Alleluia, Alleluia	Donald Fishel		
•••••	Amazing Grace	John Newton, Tune: New Britain	LMGM 173; LEV 181; SOZ 211; BH132; YL 80; HH 272	
	Angels We Have Heard	French carol	LMGM 17; VH 54; YL 207; HH 206	
•	Be Grateful	Walter Hawkins		
	Because He Lives	William J. Gaither	LEV 43; YL 265; HH 281; TFF 93	
•••	Bless The Lord	Andraé Crouch	LEV 65; YL 109; HH 105; TFF 273	
•••••	Blessed Assurance	Fanny Crosby, Phoebe Knapp	LMGM 199; LEV 185; BH 27; YL 193; HH 508; TFF 118	12
•	Certainly Lord	Spiritual	LMGM 121; LEV 132; SOZ 616; HH 678; TFF 113	
••	Christ Is All	Kenneth Morris	SOZ 180; BH 287; YL 255; HH 363	12
	Come and Go With Me	Traditional	LMGM 250; HH 596; TFF 141	
•••	Completely Yes	Sandra Crouch	HH 551	
	Do You Hear What I Hear?	Noel Regney / Gloria Shayne		
	Ezulwini Kuwebawoo	South African		
•••••	Fill My Cup	Isaiah Jones, Jr.	TFF 127	7
•••••	For God So Loved the World	Lanny Wolfe	HH 153	
•	Give Me a Clean Heart	Margaret Douroux	LMGM 279; LEV 124; SOZ 182; BH 349; HH461; TFF 216	
••	Glad To Be in the Service	Traditional		
	Glorify the Lord	Mississippi Mass Choir		
	Go Down Moses	Spiritual	TFF 87	
•	Go Tell It on the Mountain	Traditional	LMGM 22; LEV 21; SOZ 275; BH 66; YL 215; HH 202; TFF 52	

#	Song Title	Source (when known)	Hymnals (for reference only)	Appears in chapter:
••	God Be with You	Thomas A. Dorsey	LMGM 308; LEV 234; SOZ 203; YL 86; HH 639; TFF 160	6
••••	God Has Smiled on Me	Isaiah Jones, Jr.	LMGM 121; LEV 52; SOZ 196; HH 152; TFF 190	
•••	God Is	Dr. Robert J. Fryson	HH 134	6
••••	God Our Creator	Paul J. Prochaska, (S.F. Renew '88)		
	God's Holy Word	Traditional		
	Goin' Up Yonder	Walter Hawkins	SOZ 181	
	Guard Your Soul	Reed Fromer / Judith Supinski		
	Happy Birthday	Stevie Wonder (for Dr. M. L. King, Jr.)		
	He Arose	Traditional	SOZ 168; BH 104; YL 269; HH 280	
••	He Is Lord	Traditional	HH 285; TFF 95; SOZ 233	15
•••••	He Keeps Doing Great Things for Me	Dorothy Love Coates		
•••	He Who Endureth	Traditional		
	He's Able	Richard Smallwood		
••	He's Alright with Me	Traditional		1
	He's Blessing Me	Norris Garner		13
	He's Got the Whole World	Traditional		
	He's Sweet I Know	A. Jackson	YL 137; HH 510	
••	He's Worthy	Mississippi Mass Choir		
••	Here Am I	Traditional		
•	His Eye Is on the Sparrow	Charles Gabriel / C. D. Martin	LMGM 186; LEV 191; BH 204; HH 143; TFF 252	7
	His Name Is Jesus	Traditional		

#	Song Title	Source (when known)	Hymnals (for reference only)	Appears in chapter:
•••	How Do You Recognize a Child…	Traditional		6
••	How Great Thou Art	Stuart K. Hine	LMGM 181; LEV 60; BH 25; YL 39; HH 148	4
	How I Got Over	Clara Ward	SOZ 188	13
••	I Am the Bread of Life	Suzanne Toolan		4
	I Believe I Can Fly	R. Kelly		
	I Find No Fault in Him	Andraé Crouch		3
	I Get a Blessing Every Day	James Cleveland		.2
•	I Go to the Rock	Dani Belle Hall		
•••	I Have a Father Who Can	Ron Winans Family + Friends Choir		3
••••••	I Have Loved You	Michael Joncas		
••••••	I Love You	William Hubbard, Arr.: E. Hawkins	HH 580	
	I Love You Lord	Reed Fromer		5
	I Must Tell Jesus	Elisha A. Hoffman	LMGM 267; LEV 66; BH 232; YL 74; HH375; TFF 183	
••••	I Want Jesus to Walk With Me	Spiritual	LMGM 263; LEV 70; SOZ 95; BH 503; YL 381; HH 563; TFF 66	11
	I Want To Praise Him			
•	I'll Never Stop Praising the Lord	Shirley Caesar		
•••••	I'll Say Yes, Lord, Yes	Shirley Caesar		7
	I'm Glad			
	I'm Gonna Lay Down My Burdens	Traditional		
	I'm Gonna Sing	Traditional		
••	I'm Going to Work	Traditional		

#	Song Title	Source (when known)	Hymnals (for reference only)	Appears in chapter:
•••	I'm on the Battlefield	S. Bell / E.V. Banks / T. A. Dorsey		14
••	I'm So Glad	Traditional	LMGM 171; LEV 105; YL 455; HH 238; TFF 191	
	I've Been Redeemed	Traditional		
	I've Got Jesus and That's Enough	Dorothy Love Coates		13
•	If It Had Not Been for the Lord	James Cleveland		
••••	In This Place	V. Michael McKay		13
•••	Inner Call	Reed Fromer / Phyllis Kinimaka		
••••	Is Your All On the Altar	Elisha A. Hoffman	LMGM 277; LEV 135; SOZ 34; BH 183; YL 300; HH 393	3
•••	It's Good to Know Jesus	Mississippi Mass Choir		7, 14
••	It Won't Be Long	Andraé Crouch		
•••	Jesus I Love You	Edwin Hawkins		7
•••	Jesus Is the Light	Traditional		13
	Jesus, the Light of the World	George D. Elderkin	BH 514; TFF 59	
	Jesus, Oh What a Wonderful Child	Traditional	TFF 51	
••	Jesus on the Main Line	Traditional	YL 521	
	Joy to the World	Isaac Watts // Tune: Antioch	LMGM 19; BH 61; YL 210	
	Keep on Trusting By Faith	Traditional		
	Keep on Praying			
•	King of Kings			
••	Lead Me, Guide Me	Doris M. Akers	LMGM 168; LEV 194; BH 355; HH 474; TFF 70	7
••	Lean on Me	Bill Withers		
•••••	Let Us Break Bread Together	Spiritual	LMGM135; LEV152; SOZ288; YL30; BH488; HH686; TFF 123	

#	Song Title	Source (when known)	Hymnals (for reference only)	Appears in chapter:
•	Lift Every Voice and Sing	James W. Johnson/ J. R. Johnson	LMGM 291; LEV 1; SOZ 32; BH 477; YL 506; HH540; TFF 296	2
	Little Drummer Boy	James Pierpont		
	Looking for Freedom	Jon Fromer		
••	Lord Don't Move This Mountain	Doris Akers	SOZ 173	5
•••••••	Lord, Help Me To Hold Out	James Cleveland	LMGM 229; SOZ 194; HH 446	4, 9
	Lord, I'm Coming Home to You	Phyllis Kinimaka / Reed Fromer		
••••••	Lord, Let Your Spirit Fall On Me	Shirley Caesar		11, 13
•	Love's in Need of Love Today	Stevie Wonder		
•	Mine Eyes Have Seen the Glory	Julia Ward Howe	LMGM 6; LEV 226; SOZ24; BH475; YL502; HH490; TFF 297	
	More Than a Dreamer	Jon Fromer		
	Move Me	Richard Alan Henderson	SOZ 185	
•••	My Shepherd Is the Lord	Grayson Brown		4
•••	Near the Cross	F. Crosby /W. Doane/Miss. Mass Ch.	LMGM 45; LEV 29; BH 94; YL 244; TFF 73	4, 6, 12
	Never Alone	Walter Hawkins		
	Nobody Knows Me Like the Lord	Traditional		
••••	Now Let Us Sing	Traditional		
	O Come All Ye Faithful	John F. Wade	LMGM 20; BH 59; YL 203; HH 199	
	O Come, O Come Emmanuel	Latin, 9th c.	LMGM 3; BH 53; HH 188	
••	O I Want to See Him	R. H. Cornelius	BH 41	6
•	O Happy Day	Walter Hawkins, Arr.	SOZ 36; BH 246; YL 444; HH 359	
	O Holy Night	John S. Dwight	HH 201	
••	Oh, It Is Jesus	Andraé Crouch	HH 260	10

#	Song Title	Source (when known)	Hymnals (for reference only)	Appears in chapter:
	Oh, How I Love Jesus	Frederick Whitfield	LMGM 85; BH 10; YL 440; HH 29; SOZ 36	4
•	One Day at a Time	Rev. C. L. Barnes		
•••	Open Your Mouth and Sing	Reed Fromer / Phyllis Kinimaka		
••	Order My Steps	Glen Burleigh	HH 333	13
	Over My Head	Traditional	HH 169; SOZ 167	5
	Pass Me Not	Fanny J. Crosby / William Doane	LEV 139; BH 162; YL 276; HH 435; TFF 150	
•••	Perfect Praise (Excellent)	Brenda Moore	HH 296	3, 6, 12
	Praise God from Whom All Blessings	I. Watts /W. Keathe/J. Hatton/ G. Coles	LMGM 306; SOZ 230; HB 529; YL 52; HH 651; TFF 276	
••••	Praise Him	Donnie Harper	LEV 98; HH 172; TFF 285	
	Precious Lord	Thomas A. Dorsey	LMGM162; LEV106; SOZ179; BH339; YL384; HH471; TFF193	
•	Ride on, King Jesus	Spiritual	SOZ 77; HH 225; TFF 182	
	River of Sin	Hayward Antoine		
••••	Rough Side of the Mountain	F. C. Barnes, James Brown Barnes		6
••	Show Me the Way	James Johnson		
•	Sign Me Up	Kevin Yancy, Jerome Metcalf	LMGM 111; LEV 142; HH 192	2
	Silent Night	Joseph Mohr	LMGM 26; LEV 26; BH 56; YL 217; HH 211	
	Sing a New Song	Dan Schutte		
	Sing For Jesus	Reed Fromer / Judy Brown		5
••••	Somebody Prayed for Me	Traditional	HH 505; TFF 246	
••	Soon and Very Soon	Andraé Crouch	LMGM 4; LEV 14; SOZ 198; YL 168; HH 193; TFF 38	
••	Step by Step			

#	Song Title	Source (when known)	Hymnals (for reference only)	Appears in chapter:
•••	Take Our Bread	Sebastian Temple		
•	Tear Your Kingdom Down	Traditional		
•••	Thank You	Walter Hawkins		
•••	Thank You Lord	Traditional	LMGM 206; LEV 232; SOZ 228; HH 531; TFF293	
	That's What Friends Are For	Burt Bacharach/Carole B. Sager		15
	The Angels Sang			
•	The Blood . . .	Andraé Crouch	SOZ 184; BH 97; YL 250; HH 256; TFF 201	14
•	The Blood of Jesus	Andraé Crouch / Sandra Crouch		
•	The Lord Is Blessing Me	Traditional	HH 506	
•	The Lord Is My Light	Lillian Bouknight	LEV 58; HH 160; TFF 61	
	The Old Rugged Cross	George Bennard	LMGM 37; LEV 38; BH 96; YL 246; HH 244; TFF 77	
••	The Power	Rita Abrams		12
•	There Is None Like Him	Franklin Williams / Derrik Horne		
•	They'll Know We Are Christians	Peter Scholtes		
•••	This Joy That I Have	Traditional		1
••	This Little Light	Traditional	LMGM 190; LEV 222; SOZ 132; BH 401; HH 549; TFF 65	
	Through a Storm	Margaret Pleasant Douroux		
	Through It All	Andraé Crouch	YL 71	
••••	To God Be the Glory	Andraé Crouch	YL 18; HH 111; TFF 272	8, 12, 14
•	Tomorrow	The Winans		
•••	Touch Me	James Cleveland		
•••	Trouble Don't Last Always	Spiritual		

#	Song Title	Source (when known)	Hymnals (for reference only)	Appears in chapter:
	Try Real Love	Edwin Hawkins		
•••	Unwavering Faith	Darryl L. Gates		2, 4, 13
•	Use Me, Mold Me, Make Me			
•••••	Victory Is Mine	Dorothy Norwood / Alvin Darling	HH 489; TFF 266	
	Wade in the Water	Spiritual	LMGM107; LEV143; SOZ129; BH439; YL114; HH676; TFF114	
	We Are Sharing	Traditional		
•••••	We Need to Hear from You	Andraé Crouch		2
••	We Shall Overcome	Traditional	LMGM 297; LEV 227; SOZ 27; BH 372; HH 542; TFF 213	
••	We Worship Christ the Lord	Mississippi Mass Choir		
	We're All in the Same Boat	A. Schroeder/D. Grover /T. Hawkins		
••••	We've Come This Far by Faith	Albert A. Goodson	LMGM 225; LEV 208; SOZ 192; BH 222; YL 395; HH 412	2, 4
	Welcome Table	Spiritual	TFF 263	
•••••	What a Mighty God We Serve	Traditional	HH 478; TFF 295	6
	What Child Is This	William C. Dix	LMGM 29; YL 206; HH 220	
	What Do You Know About Jesus	Traditional		
•••••	What Shall I Do?	Quincy Fielding, Jr./ T. Hawkins		1
	When the Saints Go Marching In	Traditional		
	When We Eat This Bread			
	When the Praises of God	Mississippi Mass Choir		
•••••	Where God Leads Me	E. W. Blandy / John S. Norris	LMGM120; LEV144; SOZ242; BH168; YL409; HH550; TFF146	
	Where We'll Never Grow Old	James C. Moore	LMGM 145; BH 427; YL 157	

#	Song Title	Source (when known)	Hymnals (for reference only)	Appears in chapter:
	Why We Sing	Kirk Franklin		
•	Will the Circle Be Unbroken	Alda R. Havershon / C. H. Gabriel	YL 297	2
•	Wind Beneath My Wings	Larry Henley/Jeff Silbar		14
	Woke Up This Morning	Congregational Praise Song	HH 566	
•••••••	Worship Him	Bruce Ballinger	HH 174; TFF 136	14
	Yes, God Is Real	Kenneth Morris	LMGM 226; LEV 109; SOZ 201; BH 188; YL 325; HH 162	
	Yes, Jesus Loves Me	William Bradbury	BH 465	5
	Yield Not to Temptation	Horatio Richmond Palmer	LMGM174; LEV170; SOZ62; BH188; YL325; HH429; TFF195	
	You Can't Beat God's Giving	Doris Akers	HH 671	
••••• ••	You Don't Know What You're Missing If You're Not Serving God			10
	You Gotta Have Love			
•	You Must Be Born Again	Dorothy Love Coates		
	Your Grace and Mercy	Franklin D. Williams	HH 270	15
	Service Music	**Source (when known)**	**Hymnals (for reference only)**	
	Lord Have Mercy	Grayson Brown		
	Glory, Glory, Hallelujah	Grayson Brown		
	Holy, Holy	Grayson Brown		11
	Doxology	Reed Fromer		11
	Amen	Traditional	LEV 233	5, 11
	Lamb of God	Kenneth Louis		

NOTES

PREFACE

[1] Secretariat for the Liturgy, Secretariat for Black Catholics, National Conference of Catholic Bishops, *Plenty Good Room* (Washington, DC: United States Catholic Conference, 1991) vii.

[2] Karl Rahner, "Towards a Fundamental Theological Interpretation of Vatican II," *Theological Studies* 40 (1979) 717.

[3] Ibid., 723.

[4] Ibid., 718–19, 724–26.

[5] Ibid., 723.

[6] Ibid., 718–19, 725–26.

[7] Kenan Osborne, *Christian Sacraments in a Postmodern World: A Theology for the Third Millennium* (New York: Paulist Press, 1999).

[8] Ibid., 63, 62.

[9] Ibid., 121.

[10] Ibid., 198.

[11] Pope Paul VI, "The African Church Today," address given in Kampala, 31 July 1969. *The Pope Speaks,* 14:3 (1969) 219. All quotes in this paragraph from the same page.

[12] This invitation quoted by the Black Catholic Bishops of the United States, *What We Have Seen and Heard: A Pastoral Letter on Evangelization From the Black Bishops of the United States* (Cincinnati: St. Anthony Messenger, 1984) 3.

[13] Pope John Paul II, "The Pope's Address to Black Catholics," New Orleans, Louisiana, 12 Sept. 1987, *Origins* 24 (September 1987) 252.

[14] Rahner states that the open question during the contemporary church's metamorphosis into a world church is whether "the Church can legitimately perceive possibilities of which she never made use during her second major epoch because those possibilities would have been meaningless in that epoch and consequently illegitimate," Rahner, 724.

[15] Secretariat, Bishops' Committee on the Liturgy, NCCB, *In Spirit and Truth: Black Catholic Reflections on the Order of Mass* (Washington, DC: United States Catholic Conference, 1988) #70.

[16] Cyprian Davis, O.S.B., *The History of Black Catholics in the United States* (New York: Crossroad, 1990); Cyprian Rowe, "A Case for the Distinctiveness of Black Culture," in

This Far By Faith: American Black Worship and Its African Roots (Washington, DC: NOBC and The Liturgical Conference, 1977) 20–27; Diana L. Hayes and Cyprian Davis, O.S.B., eds., *Taking Down our Harps: Black Catholics in the United States* (Maryknoll, NY: Orbis, 1998); Joseph A. Brown, S.J., *To Stand on the Rock: Meditations on Black Catholic Identity* (Maryknoll, NY: Orbis, 1998); Jamie T. Phelps, O.P., ed., *Black and Catholic: The Challenge and Gift of Black Folk* (Milwaukee: Marquette University Press, 1997); Thaddeus J. Posey, O.F.M. Cap., ed., *Theology: A Portrait in Black* (Pittsburgh: The Capuchin Press, 1980).

[17] See Mary E. McGann, "Timely Wisdom, Prophetic Challenge: Rediscovering Clarence R. J. Rivers' Vision of Effective Worship," *Worship* 76 (1) (January 2002) 2–24. The summary that follows is taken from this article.

[18] Ibid., 23–24.

[19] Mary E. McGann and Eva Marie Lumas, "The Emergence of African American Catholic Worship," *U.S. Catholic Historian* 19 (2) (Spring 2001) 27–65.

[20] Black Bishops of the United States, "What We Have Seen and Heard: A Pastoral Letter on Evangelization," 31.

[21] Mary E. McGann, *Exploring Music as Worship and Theology: Research in Liturgical Practice* (Collegeville: Liturgical Press, 2002).

[22] Paul F. Bradshaw, *The Search for the Origins of Christian Worship*, 2nd ed. (Oxford: Oxford University Press, 2002) 115–16. See also John Wilkinson, *Egeria's Travels* (London 1971; 2nd ed. Warminster 1981; 3rd ed. 1999).

[23] McGann, *Exploring Music*, 56.

[24] Ibid., 43.

[25] Dalen Daniels, as quoted in *Exploring Music*, 41.

[26] Thomas Keating, *Open Mind, Open Heart: The Contemplative Dimension of the Gospel* (New York: Continuum, 2000) 71.

[27] Samuel A. Floyd, Jr., *The Power of Black Music* (New York: Oxford University Press, 1995) 5. Floyd bases his theory of Black music in the work of Henry Louis Gates's *The Signifying Monkey: A Theory of African American Literary Criticism* (New York: Oxford, 1988) and Sterling Stuckey's *Slave Culture: Nationalist Theory and the Foundations of Black America* (New York: Oxford, 1987).

[28] Joseph A. Brown, S.J., *To Stand on the Rock* (Maryknoll, NY: Orbis, 1999) 2.

[29] See Diana L. Hayes, "Tracings of an American Theology: A Black Perspective," in *Our Roots and Gifts* (Washington, DC: National Office of Black Catholics, 1989) 56–62; also McGann, *Exploring Music*, 60.

[30] Christopher Small, *Musicking: The Meanings of Performance and Listening* (Hannover: Wesleyan University Press, 1998) 10.

[31] Ibid., 13. For a fuller orientation to how music is understood in this study, see my *Exploring Music as Worship and Theology*, 20–28.

[32] Samuel Floyd describes "core culture" as "that portion of the black population that has remained closest to its mythic and ritual roots, whose primary cultural values and interests lie *within* that community, and whose concerns for racial integration appear to be secondary to its concern for individual and community survival and the perpetuation of African-American cultural and social behaviors and institutions. It is in this population that the cultural memory is strongest and most abiding," Floyd, 10, n. 2.

[33] Thea Bowman, "The Sound of Black Spirituality," in *Shooting Star*, Celestine Cepress, ed. (Winona, MN: St. Mary's Press, 1993) 45.

INTRODUCTION: BORDERLANDS

[1] These poetic reflections on music at Lourdes were inspired by several sources, including Langston Hughes' poem "I've Known Rivers," and Sandra Jackson-Opoku's novel *The River Where Blood Is Born* (New York: Ballantine Books, 1997). Several words and images of the "river's" movements in the next two paragraphs are taken directly from Opoku, 3–16.

[2] See Francis F. McCarthy, *Hunter's Point* (San Francisco: Flores Paramount Press, 1942) 26–41 for a history of the Hunters Point area, and Arthur E. Hippler, *Hunters Point: A Black Ghetto* (New York: Basic Books, 1974) 13–20 for a summary of the development of Hunters Point during and following World War II.

[3] Francis F. McCarthy, 1–25.

[4] For a description of the founding of the parish, see Francis F. McCarthy, 1–25.

[5] All quotations from Father MacKinnon in this section are taken from an interview with the author, 7/11/95. For an excellent pastoral memoir of the rebuilding of Lourdes from 1968–1990 that documents many of the important innovations that took place and their significance within the post-Vatican II church, see Father Donald MacKinnon, *Gospel Parish in the Modern World: Pastoral Reflections* (forthcoming).

[6] *Black San Francisco: The Struggle for Racial Equality in the West, 1900–1954.* Albert S. Broussard, (Lawrence, KS: University Press of Kansas, 1993) 242.

[7] Ibid.

[8] Conversation, 9/3/95.

[9] Information in the sections that follow taken from interviews with Sister Martin de Porres Coleman, S.N.D.deN. (2/22/94, 12/15/95), Sister Helen Carroll, R.S.C.J. (7/19/95), and Father Donald MacKinnon, C.S.S.R. (7/11/95). Also: Sister Martin de Porres Coleman, "Our Lady of Lourdes Parish," *Freeing the Spirit*, 4 (1) (1975) 16.

[10] Sister Martin quotes statistics from the Hunters Point Census tract in her 1975 article: 99% public housing; 90% A.F.D.C; 60% under the age of 19; 97% Black, 25% of the city's reported deaths due to alcoholism. "Did someone say that there are a few problems in our area? Yes, there are!"

[11] Sister Martin de Porres Coleman, S.N.D.deN., "Our Lady of Lourdes Parish," 16.

[12] Sister Martin, the only Black sister in the California Province of the Sisters of Notre Dame de Namur, continued to teach at Notre Dame High School, San Francisco, for a brief time before joining the Lourdes staff full time. She has served on the boards of the National Office of Black Catholics, the National Black Sisters' Conference, as well as the Pastoral Council and Sisters' Council of San Francisco.

[13] Leon C. Roberts, "The Development of African American Liturgical Music Since Vatican II," in *Our Roots and Gifts* (Washington, DC: National Office of Black Catholics, 1989) 28–37.

[14] A second replacement of windows was initiated in 1984. The images and significance of these windows will be indicated in chapters 4, 5, and *Intermezzo: Space.*

[15] When this initiative was launched, the archdiocese had not yet initiated its program for the training of permanent deacons.

[16] I came to Lourdes at the invitation of Sister Helen Carroll, R.S.C.J., who had recently retired from the Lourdes staff but was still a regular participant in Sunday worship.

[17] Several Redemptorist priests served brief terms as pastor between Father MacKinnon's two tenures. In the flux of leadership, members of the parish played a strong role in holding the parish together.

[18] For a detailed presentation of the field research methodology I followed, see *Exploring Music as Worship and Theology*, 37–57.

[19] At this juncture, I made the decision not to extend my research to include a second, Samoan musical tradition.

[20] See Don Lattin, *San Francisco Chronicle*, March 2, 1997. This decision reversed the original relationship between Lourdes and All Hallows parishes.

[21] "Interpreting the Ritual Role of Music in Christian Liturgical Practice" (Ph.D. dissertation, Graduate Theological Union, 1996.)

[22] For scholarly treatment of Black English, see, for example: Guy Bailey, Natalie Maynor, and Patricia Cukor-Avila, eds., *The Emergence of Black English* (Philadelphia: John Benjamins Publishing Company, 1991); Deborah Sears Harrison and Tom Trabasso, eds., *Black English* (Hillsdale, NJ: Lawrence Erlbaum Associates, Publishers, 1976); Malachi Andrews and Paul T. Owens, *Black Language* (Berkeley, CA: Seymour-Smith Publisher, 1973); Ila Walkes Brasch and Walter Milton Brasch, eds., *A Comprehensive Annotated Bibliography of American Black English* (Baton Rouge: Louisiana State University Press, 1974); Arthur L. Smith, ed., *Language, Communication, and Rhetoric in Black America*, (New York: Harper and Row Publishers, 1972); J. L. Dillard, *Black English* (New York: Random House, 1972); and J. L. Dillard, ed., *Perspectives on Black English* (The Hague: Mouton & Co., 1975).

[23] "Black English," in *Language, Communication, and Rhetoric in Black America*, 94.

CHAPTER 1

[1] For example, "revival" is not an entry in *The New Dictionary of Sacramental Worship* (Collegeville: Liturgical Press, 1990), nor in *The New Dictionary of Theology* (Collegeville: Liturgical Press, 1987), nor in *The New Dictionary of Catholic Spirituality* (Collegeville: Liturgical Press, 1993).

[2] Diana L. Hayes, "Black Catholic Revivalism: The Emergence of a New Form of Worship," in *The Black Christian Worship Experience*, revised and enlarged edition, Melva Wilson Costen and Darius Leander Swann, eds. (Atlanta: ITC Press, 1992) 87–88, 107.

[3] *National Catholic Reporter*, "History of revivals as an evangelical strategy," March 24, 1995.

[4] Former pastor, Father Donald MacKinnon, C.S.S.R.: interview, 7/11/95.

[5] St. Alphonsus Liguouri "Rock" Church, better known as "The Rock," is an African American Catholic parish in St. Louis staffed by the Redemptorist Fathers.

[6] Music and lyrics by: Quincy Fielding. Performed by Tramaine Hawkins.

[7] (New York: Crossroads, 1990).

CHAPTER 2

[1] "We Need to Hear From You," composer and lyricist Andraé Crouch.

[2] See Samuel A. Floyd, Jr. *The Power of Black Music. Interpreting Its History from Africa to the United States* (Oxford: Oxford University Press, 1995) 6.

[3] Olly Wilson, "Black Music as an Art Form," *Black Music Research Journal* 3 (1983) 3.

[4] Lyrics and Music: Kevin Yancy and Jerome Metcalfe.

[5] Traditional. As sung.

[6] See Maulana Karenga, *The African American Holiday of Kwanzaa* (Los Angeles: University of Sankore Press, 1988); Dorothy Winbush Riley, *The Complete Kwanzaa: Celebrating our Cultural Harvest* (New York: Harper Perennial, 1995).

[7] See Cyprian Davis, O.S.B.'s reflections on these principles and Black Catholic spirituality: "Some Reflections on African American Catholic Spirituality," *U.S. Catholic Historian* (19) 2 (Spring, 2001) 7–14.

[8] "We've come this far by faith," lyrics and music by Albert A. Goodson.

[9] See Karenga, 70.

[10] "Lift Every Voice and Sing," lyrics: James Weldon Johnson; music: J. Rosamond Johnson.

CHAPTER 3

[1] In Reed's telling, the scene unfolded thus: near the close of the liturgy, Reed sensed that he could intuit a harmonization for the song being sung. Gesturing to Charlene, who was directing, "Well, should I?" and meeting her enthusiastic nod, he started "feeling out" the unfamiliar song, inventing an accompaniment that, to everyone's delight, was just what was needed.

[2] The Freedom Song Network is an association of singers and writers who lend musical support to various progressive socio-political causes.

[3] Personal correspondence, 8/22/02.

[4] Lyrics and music by Andraé Crouch.

[5] Learned from a recorded performance by Ron Winans Family and Friends Choir.

[6] Conversation, 3/11/95.

[7] See Olly Wilson, "The Heterogeneous Sound Ideal in African-American Music," in *New Perspecives on Music: Essays in Honor of Eileen Southern,* Josephine Wright and Samuel A. Floyd, Jr., eds. (*Warren,* MI: Harmonie Park Press, 1992) 327–38.

[8] Interview with the Lourdes Choir, 1/19/94.

INTERMEZZO: TIME

[1] See Gerhard Delling, "*Kairos*," in Gerhard Kittel, *Theological Dictionary of the New Testament,* vol. 3 (Grand Rapids, MI: Eerdmans, 1965) 455–64; also James A. Wilde, *At That Time* (Chicago: Liturgy Training Publications, 1988) 9–10.

[2] M. Shawn Copeland, "African American Catholics and Black Theology: An Interpretation," in *Black Theology: A Documentary History, Vol. II: 1980–1992,* James Cone and Gayraud S. Wilmore, eds. (Maryknoll, NY: Orbis, 1993) 101.

[3] Aylward Shorter traces the first instance of this term to a little-known 1962 article (in French) of J. Masson. But it was only in the 1970s that the image received any wider use, first in the statements of African and Asian bishops (1974), then in a letter of Father Pedro Arrupe to the Society of Jesus (1978). Its first use in a papal document was in 1979. See *Toward a Theology of Inculturation* (Maryknoll, NY: Orbis, 1988) 10.

[4] Samuel A. Floyd, Jr., *The Power of Black Music* (Oxford: Oxford University Press, 1995) 6.

[5] Ibid., 8.

[6] Image taken from a celebrated spiritual entitled "Ezekiel saw the wheel."

[7] Samuel Floyd, 35–57. See also: Sterling Stuckey, *Slave Culture: Nationalist Theory and the Foundations of Black America* (New York: Oxford University Press, 1987); Melva Wilson Costen, *African American Christian Worship* (Nashville: Abingdon Press, 1993) 52–54; Albert J. Raboteau, *Slave Religion: The "Invisible Institution" in the Antebellum South* (New York: Oxford University Press, 1978) 63–75.

[8] Ibid., 6, making reference to Stucky's work cited above.

[9] Ibid.

[10] Ibid. See the "Glossary of Musical Terms" (Appendix) for explanation of many of these terms.

[11] Samuel Floyd, 6.

[12] Pearl Williams Jones, "Gospel Music: A Cyrstallization of the Black Aesthetic," *Ethnomusicology* 19 (3) (1975) 373–85.

[13] Ibid., 374–77. See also Jacqueline Cogdel Dje Dje, "Change and Differentiation: The Adoption of Black American Gospel Music in the Catholic Church," *Ethnomusicology* 30 (2) (1986) 223.

[14] Pearl Williams Jones, 381.

[15] The Akan term *sankofa* captures this understanding. See *Sankofa: Celebrations for the African American Church*, Grenae D. Dudley and Carlyle Fielding Steward III (Cleveland: United Church Press, 1997).

[16] Samuel Floyd, 9.

[17] *Anamnesis* is a Greek term for "dynamic memory" by which God's action in the past is remembered by reliving it, ritually, in the present, so as to claim God's expected action in the future. Liturgical scholars often focus on *anamnesis* as a dimension of the Eucharistic Prayer, although its broader reference is to the whole liturgical action, of which it is a primary goal.

[18] See Gordon Lathrop, *Holy Things: A Liturgical Theology* (Minneapolis: Fortress Press, 1993) 15–32.

[19] See Aimé George Martimort, ed., *The Church at Prayer: Introduction to the Liturgy* (Collegeville: Liturgical Press, 1986) 92–6.

[20] These complexities of rhythms are described by Black music theorists as cross-rhythms, polyrhythms, rhythmic clash, at times metrical ambiguity.

CHAPTER 4

[1] Lyrics and music by Albert A. Goodson.

[2] Comments made by various members of the community, including pastor Father Kirk, made at various times.

[3] Interview, 4/3/95.

[4] Material in this section from interviews with Father Donald MacKinnon (7/11/95) and Sister Martin de Porres Coleman (2/22/94).

[5] Conversation, 4/22/02.

[6] Conversation, 4/24/94.

[7] Black music scholar Wyatt Tee Walker refers to these hymns as "hymns of improvisation." See *Somebody's Calling My Name: Black Sacred Music and Social Change* (Valley Forge: Judson Press, 1979) 97–125.

[8] "How great thou art," Lyrics and music by Stuart K. Hine, sung in an improvised gospel style.

CHAPTER 5

[1] German composer and educationalist Carl Orff (1895–1982) co-founded, with Dorothee Günther, a school for the coordinated teaching of music, gymnastics, and dance. This led to his development of an approach to music education in which students play ensemble, accompanying their movements and singing with instruments on which on which they improvise freely. See, for example, Carl Orff, "Orff-Schulwerk:

Past and Future," in *Orff Re-Echoes: Selections from the Orff Echo and the Supplements*, Isabel McNeill Carley, ed. (Cleveland: American Orff-Schulwerk Association, 1977) 3–9; also his *The Schulwerk*, Margaret Murray, trans. (New York: Schott Music Corp., 1978). Also "Carl Orff," in *The New Grove Dictionary of Musical Instruments*, vol. 2, Stanley Sadie, ed. (New York: MacMillan Press, Ltd., 1984) 838. Hungarian composer Zoltán Kodály (1882–1967) developed a similar mode of ensemble, *a cappella* vocal singing for children. My reflections on the significance of children at Lourdes learning music "ensemble" were confirmed and expanded in conversation with Scott Walz, student at the Pacific Lutheran Theological Seminary, Berkeley, California.

[2] For example, the pitches of Orff's instruments for children make extensive use of pentatonic scales which, because they are constructed without semi-tones, enable free improvisation without musical dissonance. At Lourdes, the spectrum of musical sound and movement allows children to engage freely without apparent disruption of the communal performance.

[3] See John Blacking, "Movement, dance, music, and the Venda girl's initiation cycle," in *Society and the Dance: The Social Anthropology of Processes and Performance* (Cambridge: Cambridge University Press, 1985) 80.

[4] A second youth choir, also founded by Judy Brown, disbanded some seven years earlier as its young members outgrew it and the community lacked a quorum of younger children to take their places. In the meantime, Judy and former choir member Letty Woods, tried to assemble a local youth choir, but without their families tied to the church, the ensemble's sense of purpose never solidified.

[5] Music and Lyrics by Doris Mae Akers; performed and made famous by Inez Andrews. Lyrics as sung.

CHAPTER 6

[1] Conversation, 4/2/95.
[2] Conversation, 7/28/95.
[3] Conversation, 3/11/95.
[4] Conversation, 3/11/95.
[5] Conversation, 3/11/95.
[6] Conversation, 2/22/94.
[7] Sister Thea Bowman, "To be Black and Catholic," *Origins* (6 July 1989) 114–18.
[8] Ibid.
[9] Conversation, 4/24/94.
[10] Conversation, 8/2/02.
[11] Kwanzaa presentation, 2/13/94.
[12] Conversation, 1/12/94.
[13] Music and lyrics by F. C. Barnes.
[14] See James H. Cone, "Sanctification and Liberation in the Black Religious Tradition, with Special Reference to Black Worship" in *Speaking the Truth* (Maryknoll, NY: Orbis Books, 1986) 17–34.

INTERMEZZO: SPACE

[1] Images in this paragraph taken from Albert J. Raboteau, *Slave Religion: The "Invisible Institution" in the Antebellum South* (Oxford: Oxford University Press, 1978); Samuel A. Floyd, Jr., *The Power of Black Music* (Oxford; Oxford University Press, 1995); and

310

Melva Wilson Costen, *African American Christian Worship* (Nashville: Abingdon, 1993). Ronald L. Grimes speaks of "founded places" in *Beginnings in Ritual Studies,* rev. ed., Columbia, S.C., 1995) 71–73. See also, *Intermezzo:* Time for an exploration of the Ring Shout.

[2] Wyatt Tee Walker, *"Somebody's Calling My Name": Black Sacred Music and Social Change* (Valley Forge: Judson Press, 1979) 43–45.

[3] Image taken from Margaret Visser, *The Geometry of Love: Space, Time, Mystery, and Meaning in an Ordinary Church* (New York: North Point Press, 2000).

[4] Although Lourdes was not officially closed before Father MacKinnon arrived (one of the priests from All Hallows would generally come for Sunday liturgy), it was not functioning as a parish.

[5] It is interesting to note that temples/houses for God, as typified in ancient Greece and Rome architecture, were most often *atop* a hill. Situated at the foot of the hill, Lourdes inverts this perception of sacred presence in the midst of the human community. See Visser, 34.

[6] Note that separateness, being "cut off," being bounded are implicit in words such as "sacred" and "temple." "The word *templum* . . . is a cognate with Greek *tyemnein,* to cut: the special area is "cut off" by a boundary from the space around it. . . . 'Sacred,' from the Latin *sacer* meant essentially that something should be respected. . . . Separateness is an essential element of the notion of the sacred," Visser, 33.

[7] See Visser on metaphorical journey, 29–30, 32.

[8] Visser, speaking of labyrinths and round churches, 30.

[9] It is interesting to note that the tabernacle, as "place of presence," is part of this focal sphere.

[10] The entranceway to the church, already hallowed by abundant hospitality, provides a second focus for the distribution of Communion.

[11] See Sandra Schneiders, *Selling All: Commitment, Consecrated Celibacy, and Community in Catholic Religious Life* (New York: Paulist Press, 2001) 72–77. Schneiders draws on the work of Margaret J. Wheatley on the relationship of post-Newtonian science to organizations, *Leadership and the New Science: Learning about Organization from an Orderly Universe* (San Francisco: Berrett-Loehler, 1992).

[12] See Margaret J Wheatley, 79–86, 128 as source of images and quotes in this paragraph.

[13] "Filling up the musical space," creating a densely dialogic musical texture, claims Olly Wilson, is a deep predilection of all African based music. See "The Heterogeneous Sound Ideal in African American Music," in *New Perspectives on Music: Essays in Honor of Eileen Southern,* Josephine Wright and Samuel A. Floyd, Jr., eds., (Warren, MI: Harmonie Park Press, 1992) 328.

[14] Mary Collins, drawing on the work of Gregory Bateson, states: "Bateson . . . makes a case that the vehicles for statements about relationships are presentational forms other than discursive language. In any given ritual, these presentational forms are multiple and redundant. For this very reason, they are much less liable to distort the unconscious knowledge of relationships than is discursive and rational language." *Worship: Renewal to Practice* (Washington, DC: The Pastoral Press, 1987) 87.

CHAPTER 7

[1] "I'll Say Yes, Lord, Yes!" performed by Shirley Caesar. Composer and lyricist unknown.

[2] Conversation, 1/30/94.

[3] Interview with Gospel Choir, 1/19/94.

[4] Conversation, 4/2/95.

[5] "Jesus I Love You," composer and lyricist Edwin Hawkins.

[6] Conversation, 3/11/95.

[7] Interview with Gospel Choir, 1/19/94.

[8] Conversation, 4/2/95.

[9] "It's Good to Know Jesus," performed by the Mississippi Mass Choir. Composer and lyricist unknown.

[10] Hymnwriter Isaac Watts is often referred to as "Dr. Watts" within the African American community. A stanza from one of his hymns is incorporated into this gospel song "It's Good to Know Jesus."

[11] Conversation, 3/4/95.

[12] Interview with Gospel Choir, 1/19/94.

[13] Interview with the Women's Sodality, 5/22/94.

[14] Conversation, 4/2/95.

[15] Personal communication, 8/9/03.

[16] "Lead Me, Guide Me," lyrics and music: Doris M. Akers.

[17] Interview with Gospel Choir, 1/19/94.

[18] Interview with Gospel Choir, 1/19/94.

[19] Interview with Gospel Choir, 1/19/94.

[20] Interview with the Women's Sodality, 5/22/94.

[21] Conversation, 1/12/94.

[22] "Fill My Cup," lyrics and music: Isaiah Jones, Jr.

[23] Conversation, 10/15/95.

[24] Conversation, 2/26/95.

[25] Interview with Gospel Choir, 1/19/94.

[26] Interview with Gospel Choir, 1/19/94.

[27] Lyrics: Civilla D. Martin. Music: Charles H. Gabriel.

CHAPTER 8

[1] Mark Furman was the police detective involved in the investigation of O. J. Simpson who testified for the prosecution in his trial.

[2] Father Kirk employs a threefold, trinitarian profession of faith modeled on that used in current rites of Christian Initiation and in the Renewal of Baptismal Promises by the faith community during the Easter season. This ancient, threefold interrogatory profession of faith, evident in some of the earliest practices of Christian Initiation, took shape prior to the formulation of either the Apostles Creed or the Nicene Creed. See Paul F. Bradshaw, *The Search for the Origins of Christian Worship,* 2nd ed. (New York: Oxford University Press, 2002) 144–70, especially 157, 166.

[3] Conversation, 3/11/95.

[4] Conversation, 4/2/95.

[5] Conversation, 1/12/94

[6] Conversation, 12/7/95.

[7] Proposition 187 was a public referendum, passed by California voters in the November 8, 1994, general election, to prevent illegal immigration by requiring that law enforcement, social services, healthcare and public personnel report illegal aliens to state and federal officials and insure that they are denied social services, healthcare, and education. Opponents challenged the measure in state courts, which ruled that its core provisions were unconstitutional and prevented implementation.

[8] Conversation, 12/7/95.

[9] Conversation, 12/7/95.

CHAPTER 9

[1] Conversation, 3/4/95.

[2] Conversation, 4/24/94.

[3] Conversation, 2/26/95.

[4] Conversation, 4/2/95.

[5] Conversation, 1/15/95.

[6] See "The Association of Movement and Music as a Manifestation of a Black Conceptual Approach to Music-Making" in *More Than Dancing,* Irene V. Jackson, ed. (Westport, CT: Greenwood Press, 1985) 9–10.

[7] See, for example, Mellonee Burnim, "The Performance of Black Gospel Music as Transformation," in *Music and the Experience of God,* David Power, Mary Collins, and Mellonee Burnim, eds. (Edinburgh: T. & T. Clark, Ltd., 1989) 52–61.

[8] Conversation, 11/14/94.

[9] Conversation, 11/14/94.

[10] Image inspired by Philip Yancey, "A Goad, a Nail, and Scribbles in the Sand." Talk given at New College, Berkeley, CA., May 14, 1999. Unpublished. He uses "scribbles in the sand" to describe the effect of poetry.

INTERMEZZO: WORDS

[1] Arthur L. Smith, "Socio-Historical Perspectives of Black Oratory," in *Language, Communication, and Rhetoric in Black America* (New York: Harper and Row, 1972) 296.

[2] Image taken from Cheryl A. Kirk-Duggan, *Exorcizing Evil: A Womanist Perspective on the Spirituals* (Maryknoll: Orbis, 1997).

[3] Arthur L. Smith, "Socio-Historical Perspectives of Black Oratory," 296.

[4] Samuel A. Floyd, Jr., *The Power of Black Music* (New York: Oxford University Press, 1995) 230. The second, third, and fourth images Floyd quotes from the following sources: Hafiz S. F. Johnson and John Miller Chernoff, "Basic Conga drum rhythms in African-American musical styles," *Black Music Research Journal* 11 (1) (1991) 56; Donna Marimba Richards, *Let the Circle Be Unbroken: The Implications of African Spirituality in the Diaspora,* 1980: 3 (n.p.)**;** and Paul Carter Harrison, *The Drama of Nommo: Black Theatre in the African Continuum* (New York: Grove Press, 1972) 42.

[5] Lyrics of songs selected for Sunday worship are printed on a weekly "songsheet," but, since most members know the repertoire by heart, these sheets are used primarily by visitors.

[6] The instances mentioned here are not exhaustive. For a more extensive analysis of these word actions and their redundant presence in the worship, see McGann, 1996: 200–14.

7 Sister Thea Bowman identifies these words in linguistic terms as "suprasegmental phonemes," part of the "Black sounds" or "Ebonics" of the Black oral tradition, that, while defying precise interpretation, "precisely express the Black experience." See Celestine Cepress, ed., *Sister Thea Bowman: Shooting Star* (Winona, MN: St. Mary's Press, 1993) 45.

8 See Arthur L. Smith, "Making of an African Concept of Rhetoric," in *Language, Communication, and Rhetoric in Black America*, 369.

9 Arthur L. Smith, "Making of an African Concept of Rhetoric," 366. See also Olly Wilson, "Black Music as Art," *Black Perspective in Music* (1983) 1–22.

10 See Walter J. Ong, *The Presence of the Word* (Minneapolis: University of Minnesota Press, 1967) and *Orality and Literacy: The Technologizing of the Word* (New York: Routledge, 1982).

11 "God's Word: A Human Word," *Assembly* 26 (5) (September, 2000) 33.

12 *Upheavals of Thought: The Intelligence of Emotions* (Cambridge: Cambridge University Press, 2001) 1, 19, preface. The first image Nussbaum borrows from Marcel Proust.

13 See "Whatchumean, Jellybean? Or Integration in Black Catholic Ministry," in *Making a Way Out of No Way: Proceedings: Joint Conference of the National Black Sisters' Conference, The National Black Catholic Clergy Caucus, the National Black Catholic Seminarians* (August, 1982) 7–8, as summarized by M. Shawn Copeland, "Method in Emerging Black Catholic Theology," in *Taking Down our Harps: Black Catholics in the United States*, ed., Diana L. Hayes and Cyprian Davis (Maryknoll: Orbis Books, 1998) 127.

14 Gail Ramshaw points out that the "God of the Hebrews is a God who acts," from which flows the Biblical pattern of describing God with verbs. See *Christ in Sacred Speech* (Philadelphia: Fortrees Press, 1986) 53–54.

15 Arthur L. Smith, "Socio-Historical Perspectives of Black Oratory," 303–04.

16 Ronald Rolheiser, *The Shattered Lantern: Rediscovering a Felt Presence of God* (New York: Crossroad, 2001) 117.

17 Thea Bowman, spoken in the video *Fire in the Pews*.

CHAPTER 10

1 For a complete transcription of Deacon Dupre's preaching, 4/30/95, see chapter 8.

2 Conversation, 7/28/95.

3 Conversation, 1/12/94.

4 See Paul Bradshaw, *The Search for the Origins of Christian Worship*, rev. ed. (Oxford: Oxford University Press, 2002) 122 n. 29 for further information regarding the conclusion of congregational prayer with the Kiss of Peace.

5 "You Don't Know What You're Missing," composer unknown.

6 Lyrics and music by Andraé Crouch. Lyrics as sung at Lourdes.

CHAPTER 11

1 Conversation, 4/30/95.

2 Interview with the Lourdes Sodality, 5/22/94.

3 Conversation, 4/2/95.

4 Conversation, 3/11/95.

5 Conversation, 2/26/95.

6 All quotes in this paragraph from interview with the Lourdes choir, 1/19/94.

7 Conversation, 3/11/95.

8 Performed by Shirley Caesar.

⁹ Text of the Eucharistic Prayer qvouted includes portions of the Preface for Sundays in Ordinary Time I and the Eucharistic Prayer for Masses of Reconciliation I. The incorporation of additional saints' names near the conclusion of the prayer is indicated by a double indent.

CHAPTER 12

¹ See Gordon W. Lathrop, *Holy Things: A Liturgical Theology* (Minneapolis: Fortress Press, 1993) 116–38.

² "Blessed Assurance," lyrics by Fanny J. Crosby, music by Phoebe P. Knapp.

³ Conversation, 4/24/94.

⁴ Bishop Carlos Sevilla, S.J., was then an auxiliary bishop of San Francisco.

⁵ Image taken from Kathleen Norris, *Amazing Grace* (New York: Riverhead Books, 1998) 250.

⁶ Image taken from Wyatt Tee Walker, *Somebody's Calling My Name* (Valley Forge: Judson Press, 1979) 119.

⁷ The song, composed by a friend of Reed's, is now a treasured part of the Lourdes repertoire.

INTERMEZZO: FLOW

¹ *Soulfull Worship* (Washington: National Office for Black Catholics, 1974) 42. See also "Music and the Liberation of Black Catholics," *Freeing the Spirit* 1 (1) (1971) 27.

² Ibid.

³ Image inspired by Lawrence A. Hoffman, *Beyond the Text: A Holistic Approach to Liturgy* (Bloomington: Indiana University Press 1989) 149–51.

⁴ Although definitions of improvisation abound, Micheál O'Suilleabhain's is most pertinent to this claim: "The process of creative interaction . . . between the performing musician [or 'performing community'] and a musical model which may be more or less fixed." Quoted in Bruno Nettl, ed., *In the Course of Performance: Studies in the World of Musical Improvisation* (Chicago: The University of Chicago Press, 1998) 11.

⁵ See Renato Rosaldo, *Culture and Truth: The Remaking of Social Analysis*, rev. ed. (Boston: Beacon Press, 1993) 111–12.

⁶ This flow and the rhythm it creates is perhaps most evident when one of the major leaders is not present, e.g., when Brother Banks is ill, or Father Kirk is out of town and replaced by another priest who does not have a feel for this interchange.

⁷ Joseph A. Brown, *To Stand on the Rock: Meditations on Black Catholic Identity* (Maryknoll, N.Y.: Orbis Books, 1998) 26–27.

⁸ Henry John Drewal and John Pemberton III, with Rowland Abiodun, *Yoruba: Nine Centuries of African Art and Thought* (New York: Harry Abrams, 1989) 16, as quoted in Joseph A. Brown, 17.

⁹ Joseph A. Brown, 27, quoting William Ferris Thompson, *Flash of the Spirit: African and Afro-American Art and Philosophy* (New York: Random House, 1983) 5.

¹⁰ Joseph A. Brown, 27.

¹¹ Clarence R. J. Rivers, *The Spirit in Worship* (Cincinnati: Stimuli, 1978) 37.

¹² Wendy M. Wright, *Sacred Heart: Gateway to God* (Maryknoll, N.Y.: Orbis Books, 2001) 6, describing an "intuition that lies deep in the [Christian] tradition," that "the very nature of divinity is ecstatic."

¹³ Wendy M. Wright, 6.

[14] Clarence R. J. Rivers, *The Spirit*, 33–39.

[15] Joseph A. Brown, 27 (italics mine).

[16] Rhythm, as used here, does not refer to repetitive "beat" but to the articulation of sounds in time which, by its nature, requires a vacillation between opposites, sound and silence.

[17] William C. Turner, Jr., "The Musicality of Black Preaching: A Phenomenology," *Journal of Black Sacred Music* 2 (1) (1988) 25–26.

[18] Annemarie Colbin, *Food and Healing* (New York: Ballantine Books, 1996) 33.

[19] Walter Pitts, noting a similar pattern in Afro-Baptist worship, describes this alternation in Turnerian terms as a movement from "the calmness of structure to the tumultuous, billowy sea of anti-structure, then back to the smooth restructure of benedictory prayer," *Old Ship of Zion: the Afro-Baptist Ritual in the African Diaspora* (New York: Oxford University Press, 1993) 169.

[20] Interview, 12/7/95.

[21] See Clarence R. J. Rivers, *The Spirit*, 16–31.

[22] As quoted in Margaret J. Wheatley, *Leadership and the New Science: Learning about Organizations from an Orderly Universe* (San Francisco: Berrett-Koehler, 1992) 17. Reflections in the following paragraph were inspired by Margaret Wheatley.

[23] Margaret J. Wheatley, 11.

[24] *The Self-Organizing Universe* (Oxford: Pergamon Press, 1980) 196, as quoted in Margaret J. Wheatley, 23 (italics mine).

[25] Renato Rosaldo, 102. Remainder of paragraph, including quotes, taken from 102, 112.

[26] *Flow: The Psychology of Optimal Experience* (New York: Harper Collins, 1990) 59. Csikszentmihalyi's exploration of "flow" focuses primarily on the psychology of personal experience, rather than on the ritual-performative unfolding that is our concern in this intermezzo. However, many aspects of his study are pertinent to worship and music at Lourdes and specifically to *flow*.

[27] Mihaly Csikszentmihalyi, 4, 60.

[28] Mihaly Csikszentmihalyi, 60, 59, italics his. Latter part of the quote is taken from a dancer interviewed in his research.

[29] While tuning can refer to creating unisonous or monophonic sound, it most often suggests multivoiced resonance. In addition, we note that in the world of music, tuning systems differ from one cultural context to another, requiring those of us shaped by notions of "standardized pitch" to adjust our ears and our listening hearts to other sonic landscapes.

CHAPTER 13

[1] Conversation, 4/2/95.

[2] Conversation, 9/9/95.

[3] The image of the world as "God's playhouse," brought to my attention by Professor Michael D. Guinan, O.F.M., of the Franciscan School of Theology, Berkeley, CA., is suggested by William P. Brown's exploration of Wisdom in the book of Proverbs: *The Ethos of the Cosmos: the Genesis of Moral Imagination in the Bible* (Grand Rapids, MI: William B. Eerdmans, 1999). The image used in Brown's work is "Wisdom's playhouse," which is, by implication, God's.

[4] Interview with Lourdes Women's Sodality, 5/22/94.

[5] Conversation, 1/12/94.

⁶ Conversation, 6/1/03.

⁷ Image taken from Clarence R. J. Rivers, *The Spirit in Worship* (Cincinnati: Stimuli, Inc., 1978) 37.

⁸ Thomas Merton, *New Seeds of Contemplation* (New York: New Directions Books, 1972) 297.

⁹ Ibid.

¹⁰ Composer and lyricist Dorothy Love Coates.

¹¹ At the time of this visit to Lourdes, Bishop McGrath was an auxiliary bishop of the Archdiocese of San Francisco. He is currently the bishop of the Diocese of San Jose, California.

¹² This liturgy took place some five months after the Samoan community joined Lourdes. At future "combined liturgies," Samoan music would be intermingled with gospel songs throughout the service.

¹³ Traditional spiritual.

¹⁴ Father Kenneth Crowe-Hamilton, S.V.D., resides in St. Lawrence O'Toole parish, Oakland, California. He is a member of the Bowman-Francis Ministry team, working in "cutting edge" ministries with the African American community while pursuing a Ph.D. at the Union Institute.

¹⁵ Composer and lyricist Norris Garner.

¹⁶ Ibid.

¹⁷ "Order My Steps," lyrics and music by Glen Burleigh. As sung at Lourdes.

¹⁸ Most of the literature on Christian mysticism focuses on traditions that cultivate silence and the stillness of body, mind, and psyche as core elements of the mystical encounter with God. Here we find another tradition—a cultivated mystical practice, a "danced mysticism," rooted in African religious and ritual sensibilities and cultivated historically within African American religious culture.

¹⁹ Thomas Merton, 297.

CHAPTER 14

¹ Celestine Cepress, ed., *Sister Thea Bowman: Shooting Star. Selected Writings and Speeches* (Winona, MN: Saint Mary's Press, 1993) 32.

² The term musicians is used here to include all the women engage in Lourdes' musical ministry.

³ Traditional.

⁴ Stephen Henderson, speaking of "certain words and constructions" that "seem to carry an inordinate charge of emotional and psychological weight." *Understanding the New Black Poetry: Black Speech and Black Music as Poetic References* (New York: William Morrow, 1973) 44, as quoted in Celestine Cepress, ed., 63.

⁵ "My Testimony," lyrics and music by Andraé Crouch.

⁶ Conversation, 6/8/03.

⁷ Cheryl Townsend Gilkes, *If It Wasn't for the Women: Black Women's Experience and Womanist Culture in Church and Community* (Maryknoll, NY: Orbis, 2001) 135–37.

⁸ Ibid. 135. The song *Surely God is Able* was composed by Reverend Herbert Brewster.

⁹ "This is the Time," composer and lyricist V. Michael McKay.

¹⁰ Judy sings a gospel adaptation of the Grammy-winning, popular ballad performed by Bette Midler. Composers/lyricists: Larry Henley and Jeff Silbar.

CHAPTER 15

[1] Father Thomas Hamilton is a Marist priest who served on the staff of All Hallows parish for several years. He is currently parochial vicar of St. Bruno Church, San Bruno, California.

[2] "Your grace and mercy," lyrics and music by Franklin D. Williams.

[3] Testimonies given here are excerpts from the more lengthy words of each speaker.

[4] Reed's mother-in-law is Avery's foster-mother.

[5] "That's What Friends are For" is a song composed by Burt Bacharach and sung by Dionne Warwick and Friends—a group that included Gladys Knight, Stevie Wonder, and Elton John.

[6] Judy Brown, conversation, 6/8/03.

[7] Pat Goodall, conversation, 6/1/03.

INTERMEZZO EMBODIMENT

[1] See Samuel A. Floyd, Jr., *The Power of Black Music* (Oxford: Oxford University Press, 1995) 226–36.

[2] Olly Wilson, "The Association of Movement and Music as a Manifestation of a Black Conceptual Approach to Music Making," in *More Than Dancing,* Irene V. Jackson, ed. (Westport, CT: Greenwood Press, 1985) 9–23.

[3] Pearl Williams Jones, "Gospel Music: A Crystallization of the Black Aesthetic," *Ethnomusicology* 19 (3) (1975) 373–85.

[4] Ibid., 381.

[5] See Mary Collins, *Contemplative Participation* (Collegeville: Liturgical Press, 1990) 58.

[6] The image of "resonant community" is inspired by Brigitte Enzner-Probst's exploration of women's liturgies, "The Role of the Body in the Liturgical Work of Women," presented at the North American Academy of Liturgy, January 2003 [unpublished]. I am indebted to her for sparking other images/points of analysis used in this section.

[7] William C. Turner, Jr., explores the significance of rhythm for communicating a surplus of meaning in his article "The Musicality of Black Preaching: A Phenomenology," *Journal of Black Sacred Music* 2 (1) (1988) 21–29.

[8] Susan McClary, *Feminine Endings: Music, Gender, and Sexuality* (Minneapolis: University of Minnesota Press, 1991) 23. See her commentary on the body in music-making.

[9] See Enzner-Probst, 9.

[10] See Christopher Small, *Musicking* (Hanover, NH: Wesleyan University Press, 1998) 13.

[11] Edward Foley explores a related trajectory of how music-making, by ordering a community in particular ways, "contributes to the expression and creation of an assembly's ecclesial identity." See "Musical Forms, Referential Meaning, and Belief," in *Ritual Music: Studies in Liturgical Musicology* (Beltsville, MD: Pastoral Press, 1995) 145–72. Foley's analysis focuses primarily on the significance of musical forms and structures, which leaves room for much variation within the performance dynamic that unfolds in specific communities.

[12] Catherine Bell proposes that the schemes of ritualization imprint themselves on participants. *Ritual Theory, Ritual Practice* (New York: Oxford, 1990) 99, 116–17.

[13] Karl Rahner claims that this is the mysticism of the future, essential for human survival. See Michael Skelly, *The Liturgy of the World: Karl Rahner's Theology of Worship* (Collegeville: Liturgical Press, 1991) 74–84.

[14] See Clarence R. J. Rivers, *Soulfull Worship* (Washington, D.C.: National Office for Black Catholics, 1974) 15–17, and *The Spirit in Worship* (Cincinnati: Stimuli, 1978) 30–31.

[15] Clarence R. J. Rivers, exploring the worshiping congregation as the "primary witness of faith," offered this scheme as model many years ago. See *The Spirit in Worship*, 50–61.

[16] Image from Mary Collins, *Contemplative Participation*, 33.

[17] Ibid., 32–33.

[18] The image of "strong mothers" as used at Lourdes is inclusive of all those persons who nurture life in a regular and sustaining way, be they men or women.

[19] The term is taken from Catherine Bell. See her exploration of "The Power of Ritualization," in *Ritual Theory, Ritual Practice*, 197–223

[20] Joseph A. Brown, *To Stand on the Rock* (Maryknoll, NY: Orbis, 1998) 159–62.

[21] E-mail communication, 8/7/03.

[22] Pat Goodall, conversation, 6/1/03.

[23] See Catherine Bell, "The Ritual Body," in *Ritual Theory, Ritual Practice*, 94–117.

SPEAKING THEOLOGICALLY

[1] Image suggested by Aidan Kavanagh, *On Liturgical Theology* (New York: Pueblo Publishing, 1984) 146. Kavanagh speaks of a liturgical assembly as a "theological corporation."

[2] Ibid.

[3] Mary McGann, *Exploring Music as Worship and Theology* (Collegeville: Liturgical Press, 2002) 58–81.

[4] I take this image from Clarence R. J. Rivers. See my summary, "Timely Wisdom, Prophetic Challenge: Rediscovering Clarence R. J. Rivers' Vision of Effective Worship," *Worship* 76 (1) (2002) 7–8.

[5] See, for example, "What Do You Mean by Soul?" and "People Cannot Stand Much Church!" in *The Spirit in Worship* (Cincinnati: Stimuli, Inc., 1978) 33–38, 49–61, especially 58.

[6] See Ronald Grimes, *Ritual Criticism* (Columbia, SC: University of South Carolina Press, 1990) 54–56. Grimes takes the term "sensorium organization" from Walter J. Ong, *The Presence of the Word* (Minneapolis: University of Minnesota Press, 1967) 1–16.

[7] See Edward J. Kilmartin, *Christian Liturgy: Theology and Practice*, vol. 1: *Systematic Theology of Liturgy* (Kansas City, MO: Sheed and Ward, 1988) 228–32; Mary Collins, "Eucharist and Christology Revisited: The Body of Christ," *Theological Digest* 39 (4) (1992) 321–25.

[8] Images of the Spirit's action are inspired by, in part adapted from, Clarence R. J. Rivers, "What Do You Mean By Soul?" *The Spirit in Worship* 37. Additional quotes in this paragraph from the same source.

[9] Ibid. See also Mary McGann, "Timely Wisdom, Prophetic Challenge," 6–7.

[10] See Jean Corbon, *The Wellspring of Worship* (New York: Paulist Press, 1988) 6–7. Corbon, reclaiming a biblical-patristic vocabulary with which to speak about/reflect on the mystery of God's grace in liturgical action, defines "energy" as "the life-giving power of the living God and more particularly that of the Holy Spirit." He claims that "when the energy of human beings is brought into play by the Spirit and linked to the energy of God, there is a 'synergy.' The liturgy is essentially a synergy of the Spirit and the Church." Synergy, he goes on to name as the "joint activity," the "combined energies" by which "the energy of the Holy Spirit . . . permeates the energy of human beings and conforms them to Christ," 7.

[11] See, for example, Kevin Irwin, *Text and Context* (Collegeville: Liturgical Press, 1994) 46–50.

[12] James H. Cone, "Sanctification and Liberation in the Black Religious Tradition, with Special Reference to Black Worship," in *Speaking the Truth: Ecumenism, Liberation, and Black Theology* (Maryknoll, NY: Orbis, 1999) 20.

[13] Diana L. Hayes, "Through the Eyes of Faith," in *Taking Down Our Harps: Black Catholics in the United States* (Maryknoll, NY: Orbis, 1998) 60.

[14] Ibid., 61.

[15] Eugene LaVerdiere, *Dining in the Kingdon of God* (Chicago: Liturgy Training Publications, 1994) 1–5.

[16] Vatican Council II, *Lumen Gentium* #39–42.

[17] See Mary Collins, "Principles of Feminist Liturgy," in *Women at Worship: Interpretations of North American Diversity*, Marjorie Procter-Smith and Janet Walton, eds. (Louisville: Westminster/John Knox Press, 1993) 13–14.

[18] Henri de Lubac, "Du Symbole à la dialectique," in *Corpus mysticum: L'eucharistie et l'Église au Moyen Age, étude historique,* Théologie 3 (Paris: Aubier, 1944) 280–83, as quoted in Louis-Marie Chauvet, *The Sacraments: The Word of God at the Mercy of the Body* (Collegeville: Liturgical Press, 2001) 139.

[19] See Cyprian Davis, *The History of Black Catholic in the United States* (New York: Crossroad, 1990); Diana L. Hayes, "Through the Eyes of Faith," 61; and Cheryl Townsend Gilkes, *If It Wasn't For the Women: Black Woman's Experience and Womanist Culture in Church and Community* (Maryknoll, NY: Orbis, 2001).

[20] James Cone contends that the historical experience of oppression and slavery is determinative in shaping the eschatological vision of Black faith. See "Sanctification and Liberation in the Black Religious Tradition," 17–34.

[21] Ibid., 19.

[22] "Rough Side of the Mountain," lyrics and music by F. C. Barnes.

[23] Diana L. Hayes, *And Still We Rise: An Introduction to Black Liberation Theology* (New York: Paulist Press, 1996) 173.

[24] From a sermon entitled "Worship in Spirit and Truth," *The Spirit in Worship* (Cincinnati: Stimuli, Inc., 1978) 90–92.

EPILOGUE OUR LADY OF LOURDES—2003

[1] Susan Sward, "African Americans March in San Francisco," *San Francisco Chronicle* (Sunday, August 26, 2001) A24.

[2] Population has declined from from 55,000 in 1950 to 21,000 in 1980. See Patricia Yollin, "Skepticism runs deep in Bayview," *San Francisco Chronicle* (November 26, 2003) A1.

[3] See "Parochial Crisis," *San Francisco Chronicle* (Thursday, April 17, 2003) A19.

Index

322

and family history, 62–3
and spiritual power, 138, 195, 199
as cultural memory, 44, 47, 62–3, 89,
 103, 104, 186
as gift of God, xxiv, 205, 207
as holistic and embodied, 249–50
as revelatory, 50–1, 112, 207
as river, xxiii–xxiv
as vernacular music, 44
leadership of, 32, 105, 141–2, 198
musical speech, 59, 150–1
origins of, 45–6
participation in, 70, 104–5, 112–3, 136–7
performed "ensemble," 70–1
plantation and, 60
spirituals and, 46, 76, 97, 144
stored in the body/ imagination, 257–8
See also Black sacred music; gospel
 music; rhythm; songs
mysticism, 219, 254–5

oral / aural tradition, 39–40, 133,
 139–40, 144–52, 196–7
order, 201–3
and chaos, non-order, 174, 202
and control, paradox of control, 201–3
Our Lady of Lourdes
Church, xxiv–xxv, 54–5, 97–105
 windows, stained glass, 89, 98–9
community,
 children, 68–81, 180, 183–4, 267
 elders, 52–67, 83, 273–4
 identity in worship, 104–5
 mothers, 83, 228, 229–33
 religious background of, xxix–xxx
 young adults, 79–81, 105, 274–5
 See also communal life
ecumenical engagement of, xvi–xvii,
 5, 90–2
history of, xvi–xx, 54–6, 62–3, 227–8,
 272–80
Lourdes'
 Men's Choir, 229, 276

Miracles, 75–7, 274
 saints, 21–3, 89
 parish closures and, xxxii, 57, 85–6
 visitors to, 166–7, 192–4, 242–5

pneumatology, biblical, 262–4
praise, xxiv, 205–7, 220–1
and singing, 207
many voices of, 206, 207
prayer, improvised, 57–8, 119, 150, 155–8
preaching, 119–33, 144–52
and singing, 119, 133, 147–8, 150–1
as message, 119, 124–5, 146–8
biblical metaphors in, 149–50
Black, 12, 130–3
emotional intensity of, 129–30,
 133, 147–8
examples of, 5–10, 64–7, 92–3, 120–4,
 126–9, 130–3, 215–6
participation in, 129–30, 133
shaping of, 129–30, 133, 150–1
protest, 90–2, 95–6, 120, 269

racism / injustice, 43–4, 60–2, 65–6,
 120–3, 127–8, 129, 136, 149, 161–2,
 173, 223, 268, 269, 270
 See also slavery
revival, 2–3
Black Catholic revivalism, 2
Lourdes Revival, 1–15, 213–9, 238–42
rhythm, 19, 49–51, 130, 138, 200, 205–19,
 252, 257, 260, 261
as revelatory of God's presence, 200,
 205, 209, 261
Black, 19, 261
worship as rhythmic, 19, 200, 261
ring shout, 45–6, 97
Rivers, Clarence R.J., xvii–xviii, 270–1

sacramental worldview, 260–2
sacred
 and secular not dichotomous, 45,
 47–8, 103, 254–5, 261–2

time and space, 47–8
slavery, 25–7, 97, 136, 144, 223
song(s)
    as arenas of action, 104
    during the liturgy,
        Opening song, 82–4
        in the Liturgy of the Word, 115, 116
        during Preparation of Altar-table,
            173–7
        during Eucharistic Prayer, 178–80,
            253
        Communion song, 112–3, 184–5
        Communion meditation, 116–18,
            185–6, 187–8, 189–90
        "special request," 164–5, 191–4
    shaping of, 48–9, 129, 141–2, 150–1,
        198, 200
    selection of, 109, 115–6
    speech and, 150–1
    See also Black sacred music; music,
        African American; Spirit, Holy
soul, soulful, 112, 165, 195, 228
sound, 99–100, 130, 141–2
    sounded words, 144–52
space, 97–105, 134, 265
    acoustic, musical, 99–100, 104
    and cosmic geography, 102–3
    as sphere of action, 100–1
    identity mediated within, 104–5
    microcosms / metaphors for, 103–4
    qualities of, fields within, 101–2
    religious-cultural, 98–9
    transformed, 100–1, 164
    visual/acoustic convergence within,
        84, 100, 101
    worship space, 97–8
    diagrams of Lourdes', 282–4
Spirit, Holy, 99–100, 102, 114, 119, 125,
    128, 132, 136, 138, 149–50, 168–80,
    172–3, 196, 198–9, 203–4, 231, 235–6,
    238, 252, 254, 256, 262–4, 267
    and *àshe*, 198–9
    biblical images for, 204, 262–3

biblical pneumatology, 262–4
    body as "epiphany" of, 250, 261
    epicletic action of, 178, 264
    gifts of, 169–70, 199
    in song lyrics, 172, 173–6
    "incorporating the body," 234–48,
        251
    music and the, 170–3, 173–7, 204
    mystical experience of, 255
    singers moved by, 108, 114, 171, 172,
        226, 236–7
    Spirit-directed worship, 168–80,
        203–4
    Spirit-like qualities of singing,
        preaching, praying, 171, 204
    transforming power of, 170, 178
    tuning worship to the action of,
        203–4, 263–4
spirituality, 112, 221
    communal, 185–6, 254–5

tension, 19, 104–5, 142, 143, 199–200, 261
    creative, 19, 253, 261
    tension–release, in songs, preaching
        and prayers, 141–2, 200–1
testimony, 148, 158, 191, 231, 238–42
time, 30–42, 43–51, 134, 166, 265
    being "in time," 49–51
    Black sacred music and, 46–7
    intersecting cycles of, 16–29, 50
    Kairos, 43–4, 50–1
    musical, 49–50
    taking time, 30, 48–9

vamp, 140–2, 200

women, 220–33
    as liturgical leaders, 220–33, 256–7
    as witnesses, 224–7
    Black women musicians, 228
    spiritual authority of, 221, 255–7
Word of God, 120, 125, 126–7, 129, 133,
    147–8, 149, 151, 152, 251